THE PATHOLOGICAL FAMILY

10/14

A VOLUME IN THE SERIES

CORNELL STUDIES IN THE HISTORY OF PSYCHIATRY

Edited by Sander L. Gilman and George J. Makari

A list of titles in the series is available at www.cornellpress.cornell.edu.

THE PATHOLOGICAL FAMILY

Postwar America and the Rise
of Family Therapy

DEBORAH WEINSTEIN

Cornell University Press
Ithaca and London

Copyright © 2013 by Cornell University

First published 2013 by Cornell University Press
First printing, Cornell Paperbacks, 2013

Printed in the United States of America

Library of Congress Cataloging-in-Publication Data   26.95

Weinstein, Deborah, 1971–
   The pathological family: Postwar America and the rise of family therapy / Deborah Weinstein.
      p. cm.
   Includes bibliographical references and index.
   ISBN 978-0-8014-5141-6 (cloth: alk. paper) —
ISBN 978-0-8014-7821-5 (pbk.: alk. paper)
   1. Family psychotherapy—United States—History—20th century.
2. Families—United States—Psychological aspects.   3. Cold War—
Social aspects—United States.   4. Cold War—Psychological
aspects.   I. Title.
   RC488.5.W45   2013
   616.89'156—dc23   2012028439

Cornell University Press strives to use environmentally responsible suppliers and materials to the fullest extent possible in the publishing of its books. Such materials include vegetable-based, low-VOC inks and acid-free papers that are recycled, totally chlorine-free, or partly composed of nonwood fibers. For further information, visit our website at www.cornellpress.cornell.edu.

Cloth printing   10 9 8 7 6 5 4 3 2 1
Paperback printing   10 9 8 7 6 5 4 3 2 1

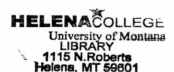

For Eric, Zach, And Lillian

CONTENTS

FIGURES

ACKNOWLEDGMENTS

These acknowledgments represent but a small token of my deep gratitude for the generosity and support of many people. I have been incalculably fortunate to have traveled through several intellectually enriching communities since this project's inception. Anne Harrington, Allan Brandt, and Evelynn Hammonds provided insightful guidance during its genesis at Harvard. Their critical feedback on points large and small contributed to making it a much better work, and I remain inspired by their mentorship and scholarship. During my postdoctoral fellowship at Brandeis, Peter Conrad, David Engerman, and Alice Kelikian provided invaluable support for my work. Throughout my multiple stints at Brown, Anne Fausto-Sterling has offered sage advice and warm encouragement. My colleagues at the Pembroke Center have made it an ideal place to finish this book, and I extend heartfelt thanks to Christy Law Blanchard, Denise Davis, Donna Goodnow, Martha Hamblett, Wendy Korwin, and Kay Warren.

I would not have completed this project without the convivial input and motivation of several writing groups. Many thanks go to Rachael Rosner, Susan Lanzoni, Conevery Bolton Valencius, Nadine Weidman, Lara Friedenfelds, and Karen Flood for shepherding my work during its earliest stages. Rina Bliss, Debby Levine, and Adrián López-Denis helped me return to the manuscript after setting it aside for several years, and our regular meetings enabled me to figure out how to finish it. Elizabeth Weed, Suzanne Stewart-Steinberg, and Lynne Joyrich showed me how to clarify my argument at innumerable points, and

I am indebted to them for their sustained commitment, good humor, and sharp questions.

At key moments, my work on this project has also benefited from the comments and support of individual colleagues and friends, including David Jones, Jamie Cohen-Cole, Nick King, Rena Selya, Kristen Haring, Elly Truitt, Hannah Landecker, Chris Kelty, Jenny Reardon, Stephanie Kenen, Sarah Igo, Bob Brain, Peter Galison, Charles Rosenberg, Mari Jo Buhle, Raymond Fancher, Joseph Fischel, Crystal Biruk, and Poulomi Saha. I am grateful for the able research assistance of Maggie Hennefeld, who was a wizard at tracking down permissions both obvious and obscure, and Michael Litwack, who helped me fix citations, check quotations, and generally clear up loose ends. Ellen Herman and Howard Brick read early versions of my manuscript, and their penetrating queries stayed with me through successive revisions. Robert Self gave me incisive and generous feedback at a critical moment of final revision. Rebecca Herzig has been a kindred spirit since early graduate school, and her keen intellect and sustaining friendship have marked this work in countless ways.

Several institutions and fellowships provided generous financial support for my work, and I am deeply grateful to them for making this project possible: a National Science Foundation Graduate Fellowship, a Henry A. Murray Dissertation Award from the Murray Research Center at Radcliffe, the Harvard Graduate Society, the Mrs. Giles Whiting Foundation, the Dibner Institute for the History of Science and Technology, a Nancy L. Buc postdoctoral fellowship and other support from the Pembroke Center at Brown, and a Mellon postdoctoral fellowship at Brandeis.

My research was also made possible by the resources of several archives and family therapy institutes. At the Bowen Archive, it was a pleasure to work with Priscilla Friesen, who made my research experience there very productive and congenial. I also thank the rest of the staff and faculty at the Bowen Center for making me feel welcome during my visits. At the Don D. Jackson Archive, Wendel Ray enthusiastically helped me to navigate the uncataloged riches of the collection. I am grateful to him for inviting me to present my work to an audience of family therapists at an early stage in my research. My thanks also go to Wade Pickren at the American Psychological Association and Diane Richardson at the Oskar Diethelm Library for the History of Psychiatry at Cornell Medical Center. For their assistance with the video collections and training films of their respective institutions, I am grateful to Andrea Mahoney-Schara at the Bowen Center, Climeen Wikoff at the Ackerman Institute for the Family, and Marion Lindblad-Goldberg at the Philadelphia Child and Family Therapy Training Center. In addition, several family therapists spoke with me about the early years of their field. For their generosity with their time and memories, I thank Donald Bloch, Barry Dym, David Kantor, Salvador Minuchin, Fred Sander, and Carter Umbarger.

George Makari has encouraged this project since I gave a preliminary talk about it at the Richardson Seminar in the History of Psychiatry, and he helped my book find a home at Cornell University Press, where I have benefited from the expert guidance of John Ackerman. Karen Hwa and Jamie Fuller were superb editors whose careful feedback made all the difference.

An earlier version of chapter 3 appeared as "Culture at Work: Family Therapy and the Culture Concept in Post-World War II America," *Journal of the History of the Behavioral Sciences* 40, no. 1 (2004): 23–46.

My own kinship networks have been the ballast that enabled me to complete this book. Edie Weinstein, Jerry Weinstein, Margie Weinstein, Laura Weinstein, and Keren Goldenberg have been cheerleaders, babysitters, and loving listeners. I am inexpressibly thankful to them for far more than fits in the space of these acknowledgments. The friendship of Rachel Gordon and Allison Smith has made my life all the richer. I am also deeply appreciative of the support of Barbara Morrow, Nathan Morrow, Lisa Morrow, David Herzstein, Maryanne Morrow, and Mark Goldstein. Eric has seen this project through all of its incarnations, and I thank him for everything that has entailed. He, Zach, and Lillian regularly remind me of the ineffable and exquisite joys of family life, and for that I am most grateful.

THE PATHOLOGICAL FAMILY

THE POWER OF THE FAMILY

"Seeds of insanity could be lurking in your own home," warned the narrator of a 1959 television program, *The Fine Line*.[1] The show's title alluded to the "fine line" between sanity and insanity. To illustrate the fragility of this boundary, the show included enactments of two versions of a family's interactions at their breakfast table, along with commentary about the hazardous implications of seemingly minor differences between the two scenarios from researchers in the newly formed field of family therapy. The pattern of communication in one scenario could induce schizophrenia in a child, these experts asserted, while the other would not.

The dangers highlighted in *The Fine Line* stand in apparent contrast to the idealized representations of family life in other 1950s television programs. Whether weighted with a positive or negative valence, however, these representations underscore the salience of postwar American investments in the family. The white, middle-class nuclear families in midcentury American television programs such as *Leave It to Beaver* and *The Adventures of Ozzie and Harriet* exemplified the model of family "togetherness" espoused by women's magazines of the 1950s and featured in the photographs of contemporaneous publications such as *Life*. During the 1990s, the Cleavers and other midcentury television families became fodder for the political discourse of "family values." In the twenty-first century, they have come to serve nostalgically as a talisman in debates about topics as disparate as gay marriage, working mothers, immigration policy, and reproductive technologies. The normative weight that these representations of postwar domesticity have retrospectively accrued stands in sharp contrast to the views of many midcentury social scientists and cultural critics, who thought the American family was in crisis. Moreover, as more than two decades of historical scholarship has demonstrated, many postwar families bore little resemblance to the fictional Cleavers or their popular-culture peers.[2]

The power of the family at midcentury becomes particularly apparent when one examines the history of family therapy, which emerged as a new clinical field after World War II. During the 1950s and 1960s, a group of clinicians in the United States developed a psychotherapeutic approach to treating mental illness that located the source of pathology and the potential for cure in the cyclical patterns of family interactions rather than in the biological or psychological characteristics of an individual. Their approach became known as family therapy, and in the field's development we can see many of the tensions that defined postwar America in a new way.

By bringing a macroperspective on the postwar period to the microsetting of the therapist's office, this book examines how families came to be seen as a site of disease and an appropriate locus of intervention at midcentury. It operates across three interconnected registers: the history of a field's formation, the history of postwar American cultural and intellectual life, and the history of scientific observation. In addition, it shows how the appropriate solution to long-standing social problems such as juvenile delinquency came to be understood as therapeutic and family-based, and it argues that an emphasis on the epistemological value of observable interpersonal interactions, such as those on display in *The Fine Line*, was critical to the field's development.

Early family therapists developed their theoretical models and therapeutic practices in a technical language that was seemingly distinct from social and political trends of the postwar period but that was nonetheless indebted to the contemporary sense that families represented the cornerstone of a healthy democratic citizenry. Their clinical evaluation of normalcy, health, treatment, and cure resonated with broader cultural ideals, such as the meaning of the good life.[3] The prospect of treating whole families drew on postwar assumptions about gender, class, race, and sexuality, which were themselves in flux. Such implicit conceptions of family life were apparent in who was included in therapy sessions and how therapists identified improvement or cure, as well as in their assessment of the distinctions between normal and pathological families.[4] Beyond their ideas about their patients, the therapists debated the implications of their interventions for their own role as "an agent of the culture."[5]

The Pathological Family thus examines the dense connections in postwar America between therapeutic culture and family life, which U.S. social and cultural historians have often analyzed separately. Indeed, it is one of the central claims of this book that the concurrent expansion of a therapeutic ethos and the growing fixation on the family in postwar America were deeply intertwined, not just parallel trends. The history of family therapy contributed to the synergy between these seemingly distinct domains.

The rise of a therapeutic ethos or culture was a key feature of twentieth-century American life.[6] There were several dimensions to the turn to psychological explanations and therapeutic solutions for social problems, including the increasingly common understanding of the good life in terms of happiness and personal fulfillment and the growing propensity of Americans to seek out psychological experts for advice and treatment. A psychological orientation supplemented or in some cases displaced other explanatory modes, from moral and religious prescriptions about sexuality to biological explanations for racial inequality.

Though it had its roots in the nineteenth and early twentieth centuries, the therapeutic was notably triumphant—to echo Philip Reiff—in the wake of World War II with the postwar boom in psychological experts and the expanded popularization of psychoanalysis. During the 1950s and 1960s, struggling families turned to experts who could provide advice and therapeutic assistance for a wide range of problems.[7] In addition, many social scientists and policymakers began to assess problems like prejudice, poverty, and delinquency as the products of psychological damage that required therapeutic (rather than social or economic) interventions. Psychiatrists in turn aimed to broaden their constituency by proclaiming the importance of their profession for promoting mental health, not just treating mental illness. Such claims echoed those of early twentieth-century mental hygienists, who promoted the value of psychiatric attention to the mental health and "adjustment" of individuals without a psychiatric diagnosis. However, the expanded purview of mental health proved to be particularly salient in the wake of the many breakdowns among seemingly normal soldiers during World War II and in the context of the ascendance of psychoanalytically oriented clinicians who treated the "worried well" in addition to chronically mentally ill patients.

By midcentury, a therapeutic ethos was manifest in domains as far-flung as the psychotherapeutic management of college students' sexual behavior, studies of the psychological deficiencies of black families, child adoption policies, views of gender roles in alcoholic marriages, and the expansion of psychological warfare in the Cold War.[8] Critics of therapeutic culture from across the political spectrum alternately derided its minimization of personal responsibility and bemoaned its emphasis on the individual psyche at the expense of social inequalities and the public good. These seemingly contradictory criticisms shared the presumption that a psychological orientation privileged an individualistic, autonomous, liberal self, although, as this book demonstrates, notions of the family were also crucial to the expansion of therapeutic culture.[9]

In turn, the midcentury therapeutic ethos shaped a heightened contemporary preoccupation with the heterosexual, middle-class family that was manifest in diverse forums ranging from political discourse to academic family studies to popular advice literature.[10] The landscapes of family life in America, along with popular and expert views on the family, underwent significant shifts during and after World War II. The wartime rise in women's participation in wage labor, the postwar return of soldiers from overseas, demographic increases in marriage and birth rates, and patterns of middle-class suburbanization and population migration all contributed to the changing social landscape.[11] The war had intensified and reconfigured prewar social, demographic, and economic trends while heightening the ideological significance of family life by underscoring the bonds between child rearing and the production of a democratic citizenry. In the postwar cultural imaginary, the family itself was seen as a means of repairing the social fabric torn by war.

One of the key arenas in which the therapeutic ethos of the postwar period was harnessed to family life was political culture. Family therapy emerged in the 1950s in the context of Cold War anxieties about family life, mass society, and the stability of democracy in the face of fascism and communism. Mental health and democracy were increasingly tied together as the promotion of democracy became framed in the language of children's personality formation, or what historian Joanne Meyerowitz has called a "biopolitics of child rearing."[12] Through parenting practices that fostered psychological health, families, particularly mothers, stood as positive guardians of democracy, domestic security, and citizenship and as a bulwark against the dangers of the Cold War.[13] Experts and popular media of the postwar period also portrayed mothers and families more nefariously as powerful potential contributors to soldiers' breakdown, fascism, racial prejudice, homosexuality, and—most pertinent for family therapists—delinquency and schizophrenia.[14]

In the years after the war, democratic citizenship thus became an ever more psychological enterprise, as well as one grounded in material consumption, and the family played a critical role.[15]

During the midcentury period in which family became invested with such significance across a range of cultural, political, and social scientific domains, family therapists manifested the same move in the clinical realm. Even as they deployed the specialized language and expertise of midcentury psychiatry, the architects of family therapy were concerned with how to help families achieve the many ambitions postwar American society delineated for them. Like their social science and public policy colleagues who aimed to address social problems through the application of scientific theories and social engineering, the therapists drew on midcentury confidence in expert intervention. They attempted to use therapeutic means to address social ills such as delinquency and prejudice while attributing those social ills to pathological families.

A crucial dimension of this history was the theoretical and methodological work entailed in moving from an individual to a familial view of pathology. Instead of invoking a linear model of cause and effect to explain why some children developed schizophrenia or became juvenile delinquents, these family therapists proposed to study the family as a dynamic system with interacting components, an underlying structure, cyclical patterns, and the capacity to self-regulate through negative feedback mechanisms. In their research projects, they often found their raw material in the textures of daily life, from "dramatic confrontations" to quotidian interactions "in which nothing, it would seem, is happening."[16] This refiguring of the subject of clinical care further inclined family therapists to look beyond a given patient's set of symptoms and attend to a host of contextual factors not conventionally seen as the province of medicine. In the words of the family therapist Nathan Ackerman, "In characterizing families as well or sick, we are reflecting on a way of life."[17]

In the process of forming their new field, early family therapists also remade the object of their analysis. They classified families as healthy or ill, normal or pathological, thereby challenging one of the central assumptions of modern medicine, including psychiatry, that pathology resides in individual people and that treatment should target a diseased individual or a specific pathogenic agent. In their therapeutic interventions, these clinicians aimed instead to treat the family "as a single organism"[18] in which one individual became the identified patient who symptomatically expressed the pathology of the whole organism. The shift from viewing family as a potential source of an individual's problems to an understanding of family itself as the patient was not straightforward, and the implications of defining family as a unit of disease were often paradoxical.

Family therapists' concomitant elevation of naturalistic observation in their therapeutic practices, pedagogical strategies, and research projects further buttressed their reframing of the locus of pathology from an interior, psychological self to the family. They were particularly attentive to what happened in the visually accessible domain *between* people rather than *within* individual psyches. In research studies based on "naturalistic observation" of families going about their daily lives, in therapeutic approaches that privileged watching families interact over listening to a retrospective description of their problems, and in their use of technologies such as films and one-way mirrors for training purposes, they emphasized the visual, performative dimensions of family life.

These efforts were emblematic of the simultaneously pessimistic and optimistic outlook of the postwar period.[19] In the so-called age of anxiety, fears of nuclear war and the spread of communism sat alongside strengthened national confidence and economic prosperity. Pessimistic concerns about the state of the American family were coupled with optimistic confidence in the potential for expert assistance, including the capacity of family therapists to use therapeutic means to address severe pathologies such as schizophrenia and to ameliorate entrenched social problems such as delinquency. That the family was seen as the crucible of so many hopes and problems, from schizophrenia and delinquency to the state of national democracy and military strength, underscores the stakes of approaching the family as a site for therapeutic intervention.

What Is "The Family"?

This book builds from the assumption that the family is not a timeless natural category but rather one that has been produced historically. However, the very phrase, "the family," in its grammatically singular form, implies a unity and homogeneity to family life, thereby potentially reinscribing its seemingly self-evident nature. Thus a note on terminology is in order.

The meanings and forms of family life have long been saturated with values and expectations from varied political, religious, social, and intellectual domains. "Family" has meant household, race, clan, fellowship, and taxonomical category of species classification. It has functioned to connect far-flung members, as in the metaphorical "family of man" or "family of nations." Families have been held together by an array of connections (biological, emotional, adoptive, economic, legal, and otherwise), and they have defined their boundaries with social, institutional, technological, and environmental means.

Family has also implied varied permutations of individuals. These range from the definition of the nuclear family given by G. P. Murdock in his 1949 book, *Social Structure* ("The first and most basic, called herewith the nuclear family, consists typically of a married man and woman with their offspring")[20] to single parents to remarriages with children from prior spouses. Other configurations included the multiple generations, distant relatives, and common ancestry of extended families; the state-sponsored, transitory composition of foster families; and the associations among members of communes or other voluntary communities who called themselves families.

Over the past century, scholars from many fields have taken the family as their object of analysis. Anthropologists have studied the cross-cultural complexities of kinship. Family historians have examined changes over time in the structure, demography, migration patterns, emotional bonds, and economic functions of family units. Family sociologists have researched the socialization processes, social roles, household forms, and courtship patterns among families, as well as the family's relationship to other social structures and institutions. Policymakers have used the family as a unit for taxes, welfare, immigration status, and legal rights. Feminists have variously championed, challenged, and deconstructed the relationships between family and gender. Psychoanalysts, sexologists, and historians of sexuality have linked family and sexuality in their assessments of desire, reproduction, pleasure, and the body. Other scholars have emphasized the connections among conceptions of family, race, and nation.

In other words, despite the apparent simplicity of the phrase, "the family" was (and remains) a multivalent, polymorphous category. The rich complexity of the category, coupled with its colloquial familiarity and ready accessibility, has productively facilitated its movement across diverse domains. It thereby functions as what science studies scholars have called a boundary object, meaning "objects which are both plastic enough to adapt to local needs and the constraints of the several parties employing them, yet robust enough to maintain a common identity across sites. . . . They have different meanings in different social worlds but their structure is common enough to more than one world to make them recognizable."[21] The problem for the founders of family therapy was figuring out how to manage, study, make comprehensible, and treat their unruly and unconventional patient.

The Family in Family Therapy

A small number of psychoanalytically trained psychiatrists, social workers, and other clinicians developed family therapy while working with patient problems related to child psychiatry, juvenile delinquency, and schizophrenia. Initially unaware of one another's efforts, in the early and mid-1950s, these scattered clinicians began to conduct therapy sessions with multiple family members present in the room.[22] In disparate locations and with diverse theoretical premises, they simultaneously began to investigate the role of the family not only in the etiology of mental illness but also in its ongoing maintenance.[23]

Early family therapists were variously interested in treating the structural, communicational, and emotional problems of family life, including what one early therapist labeled, in politically evocative terms, the "cold war" among family members.[24] These clinicians did not set out in the 1950s and 1960s to address what a contemporary cartoon referred to as "the little things."[25]

This cartoon shows a woman in psychoanalysis lying on a couch, with her analyst discreetly out of view behind her—a classic scenario, except for the two children on the couch next to her. According to the caption, the source of her problems (what drives her crazy) is what she calls "the sitter problem." The children are not there for family therapy but because there was some difficulty with child care. Like the psychoanalyst in the cartoon, early family therapists were not focused on helping families find practical solutions to the sitter problem or comparable issues, nor did they aim to ameliorate the economic conditions affecting families through structural interventions. Instead, they trained their therapeutic acumen on the patterns of interaction and communication within the individual families under their care. However, unlike the psychoanalyst in the cartoon, family therapists treated children as crucial participants in the therapeutic process rather than an inconvenience or distraction. Family therapy practices were highly unorthodox, even controversial, according to the standards and conventions

"It's the little things that drive me crazy—for example the sitter problem . . ."

SUBURBIA TODAY

Figure 1. Barney Tobey, cover cartoon for *Suburbia Today*, magazine supplement to *Valley Times Today*, reproduced on the program cover for "Campus Conference: What's Happening to the Family in Suburbia?" April 22, 1961, San Fernando Valley State College, Don D. Jackson Archive, University of Louisiana at Monroe. By permission of David M. Tobey.

of psychoanalysis, since having multiple family members in the same therapy session violated psychoanalysts' strong emphasis on the confidentiality of the individual patient and disrupted the transference relationship between patient and analyst, which psychoanalysts saw as necessary for an efficacious treatment.

Early family therapists actively defined their work as a radical break from mainstream psychiatry and psychoanalysis. Like other postwar psychotherapeutic innovators, such as the humanistic psychologists Carl Rogers and Abraham Maslow, they distinguished their new field from psychoanalysis and behaviorism, though they also cited neo-Freudians like Harry Stack Sullivan as their inspiration.[26] In his capacity as organizer of a 1967 conference on family research and therapy, James Framo urged the conference participants to rise to what he saw as the innovative spirit of their field: "In reformulating concepts about the very nature of emotional disturbances and its treatment, the family therapy movement, a tour de force breakthrough, really, has yielded a mass of undigested information about the transactional nature of intimate relationships. Family therapy is not just a modality of treatment but a philosophy which offers a wholly new theoretical model for thinking about psychopathology, contexts and systems."[27] Many people shared Framo's assessment of their field as a "tour de force breakthrough" that was as much about philosophy or "a wholly new theoretical model" as it was about therapeutics. Similarly, Framo was not alone in citing the historian of science Thomas Kuhn to buttress his claim that the family approach "represents a quantum leap forward so discontinuous from the past as to qualify as a scientific revolution."[28] In their own histories, family therapists have often drawn on Kuhn's work on scientific revolutions and paradigm shifts to justify the significance of their field.

Many of them were also explicit about their efforts to make the family into the unit of research and treatment. In an overview presentation at the 1967 conference organized by Framo, Jay Haley argued, "The family orientation in psychiatry does not merely suggest a revision of past psychological theory; it raises a basic question about the *unit* that should be studied and treated."[29] His comments further linked symptomatic behavior to an individual's social and familial context: "From this view, the difference between 'normal' people and individuals with psychiatric problems would be a difference in the current family situation (and treatment situation) in which the person is embedded."[30] While Haley qualified his remarks by noting some of the difficulties in experimentally assessing distinctions between normal and abnormal families, his comments were representative of family therapists' efforts to locate pathological difference and therapeutic intervention in the family itself.

Families made their way into therapy through several avenues, including professional referrals, ongoing hospital or clinic arrangements with family therapists, and the recommendations of probation officers or juvenile reformatories. Some went in search of treatment to alleviate the suffering of a family member and happened to end up with family therapy, whereas others explicitly sought out family therapists to help them with their troubles. In at least one case, a family reported contacting a research project on family therapy for help with a "family problem" after reading an article about the project in a local paper.[31]

The early family therapists of the 1950s drew on the work of academic and clinical predecessors in the United States, Europe, and Britain who focused on the family, but they developed a field that was historically distinct. Earlier psychological experts, such as those in the mental hygiene and child guidance movements of the early twentieth century, attended to the role of family environment in the production of mental illness and delinquency, but they retained a notion of the individual person as the patient to be treated and never conceptualized the family unit itself as the patient.[32] The marriage counselors of the 1920s and 1930s applied their backgrounds in eugenics, gynecology, sociology, social work, and religion to marital education, advice literature, and counseling to help couples avoid divorce.[33] In contrast, the newly self-identified family therapists of the 1950s came largely out of psychiatry, and they focused on psychiatric problems like schizophrenia or criminological problems, especially juvenile delinquency. The significance of these distinctions lay in the severity of the problems family therapists claimed to address and the pathologization of the family entailed in their efforts.

The scattered family therapy clinicians of the early 1950s began to learn of one another's work by the decade's end through journal publications, conferences, personal correspondence, and new institutions. The traffic in these networks contributed to the production of an increasingly self-aware community of practitioners who debated whether and how strongly to police the boundaries of their field. Throughout the 1960s, family therapists argued about the advantages and hazards of establishing a national association and accreditation standards, with many concerned that such moves would stifle the development of the field and promote the hegemonic imposition of one approach to family therapy. In 1970, the American Association of Marriage Counselors, which was established in 1942, changed its name to the American Association of Marriage and Family Counselors, to reflect members' growing interest in treating families. It again changed names in 1978, to the American Association of Marriage and Family Therapists (AAMFT), to move away from the connotation of advice giving associated with counseling and to appeal to family therapists with professional training in psychology and psychiatry. The same year, the U.S. Department of Health, Education, and Welfare designated AAMFT as the official accrediting agency to set standards for family therapy training programs. These institutional developments were indicative of the consolidation of family therapy's status as a professional field by the 1970s.

The Pathological Family

Although psychological experts and popular writers had long attributed the cause of a wide range of social ills to upbringing, the shift by family therapists to viewing the family itself as the patient, not just the source of problems, was a distinctive but difficult transition. The chapters that follow address a number of questions regarding the mutual formation of family therapy as a field and the family unit as its object of observation and treatment during the 1950s and 1960s. How did family therapists participate in the expanding domain of psychological thinking during the postwar period? In what ways did they reinforce or challenge normative visions of the nuclear family; assess the impacts of culture, poverty, or race on family life; and theorize the relationship between social problems and individual psychology? How did their interdisciplinary borrowings from nonclinical fields, particularly cybernetics, sociology and anthropology, contribute to their characterization of the family as a system, their appropriations of the concept of culture, and their emphasis on observation?

Chapter 1 situates the emergence of family therapy in a postwar configuration of several factors: the professional landscape and socially minded mission of psychiatry; a therapeutic ethos that grounded the solution to social problems in psychological treatment; and conflicting worries about the family, such as its pernicious capacity to foster racism or delinquency and the isolation and conformism of suburban families in mass society. The new techniques and practices developed by therapists for working with patients who no longer fit the psychoanalytic model of the individual also played a vital role in the field's formation.

Several clinicians became interested in family pathology through their research and clinical efforts related to schizophrenia. Chapter 2 focuses on one such research project, which was organized by the anthropologist Gregory Bateson in Palo Alto in 1952. The discussion of this project highlights the historical nexus of schizophrenia, communication, and the family through a close analysis of the research group's development of the theory of the double bind. The chapter shows how the family came to be understood as a system by analyzing the central role of cybernetics in shaping family therapists' understanding of schizophrenia and family processes.

Like the analytic category of the system, the concept of culture also contributed to the reconceptualization of the family as the unit of pathology and treatment. Chapter 3 explores how family therapists used the culture concept, as elaborated by anthropologists such as Alfred Kroeber and Clyde Kluckhohn, to justify their own field and build a community of self-identified professionals. The chapter demonstrates how therapists used culture to serve conflicting ends in debates about universal versus relativistic characterizations of the family, the viability of addressing problems like delinquency through therapeutic means, and the advisability of promoting or challenging societal values and norms through family therapy.

Moving from analytic categories to methodologies, chapter 4 considers the role of observation in the production of knowledge about families. It examines three residentially based research projects that aimed to study whole families through methodologies that emphasized naturalistic observation and visible interactions. In one of the projects, families moved for months at a time into an inpatient hospital ward at the National Institutes of Health in Bethesda, Maryland. In two subsequent projects, researchers moved into families' homes for several days or weeks. Through the lens of material practice, this chapter demonstrates the impact of place on research projects in which hospital stood for laboratory and home for natural habitat, as well as the implications of researchers' chosen techniques to document and represent family interactions.

Building on the optic orientation elaborated in chapter 4, chapter 5 turns to the visual technologies, particularly one-way mirrors and training films, that played a critical role in bringing together the realms of family life and therapeutic culture. The chapter analyzes two of the arenas in which family therapists incorporated these technologies: educational programs to train new family therapists and research efforts to understand and treat delinquency as a clinical problem. These domains were significant because of their impact on the future shape of the field.

By the 1970s and 1980s family therapy was well established as a field of psychotherapy, but, as the epilogue shows, by the 1990s the therapists' initial optimism that they could use their expertise to revolutionize the treatment of psychological and social problems had waned. Nevertheless, their field played a vital role in shaping the relationship between therapeutic culture and the changing meanings of family life in twentieth-century America.

CHAPTER ONE

PERSONALITY FACTORIES

"What's the matter with the family?" asked eminent American anthropologist Margaret Mead in *Harper's* in the spring of 1945, several months before World War II ended. In the remaining years of the 1940s, academic journals and popular magazines alike published articles that echoed Mead's query: "The American Family: Problem or Solution?," "What's Wrong with the Family?," and "The American Family in Trouble," among many others, debated such issues as the rising rates of divorce and the deleterious impact on juvenile delinquency of fathers' overseas service and mothers' wartime employment. Whether concerned with the state of marriage, the ferment of race relations, or patterns of child rearing, public commentators of the postwar years fretted over the American family.[1]

Such anxieties drew support from the contemporaneous expansions of psychoanalysis and psychiatry in American culture, for they were often framed in terms of the psychological shaping of children. The sociologist Talcott Parsons underscored this conception of the modern American family with the vivid comment that families "are 'factories' which produce human personalities."[2] The discourse of "momism" further instantiated the postwar links among upbringing, mental health, and national security. Coined by Philip Wylie in 1942 in his bestselling *Generation of Vipers*, "momism" proved a particularly influential term, suggesting the psychic damage that bad mothering could inflict on individual offspring and ultimately on the state of the nation. According to Wylie and others such as psychiatrist David Levy in his 1943 book

Maternal Overprotection, momism entailed a warped maternal instinct in overly materialistic mothers who appeared loving, doting, and selfless, but were in fact calculating and self-centered. Such mothers wreaked havoc on their children through their smothering attention, which left the children unprepared for being self-reliant.[3]

Family therapy's emergence in the 1950s was symptomatic of the culturally intertwined concern with family life and confidence in psychiatric expertise that underwrote the formulation of momism, even though it undid the logic of momism by shifting attention away from the mother-child relationship to a view of the family system as patient. Family therapists produced a new definition of what a family could be— namely, a unit of disease, which had previously been contained in individual bodies. Furthermore, twentieth-century American views of the family as the site of both reproduction and socialization, nature and culture, shored up the legitimacy of therapists' focus on the family as such.

The new definition of family as a unit of disease not only transformed the category of "family" and the meaning of "disease" but also prompted the development of new therapeutic techniques and goals. By shifting their clinical acumen from the individual to the family, early family therapists opened up space for a new set of practices that would then be appropriate for treating family-based disease. In so doing, they reconfigured the relationship between midcentury therapeutic culture and contemporaneous concerns about family life. That reconfiguration happened not just in prescriptive literature about what families should be but in the active realm of therapeutics and the development of new practices and techniques that shaped what happened in therapy sessions during the 1950s and 1960s. This chapter examines the earlier modes of expertise that informed the field's emergence and shows how the novel clinical practices developed by early family therapists made the family itself into a therapeutic subject.

A Genealogy of Family Expertise

Family therapy of the 1950s represented a new approach to psychotherapy, but it did not arise sui generis. Rather, early family therapists drew on long-standing concerns among marital relations experts, child guidance professionals, and psychoanalysts about issues such as marital stability, child rearing, motherhood, deviancy, and mental distress. The rise of family therapy similarly built on a much longer history of the intersection between the family and the state, in which the postwar period became a critical moment of transition. During the first half of the twentieth century, the relevance of family life was variably framed in terms of mate choice and sexuality, reproduction and child care, and personality and democratic citizenry. "Family" was itself an unstable category, at once naturalized and denatured. By the 1950s, it was the target of competing theories and agendas both within psychoanalytic and psychological theory and within broader social and cultural discourses in postwar America.

The proliferation of marriage experts during the early twentieth century illustrates the centrality of the relationship between husband and wife to modern family life.[4] In the United States, marital relations experts came from fields as varied as sexology, sociology, psychiatry, psychology, social work, and education. In university classes, traveling workshops, textbooks, and advice literature beginning in the 1920s, Ernest Groves and other sociologists built a family-life education movement that included material on courtship and marriage.[5] The ideal of the "companionate marriage" proved particularly influential as a model to emulate. The term was coined by Judge Ben Lindsey in the 1920s and later picked up by family sociologists such as Groves and Ernest Burgess to redefine successful marriage in terms of intimacy and emotional compatibility, in contrast to the older ideals of duty, sacrifice, economic partnership, and spiritual union.[6] As Jane Gerhard has argued, marriage experts such as Theodore H. Van Der Velde acknowledged the importance of female sexuality to successful marriages. However, they did so within a narrowly defined, psychoanalytically informed, heterosexual framework that defended women's passivity and dependency and, by the 1940s, became increasingly focused on reproduction rather than pleasure.[7]

In addition to advice and education, counseling became a medium through which professionals tried to intervene in marital relations in order to promote marital happiness, prevent divorce, improve sexual relations, and encourage eugenic marriages among native-born whites for racial betterment.[8] Marriage counseling as a field developed in the late 1920s and 1930s through the efforts of physicians (particularly from the new specialty of gynecology), clergy, social workers, and family educators such as Paul Popenoe. Its practitioners drew on the work of European sexologists with a wide range of political views, such as Havelock Ellis of Britain, Richard von Krafft-Ebing of Austria, and Magnus Hirschfeld of Germany.[9] The field also had links to Progressive

Era reform movements, including eugenics, mental hygiene, and social hygiene.

The case of Paul Popenoe is illustrative. Popenoe established one of the first marriage counseling centers in the United States in 1930. A strong advocate of eugenics, he served as editor of the *Journal of Heredity* prior to World War I and became research director at the Human Betterment Foundation in California and an advocate of sterilization of the "unfit" after the war.[10] He augmented his support for the negative eugenic policies of institutionalization and sterilization of the feeble-minded and other "defectives" with the positive eugenic goals of helping fit couples overcome marital discord and produce healthy offspring. Popenoe also popularized marriage counseling through a 1954 *Ladies' Home Journal* series, "How to Be Marriageable," which featured cases from the files of his American Institute of Family Relations; a syndicated newspaper column titled "Modern Marriage" (1947–57), later renamed "Your Family and You" (1958–72); and a television show, *Divorce Hearing* (1957–60), on which Popenoe and other "judges" listened to the problems of couples on the verge of divorce and tried to help them reconcile.[11]

The inspiration for Popenoe's marriage clinic came from the marriage consultation centers established in Austria and Germany in the wake of World War I to promote racial hygiene and race betterment.[12] Some of the European marriage counseling centers of the 1920s and 1930s were focused on encouraging eugenically "responsible" marriages, while other clinics were more oriented toward sex education, child-rearing advice, and birth control. Staffed by physicians, social workers, midwives, and psychoanalysts such as Wilhelm Reich, the centers often aimed to reach working-class populations. Some were private and independent, while others were state-sponsored and established by municipal or health insurance officials. Although the Austrian and German sex and marriage counseling clinics had nationally specific features, such as their dependence on the working-class politics of the Weimar Republic and national health insurance policies, their amalgamation of sex reform, eugenics, and marriage counseling influenced contemporaneous American efforts to establish marriage counseling.[13] Britain's marriage counseling movement, institutionalized in 1938 in the National Marriage Guidance Council, also served as a model for its American colleagues.[14]

A national organization for professional marriage counselors in the United States began meeting informally in 1942, then more formally in

1945, with the stated purpose of maintaining standards, holding meetings, and sponsoring research and publications. According to a 1948 report from a joint subcommittee of the National Council on Family Relations and the American Association of Marriage Counselors, marriage counseling as a specialty centered "largely on the interpersonal relationship between husband and wife."[15] Demonstrating a multifaceted view of marriage, this report advocated that an accredited training should cover sexual anatomy, personality development, and legal aspects of marriage, in addition to counseling techniques.

Although the field of family therapy merged with marriage counseling in the 1970s, in its early years it developed in ways that were distinct from marriage counseling. Founding family therapists of the 1950s drew their conceptions of the family more directly from psychoanalysis and psychiatry than from the eugenic, legal, religious, and gynecological backgrounds of early marriage counselors. Family therapy also differed from marriage counseling in its attention to child rearing, not just marital relations, and its early focus on schizophrenia and delinquency rather than marriage saving, sexual relations, or eugenic fitness.

Early family therapists' approaches to parent-child relations emerged from perceptions of a deepening association between family structure and democracy during the twentieth century, as well as the growing psychologization of parenthood.[16] Whereas the connection between mothering and the production of democratic citizens was long-standing, by the 1940s concerns about child rearing and political formation became increasingly informed by psychology.[17] The concentration of responsibility for the socialization of children in the nuclear family during the 1920s–1940s solidified the role of parents, especially mothers, in the "enterprise of rearing psychologically healthy and productive citizens," as historian Julia Grant has argued.[18] This conjoining of psychological health with the formation of a democratic, productive citizenry in the crucible of the family marked many of the child-oriented movements of the early and mid-twentieth century.

Given the high stakes of child rearing, experts in many guises aimed to help parents guide their children's development in the right way. They were part of a general proliferation of expert administrators in the Progressive Era. Early twentieth-century child reformers were concerned about the psychological and sociological dimensions of child rearing, as well as infant mortality, domestic hygiene, and child labor. The medicalization of motherhood and the "ideology of scientific motherhood" laid out a contrast between views of motherhood as common sense and as a profession that required training and depended on expert advice.[19] The ideology of scientific motherhood buttressed women's long-espoused maternal role in the domestic sphere but with increased emphasis on the importance of scientific and medical input for preparing women for their proper "profession" of motherhood. In baby books, magazine columns, parent education courses, pediatricians' offices, and child guidance clinics, an array of experts offered parenting advice to audiences with varying degrees of interest and receptivity.[20] Better baby contests and maternal- and infant-health programs also promoted expert guidance in child rearing that was informed by eugenic ideals.[21]

The mental hygiene and child guidance movements provided further avenues for expert interventions into family life and child-rearing practices. Rooted in Progressive Era confidence in scientific solutions to societal problems, the mental hygiene movement grew out of the joint efforts of a former mental patient, Clifford Beers, who wrote a critique of mental hospital abuses and established the National Committee for Mental Hygiene in 1909, and the prominent psychiatrist Adolf Meyer, who wanted to promote a role for psychiatry beyond the walls of asylums by focusing on the prevention and treatment of noninstitutional problems such as alcoholism, crime, and feeblemindedness. Although there remained significant heterogeneity within the movement among psychiatrists, other helping professionals, and lay social reformers, by the 1920s, psychiatrists' emphasis on prevention and the popularization of psychiatry overshadowed Beers's interest in institutional reform.

The mental hygiene movement was based on an environmental view in which childhood experiences laid the groundwork for adult mental health. Meyer defined mental health in terms of adjustment between an individual and his environment, whereas maladjustment served as the explanation for insanity, alcoholism, delinquency, prostitution, and other social problems. He believed that childhood experiences laid the groundwork for adult adjustment or maladjustment. William A. White, a psychoanalytic leader in the movement, wrote that childhood was the "period *par excellence* for prophylaxis. . . . If we are to produce a better race of adults, we must be able to control the influences which go to mold the adult character."[22] White and other mental hygienists attempted to improve adult mental health by guiding childhood "influences" through diverse venues such as educational exhibits, schools, community clinics, and eugenic legislation.[23]

With roots in the environmentalist reform efforts of Progressive child savers to combat urban crime by helping poor and immigrant children, child guidance represented one strain of mental hygiene that focused on preventing delinquency and treating conduct disorders, or in Kathleen Jones's felicitous phrase, "taming the troublesome child."[24] Its adherents viewed delinquency as an individualized, psychological problem best addressed by professional teams composed of psychiatrists, psychologists, and social workers. Beginning in 1922, the Commonwealth Fund contributed to these efforts by providing seed money for psychologically oriented child-guidance clinics around the country. But child guidance quickly moved beyond the clinic and a narrow focus on delinquents to considering "predelinquency" and the "everyday child." The theory was that the child-rearing habits of families of any social class could promote misbehavior and maladjustment and should therefore be accessible to the expert advice of professionals.[25]

By shifting the cause of misbehavior from class or heredity to bad parenting, child guidance professionals framed a set of causal associations that informed the subsequent development of family therapy and other postwar studies of parenting and psychopathology. As Kathleen Jones has argued, "Although the frenzied studies of schizophrenogenic mothers, of cold rejecting mothers who allegedly cause autism, and of maternal deprivation lay in the future, the diagnoses of maternal pathology made during the 1920s and 1930s laid the groundwork for these later incriminating portraits of motherhood."[26] Yet experts did not foist advice on passive mothers who uncritically adopted their suggestions wholesale. Even in the face of strongly prescriptive, often mother-blaming professionals, parents actively sought out and critically evaluated expert opinions in their turn to child guidance services and other forms of advice.[27]

Such advice often had political resonances. The "discourse of the democratic family" preceded World War II but drew particularly intense attention during and after the war. As Sonya Michel has argued, this discourse included descriptive attention to what early twentieth-century sociologists characterized as an increasingly democratic structure and decreasingly patriarchal pattern of authority within families, as well as prescriptive efforts by policymakers and government agencies to encourage mothers to retain their traditional maternal role rather than enter the workforce.[28] Psychologically minded experts readily joined such conversations. On the eve of the war, the influential Rockefeller Foundation officer, Lawrence K. Frank, conjoined the state of national politics with the psychological impact of child rearing when he bemoaned the threat that poorly adjusted people posed to democracy. Such people, he wrote, "have never learned to accept themselves or to manage their feelings. . . . Democracy, like charity, begins at home, where the fundamental patterns of human relationships are developed that will govern the child's subsequent adult conduct and social adjustment."[29]

America's democratic future thus began in the home but not solely under the watchful eye of domestic motherhood. Notably, Frank emphasized that fathers, not just mothers, were responsible for rearing good citizens: "The father in the family carries the major responsibility for these developments and by his attitudes and actions he is deciding the fate of our democracy."[30] In their writings on modern fatherhood, Frank and other experts such as Ernest Burgess and Ernest and Gladys Groves exhorted fathers to focus less on authority and discipline and instead to assume a more involved and loving role in their children's lives. They did so not to transform a gender-based division of labor but rather to shore up traditional gender roles by strengthening fathers' impact on the formation of their children's personalities, thereby contributing to the development of democratic values and resistance to fascism while preserving the model of a breadwinning father and homemaker mother. The concerns about fathers' roles were only heightened when the United States entered World War II and the country grappled with the impact of fathers' absence from the home while fighting overseas.[31]

The wartime context also heightened concerns about family life, psychological health, and national security because of the high number of neuropsychiatric casualties among America's military men. Studies such as *Men under Stress*, by Roy Grinker and John Spiegel, were emblematic of the normalization of mental distress during World War II. Unlike Adolf Meyer and other mental hygienists who aimed to normalize mental distress earlier in the century through their focus on adjustment, Grinker and Spiegel did so through the discourse of stress. Relying on their work with air force pilots, they concluded that given enough stress, any man has his breaking point.[32] Work by Grinker, Spiegel, and other psychiatrists raised the question, if all men have breaking points, what determines when and how a particular person breaks down?

For many, the answer lay in upbringing. In his postwar critique of the damaging impact of poor mothering on soldiers' capacity to fight for the country, psychiatrist Edward Strecker asserted, "'Mom' as I have used it, and will use it throughout this book, is merely a convenient verbal hook upon which to hang an indictment of the woman who has failed in the elementary mother function of weaning her offspring emotionally as well as physically. I might have called this spurious mother far less pleasant names than Mom."[33] In terms that echoed the momism of Philip Wylie, Strecker continued by comparing bad moms and good mothers on the basis of their ability to loosen the apron strings and allow their sons to develop and mature. According to Strecker, the stakes were nothing less than the state of national security.

Furthermore, wartime attention to the mother-child relationship among British psychoanalysts shaped widespread American attitudes toward mothering in general and informed early family therapists' intellectual views of the mother-child bond, particularly in the development of schizophrenia. The Tavistock Clinic and the Tavistock Institute of Human Relations were hubs of influential activity in England.[34] The wartime therapeutic work by Wilfred Bion and John Rickfield with shell-shocked soldiers at Northfield drew on Kurt Lewin's social psychology approach to small groups and contributed to the subsequent development of group therapy.[35] Among British psychoanalysts, Melanie Klein and later Donald W. Winnicott were influential in their emphasis on mother-child interactions. Although Klein and her followers contributed to the elevation of the mother-child dyad in British psychoanalytic theory, her focus on the role of the mother in infantile fantasies and drives distinguished her work from that of her rival, Anna Freud, whose attention to environment rather than psychic fantasies resonated with American neo-Freudians and ego psychologists. Anna Freud's wartime work with Dorothy Burlingham with orphaned infants in the Hampstead Nurseries and her publications on infants without families were fundamental to midcentury American understandings of maternal deprivation, as was work by René Spitz and John Bowlby. Their studies became part of postwar conversations about the hazards of women's work outside the home. Despite their differences, studies by Freud, Spitz, Bowlby, and others on maternal deprivation worked together with seemingly opposing publications on maternal overprotection and involvement to shore up traditional gender roles and emphasize the importance of the mother-child dyad.[36]

Bowlby's wartime work on maternal care, infant health, and psychoanalysis was a particularly notable part of the intellectual genealogy of family therapy. He also played a part in the professional development of the field. The psychiatrist John Bell visited Tavistock in 1952 and heard Bowlby describe working psychotherapeutically with families. Although Bowlby met with each member individually, Bell thought he was seeing all family members at the same time and decided to try this approach when he returned to the United States. The Tavistock was also home to other psychological experts besides Bowlby who were important to the history of family therapy, including R. D. Laing, whose work on family and schizophrenia during the 1960s drew inspiration from the work of American family therapists; Michael and Enid Balint, who developed a case conference format for training marriage counselors at the Family Discussion Bureau during the 1950s; and psychiatric social workers who staffed a family psychiatry unit in which they worked with couples referred by divorce court.[37]

In the years after 1945, the wartime experiences in Britain and the United States provoked wide-ranging professional and institutional changes in American psychiatry. The number of psychiatrists grew rapidly. Membership in the American Psychiatric Association grew from 2,423 in 1940 to 18,407 in 1970.[38] The need for clinicians in Veterans Administration (VA) hospitals in part drove this increase as well as the emergence of clinical psychology.[39] With the National Mental Health Act of 1946 and the establishment of the National Institute for Mental Health (NIMH) in 1949, psychiatrists gained an institutional base and funding source at the federal government. The National Mental Health Act was initially called the National Neuropsychiatric Institute Act when it was first introduced in Congress in 1945, and the shift to the term "mental health" captured the pivotal role of World War II in moving clinical orientation toward normalization, as encouraged earlier in the century by the mental hygienists. In 1950, the first year of NIMH operations, the institute had a budget of $8.7 million. Ten years later, its budget was over $100 million and in less than two decades, it had reached $315 million.[40]

The war's impacts were social as well as institutional. During the war, psychiatry and psychotherapy touched millions of Americans through military screenings and treatment. These included the more than a million men who were rejected from military service on neuropsychological grounds plus those who received psychiatric or psychological treatment during and after the war, not just institutionalized patients with severe and chronic mental illnesses. In 1955, the Joint Commission on Mental Illness and Health received congressional endorsement and federal funding to survey mental illness and make recommendations on how to combat it. The commission published its final report in 1961 as *Action for Mental Health*, which highlighted the link between mental health and democracy and advocated for community-based psychotherapeutic services for illness prevention. Other contemporaneous studies, such as

Americans View Their Mental Health, which was also conducted by the commission, and *Mental Health in the Metropolis: The Midtown Manhattan Study*, underscored the widespread public concerns about mental health and the value of psychiatric services in addressing such problems.[41]

The expansion of the psychiatric profession in the wake of the war also enhanced the status of psychoanalysis. The Second World War created a need for psychiatrists who could understand and treat war neuroses and psychosomatic disorders. Because psychoanalytic psychiatrists had long focused on neurotic behavior, they were better able to deal with this challenge than their institution-based colleagues. Analysts quickly moved into leadership positions and played key roles in military training programs for psychiatrists. Beyond the military and professional contexts, psychoanalysis reached a broader popular audience in the postwar period through films, plays, cartoons, and the advice literature of Benjamin Spock and others.[42]

The postwar professional and popular growth of psychiatry and psychoanalysis fueled the diffusion of psychologically oriented views of family life, but the concern with overly domineering mothers, weak fathers, and family dynamics was not unique to psychiatry. Rather, worries about parenting and mental breakdown were part of a broader set of ambivalent preoccupations with the functions and influences of American families during the 1940s and 1950s. As James Gilbert has argued, "From the 1940s to the 1960s, Americans looked at the family with double vision: with optimism and despair."[43] In magazine articles, speeches, and advice columns, a wide range of public intellectuals and commentators bemoaned the perceived rise in juvenile delinquency, the alleged reluctance of returning veterans to assume their family responsibilities, and the seeming fragility of family relations in the aftermath of wartime disruptions.[44]

Social scientists also played a vital role in framing postwar conversations about American families. Sometimes they did so in institutional settings that brought sociologists and anthropologists directly into conversation with psychologists and psychiatrists, such as the Yale Institute for Human Relations and the Department of Social Relations at Harvard University.[45] In the years following World War II, the eminent American sociologist Talcott Parsons was instrumental in the establishment of Social Relations as an interdisciplinary department for the social sciences. In his own work, he argued vigorously for the contemporary significance of the family in an era in which it had "lost" many of the functions it had previously served, such as producing its own food and clothing. In so doing, Parsons echoed a concern that had preoccupied American sociologists since at least the 1920s and 1930s regarding the alleged demise of the family in the face of social changes such as urbanization, industrialization, immigration, changing demographic patterns of marriage and divorce, and debates about sexual morality and birth control. More specifically, Parsons argued in his 1955 book, *Family, Socialization and Interaction Process*, coauthored with Robert Bales, that "the functions of the family in a highly differentiated society [like the United States at midcentury] are not to be interpreted as functions directly on behalf of the society, but on behalf of personality. It is because the *human* personality is not 'born' but must be 'made' through the socialization process that in the first instance families are necessary."[46] For Parsons, societal issues were intimately linked to individual personalities through the mechanism or "productive functions" of the family, understood as a social institution whose prime function was to produce healthy personalities who would in turn contribute to healthy societies.

While Parsons and Bales highlighted the connection between family and personality formation, the contemporaneous Midcentury White House Conference on Children and Youth underscored the causal association between personality and democratic society. The fact-finding report from the conference focused on the "development of the healthy personality," in which the very definition of healthy personality yoked together individual happiness and responsible citizenship.[47] The conference report evoked a view of personality that was crucial not just for children's welfare but for the survival of democracy: "Only individuals whose minds are free and whose personalities have developed to healthy social and emotional maturity are capable of living in accord with the high ideals which democratic society demands of us. . . . The mature, emotionally stable, healthy personality is at once the goal and the guardian of the democratic tradition."[48]

Because the family was seen as a key site for the production of healthy personalities and productive citizens, child-rearing patterns held the potential to bolster or undermine American politics and society by affecting the psychological well-being of children. In the work of otherwise diverse intellectuals such as Theodor Adorno, Bruno Bettelheim, and Gordon Allport, bad parenting became the cause of fascism, prejudice, autism, and homosexuality.[49] In their landmark 1950 book *The Authoritarian Personality*, Adorno and other scholars of the Frankfurt School who were refugees from Nazi Europe developed an "F-scale" to assess individuals' susceptibility to fascism, and patterns of child rearing and family structure were central to their psychoanalytic conclusions about the type of personality likely to support totalitarianism. Similarly, in his seminal 1944 study, *An American Dilemma: The Negro Problem and Modern Democracy*, Gunnar Myrdal focused on how a racist upbringing could damage the democratic convictions of racism's perpetrators, white Americans. Other studies focused on psychological damage among the targets of racism and attributed inequalities between blacks and whites to the family environment. For example, social scientific studies such as Abram Kardiner and Lionel Ovesey's *The Mark of Oppression* emphasized the role of matriarchal families in contributing to blacks' susceptibility to psychological damage from racism.[50] In these and other studies in the culture-and-personality tradition (discussed in more depth in chapter 3), psychoanalysts and social scientists collaboratively built up an approach to the relationship between individual psychology and sociopolitical formation that situated the family as the linchpin between those realms.

In intellectual publications as well as in popular culture, family was thus central to postwar discourses concerned with preventing the resurgence of fascism and Nazism, ameliorating American race relations, and producing democratic citizens. Such discourses framed an ideal democratic subject in terms that scholars have since analyzed as neoliberal and consumerist, as well as psychological.[51] The connection that midcentury experts drew between political ideals and notions of subjectivity was apparent in forums ranging from social scientific research to television programming. The development of a new clinical field organized around therapeutic intervention into family life was emblematic of this configuration of expertise, politics, and the self.

"Band of Brothers"

The wide-ranging postwar studies, institutional changes, and cultural concerns about therapy, family life, and political culture were part of the intellectual and cultural milieu that shaped the emergence of a clinical field that made family itself the locus of disease and the target of treatment. Some therapists reported shifting to a family orientation after observing patients improve in a hospital setting and then deteriorate after being sent home, a change they attributed to the entrenched pathology of the family setting. Others observed that there were ramifications when an individual patient did improve: another family member developed symptoms, or the whole family began to unravel. From such experiences, these clinicians concluded that the only way to heal a patient with a psychiatric diagnosis was to change the illness-inducing context of the family, and they developed a heterogeneous collection of theories and practices that were subsequently brought together under the umbrella of family therapy.[52]

The psychiatrists Nathan Ackerman, Murray Bowen, and Salvador Minuchin were among the founding figures of the new field. Though they did not exclusively comprise the "first generation" of family therapists,[53] their work illustrates the variety of therapeutic practices, patient populations, and institutional settings that became known as family therapy. The cases of Ackerman, Bowen, and Minuchin demonstrate how family therapists framed their specialized therapeutic aims in terms that explicitly evoked broader sociocultural trends. Like the field more broadly, they held a spectrum of views on psychoanalysis, and they focused on schizophrenia and delinquency as clinical problems. Furthermore, their own comments on the history of their field reflect the tensions and paradoxes that characterized the mutual formation of family therapy as a field—which they often described as a family itself—and the family unit as a patient. Cybernetics, which was also central to this history, is the focus of the next chapter.

A 1962 article by Nathan Ackerman in the new family therapy journal *Family Process* exemplified the chain of connections that he and his colleagues drew between individual problems, family systems, and social disarray, with therapy among the recommended solutions. In "Adolescent Problems: A Symptom of Family Disorder," Ackerman expressed alarm at the behavior of contemporary youth: "The adolescents of our time are hoisting distress signals. . . . Their disordered behavior today is an almost universal phenomenon. We have in the United States of America the teenage gangs and beatniks; in Germany, the 'Bear-Shirts'; in Russian, the 'Hoodlums'. . . . As J. Edgar Hoover puts it, 'Gang style ferocity, once the domain of hardened adult criminals, now centers chiefly on cliques of teen-age brigands.'"[54] Ackerman relied on FBI data to support his claims that the number of violent acts by juveniles was increasing, the severity of such acts was worsening, and the trend was universal since many countries reiterated the FBI reports.[55]

Beyond approvingly citing Hoover, Ackerman further argued that any attempt to understand and treat social ills like juvenile delinquency must consider the role of family in producing the anarchy, violence, and instability characteristic of adolescents: "The disordered behavior of the adolescent needs to be understood not only as an expression of a particular stage of growth, but beyond that, as a symptom of parallel disorder in the patterns of family, society, and culture. . . . The family, as a behavior system, stands intermediate between the individual and culture. It transmits through its adolescent members the disorders that characterize the social system."[56] In his alarm at the apparent rise in juvenile delinquency, Ackerman joined a rising postwar chorus of social critics and ambivalent Hollywood productions that looked at adolescent culture and blamed the family for the destructiveness and alienation of teenagers.[57] At the end of the article he called for therapeutic and educational solutions to these problems, thereby asserting the viability of family therapy as one means of ameliorating social disorder.

Ackerman's comments exemplified one of the ways in which family therapists connected social trends and individual disturbances. Beyond his interest in adolescent problems, he was significant for his clinical innovations and institution building. Referring to him as the "grandfather" of their field,[58] family therapists often cite two of his articles from the late 1930s as the first family therapy articles.[59] Ackerman disseminated his approach to family therapy through his published transcripts of therapy sessions, his consultations and public demonstrations across the country, and his filmed sessions.

Most of the family therapists of the 1950s had a psychoanalytic background. Of those, Nathan Ackerman remained one of the most closely identified with psychoanalysis, though he broke from orthodox practices in significant ways. He retained the strongest connection to psychoanalysis of the family therapists discussed here. He trained as a child psychiatrist, spending time at the Menninger Clinic. He underwent his training analysis at the New York Psychoanalytic Institute from 1937 to 1942 with Clara Thompson, a prominent neo-Freudian and ally of Karen Horney in the factional battles within the New York psychoanalytic community. He was active in the Group for the Advancement of Psychiatry, including the committee on social issues. He coauthored a psychoanalytically informed volume in Max Horkheimer's interdisciplinary series *Studies in Prejudice*, titled *Anti-Semitism and Emotional Disorder*. He helped found the American Academy of Psychoanalysis in 1955 in the context of acrimonious debates within American psychoanalysis about orthodoxy and medical training. In addition, he taught at a new analytic training facility at Columbia University from 1957 until the end of his career.

Despite his commitment to psychodynamics, he also broke from psychoanalytic practices in significant ways. In particular, his patients interacted with each other in the waiting room, and he demonstrated how to conduct a family interview with real families, which flew in the face not only of Freud's opposition to involving family members but also of established standards for confidentiality.[60] He claimed to have turned to the family approach because of weaknesses in traditional forms of psychotherapy, such as the emphasis on resolving transference issues rather than focusing on contemporary adult life and the inability to test a patient's image of his family relationships since they were conveyed secondhand. In contrast to these practices, he wrote, the "family approach to healing is a therapy in vivo, not in vitro. . . .; it is a means of intervention into a true slice of life."[61]

Ackerman also emphasized the naturalness of the family. For example, in his 1966 book *Treating the Troubled Family*, he asserted,

> To begin at the beginning, the human family is a unique organization. It is the basic unit of society; it provides for the union of man and woman so that they may create children and assure them nurture and strength. The human being is a true familial animal. The mother's body is structured to carry and to give birth to the child. . . . The father's body is specialized for strength and potency. He is the protector of mother and young. These are the essential, ever-present features, regardless of the endless variations of family pattern superimposed by contrasting cultures. The father sows the seed; the mother gives birth to the child.[62]

Reproductive functions and heterosexual gender roles were thus key features of family life for Ackerman. In addition to characterizing the reproducing family as a unit of "biological continuity" and a "universal design for living," he also described it as a "familial organism," by which he meant the "useful analogy between the organismic properties of the individual and the vital features of family life, for both entities are characterized by an interdependence of parts and a specialization of functions."[63] He thereby highlighted the biological as well as the psychological and social aspects of family life.

In Ackerman's own brief published discussions of the history of family therapy, he portrayed the field as both revolutionary and inevitable. For example, in his editorial introduction and article in a 1970 compilation from the first decade of the journal *Family Process*, he described family therapy in terms of its "astonishing and unpredicted directions. . . . [its] new and ingenious ways of observing and defining family interaction,"[64] though nevertheless seeing it as an "inevitable development" and "natural product" of intellectual trends in cultural anthropology, communication, psychoanalytic social science, ego psychology, and child development.[65] He also tied the development of family therapy to recent United States history when he claimed that "the revolutionary turmoil of our day has forced upon us the recognition of the extraordinary dependence of the operations of personality on the social environment. In a further step it has compelled us to a new conceptualization of behavior disorders and mental illness within the framework of the family and community transaction."[66] The "revolutionary turmoil" in his 1970 article evoked the social and political upheavals of the 1960s. Although it also contrasted sharply with the fifties-like concerns about conformity that he had expressed only eight years earlier in his article on distressed adolescents, both publications linked family therapy practices with broader contemporary trends.

In addition to psychoanalysis and child psychiatry, research on schizophrenia and clinical attempts to use psychotherapy to treat schizophrenia became key sites for the development of family therapy. The disease severely disrupted families' lives, though paradoxically it was also the very thing that brought the family together as a unit within family therapy. According to Murray Bowen, one of the early leaders of the field, "Family therapy was so associated with schizophrenia in the early years that some did not think of it as separate from schizophrenia until the early 1960s."[67] Schizophrenia formed the basis of early work by Bowen and other therapists including Lyman Wynne, Theodore Lidz, James Framo, Jay Haley, John Weakland, and Don Jackson.

This connection grew in part out of the professional context of the 1930s–1950s when some psychiatrists—including Frieda Fromm-Reichmann, John Rosen, Silvano Arieti, and Harold Searles—became interested in understanding the role of the mother-child relationship in the development of schizophrenia and in treating it with various forms of psychotherapy. The domineering mother of Philip Wylie and Edward Strecker's momism reappeared in a related yet different guise: the "schizophrenogenic mother," a term coined by Frieda Fromm-Reichmann. It referred to a mother who caused schizophrenia by her aggressive, authoritarian, yet rejecting behavior toward her children. According to Fromm-Reichmann, "The schizophrenic is painfully distrustful and resentful of other people, due to the severe early warp and

rejection he encountered in important people of his infancy and childhood, as a rule, mainly in a schizophrenogenic mother. . . . His initial
pathogenic experiences are actually, or by virtue of his interpretation,
the pattern for a never-ending succession of subsequent similar ones."[68]

The impact of Fromm-Reichmann's formulation was widespread.
Her concept of the schizophrenogenic mother was elaborated by others at the private mental hospital Chestnut Lodge where she practiced,
as well as by psychiatrists and psychological researchers across the
country, and it remained prominent throughout the 1950s and 1960s.
Psychiatrists such as Harold Searles used increasingly vivid language
to describe the pathological relationship between schizophrenogenic
mothers and their children, including the politically resonant characterizations of brainwashing and indoctrination.[69] Theodore Lidz and
Ruth Lidz argued that a schizophrenogenic mother held her children—
their patients—in bondage. They also attributed mothers' hostility to
their children to their own thwarted dreams and ambitions. In addition,
psychiatrist John Rosen targeted the damages wrought by "the perverse
mother" through his psychotherapeutic technique of direct analysis,
which he saw as a process of forceful "re-mothering." Other researchers used a variety of psychological assessment scales to investigate the
pathogenic attitudes of the mothers of schizophrenics.[70]

Early family therapists drew on this psychiatric research, though
their work ultimately turned away from the mother-child relationship
to a view of the family system as patient. Murray Bowen was an influential example of a family therapist whose early work dealt with the
role of the family in schizophrenia, though his later efforts to develop
his theory of family systems moved away from schizophrenia. Bowen
emphasized the importance of theory as well as clinical practice and
research. His approach has been considered a bridge between psychodynamic and more strictly systems perspectives.[71] His psychiatric training
began at the Menninger Clinic in 1946 after he completed his wartime
service in the army. He moved to NIMH in 1954, where he oversaw a
research project on schizophrenia in which he hospitalized whole families, then after his NIMH project ended in 1959, he joined the faculty
of the Georgetown University Medical Center.[72] In 1963, he withdrew
from his psychoanalytic training at the Washington Psychoanalytic Institute;[73] by contrast, Ackerman tried to maintain connections with analytic institutions even after he became focused on family therapy. Thus
while both Ackerman and Bowen came out of a psychoanalytic training,
they had different levels of commitment to psychoanalysis in their later

careers, a spectrum that was mirrored by other family therapists. Despite such differences, Ackerman and Bowen remained similar in their investment in institution building. Like Ackerman, Bowen built an independent center, which he established in Georgetown in 1975, to support training, research, and practice in his approach to treating families.

One of the unique aspects of Bowen's approach was his use of his own family to illustrate his theories. In 1967, after family therapy was well under way, he gave an unexpected conference paper on his own "family of origin" in which he described his efforts to work on relations within his extended family.[74] This paper fit within his broader concern with intergenerational transmission of relationship patterns. His concept of the "undifferentiated family ego mass" encapsulated his interest in the conflicting dynamics of individuation, differentiation, and fusion within families, which he characterized as an emotional system.

Bowen himself gave a historical account of the beginnings of family therapy. He reiterated his history of family therapy in some of the articles that he collected in his 1978 book *Family Therapy in Clinical Practice*. According to him, the "family movement" emerged in the mid-1950s after operating in dispersed locations for several years. "There were too many small roots, each growing independently, for any to say which was first. It was an evolutionary development that suddenly burst into the open when the psychiatric world was ready for it. Various investigators, each working independently, began to hear about the work of others."[75] Among the early researchers that Bowen particularly identified were Theodore Lidz and his colleagues at Yale, Lyman Wynne's group at NIMH, and Don Jackson and the communication group in Palo Alto, as well as clinicians Christian Midelfort and Nathan Ackerman.

Bowen's account thereby exemplified the standard origin story among family therapists according to which their field began as a "band of brothers"[76] rather than with an individual, founding father, as in the case of Freud and psychoanalysis. Evoking the rallying call of Shakespeare's Henry V to his small group of fellow fighters, "We few, we happy few, we band of brothers," early family therapists saw themselves as a sparse, beleaguered group waging battle against the orthodoxy of midcentury American psychoanalysis. This metaphor also echoed Sigmund Freud's psychoanalytic account of the origins of totemism through the murderous uprising of a group of brothers against their father. Described in *Totem and Taboo* as "the elimination of the primal father by the company of his sons,"[77] such patricidal rebellion fit the self-fashioning of the early family therapists, who positioned themselves as young Turks in the shadow of psychoanalysis. The metaphor also occluded the role of any "sisters" in the development of family therapy, which feminist family therapists would challenge in the 1970s and 1980s.[78] By appropriating the language of the family to characterize their own field, early family therapists became familial in a move that mirrored their turn to families as patients.

Bowen's version of his field's development focused on intellectual and professional history. He traced the antecedents of family therapy to psychoanalytic interest in the impact of family life on the individual patient, including noteworthy mention of Freud's 1909 paper on Little Hans, which was a psychoanalytic case study of a five-year old boy based on extensive notes from the boy's father, and a 1921 book by J. C. Flugel titled *The Psycho-analytic Study of the Family*, which included individual psychoanalytic presentations on several members of the same family.[79] Bowen also pointed to the child guidance movement, studies by sociologists and anthropologists on the family, and general systems theory of the 1930s as antecedents, but he argued that "these developments were not recognized until after the family movement was under way."[80] He ultimately related the emergence of the movement to the rise of psychoanalysis and some clinicians' efforts to find more effective means of treatment, though opposition from orthodox psychoanalysts also contributed to practitioners' early isolation.[81]

Once the family movement had surfaced as an area of multiple practitioners' research and clinical interests, the national American Orthopsychiatric Association and American Psychiatric Association meetings in 1957 and 1958 sponsored panels on family therapy and research that became touchstones for the young field. Bowen charted the field's expansion by the degree of interest expressed at those meetings: "Beginning in 1958, swarms of therapists crowded the family sections at national meetings." He characterized this rapid increase in the field as "the beginning of a healthy unstructured state of chaos."[82] Bowen himself developed an influential approach to family therapy—Bowen family systems theory—and trained scores of family therapists at his Georgetown institute.

In addition to psychoanalysis and schizophrenia research, juvenile delinquency played an important role in the development of family therapy. The therapeutic link between family and democratic citizenship became most explicit in the governmentally supported clinical management of disorderly behavior whose cause was attributed to family life. A key figure in treating delinquency as a problem of the family was

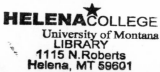

Salvador Minuchin, who became prominent a decade later than Ackerman and Bowen. Minuchin worked in a New York juvenile reformatory from the late 1950s until 1965, when he moved to the Philadelphia
Child Guidance Clinic (PCGC). He also went on a tour of other family
therapy sites during the early 1960s, which demonstrated the growing
institutional trappings of the field by that time.[83] Though the PCGC
had not previously been a site of family therapy, Minuchin transformed
it into one of the premier family therapy institutes in the country during
his tenure as director. He and his colleagues at the clinic were explicitly
concerned with providing treatment to racially diverse and socioeconomically disadvantaged communities who were traditionally underserved by psychiatry and psychotherapy. In forming his influential
school of structural family therapy, he also drew explicitly on Talcott
Parsons's structural theories of socialization and the family. Such social
scientific borrowings were commonplace among early family therapists
and other contemporary psychiatrists.

   In his historical accounts, Minuchin emphasized the role of his personal upbringing in a patriarchal Jewish family in Argentina and his
commitments to social justice in the development of his own approach
to family therapy.[84] He also wrote about the history of the broader family therapy field, just as Ackerman and Bowen had done. In the foreword
to a family therapy textbook from the late 1990s, Minuchin painted particularly vivid portraits of Ackerman and Gregory Bateson (whose work
on families and schizophrenia is the focus of the next chapter).

> Born in the late 1950s, family therapy seemed to spring fully
> formed out of the heads of a group of seminal thinkers. . . . [In]
> the beginning—as the storytellers say—there was Gregory Bate-
> son on the West Coast, a tall, clean-shaven, angular intellectual,
> who saw families as systems, carriers of ideas. On the East Coast
> was Nathan Ackerman, short, bearded, portly, who saw families
> as collections of individuals struggling to balance feelings, irra-
> tionalities, and desires. Bateson, the man of ideas, and Ackerman,
> the man of passion, complemented each other perfectly, the Don
> Quixote and Sancho Panza of the family systems revolution.[85]

Like other family therapists, Minuchin thus portrayed his field as the
product of several individuals in the 1950s. While his comparison of
Bateson and Ackerman to Don Quixote and Sancho Panza was unique
among family therapists' historical accounts, the pride of place given to

these two men was not, nor was the identification of each with a different coast of the country and a different approach.

Several themes recur in these three cases that were characteristic of the history of family therapy. Early efforts to conduct family therapy entailed more than bringing extra people into the space traditionally occupied solely by therapist/psychoanalyst and individual patient. Family research and therapy took place in diverse institutional settings, including VA hospitals, private practices or institutes, and the newly founded NIMH. There were material implications, such as the need for a larger therapy room and more chairs. There were questions of how to manage information, particularly information provided by one family member without the awareness of the rest of the family. Moreover, most of the early family therapists, who had had some psychoanalytic training, were accustomed to working with the transference relationship that developed between patient and analyst, and the presence of other people disrupted such a relationship. Given the new understanding that they were trying to treat a family rather than an individual patient, the therapists also confronted the challenge of how to understand pathology and how to produce and recognize change, treatment, and cure.

In addition, the social and intellectual context of Cold War America manifestly shaped the field's emergence, as these three cases demonstrate. The impact of broader postwar trends was visible in Ackerman's concern with prejudice, in Bowen's choice of psychiatry as his medical specialty following his military service, in Minuchin's approach to delinquency, and in expanding postwar sources of funding for all of them. Early therapists also evinced concern with deviance, especially schizophrenia and delinquency, rather than less severe family or life problems, in ways that exemplified contemporary concerns about the connection between psychological disorder and social disruption.

Family Therapy in Practice

Postwar commentators from social scientists and psychologists to public intellectuals and captains of industry worried about the American family. In contrast to the abstract representations of democratic citizenship, midcentury families had to grapple with the varied pulls of kinship and the experiences of everyday life. When those families encountered difficult problems, many of them sought out expert advice and psychotherapeutic treatment, a process that had become increasingly common since the turn of the century. When they turned to psychiatry, they encountered a profession experiencing its own "family turn," one at once deeply connected to the larger culture's obsession with the family unit and unfolding along a professionally specific trajectory with distinctive clinical techniques.[86]

Under the shared rubric of viewing the family as the unit of disease, family therapists created a wide array of theoretical frameworks and therapeutic practices. The challenge of inducing change in a therapeutic subject understood as an interactive family system or a set of relationships stimulated the development of a heterogeneous, sometimes contradictory set of approaches. Although family therapists framed their therapeutic practices in a technical language that was seemingly far removed from broader contemporary discourses, the targets of their interventions and their normative views of family life belied such a distinction.

Family therapists began the therapy process in highly varied ways. In her published training guide, social worker Virginia Satir advocated her technique for taking a "family life chronology" in the first couple of sessions.[87] In contrast, other family therapists opposed beginning the therapy process with taking some kind of history. For example, Nathan Ackerman preferred his first contact with a troubled family to begin "in a fresh, unprejudiced way, without historical data. . . . For the clinician the live, pungent and dramatic quality of spontaneous historical disclosures is a convincing experience."[88] Experience—in this case a clinician's experience of interacting with a family in therapy—took center stage, here serving the purpose of an initial assessment.

The course and frequency of therapy also varied. Ackerman reported seeing families for about an hour, once a week, though occasionally more often, over a period of six months to two years.[89] In contrast, a child guidance team at an outpatient psychiatric clinic for adolescents in Galveston, Texas, developed a brief, intensive protocol for treating families in crisis, which they called Multiple Impact Therapy. Families traveled to Galveston for two full days of alternating individual and family therapy sessions with a team of therapists that included social workers, psychologists, and psychiatrists. The team followed up with each family at six and eighteen months.[90] Similarly, other family therapists advocated a range of treatment from brief therapy consisting of six to ten sessions to long-term courses of therapy.

Family therapists also debated which family members to include, since some focused on a married pair while others included children and/or other involved family members such as grandparents.[91] Once they determined which family members to include, they faced the challenge of how to engage them all in the therapy process. In a detailed review of the transcript of an initial therapy session, Don Jackson, a Palo Alto psychiatrist, described his tendency to turn his early questions to the father. "I always go to the father first, in almost any situation. The myth is that the father is in charge of the family, but he usually knows less about what's going on and feels more insecure about it because he is out of touch and often dominated by the wife. Also, for cultural reasons or perhaps because of the nature of therapy, the fathers are the hardest to keep involved. So I try to help them make what they have to say worthwhile."[92] Jackson based his recruitment approach of early attention to the father on two presumptions about gender and power relations in the families he treated: (1) the need to shore up the fathers' roles, especially in relation to allegedly dominating wives, and (2) the imperative of keeping family members—including fathers, who were more likely to disengage than mothers—involved in the therapy. Thus even though therapists such as Jackson endeavored to undo the dyadic framework of momism, their work often retained the presumption of an overly dominating mother and further entailed recuperating the father's role in the family.

The following quotation from one family's clinical record further illustrates the strategic work entailed in bringing a family into therapy and keeping them there:

> This family was referred by a psychiatrist in Washington DC, who actually referred the identified patient, but I initiated the idea that the parents should come to [sic]. Although the patient was in the hospital, we felt that it was likely she would soon be living at home. It was explained to the parents that they would need help in handling the situation. They did not see themselves as involved causally in her illness at first. Later on, they accused the other of being the source of their daughter's difficulties. . . . When the parents began to do better together and the identified patient was doing quite well, her youngest sister became involved in an affair with a boy, which was extremely upsetting to the parents. Although they were upset, this made them realize that, as a family, they were having problems, and I think cemented their relationship to family therapy.[93]

This record demonstrates how Jackson explained to the parents why they should join their daughter in therapy, how the parents' attitudes toward their own role in their daughter's illness changed, and how on-going family problems made them more committed to family therapy.

Once the therapy process was under way, the therapists employed a range of interventions, strategies, and techniques. Some described push-ing a family to an extreme expression of symptomatic behavior to dis-rupt its pathology-maintaining patterns of interaction. Jackson called this "prescribing the symptom."[94] He might tell parents to be very firm with their grown daughter and "treat her like the child she is" in or-der to exacerbate their existing pattern of doing just that and to help them understand what they were doing since, according to Jackson, "[p]rescribing the symptom is more likely to produce insight than tell-ing people how the mind works."[95] In an interview based on close analy-sis of the transcript for an initial family session, Jackson illustrated this point when he commented, "About a week ago, I saw a family with a boy who was supposed to be mentally defective, and of course wasn't. I urged the mother to keep the father from being so benevolent to the son, because he was ruining his whole life. As soon as I touched on this, the differences between the parents started to come out. If I had tried to give them insight into what they were doing, they would have said, 'Oh, Bill is so helpless, so sick, we've got to help him,' or 'Dr. So-and-so says we should do such-and-such.'"[96] By instructing the mother to intervene between her husband and son and by labeling the father's be-nevolent treatment of their son as the problem, Jackson set up a type of paradoxical injunction, or therapeutic double bind, as if he were telling someone to be spontaneous in order to force her out of her repetitious modes of interacting. The premise that such injunctions could be cura-tive depended on Jackson's understanding of the nature of pathology as a product of communication and his conception of the patient as a homeostatic family.[97]

Another prominent family therapist, Carl Whitaker, vividly framed his related approach in terms of the Leaning Tower of Pisa. "My tactic has become a kind of tongue-in-cheek put-on; an induced chaos now called 'a positive feedback'—that is, we augment the pathology until symptoms self-destruct. It's a kind of accented irrationality with a flip kind of elaboration of the irrational components brought to therapy until the absurdity, like the Leaning Tower of Pisa, is built so high that it comes crashing down."[98] Like Jackson's, Whitaker's approach relied on the concept of feedback mechanisms. He viewed pathology as perpetuated by, and contributing to the maintenance of, a tightly self-regulating family system. Therapeutic practice entailed therapists' active intervention by accentuating the pathology in order to foster the self-destruction of the symptom-maintaining family patterns.

Salvador Minuchin and his colleague Avner Barcai also described their goal as disrupting pathological yet stable family patterns, though they did so by inducing a family crisis rather than prescribing the symptom or providing a paradoxical instruction. "The therapists deliberately intervened in ways which increased stress and conflict within the family, then directed the family to resolve these conflicts. . . . By assigning these [homework] tasks the therapists insured the continuity of the treatment process outside of the session."[99] In a case report published in the 1969 proceedings of the American Academy of Psychoanalysis, Minuchin and Barcai described a family, consisting of two parents and three children, that was referred to family therapy after other medical and psychiatric efforts to treat one daughter's recalcitrant health problems had failed. In the report they assessed the situation as follows:

> A circular feedback between the wife's control and the husband's dependency had continued for years. The wife's fear of being alone or being abandoned led her to maneuvers which were strongly controlling of her husband. She insisted that he call her often during the day and, because she was afraid he would drink heavily, that he be home by 6:15 each evening. Her husband dutifully called home twice a day and arrived home at 6:15, but he would make a point of telling her that he had taken two cocktails before getting there. This would start a typical family escalation. The parents would argue, [two of the children] would join in, alternately blaming the mother and the father, until finally the situation would dissolve into another issue without resolution.[100]

The therapists gave the husband an assigned task: to come home later than his wife expected one evening, without warning. He did so on the Friday of a weekend when his wife had planned a trip. The ensuing quarrel reached a point at which the typically gentle wife attacked her husband with scissors. According to the report, this crisis-inducing intervention destabilized the family system so that therapy could proceed.[101] Although this case involved an unusually dramatic husband-wife confrontation, it was also representative of some of the practices of family therapy in the 1960s, such as Minuchin and Barcai's emphasis on circular feedback mechanisms, their use of an assigned task outside the therapy room, their strategic induction of a disruptive crisis, and their attention to patterns of control and dependency, particularly along gendered lines.

While not all family therapists worked to induce family crises, clinicians as diverse as Nathan Ackerman, Jay Haley, and Gerald Zuk argued that a time of crisis and conflict in a family created a therapeutic opportunity, whether by providing a window for therapists to disrupt repetitive family conflicts or by maximizing the impact of their active interventions.[102] Critics charged that these techniques were manipulative or even unethical.[103]

Other family therapists assigned homework tasks that meshed with their views on the family for a variety of purposes aside from inducing crises. Virginia Satir, who advocated a communication and information-based model of the family, distributed communicational assignments, such as giving an adolescent daughter the task of communicating with her mother only in writing for a week. The task disrupted old forms of mutually upsetting interaction and encouraged clarity in communication. Murray Bowen, whose approach to family therapy emphasized individual differentiation within families and the multigenerational transmission of relationship patterns, instructed family members to visit parents and in-laws with the tasks of taking a family history by interviewing their relatives about their ancestors and shaking up the "same old two-step" of previous visits.[104]

Beyond specific techniques, the emergence of family therapy as a new field had an essential relationship with psychoanalysis, even if it was a negative one. Thus for those therapists, such as Jay Haley, who considered psychoanalysis anathema to family therapy, psychoanalysis was still the standard against which he and others defined their work and discipline. Others, such as Nathan Ackerman, maintained a more ambivalent connection with psychoanalysis in which they drew on some of its tenets while challenging others. The lines of dispute were typically drawn around the issues of confidentiality, transference, and therapeutic insight, regarding which there was a spectrum of opinion among family therapists.

For example, most family therapists deemphasized insight into unconscious processes or patient history, a practice that contrasted with the psychoanalytic approach dominating American psychiatry in the 1950s and the early 1960s. However, there was a range of views on the value of individual insight, even if there was consensus that it was not the primary therapeutic tool for producing change; some therapists remained committed to it, whereas others thoroughly rejected its therapeutic value.[105] Some, such as Haley, not only deemphasized the importance of insight for treatment but also argued that it was subsequent, even incidental, to instigating changes in family patterns or organization.[106] Family therapists also typically highlighted the importance of being aware that change in one person, or one part of the system, would induce change elsewhere in the system, so a therapist should be prepared for repercussions.

Some therapists intervening in a family system in the 1960s claimed to have more in common with an engineer modifying an experimental system or a scientist observing a biological system than with a psychoanalyst focused on individual psychodynamic issues. Murray Bowen compared his role to that of an engineer: "In broad terms, the therapist became a kind of expert in understanding family systems and an engineer in helping the family restore itself to functioning equilibrium. The overall goal was to help family members become system experts who could know the family system so well that the family could readjust itself without the help of an outside expert, if and when the family system was again stressed."[107] This theme recurred two decades later in a historically oriented section of Lynn Hoffman's 1981 survey, *Foundations of Family Therapy*, in which she explicitly drew a parallel between therapist and scientific experimenter. According to Hoffman, a therapist trying to change a family was "in the position of the experimenter in the early days of the cathode-ray oscilloscope. . . . [According to W. Ross Ashby], 'Adjusting the first experimental models was a matter of considerable complexity. . . . The system's variables (brightness of spot, rate of sweep, etc.) were dynamically linked in a rich and complex manner. Attempts to control it through the available parameters were difficult precisely because the variables were richly joined.' "[108] Yet family therapists aimed to do more than adjust variables for the sake of research, as in an experimental setup. They aimed to provoke and foster lasting, therapeutic change in the families in their care. For some, change meant alleviation of presenting symptoms, while others based their therapeutic ambitions on altering other measures of family life, such as the degree of proximity among family members which the therapists described in terms of interpersonal differentiation or overly intense enmeshment.

They thus faced the problem of defining "change" and "therapeutic," assessments that were inextricable from their understandings of disease and from normative judgments about the nature of a normal or healthy family. For example, according to Don Jackson, abnormal families sought treatment for a family member who had been identified as delinquent, schizophrenic, or underachieving, whereas normal families volunteered to participate in his research studies and had no psychiatric diagnoses or arrests among their members.[109] In this tautological formulation, the manner in which a family came to Jackson's project presaged, even defined, whether it was normal or abnormal. While not all family therapists would have agreed with his definitions, they might have recognized the mutually constitutive relationship between binary oppositions such as the normal and the pathological or health and illness.[110]

Other family therapists explicitly linked their understandings of the distinctions between normal and abnormal families to their therapeutic goals. In a published version of training outlines she developed in the 1950s and early 1960s, Virginia Satir privileged parents' self-esteem, their capacity to disagree directly, their degree of trust, and their sex-role differentiation and socialization of children as key factors in a family's functional or dysfunctional interactions. These factors were thus defining aspects of Satir's normative vision of a healthy family. In addition, before she turned to specific techniques in the section of her manual on "theory and practice of therapy," she covered communication and information theory as central to her understanding of family functioning and, as a corollary, therapeutic intervention.[111] Her presentation of this material highlighted how she integrated the processes of family functioning, the nature of disease, and the practice of therapy.

Finally, some family therapists focused on observation and enactment in their therapeutic practices. Jay Haley framed the importance of observation in terms of its utility for effective assessment and intervention: "If the father says he has difficulty talking with his adolescent son, the family therapist wants observable information about that difficulty. He will ask father and son to talk together right then in the session so that he can learn how they deal with one another and how much the mother intrudes upon them. Only by action under observation can a therapist gain this information. Ideally, the gathering of information and the intervention to produce a change occur simultaneously in the therapy session."[112] Haley thus favored action under observation over a family member's report of some difficulty. He also linked the goals of information gathering and clinical intervention through observing how a family responded to his actions. "Perhaps the most important information for the family therapist is the ways the family responds to his interventions. How the family uses him in their struggle with one another and whether or not they do as he asks is of crucial importance."[113] The information that Haley aimed to glean through observation related to the organization of

family relations—defined by generational differences, gender roles, alliances, and hostilities—and relations with extended family and the outside world. As he pointed out, "It is structural information which most
concerns a family therapist. He wants to know if there is a breeching of
generation lines, such as one parent siding with a child against the other
or a husband siding with his mother against his wife."[114]

Beyond Haley's attention to observable information and action under
observation, some therapists used visual technologies like film, video,
and a one-way mirror as a way of giving families feedback on their own
behaviors and patterns.[115] In the case of film and video, therapists recorded family sessions and then incorporated the tapes into a later stage
of therapy so family members could observe their own patterns of interaction, as well as their change over time.[116] In the case of the one-way
mirror, one group of clinicians developed a strategy that involved breaking the family into subunits. One therapist observed behind the mirror
with a subset of the family while a second worked with the rest of the
family in the main therapy room. This approach functioned both to
disrupt set alliances or antagonisms with a family and to provide family
members a view of their family patterns in action.[117]

Family therapists further solidified the connection between observation and experience in their use and advocacy of transcripts of therapy
sessions rather than case reports and training guides, which might edit
out mistakes and provide a prescriptive rather than a descriptive account
of the therapy process. For example, in their introduction to their 1967
collection of interviews and therapy transcripts with five family therapists, Hoffman and Haley wrote,

> Hopefully, the transcript of the interview provides the reader with
> an approximation of the experience of joining a family in a treat-
> ment session. *Therapists who have not yet sat down with whole families
> and observed them do not understand this new view of psychopathology.*
> Only by observing a deviant individual, such as the schizophrenic,
> in conversation with his intimates can one discover that his strange
> and bizarre behavior is meaningful and adaptive to his natural set-
> ting. It is like seeing a fish in the water for the first time when one
> has previously only seen him stranded on the shore, gasping, and
> trying to fly with inadequate finlike wings.[118]

From the therapists' perspective, a key aspect of the experience of family
therapy was observational, in the sense of seeing a patient in the context

of his or her family which they viewed as analogous to the natural habitat of an animal.

The value that Haley and Hoffman placed on experience and the link they made between experience and observation could be found in many family therapists' accounts of clinical practice. However, such an account did not provide ready access to the perspective of the "fish" (a.k.a. a diagnosed individual) who presented for treatment in the context of the "water" of family interactions. Families likely experienced the therapy process in ways not apparent in transcripts, few of which included an account of family interactions outside the therapy room or provided a family's interpretation of a session alongside the therapist's commentary.[119]

The early response to family therapy practices from psychiatrists and other clinicians was mixed. While Ackerman reported facing hostile questions and accusations of unethical behavior for breaking the confidentiality of the doctor-patient relationship with his public demonstration interviews,[120] Jackson described quiet acceptance, aside from a few disgruntled psychoanalysts and someone who accused family therapists of being "'peeping Toms' on the private lives of families."[121]

The peeping Tom accusation raised larger issues about the relation of family therapy to contemporary shifts in the line between public and private space. In *Welcome to the Dreamhouse*, Lynn Spigel argues that the changing distinction between the public and the private in postwar family life was connected to changes in consumer culture and the "experience of visuality itself. Increasingly in the postwar period the domestic environment was filled with visual spectacles previously associated with public life, and the home itself was designed as a space for looking."[122] Spigel's emphasis on the role of domestic visual culture in postwar family life paralleled family therapists' focus on visuality in their therapeutic practices. Such practices similarly had a role in reconfiguring the boundaries between private and public—for example, through films about family therapy—as well as in eliding the boundary between the individualized domain of the psychological and the communal domain of political culture.

The emergence of family therapy during the 1950s depended on the twentieth-century rise of a therapeutic ethos and psychological orientation toward understanding societal problems, as well as on changing notions of family life. In addition, the social, professional, and intellectual changes wrought by World War II heightened the psychologization of the family and its role in political culture. In the wake of the war, attitudes toward the promise of psychotherapy and the family converged in the crucible of family therapy. In turn, the evolving clinical practices of early family therapists heightened the midcentury connections between the familial and the therapeutic. Collectively, these diverse techniques and strategies presumed that the source of pathology and the appropriate unit of treatment was the family, and therapists therefore attempted to intervene in a manner that fit their understanding of its functions, organization, and processes.

A key product of their therapeutic practices was the mutually reinforcing relationship between conceptions of disease, which entailed particular understandings of the family as the unit of pathology, and the therapeutic modalities developed to intervene in pathological family processes. The families under treatment were marked in various ways: by the diagnosis of one family member, such as a schizophrenic or delinquent family; by the structure of their interrelationships or patterns of communication, such as an enmeshed family in which the boundaries between individuals were very weak; and by regional, socioeconomic, religious, or racial categories. Through their interventions and training techniques, family therapists fostered normative models of family life by defining certain patterns or structures as healthy and others as illness-inducing.

However, there was hardly a consensus across the field on what those normative models should be. While some advocated middle-class values as a family ideal in therapy,[123] others recognized that they as therapists responded differently to different sorts of families[124] and that the norm of the Parsonian nuclear family could account for neither the positive aspects of other family arrangements nor the economic, structural, or discriminatory constraints on many families.[125] Nonetheless, the families in treatment were implicitly marked as pathological by their deviation from a model of healthy, normal, functioning family life, whether that model was a monolithic ideal of the nuclear family or whether it encompassed a multiplicity of family arrangements that, despite their plurality, still functioned to define the limits of health and the meanings of pathology.

While family therapists worked out diverse solutions to these questions, they shared an emphasis on contextual change and viewing the family as the therapeutic unit. In a statement that echoed similar claims by other therapists, Jay Haley and Lynn Hoffman wrote, "Family therapists are distinct as a group largely because of a common assumption: if the individual is to change, the context in which he lives must change. The unit of treatment is no longer the person, even if only a single person is interviewed; it is the set of relationships in which the person is imbedded."[126] Family therapists' conceptions of context and relationships were multiple, including varied emphases on the analytic category of the system, as the next chapter discusses. Murray Bowen articulated some of the meanings of system in a 1966 article in *Comprehensive Psychiatry*, in which he wrote,

> The family *is* a number of different kinds of systems. It can accurately be designated a social system, a cultural system, a games system, a communication system, a biological system, or any of several other designations. For the purposes of this theoretical-therapeutic system, I think of the family as a combination of emotional and relationship systems. The term emotional refers to the force that motivates the system, and relationship to the ways it is expressed. Under relationship would be subsumed communication, interaction, and other relationship modalities.[127]

Whether family therapists variably focused on biological, cultural, communicational, emotional, or other types of systems, they shared the premise that psychopathology lay in the family context, in which their clinical practices needed to intervene.

CHAPTER TWO

- -

"SYSTEMS EVERYWHERE"

SCHIZOPHRENIA, CYBERNETICS, AND THE DOUBLE BIND

System: An organized or connected group of objects. A set or
assemblage of things connected, associated, or interdependent,
so as to form a complex unity; a whole composed of parts in
orderly arrangement according to some scheme or plan.
Oxford English Dictionary

In October 1956, the journal *Behavioral Science* published an article titled "Toward a Theory of Schizophrenia," by Gregory Bateson, Don D.
Jackson, Jay Haley, and John Weakland.[1] The article posited that the
nature and causes of schizophrenia could be understood in terms of
schizophrenics' patterns of communication, specifically their inability
to distinguish Logical Types. By Logical Types, the authors referred to
the distinction made by philosopher Bertrand Russell between a class
and the members of that class such that the class was of a higher Logical
Type than its members. They further asserted that the schizophrenics'
inability to distinguish between logical levels of meaning—for example,
their tendency to take metaphors literally—might be caused by patterns
of paradoxical communication during childhood in the form of repeated
"double binds."

The article provided select clinical examples to illustrate the double
bind theory. In one case, the mother of a young man with schizophrenia visited her son in the hospital. The son embraced her, to which she
responded by stiffening. He then drew away, and she asked, "Don't you

love me anymore?" He blushed, and she said, "Dear, you must not be so easily embarrassed and afraid of your feelings." In the words of the article's authors, "The impossible dilemma thus becomes: 'If I am to keep my tie to mother I must not show her that I love her, but if I do not show her that I love her, then I will lose her.'"[2] In their analysis of this case as well as their general articulation of the theory of the double bind, the authors analogized concepts of mechanical feedback and control to an understanding of schizophrenia as a disease of disordered familial communication. In so doing, they refigured the family as a system in a way that became a hallmark of the emerging field of family therapy.

The work of the Palo Alto-based research group that developed the theory of the double bind was key to the mutual formation of the field of family therapy and its object of study, the family as a unit of disease and treatment. This research fostered an unlikely intersection among the new field of cybernetics, long-standing research on the causes and treatment of schizophrenia, and contemporary views of the family. Headed by Gregory Bateson, the interdisciplinary group began its investigations in 1952 and disbanded a decade later. Two primary disciplinary traditions were at play: cultural anthropology and interpersonal psychiatry. The team included two anthropologists, Bateson and John Weakland, who was also a chemical engineer; one communications analyst, Jay Haley; and two psychiatrists, Don D. Jackson and William Fry. The theory of the double bind also had an immediate impact on wider psychiatric thought about schizophrenia. In the words of one psychiatrist, it hit "like a bombshell" and burst "a dam of rigid views about this mysterious disorder and loosed a flood of publications" for at least two decades, though it subsequently came under fire from various quarters for its inattention to psychoanalysis, the difficulty of testing the theory, and the questionable specificity of the double bind as a pathogenic agent.[3]

Most important, the creation of the double bind theory entailed recasting the family as a system. In the intellectual arena of postwar America, there were "systems everywhere," in the words of the systems theorist Ludwig von Bertalanffy.[4] During the 1950s and 1960s, an interest in organized, complex entities with the capacity for self-regulation developed in fields as divergent as operations research, management, urban planning, computer science, ecosystem ecology, molecular biology, engineering, cognitive psychology, neuroscience, and sociology.[5]

Viewing the family as a system therefore fit within widespread contemporary interest in systems. The double bind was a key site at which family therapists integrated contemporary understandings of family life, such as normative views of gender roles, with a therapeutic agenda. Notions of the family as a social and natural object have a long history, and systems theory productively contributed to the midcentury reconfiguration of the boundaries between the social and the natural.[6] The cybernetic approach of the Palo Alto group explicitly integrated a view of the family as social, in the sense of socially defined roles and functions, and natural, in the sense of biological reproduction; it also fashioned the family as a scientific object that was potentially pathogenic, accessible to the gaze of researchers and clinicians, and comprehensible as a self-regulating, information-processing system. By framing particular familial patterns of interaction and communication as the source of schizophrenia and eventually as the target of therapeutic intervention, the group developed a way of understanding both family and disease that would shape the practice of family therapy for many years.

Many early family therapists embraced the language of systems as a way of characterizing family patterns of interaction and their own clinical practices. This approach conceptualized the family as a system with regular patterns of communication among its members, including negative feedback mechanisms that regulated a family's response to a given event or behavior and thereby promoted stability. Though they initially focused on communication within schizophrenic families, the therapists quickly turned their attention to other types of families as well. The family system not only entailed a notion of family function but was also made concrete through clinical practice. Family therapists relied on a systems framework to justify their therapeutic interventions, as well as to theorize their own relationship as therapists to their patients. Ultimately, the language of systems served as a highly flexible framework that was used to support diverse, even conflicting, positions on the characterization of pathology and the nature of treatment.

Cybernetics and Paradoxical Communication

In 1952, with two years' worth of funding from the Rockefeller Foundation, Gregory Bateson initiated a research project titled "The Role of Paradoxes of Abstraction in Communication." The project was administered by the departments of sociology and anthropology at Stanford, directed by Bateson, and located at the Palo Alto Veterans Administration hospital. By 1954, the project had six staff members, including

Bateson, Jay Haley, and John Weakland, who were among the key figures in the subsequent development of family therapy.

For Bateson, paradoxes in communication referred to contradictions
between a primary message and a qualifying message that was at a higher
level of abstraction, indicating, for instance, that the primary message
was a metaphor or was meant as play. An early grant application included
as an example the statement, "I am lying." The primary message was
that the speaker was telling a lie. Abstracted a level and applied as a
qualification of itself, the statement meant that the speaker was telling
the truth in saying "I am lying" and was therefore not lying.[7] He studied contradictions between messages and meta-messages that generated
paradoxes such as one person directing another person to "disobey me"
or the following example:

> All statements within this frame are untrue.

Under a common agenda of studying paradoxes in communication,
project members initiated a diverse array of projects, including the study
of play in animals and children, examination of the training of guide
dogs for the blind, analysis of fictional films, examination of patient-
therapist interviews, study of the nature of humor, examination of Zen
Buddhism, examination of puppet dialogues, and development of test
procedures to assess individuals' discrimination between literal and
metaphorical messages.[8]

Analyzing communication by schizophrenic patients was initially
one of many studies subsumed in the larger project. The way in which
these patients communicated was relevant to the project because of their
symptomatic tendency to take metaphors literally, which in psychiatric
terms was labeled concrete thinking, and to react to the outside world
in a manner that Bateson called proto-metaphoric: "The schizophrenic
in reacting to the external world may talk and act as if his perception
of objects and events were proto-metaphoric or hallucinatory. Here, instead of isolating the symbol from the thing symbolized, the two are
identified. The apple *is* the breast."[9] This focus on communication and
schizophrenia fit within a psychiatric tradition that emphasized disordered language and thought association disturbances as hallmarks of the
disease.[10] However, during the project's first two years, schizophrenic
communication was but one area of investigation into paradox in communication, and project members aimed to develop a theory general
enough to cover the diverse elements of the individual studies.

This focus on paradoxes in communication grew in part from Bateson's participation in the seminal series of cybernetics conferences sponsored by the Josiah Macy Jr. Foundation.[11] These mobilized Bateson's interest in Logical Types, communication, and paradox. Norbert Wiener coined the term "cybernetics" in the summer of 1947 from the Greek word for steersman and in recognition of a classic 1868 paper by James Clerk Maxwell on mechanical governors as feedback mechanisms.[12] Wiener was an MIT mathematician whose expansive interests in servomechanisms and goal-oriented behavior grew out of his wartime work on antiaircraft gunnery.[13] According to Wiener, cybernetics referred to a theory of control and communication that integrated the problems of control engineering (including feedback mechanisms) and communication engineering (including modes of transmission) around the "much more fundamental" concept of the message, defined as "a discrete or continuous sequence of measurable events distributed in time."[14] He defined control in terms of the impact of input-output messages on the behavior of messages' senders and recipients, which could be humans, other organisms, machines, or some combination thereof. This model favored circular causality, rather than linear cause and effect or stimulus-response, because it entailed feedback mechanisms in which there was an impact on the original sender, not just on the message's recipient.

Wiener contrasted the cybernetic emphasis on the role of information in coupling individual entities to their environments with an older, energy-based model of a living organism or engine.[15] As the science studies scholar N. Katherine Hayles argues, "At the center of cybernetics is the idea of information. Rather than thinking of matter or energy as fundamental, cybernetics takes information to be primary. Cybernetics is concerned with the flow of information through and around systems and with the mechanisms that control information flow. This orientation radically changes how boundaries are conceived."[16] Such a contrast also applied to family therapy, in which the emphasis on interpersonal communication served as a departure from psychoanalytic emphasis on libidinal energies.[17]

Along with operations research and game theory, Wiener's wartime research on nonlinear, self-regulating servomechanisms contributed to a particular understanding of the enemy as a human-machine system that became the basis for postwar developments in such diverse fields as cognitive psychology, molecular biology, ecology, and computing.[18] Wiener himself had an ambitious vision of the applicability of cybernetics across domains ranging from computing machines to physiology to the nervous system to social organization, though he expressed some trepidation about the potential application of cybernetics for what he called "evil" purposes, of which he provided examples such as exploitation, the concentration of power, and unscrupulous domination over individual freedom and related values of liberal humanism.[19]

The impetus for the cybernetics conferences came from a Macy-sponsored meeting in 1942 that was officially called the Cerebral Inhibition Meeting and dealt with hypnosis and the conditioned reflex.[20] Participants at the invitation-only meeting included Bateson; Frank Fremont-Smith, who was the medical director at the Macy Foundation; the foundation officer Lawrence Frank; the psychoanalyst Lawrence Kubie; the neuropsychiatrist Warren McCulloch; the anthropologist Margaret Mead; and the physiologist Arturo Rosenblueth, all of whom became central participants in the later series of cybernetics conferences. Also present was Milton Erickson, a hypnotist who did consulting in the 1950s for members of the Palo Alto group, particularly Jay Haley, who eventually published books on Erickson's work.[21]

At this meeting, Rosenblueth made a presentation based on material he was to publish a year later with Wiener and the engineer Julian Bigelow in an article that became the springboard for the cybernetics conferences.[22] Rosenblueth's talk built on his work with the physiologist Walter B. Cannon on homeostasis, a term that Cannon coined to characterize an organism's capacity to self-regulate within narrow parameters around a given norm. For example, Cannon discussed how the body maintained a constant temperature and regulated blood sugar levels through negative feedback mechanisms.[23] Rosenblueth in turn presented a model of circular causality that could be used to analyze goal-oriented actions in analogous terms in organisms and machines. The presentation generated excitement among the social scientists in the audience, who saw its potential for explaining societal interactions, and from Warren McCulloch, who was already interested in developing models for the human nervous system based on engineering devices.[24]

At the end of World War II, McCulloch encouraged Fremont-Smith to organize an interdisciplinary conference about the ideas in the Rosenblueth-Wiener-Bigelow paper. Beginning in 1946, the Macy Foundation sponsored a series of interdisciplinary conferences initially titled "Feedback Mechanisms and Circular Causal Systems in Biological and Social Systems," later known as the Conferences on Cybernetics, after the title of Norbert Wiener's influential 1948 book, *Cybernetics, or Control and Communication in the Animal and the Machine.*[25] These conferences drew together physiologists, mathematicians, engineers, psychologists, and anthropologists around problems of information, communication, and control in what N. Katherine Hayles has called "an unprecedented synthesis of the organic and the mechanical."[26]

The initial meeting became "a major intellectual event."[27] Fremont-Smith opened the conferences with a statement of the foundation's commitment to overcoming the fragmentation of knowledge resulting from the isolation of the disciplines by promoting forums to bring together scientists from diverse disciplines around a common problem or theme.[28] Over the course of the ten conferences, participants discussed a wide range of topics, including Russell's Theory of Logical Types, positive and negative feedback, sensory perception, a quantum mechanical theory of memory, neurosis, the development of language in early childhood, a maze-solving machine, the role of humor in human communication, a mechanical chess player, and Boolean logic. Participants retrospectively described their experiences in superlative terms: "extraordinary," according to ecologist G. Evelyn Hutchinson; "the most interesting conference I've ever been in," remembered Margaret Mead; and "one of the great events of my life," in Gregory Bateson's words.[29]

The conferences also crystallized some of Bateson's earlier anthropological work, including his attempts to theorize the role of culture in shaping how people learn how to learn, which he called deutero-learning,[30] as well as the ceremonial and ritual processes governing social equilibrium and differentiation among the Iatmul people of New Guinea.[31] Bateson brought his anthropological and cybernetic interests to the problems of psychiatry in 1949, when he began a lectureship in medical anthropology at the Langley Porter Neuropsychiatric Clinic in San Francisco and a collaborative research project with the psychiatrist Jurgen Ruesch.[32]

In their research, Ruesch and Bateson attempted to integrate anthropology and psychiatry in order to find a framework for examining multiple levels of human experience, from the individual to the familial to the cultural. Ruesch and Bateson's collaboration produced the 1951 book *Communication: The Social Matrix of Psychiatry.*[33] It was targeted at social and behavioral scientists to introduce them to communications theory in the early days of cybernetics, and Wiener admired the effort.[34] Much of this study focused on psychiatrist-patient interaction and the "social matrix" in which American psychiatrists operated. In addition, in his chapter "Information and Codification: A Philosophical

Approach," Bateson discussed some of the ideas raised at the cybernetics conferences. He explicitly acknowledged his debt to the conference participants "whose thinking has deeply influenced my own," particularly Wiener, Hutchinson, McCulloch, and Walter Pitts, who with McCulloch published an influential paper on their cybernetic theory of neural networks.[35] After his collaboration with Ruesch, Bateson organized his own research program on paradoxes in communication, which by 1954 began to focus on schizophrenic patients' patterns of communication.

Schizophrenia and Communication

The increasing focus on schizophrenia came about in part because of funding options when the Rockefeller Foundation did not renew its initial two-year grant. By the spring of 1954, Bateson obtained two years of funding from the Macy Foundation for the study of schizophrenic communication and the role of mother-infant interaction in producing schizophrenia.[36] In June 1954, the Palo Alto group also applied to the Public Health Service of the NIH for $20,130 to investigate schizophrenic communication.[37] The grant application included discussion of some of the general principles regarding paradox and communication that the group was exploring.

One of these principles grew out of Bateson's earlier anthropological work on learning and deutero-learning. The application illustrated deutero-learning with the example of an experimental subject who, after memorizing a series of nonsense syllables, was able to learn another series of syllables more quickly at the end than at the beginning of the experiment. In other words, the subject had learned how to learn. Such learning became paradoxical when an individual was punished for an action as well as punished for showing, by avoiding it, that she had learned the action would be punished.[38]

Bateson eventually drew connections between his work on deutero-learning and his studies of paradoxes arising from contradictions between levels of meaning. During his Rockefeller-sponsored research on paradoxes in communication from 1952 to 1954, he studied the ways in which signals qualified other messages or behaviors—for example as play, metaphor, or fantasy. He described the qualifying signals, or meta-messages, as being of a higher Logical Type than the messages that they framed. At the same time, he was interested in how people or animals learn how to learn. By 1954, Bateson was able to formulate a connection between these research interests in a letter to Norbert Wiener:

> A question which I cannot clearly resolve is whether these two sets of two-typed communication are really identical or are both independently operating in such phenomena as play. As I understand it, type confusion leads to paradox when both message and meta-message contain negatives. On this principle we can imagine the generation of paradox in the deutero-learning system when an organism experiences punishment following some failure and learns that it must not learn that punishment follows failure. This would be approximately the picture of a man who having been punished for failure later is punished for showing his expectation of punishment after failure, e.g. is punished for cringing.[39]

This integration of paradoxical communication and deutero-learning became the basis for the double bind theory of schizophrenia.[40]

Bateson's group proposed to develop a theory of schizophrenia by applying this and other general principles of communication to an analysis of the etiology, symptomatology, and psychotherapy of schizophrenia. They laid out the relevance of deutero-learning in the following proposition about the etiology of schizophrenia:

> It is suggested that the base for later psychosis may be laid in infancy by the experience of dealing with a mother who both punishes the child for certain actions and punishes the child for learning that punishment will follow those actions. . . . [I]t is worth noting that the mother's conduct is especially likely to take this form when it is necessary for her to be hypocritical about her lack of or inhibition of love for the child. With such hypocrisy she is driven not only to punish the child's demand for love, but also to punish any indication which the child may give that he knows he is not loved, since such an indication threatens the base of her hypocrisy.[41]

The group thus began with the premise that mothers played a role in causing schizophrenia through the paradoxical messages they communicated to their children during infancy, particularly if they did not want their children to acknowledge some lack or inhibition in their expression of maternal affection.

This formulation drew on normative postwar conceptions of motherhood and increasingly psychologized views of the potentially pathological effects of mother love. Such views resonated with Philip Wylie's vitriolic critique of momism. The midcentury psychologization of mother love represented a shift away from the sentimental maternalism advocated by women reformers of the late nineteenth and early twentieth centuries. In this idealized version of womanhood, self-sacrificing, middle-class mothers at a time of economic and social upheaval provided the moral compass and nurturing, domestic care that in turn would produce good citizens, thereby serving both familial and civic duties. While midcentury critics of mother love retained maternalism's link between private care and public responsibility, they increasingly framed the ill effects of maternal affection gone awry in psychological, particularly psychoanalytic terms.[42]

The Palo Alto group combined these contemporary views of motherhood with the history of schizophrenia. Two years earlier, in 1952, the American Psychiatric Association had published a new standardized psychiatric nomenclature and nosology known as the *Diagnostic and Statistical Manual: Mental Disorders* (*DSM*). This book reflected the postwar ascendance of psychodynamic psychiatrists in its emphasis on psychodynamic conceptions of disease and its inclusion of psychoneurotic diagnoses, such as anxiety and emotional instability.[43] The first edition of the *DSM* listed psychotic and neurotic disorders together under the heading "Disorders of Psychogenic Origin or without Clearly Defined Physical Cause or Structural Change in the Brain."[44] A subset of psychotic disorders included "schizophrenic reactions" of various types (simple, catatonic, paranoid, hebephrenic, etc.).

Although the *DSM* classified the etiology of schizophrenia as psychogenic and the nature of the disease as a reaction formation, twentieth-century theories about schizophrenia and approaches to its treatment were multivalent and contradictory. The most significant early twentieth-century characterization of the collection of symptoms that were then known as dementia praecox, or adolescent dementia, by Emil Kraeplin, emphasized the phenomenology of the disease as well as its negative prognosis and chronic deterioration.[45] In contrast to Kraeplin's descriptive and somatic approach, the Swiss psychiatrist Eugen Bleuler coined the term "schizophrenia" to emphasize his dynamic and psychogenic approach that drew on Freud's work and highlighted the disordered thought processes of schizophrenic patients.[46]

However, the distinctions between descriptive and dynamic, or somatic and psychogenic, were not hard-and-fast during the first half of the twentieth century. For example, Adolf Meyer coined the term "schizophrenic reaction" to highlight the role of factors outside the individual patient in the etiology of schizophrenia, though he also developed a psychobiological conception of disease. Harry Stack Sullivan emphasized the role of culture and a patient's life history, but he also linked the emergence of schizophrenic symptoms to developmental missteps. Like Bleuler, Sullivan viewed schizophrenia as a thought-process disorder with an emphasis on language, though he saw the differences between normal and schizophrenic thought processes as qualitative rather than categorical.[47]

Efforts to treat schizophrenia were similarly diverse. During the interwar years in the United States, somatic therapies prevailed in the mental hospitals that housed most of the chronically mentally ill patients. Hydrotherapeutic baths or wet packs, malaria fever therapy, electroshock therapy, insulin shock therapy, sexual sterilization, and lobotomy were used at varying times from the 1920s to the 1940s.[48] In 1954, the first of the major tranquilizers, chlorpromazine—otherwise known as Thorazine—became available for use in the United States.[49] Practitioners linked the perceived efficacy of these varied biological or somatic treatments to their conceptions of the diseases under their care. As the historian Joel Braslow has argued, such therapeutics threaded a path between "disordered behavior, disorders of the brain, and therapeutic control."[50]

While these therapies were somatically based in varied ways and served to buttress biological views of schizophrenia, some of them also undercut a simplistic dichotomy between biological and psychological views. For example, some psychoanalysts responded positively to chlorpromazine because they thought it removed the extreme narcissism of schizophrenia that blocked transference and prevented successful analysis, thereby facilitating the psychoanalytic process.[51] In addition, by the 1950s there were multiple approaches to characterizing schizophrenia biologically, including developmental, genetic, biochemical, neurophysiological, and anatomical studies.[52]

Moreover, several midcentury neo-Freudians attended to the roles of language and interaction in their characterizations of schizophrenia. Psychoanalysts ranging from ego psychology (e.g., Heinz Hartmann) to object relations (W. R. D. Fairbairn) to interpersonal psychiatry (Harry Stack Sullivan) considered the etiology of schizophrenia in terms of the role of infant or childhood disruptions in development and interpersonal relations. In addition, they emphasized the disordered linguistic and cognitive aspects of schizophrenia, such as the loose associations of schizophrenic patients.[53]

In contrast, Gregory Bateson brought a cybernetic conception of communication to the study of the disease, a conception grounded in theories of information and control rather than psychoanalytic repression, projection, or transference. Bateson and his colleagues explicitly differentiated their work on the double bind from psychodynamically informed perspectives.[54] Rather than focus on symbols, the content of delusions, or psychoanalytic processes like projection, they aimed to study schizophrenics' use of "reality-qualifiers," meaning signals (elsewhere called meta-messages) that qualify the meaning of another message.

Thus, while other contemporary psychiatrists associated family and schizophrenia, what made the Palo Alto group unique was its addition of cybernetics to the family-schizophrenia nexus and its focus on paradoxical communication. Elsewhere, family and schizophrenia came together in the research and treatment efforts of several people who were part of the early landscape of family therapy, notably Theodore Lidz, Lyman Wynne, and Murray Bowen.[55] Despite Freud's opposition to treating schizophrenics based on their inability to form transference relationships as a result of their intense narcissism, some psychiatrists and psychoanalysts took on this challenge in the 1930s and 1940s, most significantly Harry Stack Sullivan, Frieda Fromm-Reichmann, Harold Searles, and John Rosen.[56] Though they did not treat family members together, they often invoked the family by attributing the etiology of schizophrenia to the child-rearing practices of patients' mothers. However, none of these other clinicians and researchers initially conceptualized the family as a cybernetic system.

While they took pains to distinguish their communicational approach from a more psychoanalytic one, Bateson's group also acknowledged its debt to some psychiatrists—especially Sullivan, Rosen, and Fromm-Reichmann—for their psychotherapeutic work with schizophrenic patients. The Palo Alto group's 1954 grant application to the NIH framed its project as "an attempt to construct a theoretical base for the therapeutic processes which these workers have empirically devised."[57] The researchers referred to Rosen's "direct analysis" throughout the application. For example, their sketch of the role of negative deutero-learning in the etiology of schizophrenia included the observation that "such a picture of childhood trauma fits remarkable [sic] well Rosen's description of the 'perverse' mother." In addition, Bateson and his colleagues invited Rosen and Fromm-Reichmann to visit Palo Alto separately to discuss their own approach to treating schizophrenia, and they dedicated several of their weekly meetings to discussing the psychiatrists' work.[58] They even filmed the two interacting with patients, more in the spirit of observing another culture's rituals, as in visual anthropologists' films, than with the intention of recording prominent therapists for demonstration and educational purposes as later family therapists would do.[59]

Beyond occasional meetings with outside psychiatrists, they hired a psychiatrist to consult regularly with the group. The first one on the project was William Fry, a resident at the VA hospital. However, when Fry was inducted into the navy, Bateson invited Don D. Jackson to become a regular psychiatric consultant after hearing him give a lecture on family homeostasis in 1954. Jackson's psychiatric training included medical school at Stanford and a residency at Chestnut Lodge. There he imbibed the interpersonal psychoanalysis of Harry Stack Sullivan and conducted psychotherapy with schizophrenic patients under the guidance of Frieda Fromm-Reichmann. When he set up a private practice in Palo Alto in 1951, he continued to treat psychotic patients with individual psychotherapy and drafted a research proposal to study the impact of psychotherapy on hospitalized schizophrenics.[60] However, he was also becoming disgruntled with psychoanalysts' opposition to dealing with the whole family. Unlike Chestnut Lodge, where he could avoid the patients' families, the small university town of Palo Alto enabled significant contact with parents and other family members, which altered his understanding of families' roles in the perpetuation of psychotic disorders.[61]

His observations regarding families' negative, often disruptive responses to an individual patient's improvement contributed to the talk that Bateson heard. In this lecture, Jackson discussed how changes in a patient during psychiatric treatment led in turn to changes in other family members, which then led the patient to revert to his symptomatic behavior. He used the idea of homeostasis to describe patterns or types of interaction that helped a family maintain its central modes of organization and structure within a narrow range—for example, by reinforcing the expectation that there be no disagreement in the family. This presentation and Jackson's subsequent publications reinforced his central claim that like a household thermostat, families had mechanisms for both registering and counteracting deviations or fluctuations from a particular range or norm.[62]

More specifically, he argued that they had a constant internal environment maintained by a self-regulating equilibrium or homeostatic capacity, comparable to those physiological mechanisms of the human body described by Walter B. Cannon for regulating temperature, hormone levels, and other bodily parameters. He claimed to focus on the interactions between people, as opposed to internal experiences, thoughts, or consciousness. He rejected a linear model of cause and effect, or behaviorist stimulus-response, in favor of a view of the family as tightly regulated by rules, norms, and homeostatic mechanisms for maintaining those norms. Jackson applied his model to the study of family interaction in producing psychopathology or deviant behavior.

In a later paper Jackson wrote, "The major assertion of the theory to be outlined here is that the family is a rule-governed system: that its members behave among themselves in an organized, repetitive manner and that this patterning of behaviors can be abstracted as a governing principle of family life."[63] He gave several examples of the types of rules he had in mind: "No one shall control anyone else, Father shall overtly run the show but Mother's covert authority shall be respected, Husband shall be the wooer and Wife the helpless female."[64] His selection of sample rules thus reinscribed normative gender roles through their use as illustrations of general principles, even though Jackson was not explicitly prescribing particular behaviors. He recognized that these rules were inferences or abstractions imposed by the therapist or investigator, comparable in his terms to the concept of gravity.[65]

Jackson referred to the rules of family relationship as norms, and he pointed out two of their important characteristics. First, he noted that norms were unique to each family, so the focus remained on the family unit. Therefore, individual as well as social or cultural issues became secondary. Second, the norm functioned as a baseline or setting around which family behaviors fluctuated to varying degrees. It was the homeostatic mechanisms that enforced and maintained the norms, as he later illustrated in a diagram in a 1965 article in *Family Process* (see fig. 2).

Norms for family behavior and relationship rules thus relied on homeostatic mechanisms in order to stay within acceptable limits. Pathology itself could serve a homeostatic function. For example, a child's symptoms might flare up when the parents began to argue. The disease then served the dual functions of diverting the parents' attention from the problems in their marriage and keeping the family together in order to take care of the sick child. The family therapy literature is replete with cases that follow this basic pattern, as well as those that document the

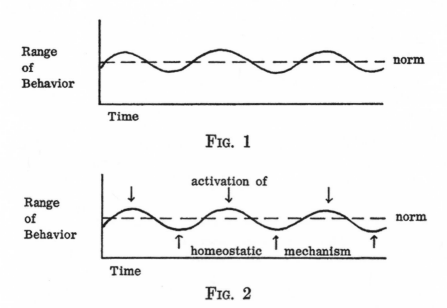

Figure 2. From Don D. Jackson, "The Study of the Family," *Family Process* 4 (March 1965): 13. Copyright © 1965 Don D. Jackson. Reprinted by permission of John Wiley and Sons.

violent responses of families to improvements in the health of the "designated patient," family therapists' term for the symptomatic individual.

Jackson explicitly framed his notion of family homeostasis in communicational terms that resonated with Bateson's research project. As he put it, "Another way of considering the topic of 'family homeostasis' would be in terms of communication theory: that is, depicting the family interaction as a closed information system in which variations in output or behavior are fed back in order to correct the system's response."[66] Although initially hired only as a clinical consultant, Jackson quickly became an integral part of the group's theoretical project.

Given their respective backgrounds, Bateson, Haley, and Weakland entered the project with their attention focused first and foremost on an anthropological study of communication, in which schizophrenia was one illustrative example among many. They were interested in theory building and "natural history"—that is, observationally based behavioral science research—and they wanted the input of a psychiatrist for clinical consultation, supervision, and case material. Their goal was not to build a new therapeutic system.

In contrast, Jackson entered the project interested primarily in the etiology and pathogenesis of schizophrenia, viewing the study of communication as a way of apprehending the causes and patterns of the disease. That a psychiatrist would turn to anthropologists or other behavioral scientists was not unusual at that time. Robert Felix at NIMH supported other efforts in which psychiatrists relied on the research skills of social scientists. Similarly, the Committee on the Family of the Group for the Advancement of Psychiatry (GAP) published a 1954 report in which it called on psychiatrists to engage with anthropological and sociological scholarship regarding the family.[67]

Despite these diverse agendas, the common thread among the members of the Palo Alto group was that they were all interested in looking at interaction rather than intrapsychic phenomena as a way of understanding schizophrenia. Within their complementary theoretical frameworks, each contingent needed the other for some purpose: the anthropologist needed the psychiatrist to help him do fieldwork with schizophrenic patients, and the psychiatrist was willing to subject his clinical material to the anthropologist's project because he could use Bateson's resources to develop a new type of therapy that would overcome the limits of psychoanalysis. Their common interest in interaction, feedback mechanisms, and control made possible a type of interdisciplinary research that would facilitate the mutual construction of the field of family therapy and the view of the family as a system.

Interdisciplinarity in Action

According to an oft-repeated story, three of the research project's members—Bateson, Weakland, and Haley—rented a mountain cabin together for a weekend, during which time Bateson deductively generated the theory of the double bind.[68] While this chronology may have legitimacy, the development of the theory was considerably more complex. The group's research proceeded by each member following the treatment of a schizophrenic individual (and by 1957, his or her whole family), and then discussing case material in weekly group meetings that they recorded on reel-to-reel audiotape (see fig. 3).[69]

The bulk of their discussions approached the double bind by working through clinical and theoretical issues arising from the patients they were following. Jackson played a central role in providing clinical guidance and explaining psychiatric concepts. For example, they discussed how Bateson should deal with his patient's poor reaction to switching wards in the hospital, the distinction between acute and chronic phases of schizophrenia, the difference between a nervous breakdown and a psychotic break, and the relationship between schizophrenia and manic depression.[70] Jackson occasionally brought in psychoanalytic issues, such as the relationship between the introjected object of psychoanalytic theory and the double bind.[71] He brought up the work of other psychiatrists: for example, he referred to the object-relations work of W. R. D. Fairbairn to aid his explanation of introjection and projection.[72] He also brought in clinical examples from his private practice, including the case of the schizophrenic son's failed embrace of his mother that the group cited in its 1956 article.[73]

Within their clinically focused discussions, the group covered a variety of topics. Bateson, Haley, Jackson, and Weakland analyzed the work of the hypnotist Milton Erickson, just as they did with Rosen and Fromm-Reichmann, and they had many conversations about Erickson's use of paradoxical directives in his practice of hypnotism. Though they focused on psychotherapy, the issue of the new psychotropic medications also arose. For example, in early 1955 Weakland asked Jackson if he was opposed to using Serpasil and other psychotropic medications. Jackson responded, "Some of the patients I've used it on . . . they have felt much more comfortable. It's not only curative . . . it's amazing. Just like taking aspirin for a psychogenic headache."[74] In the same conversation, Bateson also expressed skepticism about whether drugs made patients more open to therapy, since a drug removed symptoms, which therapy should engage. Jackson answered that the drug lowered anxiety defenses so that patients would not go blank and could face their anger or other emotions.

In addition, they talked about learning theory and experimental psychology on many occasions. In one such conversation, they tried to find parallels between subtypes of schizophrenia, such as catatonia or paranoia, and the rats in a Pavlovian maze experiment.[75] Occasionally issues related to sexuality arose, including an association between sex and machines made by the schizophrenic man with whom Haley worked, the use of hypnosis to treat "sexual malfunction," and the response from two parents to their daughter's homosexuality.[76]

A pervasive theme in the group's conversations concerned the role of mothers in the etiology and maintenance of schizophrenia. Examinations of dependence and control interlaced the conversations about mothers, as did debates about whether a child's dependence was biological, psychological, or cultural.[77] These debates underscored the simultaneously biological and social character of the family. In one of the

Figure 3. Palo Alto research group (left to right): William Fry, John Weakland, Gregory Bateson, and Jay Haley circa 1955, Don D. Jackson Archive, University of Louisiana at Monroe. The group recorded their weekly meetings on reel-to-reel audiotape, and they used the blackboard to diagram their developing concepts. By permission of Wendel Ray.

group's early meetings, Jackson proposed that a mother's helplessness was a pathogenic factor in schizophrenia and reiterated this point two months later when he commented, "If there is anything characteristic about these mothers, it is also that they are helpless, even the rich ones."[78] The group's wide-ranging discussions of learning theory included references to how mothers teach their children. For example, Haley drew a parallel between the experimenter and the animal in a Pavlovian experiment and a mother and schizophrenic child in real life. Jackson concurred with this parallel and expanded on it by describing some mothers as cold and unloving but anxious to have their children think they were loving, with their husbands complicit in this deception.[79] Jackson and others also used Fromm-Reichmann's evocative formulation of the schizophrenogenic mother on many occasions.[80] For instance, Weakland urged the group to consider what kinds of mothers they were discussing in their general conversations about the nature of dependence: "Even if we're talking about differences in degree [among different kinds of mothers] there ought to be some thought about whether we're talking about a relatively good mother or a relatively schizophrenogenic mother."[81] They thus developed their views of pathogenic motherhood in dialectical relation to a notion of "relatively good" motherhood.

Throughout the clinical conversations, the group worked on fleshing out their theoretical premises, often producing diagrams to explain their ideas. For example, the diagram on the blackboard behind the researchers in figure 3 represents the relationship between a father (F) and child (C), with the mother (M) moving between them. In August 1955, they worked on a blackboard to diagram the sequence and meaning of actions in an exchange in which person A said to person B, "I let you smoke" or in which A said, "I can hypnotize you," B said "No," and A said, "I want you to stay awake." Group members analyzed the exchanges from alternative disciplinary perspectives. Bateson brought up Logical Types and messages that frame actions, Haley mentioned hypnosis, and Jackson referred to psychoanalytic theory. The diagramming process served as a way of working through the intersections and implications of these divergent approaches. As Bateson commented, "I think we're bringing our languages together a bit." At the end of their meeting that day, Jackson observed, "We covered a lot of interesting stuff today, I think." Haley concurred and attributed it to their diagramming efforts. "Yeah, when you try to diagram it you really have to get it a lot more clear."[82] The group intermittently returned to diagramming during the fall and early winter of 1955.[83] During at least one of those meetings, the attempt to diagram a double-bind interaction was connected to an effort to bring cybernetics and psychoanalysis together, in particular Logical Types and ego formation.[84] Such diagrams served heuristic as well as generative purposes, just as illustrations, diagrams, and models have across a range of scientific fields.[85] More generally, the group's turn to diagramming, together with its emphasis on observation as research technique, exemplified the optic orientation of early family therapy.

At times the researchers debated not just the content of the theory but their methodological and epistemological approach. One debate occurred during a particularly speculative discussion[86] in December 1955 about dependence and the double bind and grew out of a conversation about how mothers respond to their infants' cries of hunger. The following extended quotation from that debate illustrates their disagreement about the relationship between data collection and theory building and gives a sense of the back-and-forth in their discussions. Haley and Weakland had just complained about the lack of evidence and observable phenomena in their research.

JACKSON (J): I have the feeling that John especially and Jay to some extent are objecting and I don't know what the hell to, certainly not to this kind of speculation. I mean look what physicists did before they were ever able to see an electron.

WEAKLAND (W): I'm not objecting to speculation at all, I'm objecting to . . . the attempt to go completely from the hypothesis which seems to me . . . a little bit like Gregory's statements we will go out with a camera and we will illustrate the double bind. Now the double bind itself is a hypothesis. And my view [is] that when you're trying to get closer to the data, you can have a hypothesis but keep it a little bit suspended. Instead of treating the hypothesis as if it were already a major fact.

HALEY (H): Don, we had some very elaborate discussions here on the difference between a hypothesis and a theory, because we felt Gregory was pulling theories out of the air and then doing his best to try to illustrate them instead of looking at the data and getting his theory from the data. Which is what John is reacting to here. . . .

BATESON (B): Look, this is a gross misstatement. . . . I was interested in the Logical Types and the awareness that a message is a message and all those questions and the nature of play. Jay then sir, started to look at schizophrenia, before I did, get the dates straight and cooked up the hypothesis, or between us I don't know what the relationship was there, that the central psychotic symptom could be phrased as a Logical Type distortion. . . . What you do in science is you start from some data.

H: Oh, now wait a minute.

B: You cook up a descriptive statement, which is in fact what happened . . .

H: Yeah, the hypothesis I'm talking about was you came up with something in the origin of double binds, on the basis of not talking to a patient at all and hardly listening to a schizophrenic. And then setting out to prove that.

B: That's what you do, that's called the working hypothesis. . . . Having gotten some degree of that description, the next thing to do is to extrapolate from it. And for that extrapolation I was responsible, I said "if that description be the correct description, then we would expect in the childhood a Logical Type traumatic system of some kind." Which is the double bind. . . .

W: Yes, but you're not treating it like a working hypothesis most of the time. . . . Where's the double bind? Gregory you're the most concrete speaker when you touch that double bind I have ever heard. You speak of the double bind as if it's that right there [referring to the solid arm of the chair]. . . .

H: All I'm doing is saying let us keep in mind that this is unobservable and hypothetical and try to work from this toward the observable.[87]

This debate underscored the indeterminacy of the meaning of research and knowledge production for their interdisciplinary research endeavor and reflected significant tensions within the group. Weakland and Haley challenged Bateson's deductive approach and pressed the group to find data by attending to the observable rather than the hypothetical, though neither Weakland nor Haley queried the meaning of "observable." Rather, they raised questions about the viability of extrapolating from observations of relationships between mothers and grown children to a characterization of mother-infant interactions, as Jackson had done, or drawing conclusions about the characterization of symptoms on the basis of the supposition that something like the symptom must have generated the symptom, as Bateson had done. In response to his critics, Bateson remained focused on theory building. He invoked a conception of science as extrapolation from a working hypothesis, which was a "descriptive statement" based on "some data."

Jackson played an intermediary role in this and other conversations. His sympathetic analogy between the group's speculative approach and that of physicists "before they were ever able to see an electron" played on the elevated status of physics as a science and on a colloquial, noninstrumental understanding of what it meant to "see" an electron. He also had the most data of the group since he could draw on case-based material from his clinical practice.

The push to find observable evidence motivated several subsequent efforts by the group, including a project to film both families with a schizophrenic member and "normal" families in order to study their respective patterns of communication. The researchers used film and audiotapes to record family interviews, rather than attempting to photograph the double bind with a camera, as Weakland had charged Bateson with doing, since photography produced single still images rather than a representation of diachronic interactions.

The use of thirty-minute film reels enhanced the need for a structured format in order to focus the family interactions during this limited time frame.[88] The design of what the group called the Structured Interview evolved over the late 1950s and early 1960s, but a few elements remained consistent. Project staff regularly asked the families to plan something together and to discuss who was in charge of the family. Without children in the room, they asked parents, "How, out of all the people in the world, did you two get together?" Project members developed additional interview techniques and family activities, some of which they administered only to families with a sick family member while others they employed with "pathological and ordinary families alike."[89] Families explicitly responded to the room's hot lights, stage-like setting, and process of being recorded.[90] Interviewers even used the setting and recording technology as a gambit at the beginning of the interview, following Weakland's prescription to "enter and make some brief 'at ease' references to the lights, camera, etc.," in a script from June 1959 for conducting family interviews.[91]

Project members recruited families with a schizophrenic member through contacts with local psychiatrists and hospitals.[92] In addition, one family from Menlo Park contacted the project reporting a "family problem" after reading a newspaper article about its research on family treatment.[93] Finally, they recruited their control group of normal families from a Stanford University sample and personal contacts of the project staff.[94] By late 1962, they had seen twenty families with a schizophrenic member in the Family Therapy Project. Of these, twelve underwent a filmed or taped structured interview, along with ten families in the control group. Six additional families participated in a limited capacity in the project, and three more "miscellaneous" families underwent Structured Interviews.[95]

The year 1956 proved to be a transitional one for the project. During the course of that year, the group's weekly meetings became increasingly focused on analyzing the audiotapes and transcripts from family interviews and discussing how to conduct therapeutic interventions in therapy sessions. Between the winter of 1956 and the winter of 1957, Bateson, Haley, Jackson, and Weakland clarified their conception of the double bind and published their seminal article on the topic.

According to the article's technical definition, the double bind had five necessary ingredients: (1) two or more people; (2) repetition so that

FIGURE 1   FIGURE 2

Contradiction and Paradox, Respectively, As Exemplified by Signs

The two injunctions in Figure 1 simply contradict each other. Therefore, only one can be obeyed. The sign in Figure 2 (a practical joke, we assume) creates a true paradox through its self-reflexivity: to obey the injunction of ignoring it, one first has to notice it. But this very act of noticing it is in disobedience of the injunction itself. Therefore, this sign can only be obeyed by disobeying it, and is disobeyed by obeying it.

Figure 4. From *Pragmatics of Human Communication: A Study of Interactional Patterns, Pathologies, and Paradoxes*, by Paul Watzlawick, Janet Beavin, and Don D. Jackson, 224. Copyright © 1967 by W. W. Norton & Company, Inc. Used by permission of W. W. Norton & Company, Inc.

double binds became habitual; (3) a primary negative injunction that entailed punishment for some action or inaction; (4) a secondary injunction that conflicted with the primary injunction at a more abstract level (e.g., "Do not submit to my prohibitions"), was also enforced by punishment, and was typically communicated by nonverbal means such as tone of voice or posture; and (5) a tertiary negative injunction that prevented the victim from escaping, such as threatened loss of parental love. In a double bind situation, Bateson and his colleagues designated one person as the "victim," typically a child, and another as the binder, who was often but not necessarily the mother.[96]

The double bind became a significant part of the landscape of the emerging field of family therapy,[97] though its diffusion also entailed some misunderstandings. For example, in the 1967 book *Pragmatics of Human Communication*, Jackson and his coauthors from the Mental Research Institute (MRI) staff, Paul Watzlawick and Janet Beavin, were at pains to correct a common misperception of the double bind as mere contradiction. They illustrated the distinction between a contradiction and a double bind-type paradox with the images in figure 4.

As the caption accompanying the images in *Pragmatics* indicated, a contradiction involves two statements that have opposite meanings ("stop" and "no stopping any time"). In contrast, a paradox presents contradictory messages at different logical levels: the literal instruction "ignore this sign" has already been disobeyed by the act of reading it. The Palo Alto group offered other examples of paradoxical communication, including "all statements within this frame are untrue," as mentioned above, and the command to "be spontaneous."

Critics of the double bind charged that the theory was too slippery to investigate, that double binds were not specific to schizophrenia and therefore could not function as a disease-specific pathogenic agent, that it was "an example of . . . mathematico-logical pseudo-psychologizing" that failed to enrich understanding of the human condition because it did not address psychoanalysis, and that the original paper presented the double bind in terms that were too concrete.[98] Some of these comments came from hostile critics, while others, such as those raised in the 1976 volume *Double Bind*, were proffered in the spirit of a "long lasting, loving relationship . . . between the idea and the reader."[99]

Criticisms that targeted the difficulty of researching the double bind and the concreteness of the concept echoed the group's own debates in the mid-1950s over the nature of theory and evidence, as shown in the weekly meetings in which Haley and Weakland challenged Bateson to find observable evidence and Weakland compared Bateson's conception of the double bind to something one could photograph, like the arm of a chair. By the late 1960s, Bateson himself had regrets about the way in which the group's original article reified the double bind and what he came to see as the premature publication of their ideas. In 1966 he wrote to Paul Watzlawick of the MRI that he was "tired of trying to fight the errors in 'Toward a Theory.'"[100] He also answered a general question about professional regrets at a 1975 conference with a comment on the double bind: "I think the first double bind paper . . . reads much too concretistic and a lot of people have wasted a lot of time trying to count double binds—which is almost like trying to count the number of jokes at a funny party. You can't do it."[101]

In the years after the 1956 publication of the double bind paper until the group disbanded in 1962, its research became increasingly diverse. Topics included close analysis of double binds based on verbatim interviews with psychotic patients; hypnosis and the double bind; classification of types of families, such as schizophrenic or delinquent; techniques for family therapy with families who had a schizophrenic member; and the development of a structured interview to collect data on family interactions.[102] In general, the project's collective approach was descriptive rather than diagnostic. According to Haley's account written in 1961, "The orientation of the Bateson project was anthropological; the research group preferred to approach a problem by observing natural history situations with as little intrusion as possible. Such an orientation is antithetical to experimentation, just as it is to a clinical approach."[103] While this summary remark overlooked the "intrusion" of the interview room, filming equipment, lights, and structured interview, it also spoke to Bateson's preference for ethnographic observation and theory building rather than therapeutics.

And yet Jackson never gave up his private practice, and it was during the course of the project that Weakland and Haley began to practice as family therapists. The tension between Bateson's theoretical orientation and the others' growing interest in therapy became more apparent by the late 1950s. This tension found expression in Bateson's response to Jackson's establishment of a new clinical institution, the Mental Research Institute, and Bateson's desire to keep his research separate from the clinical focus of MRI. In a 1964 letter to the psychologist Elliot Mishler, Bateson wrote, "There is a fundamental difference between my position and that of . . . Haley and Jackson. They are clinicians. I am a theorist. They are all the time looking for examples of generalized narrative. I am only looking for examples of formal relations, which will illustrate a theory."[104] This distinction between clinical and theoretical work also found expression in the distribution of the group members' publications. Over the course of ten years, the group generated over seventy publications. According to a survey of the group's collective bibliography by Bateson's biographer, David Lipset, the majority of the articles dealt with therapy (43 percent), and the family (27 percent), while only 24 percent addressed communications theory. Lipset noted that Bateson "not surprisingly" wrote most of the theoretical papers (80 percent), while Haley (44 percent) and Jackson (35 percent) contributed a large proportion of the group's papers on individual and family therapy, a division of labor that aligned with the members' respective interest in theory or therapy.[105]

The timeline of the project illustrates these shifts and tensions. During the first two years, 1952–54, Bateson and his research group studied paradoxes in communication in a wide variety of contexts. These included patient-therapist communication in psychotherapy and communication by schizophrenic patients, on which the group increasingly focused after 1954. From 1954 to 1956, they worked on developing their theory of the double bind and began recording interviews with whole families in addition to studying communication by individuals with schizophrenia. For the duration of the project until its conclusion in 1962, their work on the double bind served as the springboard for investigations on topics ranging from family therapy to hypnosis to family typologies. Over the course of the project, there was an increasing focus on family organization and an ongoing interest in schizophrenia, although group members also conducted research on hypnosis, humor, and the nature of psychotherapeutic change.

The Palo Alto group contributed to making family therapy into a field oriented toward visual observation as well as toward viewing the family as a system. The Palo Alto group's visual framework harnessed epistemological assumptions about the best ways to gain knowledge about schizophrenia and communication to an understanding of the nature of pathology as observable in families and their interactions, rather than hidden within individual psyches. The particular interdisciplinary configuration of the Palo Alto group fostered this orientation by bringing together cultural anthropology and interpersonal psychiatry in a manner that heightened attention to observable family interactions.

Metaphor and the Multiple Meanings of "System"

The Palo Alto group's conception of family as system emphasized interpersonal communication and control as the key features of family life, and the researchers relied on the metaphor of a self-regulating, cybernetic system to explain a family's internal patterns and processes. Their appropriation of cybernetics from its military development to the study of schizophrenia bore the marks of its historical lineage. As Peter Galison has argued, "The cultural meaning of concepts or practices, I would argue, is indissolubly tied to their genealogy. To understand the specific cultural meaning of the cybernetic devices is necessarily to track them back to the wartime vision of the pilot-as-servomechanism. . . . At the same time, it would clearly be erroneous to view cybernetics as a logically impelled set of beliefs. Nothing in the feedback device implies a representation of human beings as behavioristic black boxes."[106] In the case of family therapy, the cultural implications of the systems analogy were not uniform, nor were they predetermined or inherent in the systems framework. They were also neither infinitely flexible nor unconstrained. Some of the implications of the Palo Alto group's application of cybernetics and systems theory come into relief when these metaphors are contrasted with others used to explain family interaction and function.

By characterizing the family as a homeostatic, information-processing system, the Palo Alto group drew on the explanatory power of the metaphor of systems. In the context of family research and therapy, systems metaphors took several forms, including homeostatic and ecological systems. They performed two kinds of work: they served a productive function within scientific explanation, and they moved fluidly from the technical to the colloquial and across different disciplinary settings.[107]

A key metaphor for the double bind project was homeostasis. Jackson used the metaphor of homeostasis to describe patterns or types of interaction that helped a family maintain its central modes of organization or structure within a highly stable, narrow range. He wrote, "The term *family homeostasis* is chosen from the concepts of Claude Bernard and Cannon because it implies the relative constancy of the internal environment, a constancy, however, which is maintained by a continuous interplay of dynamic forces."[108] He underscored his focus on the "internal environment" of the family through his differentiation of family homeostasis from a sociological approach and through his attention to the psychiatric problem of the impact of an individual patient's treatment on his or her family. Jackson's use of metaphor advanced his argument in two different ways. It quickly conveyed the notion of self-regulation, constancy, and resistance to change. It also suggested that a family's response to one family member's psychiatric treatment could be predicted if psychiatrists had a better understanding of the particular homeostatic mechanisms operating in that family.

In contrast to the tightly regulated, stable model of family dynamics that emerged from Jackson's discussion of homeostasis in the mid-1950s, by the 1960s Edgar Auerswald described a more expansive approach to family systems that he called ecological. Auerswald's work provides a counterpoint to the metaphors of cybernetics and homeostasis employed by the Palo Alto group by demonstrating an alternative meaning for the phrase "family system" and by highlighting the cultural and political valences of the metaphors of homeostasis and ecology through their contrast. "Ecology" itself was hardly a straightforward term. Within the science of ecology in the postwar period, tensions arose between an older, organicist approach in which a community of species was analogous to an individual organism and a newer approach to complex ecological relations modeled on circular causal systems. Advocated by G. Evelyn Hutchinson, who attended the Macy conferences, the feedback system-based view incorporated physical and organic elements and became systems ecology.[109]

Auerswald's use of the term "ecology" bore only a vague resemblance to the science of ecology. It resonated with Barry Commoner's first law of ecology, "everything is connected to everything else,"[110] but had little relation to the nuances and debates that animated postwar scientific ecology.[111] Auerswald became involved with family therapy through working at the Wiltwyck School for Boys. Wiltwyck was a reformatory in New York that served primarily African American and Puerto Rican boys from Harlem during the 1950s and early 1960s. He later worked at a community health center in New York City. There he developed an innovative approach to mental health services that incorporated extended family, community figures, and other professionals and institutions involved in the problems of the lower-class patients served by the center.[112]

Auerswald's use of the language of ecology is exemplified in his most frequently cited article, titled "Interdisciplinary versus Ecological Approach," published in *Family Process* in September 1968. He began his discussion with a list of problems that he attributed to twentieth-century increases in scientific knowledge and technology: "The over-riding challenge is, of course, the prevention of nuclear holocaust, but such problems as crime and delinquency, drug addiction, senseless violence, refractive learning problems, destructive prejudice, functional psychosis and the like follow close behind."[113] In other words, mental illness and delinquency were pressing problems and ranked on the same scale as crime, drugs, and prejudice. His answer to addressing them lay in an integrated approach that he called ecological. He explicitly acknowledged his metaphorical use of terminology as a way to describe a form of thinking and an operational style rather than a well-constructed theoretical framework.[114]

Auerswald employed the language of ecology to argue that it was not sufficient for professionals with different disciplinary backgrounds merely to give their opinions on a given problem. Such an approach missed the important connections among disciplinary fields as well as the structure of the overall problem, such as delinquency. In contrast, he

argued, the ecological approach would focus on the nature of the interactions between various components of a system—for example, school,
mental health clinic, parents, employer. He told the story of Maria, a
twelve-year-old girl who had run away from home a few days before
a planned hospitalization for her newly diagnosed schizophrenia. An
ecologically oriented psychiatrist from Auerswald's center consulted her
parents, grandparents, mental health social worker, and guidance coun-
selor. The psychiatrist then recommended dismissing the schizophrenia
diagnosis, keeping Maria out of the hospital, reorganizing key aspects
of her home life, and bringing all the involved parties together for a
consultation. However, Maria still wound up hospitalized, which Auerswald attributed to the fragmentation and specialization of the experts
involved. The advantage to the ecological approach in this story was
not only that the girl would have avoided hospitalization and potentially
have returned home to an improved situation. The other advantage
would have been the removal of the label "schizophrenia," signifying
illness. Auerswald emphasized that Maria's behavior could just as easily have been labeled delinquent as schizophrenic had she wound up in
court rather than a mental health clinic.[115]

Auerswald's argument had several implications. The language of
ecology provided a vehicle to link his project with holism through simple association while eliding any differences that a more detailed discussion of either ecology or holism would have entailed. In addition, the
notion of ecology, in Auerswald's use, suggested focusing on a larger
social context, beyond the communicational patterns of an immediate
nuclear family or the fragmented perspectives of experts from single
disciplines. Thus his version of ecology recognized the socioeconomic
or structural factors that might impinge on a mental health problem and
the permeable boundary linking a family with, rather than separating it
from, its context.

To contrast homeostasis and ecology, both were organic metaphors
used to characterize complex systems, yet each had a divergent set of associations. The key association of homeostasis was regulated constancy,
whereas for ecology it was holistic context. Jackson emphasized the family unit to the exclusion of either the individual or the social or cultural
context. This was in contrast with Auerswald's focus on a family's extended context.

Beyond the explicit dimensions of Jackson's and Auerswald's metaphorical arguments, these frameworks had implications for what counted
as a family, as well as how one might view deviance and stability. For

example, homeostasis was useful for pointing out deficiencies or deviations from traditional norms and family rules. By characterizing the family system as homeostatic, Jackson emphasized stability and internal constancy within the nuclear family unit. Unlike Cannon's work on homeostasis, in which an organism "naturally" tended toward a healthy norm, Jackson's view of the homeostatic family incorporated pathology into its steady state, which made it difficult for clinicians to disrupt family patterns in order to induce change. Though the deviation-amplification associated with runaway or positive feedback stood in contrast to the equilibrating self-regulation of homeostatic systems and had negative connotations of destruction and breakdown in the work of Norbert Wiener and others, it became useful as a mode of therapeutic intervention.[116]

Yet a different metaphorical interpretation of system had other implications, along with a less conservative edge. The focus on context in Auerswald's use of ecology pointed to larger social changes. It was not enough to work with and change the individual or even the family; he argued that an ecological approach demanded engagement with the community as well. The clearest statement of this position would eventually come out of the radical therapy movement. A motto of radical therapy was "Therapy means change, not adjustment."[117]

Even the meaning of "family as system" was up for debate by the late 1960s. At a 1967 conference of invited family therapists and researchers, Lyman Wynne urged his fellow family therapists to consider the limits of understanding the family as a system: "The concept of the family as a system has been a useful stimulus to theory-building, therapy, and research, but the time has come to question and explore its limitations as well as its continuing conditions of applicability."[118] To illustrate, Wynne pointed to the limits of Jackson's emphasis on stability in his formulation of family homeostasis and to the alternative possibility of understanding families as non-self-equilibrating systems.[119]

The power of metaphor in family therapy lay in its capacity to bring explanatory coherence to a notion of family life as a series of interactions. The language of homeostasis suggested tightly organized family patterns centered around a well-established norm. Therapy would involve disrupting established patterns of communication and fostering a new norm around which a family's homeostatic balance could be reset without the pathological symptoms. In contrast, the language of ecology suggested the importance of a wider environmental context for understanding and treating the family. It also contained the potential for engagement with political or social change in that context.

While the "multiregister voice of metaphor"[120] enabled Jackson and Auerswald's theories to resonate with broader social and political issues, the metaphors themselves did not have inherent cultural or political meanings propelling them. Stephen Cross and William Albury have shown how Cannon and L. H. Henderson applied the concept of homeostasis to divergent political ends in the 1930s, and Anne Harrington's work on the mind and life sciences in Weimar and Nazi Germany undercuts any one-dimensional, overly romantic understanding of holism.[121]

The more general concept of systems also had contradictory cultural valences. The view of the family as a cybernetic or homeostatic system—as instantiated in therapeutic practices based on the assumption of a stable, pathology-maintaining family balance that therapists then aimed to disrupt—drew explicitly on wartime systems research that postwar academics applied to a wide variety of fields, including psychology, biology, and neurology. According to the historian Paul Edwards, "This extension of mathematical formalization into the realm of business and social problems brought with it a newfound sense of power, the hope of a technical control of social processes to equal that achieved in mechanical and electronic systems. In the systems discourses of the 1950s and 1960s, the formal techniques and tools of the 'systems sciences' went hand in hand with a language and ideology of technical control."[122] The emphasis on technical control was also part of family therapy. In the context of popular postwar concerns about the dangers of family instability, it was ironic that most early family therapists attributed the problem with pathological families not to their lack of stability but to the role of families' highly regulated, homeostatic stability in maintaining a given pathology.

However, this was not a unified vision. Some therapists, such as Wynne, challenged the early emphasis on homeostasis by considering the disadvantages of a narrow focus on equilibrium given cultural variability in family forms, and he suggested an alternative, developmental view of family life through time.[123] As Howard Brick has argued for the 1960s more broadly,

A general theory of systems and its close cousin, cybernetics (the science of communications and control), were not new to the 1960s, but they reached maturity then. To some of their proponents, they provided a basis for the unity of all science, an old positivist dream; to others, they suggested a holistic method of interpretation challenging the reductive and analytical traditions of scientific method. To some advocates, the understanding of complexity promised by systems theory and cybernetics opened prospects for social reform; to critics, they suggested only the refinement of coercive constraints.[124]

Whether the versions of systems theory and cybernetics manifest in family therapy offered avenues for social reform or coercive control, they served a productive function in defining the significant features and boundaries of the family.

Whither The Double Bind?

The significance of this collaborative project on schizophrenic communication lay in both its reframing of the family as a pathogenic system and its central role in the genealogy of family therapy as a field. A project that began as an anthropological study of paradoxes in communication morphed into one that contributed to the production of a new form of therapy that emphasized observable interactions among family members—a type of therapy that in turn bore the mark of Gregory Bateson's anthropological approach.

The ensuing careers of the project's members illustrate the project's central place in the history of the discipline. Although Bateson eventually turned away from psychiatry to study dolphin communication, the other three—Weakland, Haley, and Jackson—played foundational roles in the development of the new field of family therapy. Jackson in particular was instrumental in early institution building and the theoretical and clinical development of the field. Described as "a man of independent mind and ambitious, almost entrepreneurial character,"[125] he encouraged the group to publish their preliminary ideas on the double bind in 1956.[126] Jackson was also one of the cofounders of the first family therapy journal, *Family Process*, which began publication in 1962. He also parlayed publicity about the double bind project into financial and institutional support for establishing the MRI in 1959 as a research and training facility for family therapists at the Palo Alto Medical Research Foundation.

Through the development of the theory of the double bind, the project also significantly contributed to the view of the family as a system that was an appropriate unit for therapeutic intervention. "Everybody knows about the double bind!" wrote anthropologist Jules Henry in 1961 in response to an inquiry from John Weakland.[127] In his well-known, existentially informed critique of the biomedical model of schizophrenia, the British psychiatrist R. D. Laing approvingly cited Bateson and colleagues for their work on the double bind and their approach to schizophrenia, in which symptoms of disordered language and dissociated thoughts became intelligible in the context of the communicational patterns of the family, which Laing dubbed "knots."[128] During the 1970s, a group of psychoanalytically trained therapists in Milan, Italy, developed an internationally influential approach to family therapy that was self-consciously indebted to the Palo Alto group's work on paradox. Founded by Mara Selvini Palazzoli, the Milan team initially focused on treating families in which one member had anorexia or schizophrenia. Selvini Palazzoli and her colleagues Luigi Boscolo, Gianfranco Cecchin, and Guiliana Prata marked their Batesonian lineage in the 1978 title of their first jointly published book, *Paradox and Counterparadox*, which referred to their use of therapeutic paradoxes.[129]

The double bind's utility and appeal thus extended well into the 1970s, as further illustrated by the 1976 publication of a collection of articles titled *Double Bind: The Foundation of the Communicational Approach to the Family* and a 1977 conference titled "Beyond the Double Bind: Communication and Family Systems, Theories and Techniques with Schizophrenia," which was attended by close to a thousand people.[130] The articles in these collections and other publications demonstrated some of the efforts to revise, clarify, challenge, and/or buttress the double bind, including correctives by members of the Palo Alto group.[131] In an article originally published in 1962 and reproduced in *Double Bind*, Bateson, Jackson, Haley, and Weakland criticized the victim/binder (child/mother) formulation set forth in "Toward a Theory of Schizophrenia," and they reframed their theory to underscore a more cybernetic view of the family that highlighted "circular systems of interpersonal relations":

> The most useful way to phrase double bind description is not in terms of a binder and a victim but in terms of people caught up in an ongoing system which produces conflicting definitions of the relationship and consequent subjective distress. In its attempts to deal with the complexities of multi-level patterns in human communications systems, the research group prefers an emphasis upon circular systems of interpersonal relations to a more conventional

emphasis upon the behavior of individuals alone or single sequences in the interaction.[132]

The group thus emphasized its view of double binds as part of an ongoing system rather than a one-way interaction between binder and victim. In the late 1950s and early 1960s, project members increasingly attended to "three-party interactions" involving family members other than the mother and the child who was the "designated patient."[133]

Integral to the original conceptualization of the double bind was a historically specific model of the family. Bateson and his colleagues defined family as a self-contained unit consisting of heterosexual parents and a child or children. This definition is omnipresent in the group's conversations and publications. It was explicitly spelled out in a Mental Research Institute memo from the mid-1960s. This memo described the theory that MRI faculty members Fred Ford and Virginia Satir had stressed during an intensive training course in family therapy. It began with the following definitions: "Family = Three or more people, 1—husband, 1—wife, 1—child; Incomplete family = husband and wife without child; Family = system with a series of subsystems; System = an assemblage of objects united by some form of regular interaction or dependence; Systems have rules and rules govern systems. Neither systems nor rules exist independently Q.E.D.; Family = System = Rules."[134] This definition underscored the heterosexual and generational framework guiding their approach, as well as the centrality of the concept of the system and its governed interactions ("Family = System = Rules").

In a 1963 review of responses to "Toward a Theory of Schizophrenia," MRI faculty member Paul Watzlawick articulated more precisely the view of the family embedded in the theory of the double bind, a view that was favorably received by a number of readers, "The *specific family structure* which is conducive to double bind situations . . . [is one in which] the mother is the dominant parent whose pathological influence on the child is not sufficiently counteracted by the typically rather weak or withdrawn father."[135] This gendered vision of family life contained echoes of the portrait of domineering mothers in the work of Wylie and the influential psychiatrists David Levy and Edward Strecker. It informed the assumptions of project members, and they in turn contributed to its elaboration and perpetuation.

The Palo Alto group and its theory of the double bind received coverage not only in the professional literature but also in the popular press—for example, in a 1962 *Saturday Evening Post* article about family therapy.[136] Sixteen years later, Janet Malcolm also discussed the double bind at length in a *New Yorker* article on family therapy.[137] In addition, the double bind figured in theoretical studies of the family and became the target of criticism for contributing to midcentury psychogenic views that blamed schizophrenia on mothers.[138] Since the 1980s, most family therapists have increasingly distanced themselves from the theory that paradoxes in communication could cause schizophrenia. Instead of viewing their interventions as potentially curative in cases of schizophrenia, they advocate for the psychoeducational value of family therapy in order to help family members cope with the challenges brought by schizophrenia, understood as a biologically based disorder that should be treated psychopharmaceutically, just as they work with families facing other chronic medical problems.[139]

As this close analysis of the making of the double bind demonstrates, the theorization of the family as a system was indebted to midcentury views of schizophrenia and cybernetics. The Palo Alto project became a formative site for the development of family therapy as a field and for theorizing about the family as a system. Family system subsequently became uncoupled from schizophrenia per se and dissociated from its early framing in the technical language of servomechanisms of feedback, communication, and control; instead it became a more general characterization of family life that focused on patterns of interaction. The Palo Alto project was also a testament to the generative interface of anthropology and psychiatry during the 1950s and to the potential fruitfulness of interdisciplinary collaboration. As Bateson wrote to Norbert Wiener in 1959, "Life is not so simple that we can say that this man contributes this idea and that man that idea. There is also the mass of thoughts that are generated by interaction."[140]

CHAPTER THREE

THE CULTURE CONCEPT AT WORK

In 1952, the eminent American anthropologists Alfred Kroeber and Clyde Kluckhohn published a history and compilation of 164 of the definitions of "culture."[1] They were not interested in culture in the humanistic sense of the pursuit of perfection in the humanities, arts, and personal character. Rather, they focused on the pluralistic, anthropological definitions of world cultures with diverse value systems, patterns of behavior, beliefs, and ways of life.[2] Although the historical distinction between an aesthetic and an anthropological notion of culture was not as clear-cut as Kroeber and Kluckhohn claimed, their catalog of definitions underscored both the centrality of the culture concept for midcentury American social scientists and its mutability and diffuseness.

In the two decades following World War II in the United States, the culture concept had currency beyond the disciplinary boundaries of anthropology and sociology.[3] This chapter takes up the uses of culture as a category of analysis by family therapists in the 1950s and 1960s. The culture concept, together with the analytic category of the system examined in the previous chapter, played an integral role in the processes by which family therapists simultaneously defined the object of their research and treatment and built their new field. Their navigation of the boundary between psychiatry and the social sciences exemplified the more widespread, generative interactions among psychiatry, anthropology, and sociology during the mid-twentieth century.

Like many of their contemporaries, early family therapists were concerned with the interaction between individual personality and cultural formation, with the twist that they adapted the idea of culture to their focus on psychopathology at the level of the family. Through the lens of culture, they asked questions about differences among families or about the relationship between families and the circumstances in which they lived: How do cultural change and migration affect a family's expression of psychopathology? Are there family structures or processes that are pathological in one culture but not in another? How do family cultures contribute to socially destructive conditions such as prejudice and poverty? Unlike previous intersections between anthropology and psychiatry, most notably in culture and personality studies, family therapists were neither psychoanalytic in orientation nor primarily concerned with the determinants of individual personality, typical personalities in a given culture, or psychological types of cultural configurations. Instead, they predominantly defined their work in contrast to the individualistic, intrapsychic focus of psychoanalysis while still drawing on the theoretical frameworks and ethnographic accounts of culture and personality advocates.

The vagueness of the concept of culture in family therapists' hands proved to be productive for the field because it enabled culture to serve as an explanatory framework for a wide variety of issues, such as the nature of prejudice and the relationship between family and poverty. Culture served as both justification for and target of investigation by psychiatrists interested in the family. Interdisciplinary borrowings from anthropology and sociology provided useful perspectives and tools of analysis for the therapists, who appropriated culture to further their own aims, namely, to legitimize their new field and reconceptualize psychopathology as a familial rather than an individual problem.

However, culture was not infinitely malleable as an analytic category. Family therapists' attention to culture raised questions about the field's basic assumptions, like the universality of the form and functions of the family. Their varied uses of culture also contained tensions and contradictions, most notably those between universal and relativist views of family and psychopathology and between views of family therapy as a conservative force for maintaining the nuclear family and a progressive force for overcoming social inequality. In addition, as a scientific object that has been variably salient and productive at different historical moments, culture carried the traces of long-standing debates in anthropology and sociology that impacted how family therapists could then put culture to work at midcentury.[4]

Why Culture?

Family therapists' explanation for their attention to culture drew in part on their shift from an individual approach to mental illness to a family perspective. For them, context mattered. They initially defined context in terms of the family of a psychiatric patient, but that definition quickly broadened.

Some of the psychiatrists interested in family therapy extended their focus to include contexts beyond the family, with the justification that once one began to consider the contextual setting of a psychiatric problem, the boundaries of that context would keep expanding. A 1954 report produced by the Committee on the Family of the Group for the Advancement of Psychiatry (GAP) articulated this idea:

> To change the object of inquiry from the individual to the family . . . means the employment of different methods of observation and of different conceptual tools. . . . In brief, it turned out that the family could not be identified as a structural unit except with reference to the surrounding social system. . . . As psychiatrists, we lack *gestalten* for perceiving phenomena of such magnitude and complexity. . . .This means that we must add to our already existing stocks of concepts related to physical, chemical, biological and psychological events, a new cluster of concepts, of equal scientific rigor and seriousness, related to the group-dynamic, sociological and cultural-anthropological descriptions of events.[5]

A shift from an individual to a family perspective necessitated an additional shift in perspective to include the wider social context, so the GAP report argued, which further necessitated that psychiatrists become interdisciplinary and turn to sociology, anthropology, and other social sciences in order to study phenomena on such a large scale. This call to interdisciplinarity fit within the many interactions between postwar psychiatry and social sciences, in which the formation of GAP was an important piece.[6]

GAP was created in the spring of 1946 by psychiatrists who wanted to reorganize their national association, the American Psychiatric Association (APA), in the wake of World War II. The war had extensive impacts on the psychiatric profession. Before the war the profession had consisted largely of institutionally based psychiatrists who treated the severely and chronically mentally ill residents of mental hospitals and who favored somatic treatments such as shock therapies and lobotomy. The APA itself had the narrow agenda of putting out a journal, *American Journal of Psychiatry*, and organizing an annual meeting. World War II brought in many new young practitioners who had served in the military medical corps as psychiatrists and who had been exposed to psychodynamic approaches to therapy. The war strengthened the environmental perspective on the causes of mental illness since a key message of the war experience was that the stress of combat had induced breakdowns among soldiers without prior symptoms. The war focused attention on the fragile mental health of seemingly normal people, in addition to the extremes of severe mental illness. It also revitalized the preventative and socially activist goals that had motivated the mental hygienists of the 1920s and 1930s and highlighted a role for psychiatry in community settings like the military, not just in mental hospitals.[7] GAP, originally led by William Menninger, served as a forum for those who supported more expansive goals for the psychiatric profession, and its members soon took over some of the top positions in the APA.

However, GAP was only one faction of the APA, and its organization solidified the ongoing tensions between psychodynamic, environmentally oriented psychiatrists and the biological, institutional psychiatrists who had dominated the profession prior to 1941.[8] In the 1940s and 1950s, its approach became mainstream with the ascendancy of psychoanalysis and as increasing numbers of psychiatrists built up their practices in nonhospital settings. Over the next few years, GAP's members reorganized into an independent association that operated through working groups designed to address problems such as public education and racial and economic tensions. Overall, the group maintained an activist stance based on support for psychiatry's role in promoting mental health and the adjustment between self and society rather than merely treating mental illness.[9]

Interest in the family fell within the purview of GAP, since the family was a crucial site of potential intervention in the adjustment between individual and community. The association between family upbringing on the one hand and mental illness on the other was certainly not an original product of the 1940s and 1950s. The history of this link could be traced most immediately to the child guidance clinics, Progressive reformers, and mental hygiene movement of the first half of the twentieth century.[10] Nonetheless, the idea that families—whether this referred to mothers or to a larger configuration of people—caused mental illness did receive renewed impetus and articulation in the wake of World War II.

The GAP Committee on the Family was appointed in 1951, and its founding members included the psychiatrist John Spiegel and the sociologist Florence Kluckhohn.[11] The committee's early work and initial report of 1954 articulated a vision for a psychiatric approach to the family that resonated with early theoretical frameworks for family therapy, even though practicing family therapists did not join this committee until later in the decade.[12] One of the central themes of its 1954 report, "Integration and Conflict in Family Behavior," was the value of interdisciplinarity. This interest echoed the agenda and priorities of Robert Felix, who headed NIMH from its inception in 1949 to his retirement in 1964.[13] Felix believed that the social environment was a key factor in the etiology of mental illness but that psychiatrists did not have the training in statistics and research design or the appropriate social perspective to investigate environmental factors. He supported the application of knowledge and research techniques from the social and behavioral sciences to the study of mental illness, and he put his belief in the value of interdisciplinary scholarship into action in NIMH funding for training and extramural research.[14] GAP members' interest in interdisciplinarity also echoed broader postwar associations between interdisciplinarity, science, and democracy.[15]

This was the backdrop to the invocation of sociocultural analysis by the Committee on the Family. The committee's 1954 report began with a statement of its charge "to bring this area [of the family] into a specific psychiatric focus."[16] It found this charge particularly salient because of the extensive contemporary concern with family affairs among child welfare agencies, educators, clergy, politicians, market researchers, lay public, mass media, sociologists, anthropologists, psychologists, and psychiatrists. The report framed the impetus behind its project in the following way:

> In short, it appeared as no surprise that the United States is a family-minded nation, and that practically every visible group had some kind of stake in the family area. In consideration of this extensive, but unfocused activity, the Committee asked itself what it could contribute to an understanding of family behavior as a psychiatric organization. With this tentative idea in mind, we arrived at the following hypothetical question: Is it possible to make any generalizations regarding processes within the American family which affect the mental health or illness of the various members of the family?[17]

The report thereby emphasized the importance of the pathological family in the production of mental illness: "How to distinguish the normal—dominant or variant—from the pathological or deviant states conducive to illness is a primary task."[18] This goal evocatively defined "normal" family states in relation to "pathological or deviant" family states, but it retained an individually based conception of disease that subsequent family therapists would challenge.

Beyond the call to arms for psychiatrists to turn their attention to the family and to borrow from other disciplines in their efforts, the GAP report focused on laying out a frame of reference for analyzing the family in a rigorous way. It prefaced its analysis with comments on the difficulty of defining and locating the boundaries of the family since families varied widely in their inclusiveness, structure, and function. Given that qualifier, the report outlined five axes or points of reference for understanding the family: as a collection of individuals, a small group or organization, a structural and functional unit in a larger social system, an agency for the transmission of cultural values, and a unit residing in a particular geographical setting. The report focused in particular on the social system and cultural values because they were seen to be "of the greatest strategic importance."[19]

The report highlighted two approaches to the relationship between family and culture. The first employed cross-cultural studies to make generalizations about universal relationships between family and social system: "Extensive cross-cultural surveys have shown that some form of family is found in every society. . . . The patterns vary with respect to size and kinship lines but the basic structure is universal. Furthermore, in all societies the family system is structurally related to all other units of the social system."[20] In support of its universalizing claims, the report footnoted a diverse spectrum of literature on the family, including history of the family, anthropological studies of family in literate and nonliterate societies, sexual aspects of family life, sociological studies of the family as a social institution, and psychoanalytic writings on family and individual psychology. The report characterized the structural and functional aspects of family in terms of the adaptive differentiation of roles, such as the separation of social functions between husband and wife. The GAP report acknowledged the diverse ways in which role theory had been used, but it identified the source of its concept of role as the 1951 book *The Social System* by Talcott Parsons.[21] Parsons's work dominated midcentury sociology and helped to organize the terms of the field's main debates of that period, such as the relative merits of a structural or functional approach. His focus on a theory of socialization as the connecting mechanism between social system and personality was useful for family therapists because the family was the milieu in which social role formation took place. While the GAP report drew on Parsonian theory in the context of discussing cross-cultural studies, it ultimately used those studies to make universal claims about the relationship between family and social system, an emphasis that was in line with Parsons's work, rather than emphasizing cultural difference.

In contrast, the report's second approach to the relationship between family and culture focused on family as the transmitter of cultural values and emphasized the cultural variability in human behavior, moral standards, systems of belief, and patterns of interpersonal relations. This approach highlighted scholarship by proponents of culture and personality studies, which was an influential perspective among many social scientists who, from the late 1920s to the 1950s, decried biological, race-based explanations for group differences and turned instead to cultural explanations for patterns of human behavior.[22] It was based on the intersection of particular strains of anthropology and psychoanalysis: Boasian cultural anthropologists and neo-Freudian psychoanalysts sympathetic to ego and interpersonal psychology were among its most prominent representatives.[23] In a 1961 historical survey, Milton Singer identified three central problem areas for the field: "the relation of culture to human nature; the relation of culture to typical personality; and the relation of culture to individual personality."[24] Singer related these to the three possible relationships between an individual and a group identified by Clyde Kluckhohn and Henry Murray in the introduction to their influential collection of articles on culture and personality studies: "that every man is in certain respects like all other men, like some other men, and like no other man."[25] Thus questions of similarity and difference, on both the group and individual levels, were at the heart of the culture and personality movement.

The social scientists studying culture and personality were interested in the relationship between the group and the individual, and they saw the family as key to that relationship. The GAP report by the Committee on the Family testified to the impact of such work by claiming, "We now have a clearer understanding of the relationship between the psychology of the individual and the culture in which he develops and to which he is adapted."[26] The report outlined several factors in any culture's "value orientation," such as the relationship between man and nature and views about time, and it then applied this approach to a comparison of family life among Spanish Americans of the southwestern United States and middle-class Anglo-Americans in urban centers. The theoretical assumption underlying this analysis was that "there is an ordered cultural variation (a web of variation) in all social systems."[27] The GAP report thus drew on research and theoretical frameworks from both sociology and anthropology with the premise of broadening the domain of psychiatry to include family life. Yet, in contrast to anthropology and sociology, the clinical context of family therapy carried the presumption of instigating change through therapeutic intervention, beyond the goal of scientific study for the sake of knowledge about culture itself.

Discipline Building and the Culture Concept

When the GAP Committee on the Family released its report in 1954, there were few publications on clinical efforts to treat whole families. Over the next several years, an increasing number of clinicians began to do therapy with whole families, and they gradually became aware of one another's work at national conferences, through word-of-mouth, and in scattered publications.[28] By the late 1950s and early 1960s there was sufficient interest and momentum in the new field for the inauguration of its own journal. When publication began in 1962, *Family Process* became a site of professional identification and consolidation, and it articulated a vision for the field, even if it did not uniformly represent the views of all family therapists.[29] The importance of the culture concept to the development of family therapy was evidenced in the programmatic statements on culture made in the inaugural issue of *Family Process*.

The impetus for the journal came from Don Jackson. In a proposal circulated to prospective editorial board members in 1959, he reiterated two key themes from the 1954 GAP report: (1) any therapeutic assessment and treatment of families by psychiatrists and other clinicians necessarily entailed attending to the social and cultural setting of the families; and (2) clinicians should draw on the work of social and behavioral scientists who were already addressing such aspects of family life.[30] Although Jackson's own work on family homeostasis emphasized the internal stability of family life to the exclusion of contextual or environmental factors, he also recognized the importance of contextual analyses for the field of family therapy.

As in the GAP report, the journal proposal framed the shift to a family orientation in clinical work in terms of the need to pay attention to families' social and cultural contexts. It identified five areas of research on the human family on which the journal would publish articles: the relationship between types of individual psychopathology and types of families, family diagnosis and treatment, cultural differences in family organization, social institutions and organizations as an expanded family, and attempts to find a theoretical model for family interaction. Of these five areas, two engaged directly with ideas about culture—namely, those on cultural differences in family organization and the view of social organizations as "expanded family."

Jackson justified the turn to culture with a comparative argument. He wrote, "When the family is conceived of as a disturbed system in contrast to other family systems, the question of cultural deviance is immediately raised."[31] Thus the very notion of a disturbed family implied a culturally normative standard for a nondisturbed family. Jackson further asserted that anthropological studies of families in different cultures were relevant to research on disturbed families because such norms might vary across cultures.

However, in his proposal Jackson did not explicitly state what he meant by culture or cultural deviance. Instead, he painted in broad strokes, calling for a journal that would serve as a common source of information both about families in diverse cultures and about the impacts of cultural change on family structure and function in a given culture.[32] He simply identified culture as an important category of analysis—significant as a marker of difference among families and as an external force that could act upon and change family structure.

He paid particular attention to the impact of cultural change within the United States:

> In America the effects of cultural change upon the family unit are being studied by research men in anthropology, sociology, social psychology, and allied fields such as mass communication research. Investigations are being made of the effect of the mass media upon the family as well [*sic*] studies of the portrayal of families in the drama of the mass media. Cultural changes relevant to disturbances in families are the shifting status of women, the social mobility of families, the geographical shifting of family members, and the increasing longevity of parents.[33]

The net effect was an attempt to situate the journal among interdisciplinary efforts in the social and behavioral sciences to understand the family and to establish the relevance of family therapy for social issues not directly related to mental illness, such as the changing status of women.

Jackson further developed the expansive agenda of the proposed journal (and by proxy the whole field of family therapy) in his description of the "expanded family." He wrote,

> The fact that every individual learns how to organize with others from the type of family organization in which he matures has profound effects upon the kinds of social institutions he creates. . . . From the cultural point of view, the organization of business and government is inevitably influenced by the kind of family organization in a particular culture. . . . The proposed journal will welcome articles dealing with the reciprocal effects of family organization on treatment and other social institutions as well as national and international organizations and conflicts.[34]

The journal's purview would thus cover the organization of social institutions, businesses, and governments, not just the treatment of psychopathology.

Jackson provided several illustrations of how family organization in a given culture could affect the structure of larger institutions and relationships:

> Studies of paternalistic industry and maternalistic societies suggest how often family terminology as well as ideas of family organization influence the cultural structure of society. The shift in business organization from authoritarian leadership to committee and conference leadership would presumably be related to shifts in family organization. Just as family organization will influence national political structure, so will the political structure influence the family, as is apparent in an extreme way in China at the moment. In the international field as well, the "family" of nations will interact with each other in ways related to the patterns of interaction in the individual families of those nations.[35]

An additional example came from the familial structure of the mental hospital, in which doctors and nurses frequently became parental figures for the patients. The analogy between mental hospital and family can be traced at least to the moral therapy of the eighteenth and nineteenth centuries.[36] However, unlike asylum superintendents such as Thomas Kirkbride, Jackson was interested in the familialism of the hospital not as an intentional therapeutic technique but as a potential research topic regarding the ways in which patients' family patterns influence their interactions with a hospital system or their transference in individual or group psychotherapy.

Three years later, in March 1962, the first issue of *Family Process* appeared under the joint sponsorship of Jackson's Mental Research Institute in Palo Alto and the Family Institute of New York City, which had been established in 1960 by Nathan Ackerman. In that issue the journal's editors emphasized the importance of studying the family by outlining the deficiencies of prior research in the human sciences: "In the purview of history, the study of the human being has gravitated to two extremes: the investigation of the isolated, individual personality and the study of society and culture. The family, which is the link between the individual and his socio-cultural organization, has been curiously neglected. This polarization of the study of the human being continues."[37] The editors of *Family Process* continued their clarion call by emphasizing the family as the key to overcoming the misleading focus on the extremes of either individual personality or broader society and culture. They asserted, "To bridge the gap, it is essential to study the natural habitat of the person, his family. We can no longer afford the error of evaluating the individual in isolation from his usual environment or appraising that behavior in artificial settings. We must study the person where he breathes, eats, sleeps, loves and where he learns his place in society: in the intimate climate of his day-by-day family relationships."[38] This depiction of the family as a cultural mediator thus complemented the argument put forward in the 1954 GAP report that an understanding of the relationship between pathology and the family required that researchers broaden their area of focus beyond the boundary of the family unit to include society and culture.

Beyond the programmatic statements of the founding editors of *Family Process*, other leaders of the field echoed the call for cultural analysis. The remainder of the chapter traces four significant invocations of the culture concept within the family therapy literature of the 1950s and 1960s. The first case concerned the role of family life in generating prejudice and anti-Semitism as part of postwar attempts to explain the roots of fascism and the Nazi rise to power in Germany. The second case invoked contemporary social scientific studies of poverty and delinquency. In addition to studies of prejudice or the culture of poverty, *Family Process* published articles by several family therapists engaged in cross-cultural research and therapy projects. Finally, some family therapists raised questions about their own cultural role and the impact of family therapy on maintaining or subverting cultural norms. Together, these diverse engagements with the culture concept demonstrate the powerful, though at points contradictory, ways in which culture contributed to family therapists' reframing of the meaning of family and pathology.

Scapegoating: The Pathology of Prejudice and Psychodynamics of Family Life

Postwar invocations of culture often had political as well as psychological implications. In his work on anti-Semitism and prejudice in the 1940s, Nathan Ackerman referred to the family as the mediator between individual and culture. He used this framework as a means of cultural critique by depicting family problems as symptoms of cultural ills. He also used cultural comparison as way of reinforcing universal claims in his approach to family therapy in the 1950s and 1960s.

In *Anti-Semitism and Emotional Disorder* Ackerman argued that the family played a central role in perpetuating social ills. This book was published as part of Max Horkheimer's series "Studies in Prejudice," which included the well-known volume *The Authoritarian Personality*.[39] Ackerman and his coauthor Marie Jahoda introduced their psychoanalytical, case-based study on anti-Semitism and personality with a self-acknowledged "explicit admission" of "emotional involvement" and a statement on the status of anti-Semitism as a social pathology: "Both authors of this study . . . believe that anti-Semitism in whatever form it appears is a symptom of social pathology, indicating a form of social disorganization that menaces the stability, if not the very foundation of a culture, even beyond the suffering that it entails for its victims."[40]

In this account, the family became important as the means of transmitting prejudice and anti-Semitism. This was no simple matter of acculturation. Rather, the family became the specific catalyst or means of production of individual behaviors and attitudes, which would then go on to have social manifestations and implications. According to Ackerman and Jahoda,

> Frequently the assertion is made . . . that this attitude is passed
> on from one generation to the next within the family, which is
> the main agent for transmission of culture. Just as the child is ac-
> culturated by his family to such things as the kinship system, the
> value of money, the respect for authority and law and the use of
> fork and knife, so, it is held, does he acquire anti-Semitism. . . .
> But this hypothesis of culturally imitated anti-Semitism tends to
> be disproved by our case material. . . . The relation between the
> parents' and the child's prejudice must be regarded as a function of
> the dynamic outcome of the Oedipal development and the vicis-
> situdes of early identification attempts as well as of the receptivity
> to cultural pressures coming from inside and outside the family.[41]

Ackerman and Jahoda supported their claim for the importance of
the Oedipal complex, ego development, and the process of identification with case material from practicing psychoanalysts and two social
welfare agencies in New York City, in which anti-Semitic patients did
not necessarily have anti-Semitic parents.[42] Instead, the key feature of
anti-Semitism-generating families was a violent, argumentative, cold,
and unsympathetic relationship between the parents, often defined by
an asymmetry of dominance: "Thus, the absence of affectionate human
relations and the existence of hostility . . . represented the earliest childhood conditioning in human relations. This pattern seemed often to be
reinforced by the sharp contrast between the parents. . . . One parent was
dominant and overaggressive; the other submissive, weak, and masoch-
istic. More often than not, it was the mother who represented aggressive dominance."[43] Thus, a family milieu with antagonistic parents and
an overly aggressive mother was a common setting for the creation of
prejudice. This gendered pattern was the target of other contemporary
commentators on the dangers of bad mothering for producing not only
prejudice but also problems such as delinquency and homosexuality.[44]

While Ackerman and Jahoda favored a psychodynamic explanation
for the transmission of anti-Semitism over an explanation based on acculturation, they still highlighted the interface between culture and individual psyche: "Cultural traditions and social forces do not exist as
abstractions. Although they have been profitably studied in isolation,
they actually exist only in so far as they express themselves dynamically in the behavior of human beings. Ultimately . . . it is necessary to
study the continuous and intricate interaction of intrapsychic tenden-
cies and environmental forces as they shape and develop each other."[45]

The place in which this intricate interaction occurred was the family. In their concluding chapter, "Anti-Semitism in Context," they turned to the (unmarked and apparently unitary) American family by addressing salient features of contemporary American culture, particularly its competitiveness and acquisitiveness, the isolation of individuals and lack of group cohesion, the absence of a system of ethics and values with the decline of religion and the secularization of society, and the ambiguous social position of women. Ackerman and Jahoda asserted that all these trends were reflected in the family. At the root of most of them, they further asserted, lay the pattern of domination and submission that defined husband-wife relations in families that produced anti-Semitic children: "Theirs is a world in which the concept of cooperation and equality does not exist. Unless they dominate, they are crushed. This, then, is the answer to [psychoanalyst Otto] Fenichel's question as to the nature of the mass discontent which disturbs intergroup relations in American society."[46]

Thus the family was both the basis for and a reflection of trends in American culture and society, which Ackerman's work on family therapy also asserted. According to the editors of a collection of his published papers,

> Ackerman's account of anti-Semitism in 1950 presaged the framework in which he developed his approach to family therapy in the late 1950s and 1960s. He continued to view the family as a means of accessing both individual suffering and social distress. It is not too difficult to guess that Ackerman hoped to have the best of both worlds, to turn inward to mental life and outward to social life, and thereby reconcile the moral conflict that is entailed in choosing between these. These perspectives informed his professional life, made inevitable his interest in anti-Semitism and scapegoating, and influenced the eventual development of family therapy.[47]

Ackerman's publications on family therapy used culture as a means of discussing the universal and variable aspects of family life, as well as the importance of family as the membrane between individual and culture.

He repeatedly described the family as a universal, basic unit of society but with culturally variable forms. In his influential 1958 book *The Psychodynamics of Family Life*, he argued, "The family is the basic unit of growth and experience, fulfillment or failure. It is also the basic unit of illness and health. . . . It is the same everywhere; yet it has never remained the same. . . . There is nothing fixed or immutable about family, except that it is always with us."[48] In later work, he identified several common goals of family life: "union and individuation, the care of the young, the cultivation of a bond of affection and identity, reciprocal need satisfaction, training for the tasks of social participation, including the sex role, and the development and creative fulfillment of its members."[49] However, he also insisted that the forms of families and the means by which they coped with problems and conflicts varied with social status and cultural position.[50] He similarly painted a dual portrait of universal and culturally specific conceptions of health by both categorically defining the nature of a healthy family and describing the cultural, historical variations in definitions of health, sickness, and the role of a healer.[51]

In addition to using culture to demarcate universal and variable facets of the family, Ackerman engaged with the category of culture in his analysis of the family as the link between individual and community. Of his many articulations of the relationship between individual, family, and society, one of the most evocative appeared in *The Psychodynamics of Family Life*, where he wrote, "The family may be likened to a semipermeable membrane, a porous covering sac, which allows a selective interchange between the enclosed members and the outside world. 'Reality' seeps through the pores of the sac selectively to affect the enclosed members in a way predetermined by the quality of the sac. The influence exerted by the family members on the outside world is also affected by the quality of the sac. . . . Basically, the family does two things: It insures physical survival and builds the essential humanness of man."[52] Framed in a biological metaphor suggesting the physiological studies of homeostasis that Ackerman discussed later in the book, this depiction of the family as a membrane served to highlight the power of the family in the interchange between psyche and culture. In this vein, Ackerman criticized both the individualistic focus of mental hygiene and psychoanalysis for ignoring the significance of socialization and the social system focus of sociology that ignored psychoanalytic insights about personal identity and suffering.[53]

The Culture of Poverty: Framing Class and Race in the Language of Family and Culture

Ackerman's work on family, prejudice, and scapegoating grew out of World War II and developed during the 1950s into a more general framework for understanding family dynamics and treating family pathology. In addition to Ackerman's work on culture and family, another approach to culture grew out of the culture-of-poverty argument that was developed by the anthropologist Oscar Lewis, popularized by the sociologist Michael Harrington in his 1962 book *The Other America*, and expressed in the work of Salvador Minuchin. In the impassioned prose of *The Other America*, Harrington argued for the consideration of poverty as a culture, meaning a way of life and worldview, rather than merely an economic status. He wrote, "Poverty in the United States is a culture, an institution, a way of life. . . . Everything about [the poor], from the condition of their teeth to the way in which they love, is suffused and permeated by the fact of their poverty. . . . There is, in short, a language of the poor, a psychology of the poor, a world view of the poor. To be impoverished is to be an internal alien, to grow up in a culture that is radically different from the one that dominates the society."[54] Writing against the widespread contemporary assumption of nationally shared abundance, Harrington identified several specific groups who lived within the culture of poverty: the factory rejects, migrant farm workers, Appalachian farmers, southern black poor farmers, blacks in northern urban slums, alcoholics, beatniks and bohemians, urban hillbillies, the aged, and finally, the mentally ill. In Harrington's account, it was not mental illness that led to poverty but the grinding experience of poverty itself that produced "the twisted spirit."[55]

Minuchin incorporated the culture-of-poverty approach into family therapy in his work during the early 1960s at the Wiltwyck School for Boys, a residential treatment center in New York City for delinquent boys aged eight to twelve. Like Ackerman, Minuchin was a psychoanalytically trained psychiatrist practicing in New York. However, they treated different patient populations and used the category of culture in different ways. Ackerman treated families at his private practice and through Jewish social welfare agencies, whereas Minuchin worked with the families of delinquent boys.

Minuchin initially began working at Wiltwyck in the late 1950s as an intake psychiatrist in order to support his psychoanalytic training at the William Alanson White Institute.[56] In 1959 he received a grant from NIMH to study families in which multiple children had become juvenile delinquents. He organized a clinical research team composed of two additional psychiatrists, two psychologists, and two social workers for the project. Through the mid-1960s, they researched and conducted therapy with poor, predominantly Puerto Rican and African American families from Harlem who had at least two sons identified by the courts as delinquent.[57] On the basis of their research and clinical experiences, Minuchin and his colleagues published several articles and the 1967 book *Families of the Slums*. They devoted the bulk of their book to transcripts from therapy sessions with three families and to the development of their assessment and therapeutic techniques.

In addition to describing the authors' research and clinical practices, *Families of the Slums* emphasized the role of family structure and function in "the disorganized and disadvantaged family" in perpetuating poverty as a way of life, even in the face of available jobs or community resources. Minuchin and his colleagues at Wiltwyck focused on the impoverished urban background of the families they studied as the unifying feature among otherwise varied families: "We are especially interested in the ghetto-living, urban, minority group member who is experiencing poverty, discrimination, fear, crowdedness, and street-living in slums. . . . We have some evidence that many of the same problems characterize different impoverished groups living in urban areas everywhere; that is, it seems that a number of variables cut across *all* cultures of poverty."[58] They cited Oscar Lewis and Michael Harrington's conception of a culture of poverty as a framework for their characterization of life in an urban ghetto.[59]

Two key facets of this conception were particularly relevant to the Wiltwyck project: the deleterious psychological consequences of poverty and its familial, intergenerational transmission, referred to as a kind of inheritance.[60] More specifically, Minuchin's team proposed that the link between slum life and delinquency lay in a culture of poverty fostered by "disorganized, pathological families,"[61] rather than being a direct consequence of structural inequalities, lack of resources, or discrimination. This linkage entailed a complex set of associations that, when unpacked, demonstrate how the concept of culture operated in their work.

Culture here referred to a way of life, set of attitudes and values, patterns of family organization, and distinctive behavioral, communicational, and cognitive styles.[62] To support their claim that social class, rather than racial or ethnic factors, accounted for the particular cultural configuration that characterized the families they studied, the Wiltwyck researchers cited the work on a Boston slum by the sociologist Herbert Gans.[63] They thus connected culture to income level rather than nationality, ethnicity, religion, tribe, or other group distinctions. They further identified differences among low-income groups based on their degree of stability and disorganization: "The [unstable and disorganized] group, although sharing certain characteristics with others in the low-income population, also shows social pathology: alcoholism, disease, mental illness, addiction, crime and delinquency, etc. . . . Our book is concerned with conceptualizations concerning disorganized, unstable, lower-class families rather than those coming from the working class or more stable elements of the lower class."[64] In their depiction of disorganized poor families, they aimed to avoid what they saw as the one-sided perspectives in other scholarship on poverty, which either overestimated or ignored the strengths and adaptability of the people under study.[65]

On the "romanticizing" side were scholars like Gans who emphasized the positive, adaptive values and qualities among those living in a culture of poverty, such as a sharing of problems and regularity of routine. The Wiltwyck team did not find these "strengths of the poor" among the families they studied, which they attributed to the instability and disorganization of their patient population in contrast to other low-income but stable families. Conversely, they argued against the concept of "cultural deprivation," which implied that the life of impoverished people was defined by its deficits in, distortions of, or deviations from middle-class norms and core culture rather than by the presence of its own culture (however pathological it might be). They also argued against the remedial implication of the cultural deprivation approach, which implied that poverty and delinquency could be addressed through "enrichment" and teaching middle-class values.[66] These distinctions made by the authors of *Families of the Slums* and other contemporary studies of poverty pointed to the nuances among various culture-of-poverty arguments, but these easily fell away in generalized references to a deviant, pathological culture of poverty, despite qualifications to the contrary.[67]

In their own study, the Wiltwyck team members summarized the key features of the "disorganized and disadvantaged" family in terms of patterns of communication, socialization of affect, and family structure.[68] More concretely, they described the families they treated as having an impermanent home environment, in which meals had no set time or place and the occupants of any given bed kept changing. In the portrait painted by *Families of the Slums*, the care of young children was shared by mothers, aunts, grandmothers, and older siblings, who unpredictably provided extensive amounts of attention or left a young child alone for long stretches of time. Parents responded randomly to children's actions according to their moods rather than consistent norms and provided "traffic signals" to direct current behavior rather than guidance for the future. These and other features of family life, such as the prevalence of female-headed households and transient father figures, were seen as part of the culture of poverty in which the families lived. The disorganized and disadvantaged family garnered the designation "pathological" by socializing children in ways that contributed to delinquent behavior.[69] A model of socialization thereby clinched the complex linkages among class, culture, family, and delinquency, which became fluidly, almost seamlessly intertwined in the account put forward by Minuchin's team of researchers.

Other sociological and psychological experts of the time made parallel sets of associations, though they did not necessarily rely on socialization and the culture of poverty as the linking mechanisms. In diverse influential studies such as Eleanor and Sheldon Glueck's *Delinquents in the Making*, Albert Cohen's *Delinquent Boys: The Culture of the Gang*, and Richard Cloward and Lloyd Ohlin's *Delinquency and Opportunity*, delinquency went hand in hand with problems in the family and home environment, a "subculture" of delinquency that held values contrary to those of the middle class, a peer-oriented youth or gang culture, and the disparity between cultural aspirations and blocked opportunities for poor adolescents.[70] In these studies, as at Wiltwyck, the focus was on delinquent boys rather than girls.

However, the studies also had important points of disagreement, including the weight they gave to cultural analyses that aimed to identify and assess the particular practices, concerns, and patterns of behavior among lower-class people on their own terms rather than as an absence or distortion of middle-class values.[71] There were also debates about the ties between delinquency and poverty. As James T. Patterson argues in his history of poverty in twentieth-century America, "By the mid-1960s it was becoming clearer that juvenile delinquency was neither rampant nor clearly correlated with poverty."[72] Following the logic of this dissociation of delinquency and poverty would have meant untying delinquency from the culture associated with poverty. Critics of the notion of a culture of poverty posed challenges on several levels—the lack of substantiation for claims that poor people were passive or "present-minded," evidence that most poverty was neither long-term nor intergenerational, the persistence of racial discrimination and lack of opportunity, and the importance of understanding culture as integrally related to socioeconomic environment rather than as a separate variable.[73]

Although primary identification of the population under study in *Families of the Slums* was based on the families' status as poor urban-ghetto residents, Minuchin and his research team also used a concept of culture to differentiate among the families that composed the bulk of the clientele at Wiltwyck: "Negro and Puerto Rican slum families share many characteristics of the culture of poverty, but they differ in certain aspects, many of which are culturally determined."[74] They thus analyzed cultural differences between their research subjects from different racial and ethnic backgrounds, even as they subsumed those differences within the framework of the culture of poverty. As Alice O'Connor has argued, postwar social scientists "explained differences of race *and* class in terms of culture rather than biology while implicating cultural exclusion and pathology in the persistence of black poverty."[75] Thus the concept of culture became tied to race and ethnicity, as well as poverty and delinquency, with the family playing the linchpin role.

The Wiltwyck team's approach to African American families in particular fit within a multistranded social science lineage of scholarship focused on race, family, and psychological damage.[76] This lineage included work by E. Franklin Frazier, Kenneth Clark, Thomas Pettigrew, and Abram Kardiner and Lionel Ovesey, and it received its best-known expression in Daniel Patrick Moynihan's 1965 report for the Labor Department, *The Negro Family: The Case for National Action*. Moynihan argued that the chief obstacle for African Americans to racial equality in standard of living, education, income, and other indices was the state of the African American family: "At the heart of the deterioration of the fabric of Negro society is the deterioration of the Negro family."[77] He attributed this problem to the weakening of the black man under slavery, during Reconstruction, and through urban migrations. His diagnosis of the "tangle of pathology," including higher rates of drug use and delinquency among black than among white Americans, pinpointed the matriarchal structure of the black family, in which women gave birth out of wedlock and were the primary wage earners in the family, while men were unemployed, absent, or transient.[78] His recommendations for strengthening the black family were structural rather than therapeutic or psychological, and they included improved housing, education, employment opportunities, and rates of pay.

Minuchin and his colleagues favorably cited Moynihan's 1965 report and some of the studies on which it drew, including work by Thomas Pettigrew and Kenneth Clark.[79] They praised Moynihan for his emphasis on family structure and his advocacy of a multilevel intervention to change both familial and societal systems. Though they generalized their description of unpredictable family life to all the families in their study (defined by economic status), they differentiated African American from Puerto Rican families on the basis of the role of the father. In this, they echoed the title to a 1965 *New York Times Magazine* article by C. Eric Lincoln, which proclaimed, "The Absent Father Haunts the Negro Family."[80] The Wiltwyck team particularly bemoaned the fact that absent fathers could not serve as "models for male identification" in sons' development of culturally appropriate masculinity.[81] *Families of the Slums* included cases involving women seen as overly strong—for example, one with a "submerged, peripheral man and an overcentralized woman who constantly displaces her husband in his attempts to engage the children."[82] The authors argued that this arrangement was "robbing the children of their father"[83] and that the lack of a strong father figure was producing delinquency and other psychological problems. Their approach conveyed the more widespread contemporary view of matriarchy as pathological and relied explicitly on Talcott Parsons's model of the heterosexual nuclear family as the cultural norm against which they compared the families in their study.[84]

Such assumptions were not unique to the Wiltwyck study, nor would they remain unchallenged. The Moynihan report sparked immediate criticism from many quarters and on diverse grounds, one of which was that he failed to control for income in his comparisons between blacks and whites, thereby conflating the culture of poverty with the racialized tangle of pathology of the allegedly matriarchal black family.[85] Black activists also targeted the presumptive goal of "cultural assimilation" to white, middle-class values.[86] Opposition to the representations of black women distilled in Moynihan's report and reiterated in *Families of the Slums* sparked sharp rebuttals from black feminist scholars and others.[87] Minuchin himself warned in 1974, "The extended family, in particular the 'urban matriarchal' extended family, received a great deal of publicity from propaganda generated by the helping professions during the 'war on poverty.' As a result, a therapist may be preconditioned to pounce on this form as inherently pathogenic. Careful structural mapping, however, may show that the system is functioning adequately."[88] He thus came to place more emphasis on his structural model of the family as an indicator of function or dysfunction than on the presumption that a poor matriarchal family was inherently pathogenic.

In their suggested solutions to problems of delinquency, poverty, and family disorganization, the authors of *Families of the Slums* echoed the political implications of Harrington's argument regarding the culture of poverty. In *The Other America*, Harrington argued that the culture of poverty, invisible in the otherwise affluent United States, was destructive, and he advocated for specific political actions to alleviate that poverty. Providing additional resources was crucial but not enough; the culture itself needed to change.[89] Similarly, Minuchin and his co-researchers pointed out the need for multilevel interventions to change family structures and processes, in addition to providing housing or employment opportunities.[90] In a statement combining the concepts of systems and a culture of poverty, they claimed, "The family system is at a crossroads between society and the individual, transmitting social rules and regulations to the growing child and providing blueprints for his cognitive and emotional development. Investigations of family organization can provide vantage points from which to understand how social phenomena are incorporated into the intrapsychic life of the individual—the relationship, specifically, between the subculture of poverty and the person who is poor."[91] They thus saw family therapy as a means of combating delinquency and cultural pathology on a family-by-family basis, which they thought should go hand in hand with larger-scale social changes.

Cross-Cultural Studies

In further invocations of the culture concept, some family therapists conducted or drew on cross-cultural studies of family and psychopathology. These studies included research on specific cultural groups, often defined in ethnic or national terms, in their own context or in the process of cultural change or migration. Some studies were devoted to identifying culturally unique characteristics of families in particular settings, while others were invested in confirming universalistic claims about the family qua family by finding commonalties across cultures.

A selection of articles from the first decade (1962–72) of *Family Process* suggests the range of issues raised by cross-cultural research, as well as the response to the journal's editors' initial statement on the importance of social and cultural studies. The boundaries of a given culture extended from nations (the Greek family) to culturally specific social roles ("mentally ill housewife") to spatially and socioeconomically defined groups (urban ghetto) to individual families.[92] Family therapists did not limit their discussion of culture to the primitive, tribal "other" of classical early twentieth-century ethnography; instead, they turned to industrialized countries and their own contexts for cultural analysis. The articles also exhibited a wide spectrum of anthropological and cultural acumen, ranging from a nuanced characterization of social and cultural patterns in sailor families in Norway to an Orientalist portrait of the modern and the primitive in Turkish culture.[93]

There were at least three key issues raised by these articles. The first was the variability in what counted as family, including variation in parameters such as size, extent of kinship, functional relationships and roles, sexual practices, economy, and connection to other social structures.[94] The second issue was the applicability of particular diagnoses, such as schizophrenia, and specific family processes, such as the double bind, to cultural contexts beyond the United States or to diverse groups with the United States. As Lyman Wynne wrote in 1968, "Interactional studies of families of schizophrenics have mainly been carried out with middle-class, white American and northern European families for whom the concept of the nuclear family (parents and children) as a relatively isolated and autonomous social unit has been generally, but too often uncritically, accepted."[95] In his work at NIMH, he aimed to incorporate a cross-cultural framework for understanding the applicability of schizophrenia research for families in other cultural contexts. Finally, the articles implicitly and explicitly raised the issue of the relationship between the cultural background of the therapist or researcher and that of the people under treatment or study. As David Kinzie, P. C. Sushama, and Mary Lee asked in their article on family therapy in Malaysia,

> To what extent does [cross-cultural psychotherapy] reflect the therapist's own values rather than those of absolute mental health? Are the values and techniques implicit in Western therapy applicable to families in other cultures? Does one attempt to change the basic approaches to life, which may be pathological, or to have a family adapt more closely to its own culture, irrespective of how maladaptive this seems to the outsider? Finally, to what extent is communication even possible between Western therapists and families from a totally different background?[96]

Such questions raised issues about the transferability of Western psychiatry, the normative rather than descriptive assumptions of some therapeutic interventions, and the potential incompatibility of different cultural modes of communication. Family therapists thereby echoed the concerns of contemporary ethnopsychiatrists, such as Alexander Leighton and Georges Devereux, who in their studies of folk or indigenous conceptions of mental disturbance also queried the cultural specificity of psychiatric categories and treatments.

"An Agent of the Culture"

Some therapists explicitly considered the relevance of their own cultural position to their therapeutic goals and activities. For example, Jackson considered the concept of culture in notes from the 1950s for an unfinished book on psychotherapy. He characterized the therapist as "an agent of the culture" who might seek to change nonbeneficial aspects of his own cultural context.[97] Despite his claim of support for cultural change, the example he gave for this proposition was more in line with bending patients to the status quo, harking back to the mental hygiene movement's goals of social adjustment, even as he invoked the more recent concerns with communism of the Cold War period. Jackson wrote, "If, for example, he [the therapist] had a nuclear physicist who wanted to join the communist party he would emphasize strongly the destructive aspects of such a move in our culture at the present time. If he were not an agent of the culture he might let the [physicist] join the communist party, discover its defects and grow out of the feeling himself."[98] Thus Jackson's psychotherapeutic approach fit within a framework of individual adjustment and social conformity rather than social transformation.

This approach stood in contrast to the radical family therapy movement of the 1960s, whose motto was "change, not adjustment." Similarly, antipsychiatrists such as R. D. Laing and his colleagues drew on the family systems theory from the Palo Alto group in order to argue against the contemporary view of psychiatric treatment as restoring individual behavior to social norms.[99] The historian Alice O'Connor characterizes this contrast between individual adjustment and social transformation as "a central tension within liberal thought about the nature of inequality—not so much over whether inequality is innate or environmental in origin, but whether it is best understood and addressed at the level of individual experience or as a matter of structural and institutional reform."[100]

In contrast to those concerned with cultural change, whether at the individual or structural scale, Robert MacGregor, a well-known family therapist from Galveston, Texas, argued for the utility of transmitting middle-class values, such as appropriately delineated gender roles and child-rearing practices, at a 1964 conference titled "Family Process and Psychopathology: Perspectives of the Social Scientist and Clinician."[101] He made this argument to rebut what he saw as overzealous concern that family therapists might be erring on the side of advocating "the value system of the American middle-class family"[102] and not attending to patients' unique value systems. MacGregor used a case example to illustrate the desirability of fostering more conventional middle-class values in order to promote growth, which was central to therapists' value system and might be impeded in an alternative family system: "When working with families in which the father fails to exercise a leadership function in the home and allows his wife to become excessively dependent on a child for emotional expression, the multiple impact therapy team not only advocated the more conventional roles, but also demonstrated comfort with leadership by the way in which a male therapist exercised authority with the team-family situation."[103]

MacGregor focused not on technique or how therapy should be done but on the end goal of changing roles and values that governed how a family functioned. He justified his approach with an adaptive argument: "It is worth considering that perhaps the value system of the middle-class family survives so well because as a product of the adaptive mechanism of a living system it reflects the survival requirements for humans in society. . . . It places, for example, a value on competition. . . . Mental health seems associated with the ability to become known and hence to enjoy competition."[104] He claimed that his interests were vested in promoting growth and "the vitality of living systems," not in the "family romance" of a father as boss, mother as homemaker, and children in training to follow this pattern, a romance against which he favorably cited Betty Friedan's critique in *The Feminine Mystique*. Whether justified by a conventional ideal of the nuclear family or by a therapeutic rationale emphasizing growth, MacGregor's approach represented a differential appraisal of class-based value systems, here described in terms of pathology rather than the evolutionary hierarchy of nineteenth-century anthropology and social evolutionism.

Finally, by the late 1960s and early 1970s some family therapists and researchers such as Albert Scheflen and his colleagues confronted the issue of who benefited from their research. Scheflen was involved in a two-year study of the social and temporal structuring of living space in the East Tremont area of the Bronx. His research team was interested in how "territorial behavior" exhibited the social order and cultural patterns of life in an urban ghetto.[105] Scheflen's 1971 description of the project focused on the black and Puerto Rican residents of the East Tremont neighborhood and their use of household space, with the comment that he and his colleagues also intended to study business establishments, social institutions such as clubs, and street zones. However, in a postscript added after the article was prepared for publication, he reported that the group had decided to end its research. "We suspended video-recording in the homes of minority group and poor families and stopped collecting data in East Tremont. This decision was in part imposed upon us by the wishes of certain people in East Tremont; it represents an increasing insistence by minority peoples that they no longer be subjects of research. But in part our project members made the decision because they agree with the objections raised by Black, Puerto Rican, and other people."[106] This postscript richly conveys how family researchers' interest in the relationship between family and culture, broached in this case through the analytic of "human territoriality," was inextricable in historically specific ways from the politics of knowledge production about research subjects marked as other. According to Scheflen,

> First of all, there is no evidence that the research of past generations had been of any use or advantage to these people. Secondly, the findings of many research efforts have ultimately been used to discredit the peoples studied . . . and to support in general the prevailing stereotypes and discriminatory ideas about them and their alleged shortcomings. And finally, the data collected about minority and poverty peoples are not matched by comparable data about the middle class in America. So direct data such as we have been collecting are likely to be compared to idealized myths about middle class American households, again to the unwitting or deliberate detriment of our subject.[107]

These were also pressing issues within anthropology, in which they became part of debates about the imperialism of anthropology, the agency and interests of those being studied, the reflexivity of anthropological knowledge, and the potential function of anthropology as "cultural critique."[108]

Early family therapists saw attention to culture as being of a piece with their shift from an individual to a familial approach to pathology and treatment. In professional publications such as the 1954 report from the GAP Committee on the Family and in discipline-building efforts such as the 1962 introduction to *Family Process*, they presented culture as a central analytic category for the establishment of their field. They also depicted it as an inevitable extension of their contextual understanding of psychiatric disorders. Such characterizations emphasized not only the importance of culture but also the value of incorporating theories and methodologies from the social sciences, particularly anthropology and sociology.

Family therapists provided several justifications for the importance of the culture concept in the study of family and mental illness. These included adjustment (or lack thereof) to cultural norms as a factor in psychopathology, the designation of the family as the mediator of culture between individual and society, and culturally variable expressions of pathology. Beyond the clinical context of treating patients, many family therapists also embraced the activist mandate promulgated by a wing of the psychiatric profession, which called for psychiatry to address social and political issues such as delinquency and racism, a goal resonant with yet distinct from the earlier mental hygiene movement.

Under the umbrella of cultural analysis, heterogeneous conceptions of family and approaches to psychotherapy found space. Questions of culture arose in the context of treating psychotic, schizophrenic, delinquent, and neurotic patients. Some family therapists underscored the universality of the family by pointing to cross-cultural similarities, while others emphasized cultural variability. They also debated their own roles in fostering culturally and socially normative models of family life. Collectively, these invocations of culture served to promote the development of family therapy as a profession and to reconfigure the family as the locus of pathology and appropriate target of therapeutic intervention.

CHAPTER FOUR

OBSERVATIONAL PRACTICES AND NATURAL HABITATS

I feel I have to remind the reader what happened here, from the scientific point of view. Merely by being present for a few hours in the home, the observer was able to see with her own eyes, on the very first day, the essence of Mr. Keen's relationship to the boys.

JULES HENRY, *Pathways to Madness*

Social scientists became increasingly interested in studying the family as a scientific object during the middle third of the twentieth century, and family studies proliferated in fields including psychology, sociology, human development, and anthropology. In research on wide-ranging topics such as small groups, identity and socialization, prejudice, schizophrenia, delinquency, and the "Negro family," scholars grappled with understanding families and their functions, patterns, interactions, and pathologies. They also faced methodological challenges in designing their research protocols, establishing the boundaries of their projects, and developing standards for sampling and controls.[1]

Among clinicians engaged in family studies research, carefully prescribed practices of observation were central to legitimizing their claims to knowledge about families. As Lorraine Daston and Elizabeth Lunbeck argue in their introduction to *Histories of Scientific Observation*, scientific observation deserves to be studied "as an epistemic category in its own right," with a history whose contours have been shaped by the related cultural histories of experience, the body, the senses, observational techniques, and scientific practices.[2] Despite the seeming ubiquity of observation in scientific investigation, the meanings and status of observation have varied significantly across scientific fields and at different historical moments, as has the relationship of observation to experimentation and scientific practice more generally.

In addition to observation, "place" had a significant role in shaping the course of research.[3] Family therapy research occurred in a range of settings, including hospitals and homes. The differences between hospital-based and home-based studies of family life in many ways paralleled those between laboratory and field studies in other scientific disciplines.[4] In the case of a 1950s project at the National Institute for Mental Health (NIMH), Murray Bowen hospitalized whole families as part of a study on schizophrenia. For Bowen's research, the hospital ward was the defining site in which, as in a laboratory, the researchers could control certain variables. In contrast, other contemporary studies tried to record and analyze the everyday exploits of families in action in their natural habitat of the home. Two such studies were Jules Henry's *Pathways to Madness* and David Kantor and William Lehr's *Inside the Family: Toward a Theory of Family Process.*[5] Both operated according to a similar logic, according to which living in the home of a particular family, even for as short a period as a week, revealed meaningful patterns in the interactions of that family and knowledge about families in general.

The relationship between observation and place was itself substantive. The sites of the research projects made possible certain kinds of observations. For example, Henry found that the setting of the home made it possible for the observer to discern what was significant about a given family, "the essence" of their relationships.[6] The capacity of a researcher to see without the enhancement of a scientific instrument stood in contrast to the biologist's use of a microscope to study cells, the astronomer's use of a telescope to study planetary motion, and the physicist's use of photography to study radioactivity. The family patterns that occupied Henry and other family researchers were neither too small, too far away, nor too ephemeral to escape detection by the unaided eye but instead were readily visible to a researcher's own eyes. Furthermore, Henry framed these place-based observations "from the scientific point of view," thereby marking the epistemological stakes of the research.

In all three projects, one of the central challenges was to define what counted as a relevant observation. Researchers had to identify what they considered the significant facets of family life and how such things were knowable; in other words, the objects of their studies and their observational methods for gaining knowledge about those objects had a multifaceted and intertwined relationship, even if not explicitly articulated. For example, Bowen and his colleagues emphasized close observation of families conducting their everyday activities and participating in therapy sessions, rather than relying on other methods such as surveys, psychological tests, and scheduled interviews. They faced methodological challenges regarding who on the project had the status of an observer; how the research subjects (i.e., the families) participated in the production of the project's results; which events were noted as important, thereby becoming part of the data set; and how those data were represented.

Researchers' assessment of certain aspects of family life as relevant or significant enough for investigation also went hand in hand with their decisions regarding how to obtain and record data about the families they were studying. Family studies used diverse techniques of representation and inscription, including nursing notes on the daily activities of whole families on a hospital ward, diagrams of the types and degree of interpersonal interactions during family therapy sessions, ethnographic reports of observers living in a family's house, and audio recordings of group therapy sessions at NIMH and of events in each room in the homes. Their research practices and modes of documentation thus warrant analysis together.[7]

The researchers in all three projects were also concerned about distortion in their observations. These concerns arose from the fear that they would disrupt family life by prioritizing treatment interventions over research protocols, moving a family to a hospital ward, or placing a researcher in the home, any of which could shape results in ways that the researchers characterized as contamination or interference. The researchers thereby assumed that families had ways of being that existed prior to their participation in a study and that the aim of the research was to observe and document the families in as close to their natural state as possible.

In these efforts and their general interest in knowledge through observation, the projects shared some of the working assumptions of conventional documentary and ethnographic films during the 1950s through the early 1970s. Even though these researchers did not produce films, their repeated references to performance and cinema underscored that their work shared discursive resonances and similar presumptions with documentaries. These included the importance of observing and documenting the visible, mundane interactions of everyday life; the attempt to ensure the minimal impact of an observer on the events under observation; and the faith that their results could represent "messy human life reduced to chunks of explainable phenomena," as one critique of scientific ethnographic film put it.[8] Such presumptions faced criticisms at the time but came under particularly withering attack by the 1980s and 1990s.

Working within such understandings of vision and observation, family researchers grappled with several recurring tensions in their practices of looking, tensions that were symptomatic both of the complexity of observation, despite its status as an allegedly self-evident mode of acquiring knowledge, and of the instability of the family as an object of study. Their observational research techniques operated through a set of interrelated and unresolved tensions: between observation and participation, sight and insight, proximity and distance, natural and artificial, and nonintervention and experimentation. Moreover, in their varied attempts to draw conclusions about "all families as families,"[9] the researchers articulated the difficulties and possibilities of the relationship between the normal and the pathological, particularly regarding the issue of what one could learn about family life in general from studying schizophrenia. At stake was not only observation as a research methodology or even epistemic category but also the very making of the family, through observation, into an object of study, unit of disease, and subject of therapeutic intervention.

Living at NIMH

During the second half of the 1950s, NIMH sponsored a study in which schizophrenic patients in their teens or twenties, their parents, and their siblings were jointly hospitalized on a ward dedicated to the project at the National Institutes of Health (NIH) Clinical Center in Bethesda, Maryland. Families traveled from as far as Minnesota, Michigan, and Florida to participate for months or, in some cases, years. Murray Bowen was the principal investigator from the project's inception in 1954 until its termination in 1959. Schizophrenia thus played a critical role in early family therapy research, just as it did in the contemporaneous development of the theory of the double bind.

Bowen's research began in the summer of 1954. Initially titled "Influence of the Early Mother-Child Relationship in the Development of Schizophrenia," the project began with the hospitalization of three mother-daughter pairs on the 3-East ward at the center. In addition to Bowen, the project team included Robert Dysinger, MD; Betty Basamania, MSW; and Warren Brodey, MD. This team served as both researchers and clinicians, though at times those roles had competing priorities. In December 1955, they began admitting fathers and siblings with the patients and mothers and changed the project's title to "The Study and Treatment of Schizophrenia as a Family Problem." By the time the clinical research terminated at the end of 1958, eleven live-in and six outpatient families had participated for months or years each, and NIMH had spent close to a million dollars.[10] Among family therapy research projects, Bowen's study was unique in many ways, such as its longitudinal perspective, expensive cost, extensive facility and staff requirements, institutional home at NIMH, and degree of commitment from its research subjects, the families themselves.[11]

Both Bowen's professional background and the institutional context of NIMH contributed to the initial goals and shape of the 3-East project, as it was known colloquially. He had come to NIMH after spending eight years at the prominent Menninger Clinic in Topeka, Kansas, where he became interested in psychoanalytic research on schizophrenia and alcoholism. He felt, however, that he could not actively pursue his research interests in a clinical setting that focused on treatment rather than research.[12] After an extensive search for a research site, he moved to Bethesda in 1954 because NIMH offered "maximum freedom of the human spirit and minimal anchorage to tradition," in contrast to a medical school or private clinic with more pressing clinical needs.[13] Even after the project ended and he had become disgruntled with the NIMH leadership, Bowen continued to praise the "very idealistic research philosophy" that guided the institute in the midfifties and that, combined with the unique institutional setting, made possible "new and imaginative research" that could not have happened in a poorer or more restrictive setting.[14]

Bowen's project was part of the intramural research program at NIMH, which included all research conducted at the institute itself, while the extramural program included the grants for research conducted at other institutions. NIMH had two large intramural research divisions, Basic Research and Clinical Investigations, along with a smaller division, Biometics. Within Clinical Investigations, the Laboratory of Adult Psychiatry housed Bowen's research. Although his effort to hospitalize multiple family members together was unusual, his interest in schizophrenia fit well with similar interests in the broader psychiatric community and among researchers in both divisions of NIMH.[15]

While serving as acting chief of the Laboratory of Adult Psychiatry, Bowen presented a report to a general NIMH staff meeting on March 15, 1955, in which he justified the focus on schizophrenia by many of the projects in the Adult Psychiatry Branch, including his own. His justification rested on the assertion that schizophrenia did not fit into the traditional medical model of clearly bounded or differentiated disease entities, each with its own unique origins and manifestations. Rather, he argued, it was "one of the more severe symptom complexes in a long continuum, and one that encompasses almost every experience in human living."[16] By focusing on schizophrenia, the assorted projects were contributing to general knowledge of the human state. "[W]hen we have understood schizophrenia," he declared, "we will have understood mankind."[17] In framing schizophrenia as a microcosm of human life, he thereby echoed nineteenth- and twentieth-century physiologists who stressed the value of studying disease processes in order to learn about normal physiology.[18]

The study of schizophrenia could provide such global knowledge, Bowen continued, because unlike diseases caused by a "hostile element," the discovery and elimination of which would cure the disease, schizophrenic symptoms arose from coping with life problems. In fact, Bowen argued against labeling schizophrenic symptoms as pathological.

> The symptoms are not pathologies at all but instead are hypertrophies of the very mechanisms we all use to a lesser degree. . . . Instead of the symptom being pathological and a weakness to be eliminated, it is more nearly an overworked strength that maintains life under adversity. . . . For instance, it can be said that the pathology is schizophrenia and the etiological agent is a schizophrenogenic mother. Application of our traditional medical thinking would then infer "eliminate the mother and cure the schizophrenia.". . . Schizophrenia is something entirely different when we see it as the best mechanism available with which to deal with a mother who, though difficult, is as necessary to the life of the patient as oxygen or water.[19]

Bowen thus reframed schizophrenic symptoms as an extreme version of typical behaviors that served an adaptive purpose. In contrast to a biomedical model, he did not advocate a magic-bullet approach focused exclusively on curing a disease by eliminating its pathogenic agent. Instead, he invoked Frieda Fromm-Reichmann's psychogenic formulation of the schizophrenogenic mother in order to reaffirm the mother's role in the production of schizophrenia even as he recast the condition as an adaptation to adverse conditions and a mechanism for dealing with a pathogenic yet still indispensable mother.

Bowen's live-in study initially aimed to define the importance of the mother in the development of schizophrenia by studying mother-child pairs in which the child had severe psychiatric impairment. According to an annual project report submitted to NIH in December 1955, over a year after the project began, "Patient-mother pairs are chosen who have intense emotional attachments to each other of the type found in many chronic or severely impaired patients. . . . It is hypothesized that emotional needs in the mother not fulfilled in other relationships brings [sic] about the intense mother-child relationships and that these individuals, who go on to adulthood with some degree of unresolved attachment to their mothers, are the ones who develop clinical schizophrenia and other such severe psychiatric illnesses."[20]

Bowen framed the intense mother-child relationship as "symbiotic" and worthy of investigation for what "this very pathological condition between two adults"[21] could reveal about interactions during the child's infancy. Like other contemporary psychiatrists interested in schizophrenia—such as Theodore Lidz, John Rosen, and Frieda Fromm-Reichmann—Bowen attributed the etiology of the disease to child-rearing practices and mothers' early relationship with their children.[22] He also thought that evidence of this early relationship was observable in adult relationships, in which the results of the early pathology were treatable.

Bowen's interest in the role of the mother-child relationship in the etiology and maintenance of schizophrenia preceded his work at NIMH, and his earlier notion of a symbiotic relationship—which grew out of his work at the Menninger Clinic—served as the initial framework for the NIMH project. In his psychotherapy progress note from a patient seen at the Menninger Clinic on January 13, 1954, Bowen used the phrase "intense 'symbiotic' relationship" to describe the patient's relationship with her mother, and he lamented the difficulty of therapeutic success in this case as long as the mother was on the scene.[23] He described a similar type of intense relationship in another patient for whom he did a consultation, which he labeled, "the one-hour drama:"

There was acted out in the office for almost the entire hour the amazing intensity of the relationship between a mother and her schizophrenic daughter. For a number of years now, this examiner has been very interested in the whole problem of schizophrenia and particularly interested in the mother-child relationship in schizophrenia. . . . Seeing these two people together was a new experience. I have never seen a previous case of the dependent intensity of both the mother and the daughter that is present in these two people. . . . Because the entire consultation time was taken up in this relationship between mother and daughter, I could get very little historical information. I did not particularly want it and certainly think *this opportunity to see the mother and daughter together was worth a great deal more than volumes of carefully recorded objective historical data.*[24]

This note highlights the contrast between traditional history taking and observation of current relationship interactions. Bowen suggested that the insight he gained from watching a mother and daughter interact was more valuable and informative than the oral recounting he would have received in answer to the questions of a clinical history. In other words, the present rather than the past and observable interactions rather than the narrative recounting of psychic trauma or conflict received preferential attention.

Bowen derived his research framework at NIMH from prior clinical experiences and then used his opportunity to hospitalize dyads together to follow up on previous anecdotal experiences. His model of accessing knowledge about the phenomenon under study (witness interactions rather than take a detailed history) would not have held value for him had it not meshed with his theory regarding the phenomenon itself (that schizophrenia resulted from *observable* defects or pathologies in the mother-child relationship that occurred during infancy but continued to manifest themselves in the pair's ongoing relationship). According to one project report, "There are a large number of clinical experiences that suggest that it would be rewarding to give close scrutiny to what goes on between the patient and his family and in the family group. Much has been noticed by individual therapists and doctors in hospitals that offers glimpses of these processes. . . . We have in our setting an opportunity to observe the family life as it happens under circumstances that make close and extensive observation possible."[25] By constructing a setup in which the researchers could "observe the family life as it happens," the 3-East project gave weight to a particular target of investigation (real-time interactions between mothers and daughters) that was inextricable from the means of accessing it (observation).

As Bowen argued before an NIMH general staff meeting in March 1955, "It is hoped that this close living with these pairs will give more intimate observational material than would be otherwise available."[26] The residential, inpatient setting of the project thereby made possible certain kinds of research procedures and types of data. This complicated nexus among theoretical framework, object of study, place of research, scientific methodology, and types of data depended on a documentary-like notion of observation, which continued through the duration of the project, as well as on a particular conception of family relations and schizophrenia, which underwent significant revision over the course of the project.

During the NIMH project's first year, the research staff studied their hypothesis regarding the intense emotional attachment between mother and child by observing three main inpatient mother-daughter pairs and working less intensely with six to eight patients on an outpatient basis.[27] The first research subjects came from the Washington, DC and Baltimore areas. They participated in the project following referrals from their physicians and a Jewish welfare agency. Two of the three inpatient pairs were on public assistance prior to their admission to the project.

For the inpatient pairs, the primary admission criterion was the existence of an intense attachment between the patient and her mother.[28] As Bowen wrote in the clinical history of one of the pairs, "The essential criteria had been to find the most intense possible clinical examples of this [mother-patient symbiosis] in which the mother still maintained her position as mother."[29] In addition, the project looked for research subjects from families with one, two, and multiple siblings in order to investigate how or why the mother "chose" a particular child for an intense relationship.[30] The initial rationale for including daughters rather than sons was not a specific interest in schizophrenic daughters per se but the convenience of having a single-sex ward for the ease of ward life.[31]

The daughters all lived on the unit, while the mothers' degree of participation ranged from living in the hospital to spending daytime hours there.[32] The mothers and daughters stayed for months or years. The shortest-staying pair lived on 3-East for nine months, while the pair with the longest admission stayed for almost three years. The daughters and mothers did not leave behind written statements explaining why they had agreed to participate in the project. In the case of at least one pair, the welfare agency on which the mother and daughter depended urged them to participate. The pair had repeatedly been evicted from apartments after "paranoid fights" with landlords, and the agency was eager to find a placement for them.[33] This contradicted the impression held by some outside the project. At the March 13, 1956, weekly meeting of Gregory Bateson's research group in Palo Alto, Don Jackson briefly described Bowen's project, and Jay Haley remarked, "To get them to live in the hospital is quite a feat." In response, Jackson described the impression of a friend of his, who "thinks it's partly because these are wealthy people that have had their children at the best places and are discouraged and willing to try anything, and realize they can't buy it."[34] Although this impression may have fit some of the families who later joined the live-in study, it did not describe the class backgrounds of the initial group of participants, though it did attest to the difficulty of treating schizophrenia.

Once the project had recruited its research subjects, Bowen and his colleagues aimed to study them from a longitudinal perspective.

> In this study we have been interested in the family processes that extend over time,—we have an interest in gaining some long-range perspective on the family's living as contrasted with a microscropic [sic] picture of the family's situation at a particular time. It is our feeling that if something can be learned about the stable or recurrent patterns in the family's living over the weeks and months, we would then have a better perspective on the more immediate day-to-day situations. We want something clear about the gross anatomy,—the structure of family action over time,—before we go to the histology.[35]

In focusing on family action over an extended period rather than at a particular time, the 3-East researchers framed their project in an optic register that echoed the temporal dimension of cinema, rather than the static image of the microscope or the photograph.[36]

In addition to researching the role of the mother-child relationship in schizophrenia based on observation over time, a second early objective of the project was to create a therapeutic milieu that was conducive to treatment as well as research.[37] The intent was to develop a clinical program aimed at facilitating patients' improvement, which likely meant reducing their symptoms and the intensity of their attachment to their mothers.

> The ward milieu was regarded as an important part of the therapeutic plan. The effort was made to maintain on the Unit as near a "normal" family atmosphere as possible. This was done to facilitate the usual "emotional climate" in which these two persons related to one another and, thus, to add to the accuracy of observations as well as contributing to the therapeutic process. The usual administrative ward rules were minimized because of the way in which mother and child invoked the rules with one another rather than to work upon their problems in relating to one another.[38]

Put another way in the treatment plan for one of the patients, the aim was to create a therapeutic environment "which would offer a maximum of support and a minimum of direction in the belief that this would furnish a more accurate picture of the real character of the relationship and a maximum opportunity to mature out of the immature dependent states."[39] Bowen and his colleagues emphasized the importance of the ward environment in their reported findings of clinical improvement.[40] They also staked their claims to an accurate portrait of family life on the ward's "'normal' family atmosphere," by which they meant its lack of structure and the minimal institutional demands made on its residents, which were intended to allow the pairs' "usual 'emotional climate'" to emerge. The researchers thus designed the ward environment to foster the joint clinical and investigative goals of providing treatment by maximizing opportunities for the patients and mothers to become less dependent on each other and observing them with minimal interference. Treatment goals and research agendas were separate but intertwined, and the ward environment was key to both.[41]

Though they emphasized psychotherapy and their variation on milieu therapy, 3-East staff used other standard techniques of psychiatric hospitals, such as a seclusion room, wet packs, and continuous tub schedules, during patients' periods of decompensation.[42] If parents wanted their children to take drugs such as Thorazine, Bowen did not prohibit it, but he made it clear that psychopharmacology was not his preference. As he explained in his correspondence with the mother of an interested family who ultimately did not enroll in the project,

We are not using drugs as a primary treatment method. If a family wanted to use one of the drugs as a palliative measure, there probably would be no objection, but our conviction and thinking is that schizophrenia is something else and we are trying as hard as we can to come to some resolution of a single area rather than to jump around from one approach to another. . . . It is our thesis that the origins of schizophrenia lie in subtle disruptions in family relationships that find their focus in one family member. It is also our belief that if these disharmonies can be understood, the stage is then set for the schizophrenic process to reverse itself more or less on its own.[43]

Thus Bowen did not object to prescribing drugs to soothe anxieties or other symptoms. However, he emphasized that his project focused on family "disharmonies," which he characterized as "more undercover than overtly recognized." He remained noncommittal in his correspondence with families about whether such disharmonies were a cause or an effect of schizophrenia but maintained that resolving them would help the person with schizophrenia to improve.[44] Therefore, he generally discouraged the use of psychotropic medication on the grounds that "we found that drugs only slowed up working on family problems."[45]

Beyond managing families' internal disharmonies, the project had to manage the stability of the staff in concert with the treatment of patients. One of the major findings of the first year was "an ever-increasing respect for the difficulties of getting a staff together and welding it into a smooth working unit capable of dealing with a problem of this intensity."[46] One patient's clinical record notes that her "down periods" came at times of high staff tensions, when the staff was least capable of dealing with her, which revealed the challenge of maintaining minimal staff interference in patients' lives.[47]

The correlation between patient difficulties and staff struggles was not an incidental one, and it had therapeutic implications. "The mother and child used their relationships with staff to escape the problems implicit in their intense relationship. . . .Thus, a staff member could, unknowingly, become involved in the mother-daughter conflict."[48] The clinical challenge related to the transfer of the intense emotional conflicts within the families to conflicts among staff members, who disagreed about how to treat certain patients on the basis of their sympathetic or antagonistic relationship with those particular patients. The challenge was how to reach "a workable capacity to deal objectively with

the emotional problems of these families."[49] Bowen attributed these
difficulties to the "error" of employing individual psychotherapy techniques to treat "the more intense and involved family group problem,"[50]
but they also suggest implicit tensions in the project's practices of looking.[51] The 3-East group valued the observations made possible by the
regular proximity of staff to the mother-daughter pairs on the one hand
and the perspective garnered by distance on the other. By invoking the
capacity of the staff to work with the families' challenging relationships
in the same sentence with the project's goal of objectivity, Bowen ges-
tured to the pragmatic as well as epistemological dimensions of observation in the project.

To address these intertwined personnel and therapeutic challenges,
the research staff inaugurated regular group meetings that included all
patients and staff affiliated with the project, rather than separate sessions for family and staff, with the goal of "developing concepts and
techniques to help the staff to work with the families without becoming involved in the family problems. The immediate motivation for the
change was to make the clinical operation into one that was liveable
and operable both for families and for staff and that also seemed to offer some hope for treatment successes."[52] Initially, patients and mothers continued their individual psychotherapy, but after several months,
the project did away with individual therapists. The staff-family group
therapy meetings, designed to manage staff disagreements, ended up
becoming the centerpiece of the therapeutic and research agenda of the
project.

During the first year, research efforts focused on the symbiotic
relationship and the "closeness and distance problem,"[53] in part evidenced by how rapidly mothers and daughters would move to include
staff members in their relationship. "Detailed objective observational
data"[54] on the mothers and daughters came from reports by each daughter's individual psychiatrist and each mother's individual social worker
and from daily charting by nurses. The nurses particularly attended to
the "moves," which the project defined in a technical way, made by the
daughters and mothers toward each other or toward staff.[55] Their focus on standardizing the move as an observable entity was a means of
overcoming problems of random data selection that might slant their
results and ensuing picture of family life by providing structure to their
data collection process. It was also a means of presenting their data in
meaningful, vivid, and manageable terms, given the massive amount of
information available from observing daily life.[56]

During the mother-daughter phase of the project, which lasted until December 1955, the project's staff did not formally write up their material. As Bowen later explained to a colleague, "By the time reports were formal enough for presentation to a larger audience, the mother-patient phase of the project was little more than an introduction to the total family period that followed."[57] Even though the project did not produce conference presentations or publications during its first year, that initial period of the study was formative for the project's subsequent investigations of family interactions and Bowen's increasing attention to the family as the relevant unit of study and treatment.

The "Family Unit"

In late 1955 the 3-East project admitted as a "family unit" a young woman who had been psychotic for four years, along with her sister, mother, and father.[58] The shift in admission practices from admitting mother-daughter pairs to including fathers and siblings had implications for the project's conceptual framework, its therapeutic modality, and its research approach.[59] This admission marked a fundamental transition in the project, though the nature of that transition took on different meanings in subsequent project reports, conference papers, publications, and correspondence, which provided shifting narrative accounts of the course of the research.

These successive rearticulations of the project's approach highlight the work involved in Bowen's shift to viewing the family as the relevant category of analysis, whether characterized as a unit, an organism, or a patient. Initially he framed the inclusion of fathers and siblings as a supplement or assistance to the mother. As he wrote at the end of 1955 in his annual report, one of the major findings of the first year of the study was a "rapidly growing awareness of the father or other family figures important to the mother."[60] The significance of these other family members was defined by their impact on the mother and/or on the mother-child relationship: "It would appear that mothers can shift more rapidly when the father can begin to shift and increase his helpfulness to her. . . . The mother-patient study will be continued but in the context of the family group rather than an isolated entity within itself. In brief, it seems that the mother-patient relationship is the axis in the development of the patient's incapacity, but that other relationships are important in influencing the mother-infant relationship."[61] The project emphasis thus remained on the mother-child axis, with other family members important but auxiliary to that relationship. However, the idea of the family as a unit was present at the end of 1955 in the formulation of the project's future therapeutic course, which would entail "an attempt to work out techniques to be therapeutically helpful to the family as a unit rather than isolating the various family members for individual help through psychotherapy."[62]

One year later, Bowen described the changing course of the project in a letter to a former patient's parent:

> When I came to Bethesda 2 1/2 years ago, my thinking started at the point it had left off in Topeka. In the Fall of 1954, I began a small project in which I asked mothers to come into the hospital and live in with their daughters. . . . I chose mothers because they, as a rule, are more intimately connected with the patient's problems and because it was believed mothers would be more available for the study. . . . Something was lacking, and, without going into details, we began a year ago to ask both father and mother to come in. . . . It has been in the course of working with these families that my perspective on schizophrenia, psychiatry, life and on myself has shifted so much. . . . We tentatively are seeing the problem as one in which the patient reacts intensely to family problems.[63]

Here he did not explain why the project began to admit fathers, but he attributed the change in his understanding of schizophrenia—from viewing it as an outgrowth of a symbiotic mother-child relationship to regarding it as a product of family problems—to the yearlong experience of working with the families, rather than presenting this shift as the precondition or rationale for admitting fathers in the first place.

In his 1957 annual report to the NIH, Bowen depicted the major shifts in the project's theoretical formulation and treatment plan as growing out of practical clinical problems, if not the families' pathologies themselves. He reported, "The first efforts to perceive the family as a unit began as a clinical necessity."[64] This necessity, according to Bowen, derived from the inherent, preexisting intensity of the families' relationships[65] and from the arrangement of the study in which the research subjects, the families, lived in close proximity with the researchers, the unit staff; together they had to manage the routines of daily life in a hospital. His report asserted, "It is necessary for family and staff to negotiate with one another in dealing with responsibility with such situations as, obtaining a pass to leave the unit, periodic physical examination, passing the food at the dinner table, etc. These families were chosen because of the primitive intensity of their intra family relationships. It has been found that this intensity readily spills over into family-staff relationships, and that even simple negotiations frequently break down in an atmosphere of intense family-staff emotions."[66] Although the project worked to shore up the family as unit, Bowen's references to the primitive intensity of the families' internal relations readily spilling over suggest that the boundaries of that unit were simultaneously being undone. In this account, the practical demands of managing conflict on the unit drove the creation of the family-staff therapy sessions and the directive for nursing staff to focus on family units rather than individual family members.

By contrast, in a 1959 grant proposal, Bowen narrated the change in the project as a sharp conceptual transition. "At the end of 1955, the hypothesis was changed from one which saw the schizophrenic psychosis as a phenomenon in one person, to one which regarded the psychosis in the patient as a symptom of an active process that involved every member of the family. . . . Just as a generalized disease in a single person can focus in a single organ, so a generalized family illness can focus on and disable a single part of the family organism."[67] While the grant format may have contributed to a different type of narration than that of personal correspondence, nonetheless Bowen had effectively reframed as a single-step change in hypothesis that which he had previously described as a tentative and more gradual transition. In the process, he underscored the link between the production of knowledge and the production of a notion of the family itself, which was here rendered analogous to an organism.

The significance of a more complex perspective on this transition can be seen in a 1958 letter that Bowen wrote to Alexander Gralnick, a psychoanalyst who was interested in psychotherapy and schizophrenia.

For a long time, my concept of a family unit was intellectual. Even though I used the right words and I was able to outwardly appear objective, my inner feelings would cheer the hero, identify with the victimized one, and hope that someone would neutralize the villain. Then came the time when I could see the family struggle as a problem of the group and a phenomenon to be understood. I simply did not take emotional sides with any one family faction. . . . I liked particularly the statement in which you said that you view the family member as much a victim of the patient as vice versa. I think that most people, who speak of "the family unit", have an intellectual rather than a feeling or emotional orientation to the family unit.[68]

Similarly, in an article published in 1961, Bowen described several stages (conceptual, clinical, and emotional) in his transition to the family unit perspective.[69] These writings indicate that his shift was gradual, not that family theory and therapy appeared fully formed when the project admitted its first father and sibling in 1955.

Moreover, his characterization of this shift as one of moving from emotional reactivity to individual people (hero, villain, victim) to seeing the family struggle as a problem of the group, without taking sides, was indicative of his effort to define the boundaries of the family unit. Bowen's conception also assumed that the two-parent family was the full family unit, since he regularly described the introduction of fathers as the key factor in switching to this new perspective. However, some writings about the first phase of the project elided the distinction between mother-daughter dyad and family—for example, the discussion of the "normal family atmosphere" of the ward milieu. In addition, for at least one of the initial mother-daughter pairs, the parents were divorced, the father was nowhere to be found, and the daughter was an only child, so there were no additional members of the family unit.

More concretely, the shift from mother-daughter pairs to nuclear families had practical and material implications on the ward. The project began to admit sons as well as daughters, since the inclusion of fathers had already disrupted the single-sex status of the ward. Patients gained access to the study though several avenues: physician or guidance center referrals, project contacts at a state hospital, and a congressman.[70] Some families even corresponded directly with Bowen after learning about the project, rather than having communication go through medical professionals or another type of intermediary.[71] The primary admission criteria shifted from the intensity of the mother-daughter bond to other familial characteristics: small family size (no more than one or two children), young parents in their forties or early fifties who "still have enough life and zip ahead of them to want something enough to fight for it," and young patients with energy ("I had rather have a person who fights hell out of the environment than a withdrawn one who has given it up").[72] As Bowen wrote to a psychiatrist at the Menniger Clinic who referred him patients, the degree of the patient's psychopathology was not a significant factor in successful admissions, nor was the extent of the business commitments of the fathers, to Bowen's surprise.[73]

Once accepted into the study, the families had to make arrangements to move to Bethesda. For example, in a letter to a Minnesota family regarding their upcoming admission, Bowen wrote, "We have been planning on space for all five members of [your] family. Dr. Brodey is in charge of administrative things for the family groups but our general policy is that the parents determine how much they wish the patient member to go and come. As I understand your plans, you are giving up your house, storing your furniture, and coming to Washington by automobile. . . . We would like to know your general schedule and some idea of your expected time of arrival."[74] This letter indicates what some families had to do to participate, including managing their home, job, or other relatives. For one family, the challenge was saving enough money to cover the move to Bethesda, whereas for another it was managing to run their small, family-owned store from afar.

A limited amount of socioeconomic information about the families remains extant in their clinical files. Their income sources included two insurance salesmen, one saleslady, one family-owned department store, a dentist, a member of the military (unspecified), and a chemist. The families of a Baptist minister and a county treasurer expressed serious interest in the project but ultimately did not participate. The clinical files contained few references to patients' religions, with the exception of one Jewish mother-daughter pair. There were also no references to race or ethnicity, so presumably all the families were white, since it is likely that other racial identities would have been noted. Most of the patients had extensive previous hospitalization and psychiatric records, with treatments ranging from insulin and electric shock treatments to psychotherapy to assorted drugs such as Thorazine and Serpasil. Bowen's critical attitude toward psychotropic medications on the unit thus stood in contrast to families' previous treatment experiences.[75]

The families arrived in Bethesda to find themselves on one of the twenty-four nursing units at the Clinical Center. They had access to the general recreation floor of the Clinical Center—which housed a chapel, gymnasium, auditorium, solarium, and two sun decks—as well as a second floor with a cafeteria, bank, barber shop, beauty shop, newsstand and variety shop, all of which were available to any patient there. The 3-East unit itself contained a nurses' station, adjacent to which were a large living room, amenable to meetings and social gatherings, and a dining area with a large table where the families ate together. Two members of the nursing team were assigned to eat with the families. The hospital's nutrition department supplied cooking staples, and the dietary staff prepared the meals; the families could supply special items if they wished to cook, and they were responsible for keeping the kitchen clean. For personal space, each family had two rooms, one of which they typically designated for the parents and the other for the children, though they could use the space however they saw fit. The rooms were furnished with beds, desks, armchairs, and ottomans. The housecleaning staff took care of basic cleaning, and family members did everything else.[76]

Daily life on the ward was unstructured, with the exception of the daily, hour-long staff and family therapy meeting, which became "the center of ward action."[77] Initially arranged to prevent intrastaff divisions provoked by disagreements over patient care, these meetings became the cornerstone of the project's therapeutic and research agenda. The project staff came to view the meetings as therapeutically more effective than individual therapy because they drew family "tension" together where it could be addressed, rather than being diffused among individual therapists.

The families also identified the daily meetings as a key part of their experience on the project.[78] According to Betty Basamania, the social worker on the research staff, one potential family responded positively to attending a meeting while visiting to assess whether it wanted to participate in the project. "They attended the Group Meeting on Monday which proved to be a very intense experience for them as the family discussed not only their marital problems but also how this has affected [their daughter]. Directly after the meeting, [the husband and wife] turned to me and [he] was deeply moved as he said, 'This would do us a lot of good.'"[79] In spite of their apparent enthusiasm for the group meeting, the family did not enroll in the project because there was no space on the ward when they were available to move.

The staff-family meeting, along with other group activities like meals, also became central to the work of the unit's nurses. According to the project's head nurse, Marjorie Kvarnes, "The greater part of the nursing personnel's time is spent in observing and recording families' activities, and participating in the group activities with the entire group. . . . Meals play an unusually important part in this project, since they are the instances in which the entire patient group is together. Two members of the nursing staff are assigned to each meal; their responsibilities consisting specifically of observing the inter and intra-family actions."[80] In addition to their therapeutic purpose, group activities thus formed an important venue for data collection, since the research and nursing staff took multiple types of notes during the daily meetings regarding both the content of discussions and the interpersonal interactions.

Bowen himself underscored the importance of the project's site for his research aims. As he wrote in an annual report to the NIH, "The presence of the family group in a setting where they could be observed constantly provided a source of detailed objective data that would be hard to obtain in any other setting. Many promising observations were marked 'for future study' and passed over during the early stages when the main effort went to stabilizing the clinical operation."[81] This program report highlighted two key dimensions to the role of place for the project. First, the project was situated in a hospital in which clinical operations initially took priority. In the balance between treatment and research, the staff could focus on research only after they had stabilized the ward milieu. Second, the setting enabled the researchers to watch the families continuously. The process of uninterrupted surveillance made possible by the project's space was then tied to a valuable outcome: "detailed objective data that would be hard to obtain in any other setting." By framing constant observation in the structured environment of a hospital ward as the condition for the production of objective data, Bowen worked with and against common presumptions of observation as merely passive perception in contrast to the active, controlled manipulations of experimentation. He aimed to frame his research as noninterventionist, such that families' "natural" patterns could emerge for the research staff to observe and document. However, he also drew implicitly on the advantages of the controlled environment of the laboratory by moving his research subjects into the monitored setting of a hospital ward.

The forms of data that the project produced also belied any simplistic notion of observation as unmediated registering. Once they moved past the mother-daughter phase of the project, the 3-East staffers no longer discussed tracking moves but instead compiled data from numerous sources.[82] By September 1956, a chart titled "Data Collection and Its Use" itemized the textual format, content, and use of data records according to who was responsible for collecting the data (including the nursing staff, research assistant Clare Thompson, individual researchers like Bowen and Brodey, and an occupational therapist, Janice Matsutsuyu). The textual formats for data collection included nursing notes, daily unit-environment charts, and sociograms, which were diagrams of the relationships among the people participating in each group meeting.

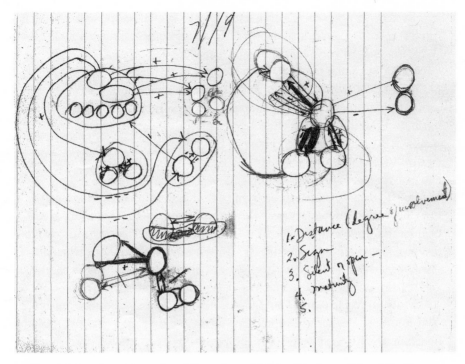

Figure 5. Sample sociograms from Murray Bowen's National Institute of Mental Health research project. Bowen Archive, drawer 2, folder "3-East Project."

Producing a sociogram entailed identifying salient interactions from the many complicated exchanges that occurred during an hour-long group meeting, abstracting those features of the interactions that the staff deemed important enough to warrant diagrammatic representation, and translating them into the inscriptional code of the sociogram. Sociograms were intended to represent who interacted with whom, the strength and direction of their interaction, and the positive or antagonistic quality of that interaction. Plus and minus signs, thickness and color of the lines, and numerical qualifiers next to the lines all indicated the nature and intensity of the interactions. The distance between the circles, which represented individuals, indicated the degree of involvement between two particular people.[83] The graphic representation of individuals as circles in which nothing of note happened internally was emblematic of the project's observational and representational focus on interpersonal rather than intrapsychic dynamics.

The sociogram was only one part of the project's multifaceted approach to producing research data, which Bowen described in the following terms:

There is voluminous research data. Every psychotherapy hour was
tape recorded. In addition, there were three simultaneous written records of each hour. One observer made a summary of the
content of the hours, another made a set of process psychotherapy
notes, and a third observer made a process sociogram. The nursing staff made detailed observations on each family member, and
on each family unit for the 24-hour period of each day. Research
assistants have abstracted much of the voluminous data into daily,
weekly, and monthly summaries.[84]

While the text-based data was hard to manage, processing the recordings proved particularly overwhelming. Bemoaning the hazards of
proliferating audiotape data, from which the project would ultimately
produce two thousand recordings,[85] Bowen borrowed Ray Birdwhistell's
phrase "perishing in a plastic jungle of tape recordings."[86] He thereby
echoed the anxieties of earlier twentieth-century cultural critics who,
according to Mary Ann Doane, described the "excess and unrelenting
continuum of mechanical reproduction" as a "flood" or "blizzard" produced by the increasing speed of modernity.[87]

In 1959, after the 3-East project ended, Bowen described his overall
approach to data collection as one of induction, "rather than the more
popular deductive method" favored by those in the basic sciences. "The
inductive method, the one used by Freud and Pavlov, was used to focus
on a broad clinical area and to utilize 'emergent' findings to determine
the course of the research. At the beginning of the study, there was
no way to guess that the 'family unit' hypothesis and 'family psychotherapy' would emerge as a central theme of the study."[88] Bowen thus
held up an incongruous pairing of Freud and Pavlov as standard bearers
and portrayed the concept of the family unit and the practice of family
therapy as the project's "emergent findings."

Despite the apparent similarities between Bowen's methodological
approach and observationally based, qualitative research in the social
sciences, he and his team did not draw on available sociological or
anthropological sources on methodology. To the contrary, he protested
the alleged need for psychiatrists to consult social scientists regarding
methodological considerations. For example, in correspondence with
fellow psychiatrist Leslie Osborn in late 1958, as the NIMH project
wrapped up, Bowen wrote,

When I came here [to NIMH], I believed that I knew very little about the "scientific method" and I either had to learn about

these things from psychologists and sociologists, or at least take my methodology cues from them. Leslie, this is one of the biggest hoaxes of psychiatric research. . . . So I started off accepting this line of thinking and believing that I did not know enough to be "scientific." How in the world did psychiatrists, with their medical background and training, ever get themselves into the position of believing this stuff? Physicians and psychiatrists are uniquely qualified as natural scientists and they have permitted their science to be "chi-squared" until they no longer have science, they have worthless junk.[89]

Bowen's opposition to having his research chi-squared into worthless junk reflected resistance to the scientific status accorded to sociologists and psychologists at the expense of psychiatrists rather than antagonism toward sociology or psychology per se: "I think that psychologists and sociologists have their own unique contributions to make. I do not mean to detract in the least from them. I am pointing the finger more at psychiatrists for permitting this crazy business to exist and for selling themselves short."[90] Bowen's comments were also indicative of larger tensions between the professions of psychiatry and psychology over control of research standards and clinical practice. These tensions flourished in the 1950s, despite the contemporary emergence of social psychiatry and other indicators of cross-fertilization between psychiatry and the social and behavioral sciences designed to address the relationship between social environment and psychopathology.[91]

Exacerbating Bowen's views on the distinction between his project's approach to data collection and that of a social scientist were the project's ongoing disagreements with hospital administrators regarding the differences between social science and clinical research. Writing in May 1956 to a colleague at the Pinel Foundation in Seattle, Bowen lamented the differences between "pure" and clinical research and sided with the clinicians. "The clinician has clinical responsibility for his patient . . . and it is not hard for him to make a move that is scientifically 'unclean.' One might say that the goal of the researcher is to keep the design and damn the patient, and the goal of the clinician is treatment and damn the design."[92] Bowen further illustrated this difference by borrowing an analogy suggested by the psychoanalyst Elsa Brunswick when she visited NIMH:

In our family project, the "pure scientists" would want to take their readings from a fixed position with controls on as many variables as possible. She [Brunswick] used the example of a fixed camera focused on one small area that looks productive. The camera stays focused on that spot no matter how interesting or seductive becomes the action in another area. This sounded so much like some of the scientific people who have said "But you have to pick one small area and stay there. You never get anywhere by moving every time something new and interesting comes along." She suggested a situation analogous to moving cameras that ride alongside the action with the effort being to get as much interesting action as possible and to hope that also included will be some idea about what causes the actions.[93]

By likening his approach to a moving camera that tried to stay with the action, Bowen not only underscored the divergence between his approach and that of the social scientists who provided a one-time consultation on his project. He also highlighted the cinematic framework that guided the project and echoed the allusion, made two years earlier regarding the "one-hour drama" of a consultation at the Menninger Clinic, to the performative aspect of a clinical setting structured around observation of family interactions.

Aside from research methods, medical care posed some of the most notable problems for the project, which the hospital setting only exacerbated rather than alleviated. Since the families were responsible for taking care of their sick members, even when medication was involved, the main physical duties of the nursing staff included "weighing patients, counting sharps, passing out linen and collecting laundry, and participating in a family medical clinic which is held once a week."[94] Despite this circumscribed list of responsibilities, the unit's nurses, physicians, and other staff members found it easy to become involved in patients' medical issues and thereby their family problems. From within the project, the research staff repeatedly noted that family members used medical or somatic complaints as proxies for their interpersonal issues. In a memo to the staff and family residents, the project's psychiatrists wrote, "These problems appear to bring on the psychological problems involved when a family member makes a 'somatic' complaint."[95] In other words, the families expressed family patterns and fought family battles through attempts to manage (or not manage) medical problems. In response, the research staff members developed specific protocols for handling medical issues in which they aimed to deal with somatic problems "in a medically responsible way while avoiding the 'taking over' position."[96]

However, the project's efforts to delegate medical responsibility to the families generated tension between the 3-East team and the NIMH administration. Despite administrative assurances of support for giving responsibility to patients, Bowen found that each time the project members did so, they faced a series of new questions about research design. He attributed this discrepancy to societal expectations for the role of the hospital in managing mental illness: "This problem seems to come down to the fact that society holds the hospital superintendent responsible for supervising the people society has called incompetent. Even though we have a director who tried hard to interpret a liberal attitude to society and to permit inner freedom, the anxiety is still there."[97]

This debate brought Bowen back to the balance between research prerogatives (minimal medical oversight, according to Bowen) and clinical responsibility (supervising medical care, according to the NIMH administration), though he stood on the research rather than the clinical side in this particular debate.

In the midst of its research, the team was aware of the unique status of the project and its eyebrow-raising description. "Many when told of the family project express surprise and interest in learning that the whole family lives on the ward. This is the most unique feature of our study."[98] Early on, they emphasized the unique premise of their research, which they attributed in part to the unique resources of NIH. They were not aware of other researchers who had "ever approached the problem by actually bringing the mothers into the hospitals with the patients. The expense involved, the high degree of clinical flexibility required, the staff requirements, and the necessary hospital facilities make this into a project that would be difficult to impossible in a less well staffed and equipped setting than the Clinical Center."[99] However, as the project progressed, they became aware of other efforts to hospitalize multiple family members together, particularly in cases in which some family members contributed to the care of other members.[100]

As the project proceeded, the research team began to publicize its findings in conference papers, correspondence, and eventually publications. Aside from local presentations, the first talk that the 3-East researchers gave was at the American Psychiatric Association annual meeting in 1957. In the remaining years of the project, Bowen, Brodey, Dysinger, and Basamania gave several conference papers.[101] These omitted the tedious details of daily life on the unit, as well as the project's conflicts with NIMH administrators about patient responsibility and social science methodology, in order to focus on the clinical setup of the project, family therapy, family theory (including the role of the father), and the nature of schizophrenia. The group aimed to communicate its research as a contribution to topics of broader interest in contemporary psychiatry. For example, Bowen's presentation at the 1958 APA meeting fit within a block of papers on schizophrenia, which he evocatively characterized as "putting diencephalons, ids, sagging egos, mean mothers, psychoanalysis, weak constitutions, and families into one blenderized concoction to be seasoned with drugs and sparked by EST."[102]

The 3-East clinical work ended on January 1, 1959, at the directive of the NIMH leadership, at which time all the families were discharged or transferred, while the research staff continued on the project until mid-1959.[103] At least one of the project's family participants considered it a privilege to have participated in the study and was sorry to have it end, as she indicated in a letter to Robert Cohen, the director of Clinical Investigations.[104] At the time of the project's termination, Bowen had explicit discussions with NIMH administrators regarding ownership and storage of the project's records and data, as well as attribution of credit to NIMH in subsequent publications. He tried to obtain foundation or private funding to support the work of writing up the project. However, despite a book contract with Basic Books, he never obtained the necessary funding for additional time to finish it.[105] Instead, he moved on to a faculty position at Georgetown University Medical Center and to other work on family therapy that became the basis for his theory of family systems, his institution building through the Georgetown Family Center, and his leadership role in professional organizations such as the American Family Therapy Association, for which he served as the first president in the late 1970s and early 1980s.

Even without completing a book on the NIMH research, the efforts at knowledge dissemination by Bowen and others on the 3-East project became significant because of their generative and influential role in the development of family therapy as a field and their contribution to the coalescing view of the family as a unit of disease and treatment by the late 1950s. A few of the group's conference papers appeared in publication, including an article in the *American Journal of Psychiatry* on family therapy that attracted four hundred reprint requests.[106] According to Bowen and his coauthors on that paper, "Psychotherapeutically, the family is treated as if it were a single organism."[107] This view of the family as a single organism or as a unit became one of the distinctive hallmarks of the field of family therapy.

Bowen also argued for the value of communicating the project's results not just as a way of understanding schizophrenia or sharing therapeutic innovations but because they had broader relevance for learning about normal families:

> The patterns [of family interaction observed in the project] are intense and striking in disturbed families but they are also present to a lesser degree in "normal" families. We believe that the disturbed family with its exaggerated patterns and mechanisms, is not sufficiently recognized as a profitable avenue for the investigation of "normal" behavior. Once it is possible to see exaggerated patterns in a disturbed family (or individual), it is then possible to see the same pattern in a much less obvious form in the "normal."[108]

Observation thus played a central role in Bowen's claim to learning something about normal families from disturbed ones—in particular, his claim that *seeing* exaggerated patterns would help the researcher to see similar patterns in subtler form in normal families.

These ideas resonated with Georges Canguilhem's meditation on the relationship between the normal and the pathological. Canguilhem made two points that pertain to Bowen's project. First, "normal" can mean both a value ("that which is such that it ought to be") and a fact ("that which constitutes either the average or standard of a measurable characteristic"). The abnormal or anomalous is also not inherently diseased, though the distinction between anomaly and disease is not always clear-cut.[109] Thus Bowen's distinction between disturbed and normal families entailed collapsing the multiple meanings of the normal—whether defined as ideal type, statistical average, or healthy—in order to juxtapose the normal with the disturbed. Second, Canguilhem argued that the abnormal state is prior, rather than subsequent, to the normal state and that the normal itself is "the effect obtained by the execution of the normative project. . . . Consequently, it is not paradoxical to say that the abnormal, while logically second, is existentially first."[110] The point here is not merely that one might see exaggerated patterns in families with schizophrenic members that were present in families without a schizophrenic member but that the very process of studying disturbed families produced the notion of the normal family unit.

More broadly, Bowen's NIMH project illuminates the central role of observation in the shifting view of families as the locus of disease and the establishment of family therapy as a field. Although he later invoked the family unit as a naturalized object, unmarked by the traces of schizophrenia research and hospital-based observational practices, his own writings from the 1950s emphasize the difficulties he faced in viewing and managing the family as a unit. Making the family into a site of disease and treatment required significant effort, as the NIMH project demonstrates, and observation of daily family life on a hospital ward helped to produce its very object of observation, in this case the family unit.[111]

Observing Families In Situ

In contrast to the researchers in the 3-East project, most midcentury clinical and social science researchers interested in family life used methodologies such as psychological tests, surveys, questionnaires, or structured interviews, or they focused their ethnographic observations on families who did not have a member with a diagnosed mental illness.[112] However, a few researchers interested in observing whole families with a schizophrenic member tried to capture the essence of family life by studying families in situ, in their "natural habitat"[113] of the home. Two such studies were conducted in the late 1950s and 1960s, the first by anthropologist Jules Henry and the second by family therapists David Kantor and William Lehr, and they provide an illuminating foil to Bowen's research at NIMH. Like the investigators in the 3-East project, Henry, Kantor, and Lehr were concerned with the relationship between family and schizophrenia, they saw their projects as contributions to clinical work as well as research, and their methodologies focused on close observation of daily family life in a residential setting. Yet they observed families in their homes rather than on a hospital ward, and they generalized their results to include, in Kantor and Lehr's phrase, "all families as families," rather than confining their conclusions to the families under study.

In the first of the home-based studies, Jules Henry began what he called a "naturalistic study" of families with psychotic children in 1957. He published his account of two such families in a chapter in *Culture against Man*, his self-described "passionate ethnography," and his account of five additional families along with his overall conclusions in *Pathways to Madness*. Henry is perhaps best known for his work on education and *Culture Against Man*, in which he argued against the conformity, competitiveness, and consumerism of modern American culture.

His critique of mass society fit within a chorus generated by diverse social critics of the 1950s, including Irving Howe, C. Wright Mills, David
Reisman, and William Whyte.[114]

Trained as an anthropologist at Columbia University by Franz Boas
and Ruth Benedict, Henry first recommended in a 1948 article in the
American Journal of Orthopsychiatry that researchers live with families
of the mentally ill in order to overcome the obstacle to understanding
mental illness posed by a "lack of scientific knowledge of family life."[115]
Eleven years later he began his ethnographic observations of families
with psychotic children at the behest of the psychiatrist Bruno Bettelheim, who supported his research with funds from a Ford Foundation
grant to the Sonia Shankman Orthogenic School at the University of
Chicago. At a historical moment of significant traffic between psychiatry and anthropology, interest by an anthropologist in mental illness
fit within the contemporary intellectual climate, as did investment by a
psychiatrist in ethnographic research.

Although Henry was an anthropologist and not a clinician, he still
explained the rationale for his research in therapeutic as well as methodological terms. According to his introduction to *Pathways to Madness*,
"I have done this study because I believe that direct observation of families in their native habitat, going about their usual business, will furnish
new insights into psychotic breakdown and other forms of emotional illness, and suggest new ideas for prevention and treatment."[116] Beyond
the clinical justification, he saw the study as being of a piece with his
broader intellectual project:

> Other motivations were my wish to understand family life better
> and to study man in his day-to-day surroundings. The last is the
> compelling goal of my scientific life. I am repelled by the artificial-
> ity of experimental studies of human behavior because they strip
> the context from life. They take away from it the environment,
> without which it has no meaning, without which it has no enve-
> lope. . . . A result is that in my studies I try to combine disciplined
> observation with a comprehensive interpretation of life in its com-
> plex interrelations.[117]

This passage articulates several key features of Henry's study. First, it
highlights the centrality of direct observation conducted in a disciplined
way, or what Henry elsewhere called "naturalistic observation."[118] This
approach privileged the perspective of the observer/writer and assumed

the transparency of the interactions, events, and emotions seen and re-corded, the "data," that Henry aimed both to let "speak for itself" and to interpret.[119] He compared his method of direct observation to an optical scientific instrument such as the telescope or microscope that reveals "new dimensions of the universe" and makes possible new theoretical developments. This analogy was ironic since such instruments were of-ten valued precisely for their capacity to aid, extend, surpass, and correct human observation.[120]

Second, Henry advocated studying families in their natural sur-roundings rather than in the laboratory or a psychiatrist's office.[121] This approach underscored the importance of place in scientific research by mapping a well-worn dichotomy between the natural and artificial (which carried powerful associations about modernity and authenticity) onto a distinction between field and laboratory, in which the home as natural habitat contrasted with the artificiality of experimental settings. The distinction between the natural and the artificial was similarly central to his critique of contemporary society, such that artificiality became the problem, according to Henry, with both the method and object of analysis in research on modern life.

Finally, Henry had the immediate goal of understanding psychotic breakdown by producing a more intimate, detailed picture of family life, but this fit within his larger project, "the study of man in his day-to-day surroundings." He hoped that his research would enrich psychiatric knowledge and treatment, as well as provide insight into more wide-spread features of family life. He also aimed to show that the disturbed families of his study were "very much like all of us—that the main dif-ference between 'them' and 'us' is that they seem to go to extremes and do too many things that are upsetting."[122] Henry based his claim for commonalities between them and us on the routine, recognizable pat-terns in the families' lives. As he asserted in the introduction to *Pathways to Madness*, "So much of their activity seems within 'normal limits' that in much of what I have written I do not use the word 'pathology'! Thus much of this book is simply a description of family life, with judgment regarding health or pathology reserved."[123]

Henry observed each of the seven families for an average of a week, equaling approximately one hundred hours, and took notes that formed the basis for his study. With three families, he had his own room in their house and lived with them for a week. For three others, he ar-rived at breakfast time and left when the family went to bed. Another researcher—a young woman whom he called Susan—stayed with the last family for a week, arriving at 7:00 a.m. and staying until bedtime.

Henry's published reports on the research do not indicate his criteria for choosing the particular families under study, other than the presence of a family member with a psychiatric diagnosis and the willingness to participate. Though he made no claims about choosing representative families from particular class backgrounds, he did provide information on the professions of the parents and made generalizations about middle-class and working-class families, drawing at points on other anthropological and sociological research to support his claims.[124] He gained access to some of the families with assistance from the Jewish Children's Bureau[125] and by telling potential participants "that science was of the opinion that their child's illness was somehow related to family life, and that the best way to discover the relationship was by having a scientist study their family. It was further explained that, hopefully, my findings might contribute to the treatment of their child; and if not to their child, surely to future generations of children."[126] His recruitment efforts thus held out the promise of treatment, though unlike Bowen, Henry did not provide any sort of therapeutic intervention himself.

In response to one of the questions regularly raised by his research, Henry made a case for why his presence did not disrupt or distort family processes. He argued that an observer could not disturb the realities of family life because of familial and individual resistance to change, as evidenced in the stability of what he called the family culture, the lack of individual control over unconscious impulses and fixed behaviors, the habitual behavior and needs of children, and the inflexibility of personality structure. He also maintained that his research subjects likely did not understand the implications of their behavior, so they were not even aware of what should be concealed or exaggerated. Finally, the parents wanted to participate in the research in the hope of helping their disturbed child, Henry claimed, so they were less inclined to dissimulation, but even if they had wanted to present a false front, the rigidity of individual and family processes would have prevented it.[127]

Regarding the content of his observations, Henry described his approach in terms of his close attention to detail, appreciation of the complexity of family life, and antagonism to reductionism in explanations of psychopathology.

In disturbed families, as in others, difficulties arise from many causes, and for this reason I have gone to great lengths to illuminate the complexity of family life. . . . I do not believe in the "commonplace." If a woman peels an onion; if a man reads a newspaper or watches television; if there is dust or no dust on the furniture;

if a parent kisses or does not kiss his child when he comes home; if the family has eggs or cereal for breakfast, orange juice or no orange juice, and so on through all the "trivia" of everyday life— this is significant to me. . . . I proceed on the basis that science advances by relentless examination of the commonplace.[128]

In all his case studies, Henry presented a picture of the families based on the minute, mundane interactions that constituted daily life, such as mealtime activities and grocery shopping trips. While he acknowledged in a footnote that some of his descriptive characterizations might reflect "observer bias" (for example, his assessment that one mother treated her infant daughter "willfully and callously"), he also claimed that his training as a professional observer and his direct observation methodology revealed the most salient features of family life.[129] As he asserted in one of his cases, the Keen family, "I feel I have to remind the reader what happened here, from the scientific point of view. Merely by being present for a few hours in the home, the observer was able to see with her own eyes, on the very first day, the essence of Mr. Keen's relationship to the boys."[130]

The conclusions that Henry drew from his research were neither quantitative nor typological.[131] Instead of statistically analyzing the interactions among family members or developing a classificatory scheme for identifying families with psychotic members (both of which came out of other contemporary research projects), he developed a set of qualitative "invariants" of human existence from which he drew generalizations about defining features of family life (time, space, motion, objects, and people), as well as parameters of interaction (e.g., quarreling, feeding, cruelty, and tenderness). In the end, he argued that no single factor, except perhaps cruelty, could produce psychopathology but that a "configuration"—borrowing Wilhelm Dilthey's term—could become psychogenic.

Henry specifically addressed family therapy, which he praised for avoiding simple-minded parent blaming. While he saw such work as movement in the right direction, he argued that family therapy still diverted attention from the corrosive effects of culture more broadly. "Through this theory we attack what is nearest, what has inflicted on us the immediate, the most memorable pain. The family, however, is merely the place where the general pathology of the culture is incubated, concentrated and finally transmuted into individual psychosis. Family therapy is a good thing, and 'family dynamics' is a valid theory, but let us remember that the family merely distills into a lethal dose what exists in the culture at large."[132] His work thus contained a more pointed cultural critique of "the destructiveness of the culture as a whole" than did Bowen's writings on his NIMH research or the subsequent work of David Kantor and William Lehr.

In the 1960s, other family therapists picked up Henry's work as a relevant research model for their own studies.[133] While schizophrenia remained a key area of interest over the course of the 1960s, therapists turned increasingly to other family problems like divorce, eating disorders, and delinquency. They focused more attention on the normal as well as the abnormal family. They also drew increasingly on the cybernetic and systems perspectives discussed in chapter 2.

This expanded purview formed the context for David Kantor and William Lehr's research that they began in the mid-1960s and published ten years later as *Inside the Family*. According to their stated goal, "Our primary focus throughout this book is on the intrinsic nature of family process. The naturalistic study of family households we began in 1965 reflects this concern."[134] Like Jules Henry, they based their study on the findings of researchers who moved into the natural habitat of families' homes, but they differed in significant ways from Henry in their conceptual model of family functioning. Their methodology was similar to his, but they added control families without a member under treatment for psychiatric problems, and they included supplemental recording and assessment procedures as well as observer reports. On the basis of this naturalistic study, Kantor and Lehr claimed to explain the structures, patterns, and processes governing functional as well as dysfunctional families.

They grounded their study on a model of the family as an information-processing system—"a cybernetic-like model for understanding family process"[135]—which they illustrated with the diagram in figure 6. This represented a prototypical feedback loop showing how a system such as a family processed an input signal. In a similar diagram of a family system not shown here, Kantor and Lehr aimed to show how a family, "as a complex informational field,"[136] managed the ongoing events, actions, and strains that occurred within it and that arose from its environment. Summarizing the message represented graphically in these diagrams, they articulated their thesis in the following way: "Through the transmission of matter and information via energy in space and time, family members regulate each other's access to the targets of affect, power, and meaning."[137] With this conception

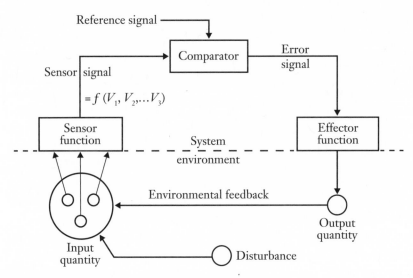

Figure 6. From David Kantor and William Lehr, *Inside the Family: Toward a Theory of Family Process* (San Francisco, 1975), 13. By permission of David Kantor.

of the family as a goal-seeking, information-processing system organized by feedback loops, Kantor and Lehr built on the family systems thinking developed in the 1950s by Gregory Bateson and his colleagues in Palo Alto.

With funding from NIMH, they recruited twenty families from clinics of Boston State Hospital and community sources. Families with a schizophrenic member and control families were roughly matched for class, ethnic background, family composition, and neighborhood. The researchers particularly attempted to study families living in public housing and working-class families.[138] The observers lived with the families for a month, day and night. To supplement the observer reports, there were also tape recorders in all rooms, psychological tests, and individual and family interviews by team researchers over the course of the study. They hired nineteen typists to transcribe all the tapes.

Like Henry, Kantor and Lehr attended to the quotidian aspects of family life. For example, they provided a close analysis of a child coming into his parents' bedroom. However, unlike Henry, who provided a narrative description of such mundane events, Kantor and Lehr systematized and diagramed the pattern of interactions.[139] In contrast to Henry's principled opposition to typology, they structured their conclusions around typology.

In so doing, they followed a trajectory in family therapy that focused on family classifications. In particular, other work on schizophrenia produced typologies of family processes.[140] Though such studies initially focused on classifying the type of family likely to produce schizophrenic symptoms, they eventually expanded to describing other types of family dynamics. For example, some therapists' attention shifted from static typologies to a developmental model of family life in the 1960s. This model drew on Eric Erikson's work on individual life stages and focused on normal, expectable transition points in the course of the family life cycle, like the birth of a child.[141]

Kantor and Lehr proposed three ideal types (in the Weberian sense) of families, based on a spatial metaphor: closed, open, and random. One commentator mapped the types onto "the familiar political categories of authoritarian, democratic, and anarchic regimes," thereby linking familial structure and politics in explicit terms.[142] According to Kantor and Lehr, "These stereotypic systems differ in both their structural arrangements and strategic styles. *The three basic types are based on three different homeostatic models. Each is a variant of the generalized concept of family as a semipermeable system.*"[143] This model included the possibility of multiple homeostatic ideals rather than an idealized state of tranquility. No one type was inherently pathological or dysfunctional; each had a mixture of ideal traits and flaws. Thus, dysfunctional families did not fit within a single type or category but rather were flawed deviations from normal types.[144] Kantor and Lehr also commented briefly that different ethnic, religious, and economic subcultures in Western communities would make their own assessments of which typal design they considered a more viable model of family organization.[145]

In the end, they used their typology to argue that professionals should recognize the viability of all three basic family types and give credence to families' own value judgments rather than imposing a normative model. "It is incumbent upon family theorists, social planners, and agency practitioners . . . to discover and sustain a family's typal style based on the family's own interior criteria rather than attempt to impose a typal style upon it that is based on external criteria."[146]

Regardless of the differences between Henry and Kantor and Lehr in their respective approaches to typology and their choices of families to observe, their studies similarly valued the observation of family life in situ, in its own place. For both studies, that meant the habitat of the home. By framing the observational methodology of their projects as naturalistic and the place of their research as a natural habitat, they also shored up the "natural" status of their object of study, the family.

Shaped by the places in which they occurred, practices of observation and documentation became crucial dimensions to the development of family therapy as a field and to the constitution of the family as a therapeutic subject. Researchers regularly considered the impact of the process of observation and the presence of an observer on the families under study. As Jules Henry remarked, "Although I have spoken to many professional groups, there has scarcely been a time when I have not been asked, 'Doesn't the presence of the observer distort the picture?' "[147] He justified the position that his picture of the families was not distorted by pointing to the stability of families' individual cultures, their resistance to change even with a nonfamily member in their midst, the difficulty of controlling fixed behavior and impulses, the inflexibility of personality structure, and the pressure applied by children toward habitual behavior.[148]

Bowen's research team also had to consider the impact of the ward setting and the presence of other families on a given family's interactions. Beyond dislocating families from their natural habitats and subjecting them to the spatial, temporal, and material limits of inpatient living, the hospital site also contained a clinical imperative. The impetus to provide treatment, in addition to conducting research, affected the design of the research project, the administrative relationship between the project staff and the hospital directors, and the expectations and motivations of the participating families.

As in the case of documentary filmmakers, much of the power of the researcher lay in the editing process. The researchers' work unavoidably entailed various types of selection, grouping, and highlighting, which inevitably served to edit the picture of pathology and family life that they presented. In their publications and talks, Bowen, Henry, and Kantor and Lehr provided background on families' history and current state, descriptions of their interactions, and quotations from individual family members. However, the families' lives could never be represented in toto, nor did they speak for themselves. Related questions about visuality informed early family therapists' efforts to train future members of their young field as well as their use of technologies such as film and one-way mirrors, which the next chapter discusses.

- -

CHAPTER FIVE

VISIONS OF FAMILY LIFE

In an early sequence from the 1955 film *Rebel Without a Cause*, the film's main teenage characters glimpse each other at a police station after they are brought in on separate charges. The meeting between Sal Mineo's character, Plato, and his delinquency officer focuses on Plato's absent parents and leads to a referral to a psychiatrist. In a parallel scene, Natalie Woods's character, Judy, worries about her troubled relationship with her father. Finally, James Dean's character, Jim, leaves his delinquency officer to find his father, mother, and grandmother dressed in evening wear and waiting for him. After his mother and grandmother make several critical comments, Jim screams, "You're driving me crazy!"[1] The cumulative implication was that for these white, well-off adolescents, family life was the cause of their problems, the damage was psychological in nature, and psychiatric treatment made sense as a potential solution. This chain of connections was part of the same cultural logic on which family therapy drew, as was the visual mode of knowing suggested in the glances exchanged between Plato, Judy, and Jim.

In addition to sharing the presumption of a relationship between family life and psychiatric pathology represented in *Rebel Without a Cause* and other contemporary cinema, family therapists actively turned to visual technologies such as film, video, and one-way mirrors to facilitate their pedagogical, clinical, and research efforts. They produced a vision of family life in multiple senses of the phrase: they relied on optic technologies for a wide range of practices (pedagogical, therapeutic, and research); they analyzed popular representations of families in terms of their field-specific theories of the salient features of family life; and they highlighted the performative dimensions to family interactions as well as their own interventions. The growing imperative to train new therapists by the early 1960s contributed to these efforts, as did the desire to move beyond the focus on schizophrenia that had been characteristic of the fifties. Unlike the researchers discussed in chapter 4 who argued against disrupting family life under the mantle of naturalistic observation, other family therapists embraced their roles as catalysts and instigators in family dynamics. They also brought in visual instruments such as film for purposes other than research, including education and treatment.

In his 1966 book *Treating the Troubled Family*, Nathan Ackerman strongly endorsed the use of recording technologies for learning and understanding how therapy works, specifically family therapy.

> The challenge of communicating the very core of the therapeutic process by the written word is a very sensitive one. Who of us can really do it well? . . . [I]t is the utter frustration of these past efforts that explains the avid hope of our time for a more adequate recording of treatment sessions with the use of sound tape, closed-circuit TV, and motion picture. The value of a permanent recording of therapeutic experience in motion pictures is self-evident. It is, in my view, the only known method to date that provides a satisfactory permanent record of a Gestalt, a merging of the image of face, voice, emotion, and bodily expression.[2]

Ackerman had been making films since the late 1950s as a means of eliminating the selective verbal translation that occurred when therapists retrospectively described what happened in therapy sessions. His interest in such technologies attested to the value of a recorded therapy session for preservation, reproduction, and sequence replay.[3] However, family therapists' investment (intellectual and economic) in visual technologies was neither "self-evident," as Ackerman claimed, nor based solely on the technologies' convenience for "communicating the very core of the therapeutic process."

Rather, family therapists' early commitment to visual technologies such as film and closed-circuit television materialized key aspects of their shift from individual, one-on-one psychotherapy to family therapy. The shift among a few psychiatrists in the 1950s from treating individual patients to treating whole families entailed new attention to observable interactions among family members, as opposed to the psychoanalytic examination of unresolved, inner psychic conflicts. The goal of the new field of family therapy became changing family communication and structure rather than producing insight. Although a few other psychotherapy researchers also began recording therapy sessions in the 1950s,[4] family therapists had a particular stake in the suitability of films and one-way mirrors to capture family interactions. Moreover, their orientation toward observable interactions within families stood in contrast to the psychoanalytic orientation toward an individualized patient's psyche whose unconscious drives and conflicts were accessible through free association, dream analysis, and other verbal techniques of depth-oriented psychoanalysis. Beyond the clinical implications, their use of visual technologies for pedagogical purposes entailed the surveillance and disciplining of therapists and their practices, not just patients.

Early family therapists' visual orientation combined assumptions about the best ways of gaining knowledge about families with an understanding of the ontological nature of pathology based in families and their interactions rather than hidden within individual psyches. Family therapy training programs, clinical practices, and research projects crystallized this alignment of how to know and what to know. The therapists turned to visual technologies not just because of their seeming objectivity and superiority in recounting family events or therapy sessions, though those were also key factors. They also incorporated these technologies because such tools enabled them to engage with the performative dimensions of family pathology itself.

Becoming a Family Therapist: Behind the Mirror and on Film

The first generation of family therapists very quickly faced the challenge of training others to follow in their Young Turk footsteps, which initially meant postgraduate training for psychiatrists, psychologists, and social workers whose graduate education had focused on individual therapy but who wanted additional training in a family perspective. The problem of training new family therapists was more involved than helping them learn to manage additional people in a therapy session. According to Murray Bowen,

> It is difficult for therapists and personnel to remain objective even if they are trained in handling countertransference problems.

A nonparticipant observer might aspire to objectivity, but, in the emotional tension that surrounds these families, he begins to participate emotionally in the family drama just as surely as he inwardly cheers the hero and hates the villain when he attends the theater. . . . Once it was possible to focus on the family as a unit, it was like shifting a microscope from the oil immersion to the low power lens. . . . Broad patterns of form and movement that had been obscured in the close-up view became clear.[5]

Though he was not directly discussing educational strategies, Bowen's comments regarding the difficulties involved in shifting to a family perspective apply to pedagogy as well as clinical practice. By describing the family therapist as a person who refrained from taking sides in the family drama and whose shift to a family perspective was comparable to changing the lens in a microscope, he emphasized certain theatrical and visual aspects of family therapy that played out in teaching situations as well—the sometimes dramatic aspects of family problems and the orientation toward viewing broad patterns of form and movement.

Moreover, the challenge in education was to help students shift not just from any individual perspective to any family perspective but more particularly from an interior, psychological (especially psychoanalytic) self to a view of the family as a system with patterns of interaction and communication, even cybernetic feedback loops. In a retrospective written in 1969, Jay Haley, the inaugural editor of *Family Process*, described the early years of family therapy training and the challenge of introducing new practitioners to family therapy as something other or more than mere treatment modality: "By the end of the 1950's a few individuals were training students, almost as an apprentice system. More formal training has brought new questions–what family knowledge is relevant to therapy, and how can an experienced family therapist teach what he knows how to do but has difficulty describing? A particular problem is the recognition that family therapy is not a method of treatment but a *new orientation to the human dilemma*."[6] Early attempts to introduce family therapy students to this new orientation incorporated visual technologies and techniques that could account for observable phenomena such as nonverbal behavior and family interactions.[7]

Family therapy education took place through watching and doing, observing and intervening. During the late 1950s and early 1960s, training took place in private offices and newly founded institutions, not established academic centers. The Family Institute in New York City and the Mental Research Institute in Palo Alto were the first two institutes devoted to family therapy practice and training. Outside these institutional settings, prospective clinicians could learn how to conduct family therapy by attending live demonstration therapy sessions conducted by traveling family therapy leaders and by watching training films, including a film series that included separate sessions conducted by four therapists with the same family.

These visual pedagogical practices embodied the field's clinical focus on observable phenomena and served as a primary means by which the founders of family therapy encouraged future generations of therapists to shift their attention from the individual to the family. For example, the New York-based family therapist Peggy Papp argued that the technique of family choreography was "an excellent training tool, due to its ability to demonstrate visually the cybernetics of a family."[8] Papp developed her technique on the basis of work in the 1960s by David Kantor, Fred and Bunny Duhl, and Virginia Satir on family sculpting. She produced a training tape on family choreography titled *Making the Invisible Visible*, which underscored the link of choreography with visuality. Papp argued that the visual and physical aspects of choreography gave it wide applicability: "The power of the choreography comes through *seeing* and *physically moving through* the situation. . . . Family choreography speaks with the universal language of sight and movement; therefore it is comprehensible to any family, from the most highly educated and articulate to the most impoverished and inarticulate."[9] Papp thus highlighted the visual and active dimensions of choreography as a pedagogical tool that could not only illustrate family cybernetics but could also overcome disparities in class and educational background among families.

Nathan Ackerman also conducted active interventions designed to rearrange current patterns of interaction. He conveyed his vision of the therapist as a "catalyst" to future family therapists in his traveling demonstrations, therapy sessions in front of a one-way mirror, and films. In a 1962 article in which he compared psychoanalysis to family therapy, he argued,

> The [family] therapist must be active, spontaneous, and make free use of his own emotions, though in a selective and suitable manner. His prime function is to foster the family's use of his own emotional participation in the direction of achieving a favorable shift in the homeostasis of family relationships. He loosens and shakes up preexisting pathogenic equilibria and makes way for a

healthier realignment of these family relationships. In this role, his influence may be likened to that of a catalyst, a chemical reagent, a re-synthesizer.[10]

Thus Ackerman did not focus on the past or psychoanalyze the therapist-in-training, techniques used in psychoanalytic training, nor did he exclusively privilege patients' privacy, focus on patient history, or offer a neutral, blank screen for patient's transference and projections. The performative quality of his interventions, which were explicitly dramatic, was conveyed in his presentation format. Beginning in the late 1950s, Ackerman began conducting interviews across the country in which he led an evaluation or diagnostic session with a family in front of a live audience. He also conducted therapy sessions in front of a one-way mirror and recorded sessions on film. He thereby undermined the sanctity of individual patient confidentiality in psychoanalysis, first by bringing in other family members, then by having observers behind a mirror, and then by distributing his films to a wider audience.

Among the various technologies used by family therapists for such visually oriented pedagogical and therapeutic purposes, the one-way mirror was one that family therapists incorporated from the beginnings of their discipline. This kind of mirror has a reflective coating sufficiently opaque to reflect light when well lit but thin enough to let some light pass through, such that those on the darkened side of the glass can see through it, while those on the lit side see their own reflections. The one-way mirror enabled therapists to structure a situation in which people on one side of the viewing apparatus could observe those on the other side without being seen in return. From behind a mirror, students learned from watching their teacher interact with a family, and teachers supervised how their students conducted therapy. Some therapists even incorporated the mirror into their interventions by working with a portion of a family in front of it while other family members observed from behind the mirror. These practices raised a key question: what was the value of looking without being seen in return?

Family therapists' own accounts of their early deployment of one-way mirrors and viewing screens typically present the mirror as a self-evident improvement over therapists' selective recounting of what happened in therapy sessions since it, like film, allegedly provided a more objective view of the therapy process. Despite such claims, the one-way mirror as a technology was not inevitable but was constructed and employed for particular functions. Historians of science and medicine interested in

Figure 7. Arnold Gesell's one-way vision dome. Courtesy of the Arnold Gesell Papers, Library of Congress, and by permission of Rex Walden and the Gesell family.

visual culture have written extensively about film, photography, microscopes, telescopes, and X-rays as scientific instruments. The use of the one-way mirror by psychological and clinical experts deserves similar analysis, since it raises questions about the epistemology of observation, practices of surveillance and spectatorship, and the production of objectivity in therapeutics.

The use of one-way mirrors has, over the past century, become routine in fields ranging from developmental psychology and pediatrics to nonclinical fields such as education, law enforcement, and market research. Around the turn of the twentieth century, magicians used partially silvered mirrors to aid their sleights of hand. A similar viewing apparatus came into use in early twentieth-century child development research. For example, the child psychologist Arnold Gesell developed a nine-foot-high, one-way viewing dome made from iron mesh screening painted white, which he used for his research on infants and young children in the 1920s and 1930s. By the 1950s, the Bank Street College of Education employed a one-way viewing screen to train teachers.[11] The subsequent substitution of large glass mirrors for mesh screens depended on the development of industrial plate glass production.[12] Though Gesell and the Banks School relied on mesh screens rather than glass mirrors, they put the screens to use in ways that presaged family therapists' subsequent efforts by enabling unseen observers to watch the events taking place on the lit side of the screen.

One of family therapists' primary uses for one-way mirrors was to teach new therapists. In 1960 Nathan Ackerman established the Family Institute in New York City for clinical and educational purposes. He initially had a small one-way mirror installed between a room designated for therapy and a small adjoining room, which became an observation room. From behind the mirror, students learned from watching Ackerman and others interact with a family, and instructors observed how their students conducted therapy, in what Ackerman called "live supervision."[13] Eventually the small mirror was replaced with a larger one that filled most of the wall between the observation and therapy rooms.[14] The presumption was that extra people in the therapy room would be distracting for the participants but that once the observers were ensconced behind the mirror, the session could proceed as if they were not there.

In Palo Alto, Don Jackson founded the MRI in 1959 to provide a site for family therapy practice and a training course "in the principles of family diagnosis and family therapy."[15] Like the Family Institute in New York, the MRI relied on the use of one-way mirrors. Jackson recruited Virginia Satir and others to teach family therapy at his new institute. The training program initially received a year of funding from the Hill Family Foundation, and then in 1961 it received a five-year grant from NIMH to expand. Training options included survey courses, which consisted primarily of lectures and demonstrations that focused on diagnostic skills and theoretical concepts, and an intensive course that admitted eight practitioners a year who graduated as "qualified family therapists."[16] Satir based her influential 1964 publication *Conjoint Family Therapy* on the training handouts she developed at the MRI and during her earlier work with families in Chicago. The intensive course began with didactic lessons, examination of recorded family interviews, and observation of live family therapy sessions; it then progressed as each student began to conduct therapy with one family under close supervision.[17] Trainees first watched behind one-way viewing mirrors while experienced family therapists conducted family interviews; then they studied the audiovisual recordings of those sessions in detail "for the diagnosis of patterns of interaction in the family."[18]

However, observation without interpretation proved insufficient for conveying the nature of the clinical problem at hand or the rationale for particular therapeutic maneuvers; the families in treatment and the interventions used by Ackerman, Satir, and other clinicians were not as transparent or self-evident as the one-way mirror through which observers might watch them. To address this issue, the MRI staff developed an interview technique that they called the Structured Family Interview. It was designed to bring out families' typical patterns of making decisions, handling stress, and generally interacting by asking them to perform tasks such as designing a family trip with a given budget or describing how, out of all the people in the world, the parents had found each other. The MRI staff developed this tool for use in its combined research and clinical activities. One person at the MRI described the utility of the Structured Family Interview in terms of its transparency: "Its usefulness lies in the fact that its results are evident and directly accessible through observation. . . . In fact, this makes it possible for the therapist, having observed the interview through the one-way vision screen, to take a family over for treatment directly from the interviewer at the end of the Structured Interview and to establish the first therapeutic contact already with an understanding of the family's dynamics and patterns of interaction."[19] Beyond its clinical accessibility and efficiency as an assessment tool, the Structured Interview also had educational advantages, as a description in *Family Process* pointed out:

> The Structured Interview has also been found to be a simple, inexpensive and very effective teaching and training aid. . . . At the Mental Research Institute, all demonstrations of family therapy and all supervised work of the trainees now begin with the administration of a Structured Interview. These interviews are then discussed during subsequent training sessions, and the trainee's attention is drawn to the emerging patterns which can be expected to repeat themselves during the course of therapy and are the main object of therapeutic intervention.[20]

One of the pedagogical assumptions built into the technology of the Structured Interview was that it would lead families to display patterns of interaction that not only would repeat during the therapy process but were the very locus of pathology, therefore the target of clinical attention.

Despite the Structured Interview's alleged transparency, the MRI staff members themselves acknowledged that "an important early phase in the training of family specialists will involve teaching them *how to look*."[21] Thus, watching behind the mirror was not enough; trainees needed to be taught *how* and *what* to observe. Don Jackson and others at the MRI argued that the key features of family life were the patterns that maintained balance and stability, the homeostatic, negative feedback mechanisms that kept a family functioning within an emotional range. For example, a child's delinquency would appear in response to parental arguments but would then have the impact of keeping the parents together to manage the delinquency.[22] The combination of the one-way mirror and the Structured Interview would teach future family therapists to look for these kinds of interactions.

In this emphasis on teaching trainees how to look, we can hear echoes of what Lorraine Daston and Peter Galison have characterized as trained judgment, "the necessity of seeing scientifically through an interpretive eye" via the cultivation of perceptual expertise in how to interpret images.[23] Similarly, newly specialized radiologists of the early twentieth century called for expertise in reading X-rays in legal as well as clinical contexts, with the claim that X-rays did not speak for themselves, particularly in the courtroom, but instead required specific expertise for their interpretation.[24] Family therapists' attentiveness to teaching students how to look was thus not unique but part of a more widespread call over the course of the twentieth century for expertise in observation in order to secure a particular kind of objectivity; at the same time observation was justified in terms of its self-evidence and transparency.

One of the features of one-way mirrors in these pedagogical contexts was that students could watch a therapy session unfold without reminding patients of their presence and disrupting the therapeutic process. Other therapists used the mirrors in ways that suggested they could function as more interactive, even permeable boundaries. For example, Salvador Minuchin first began using one-way mirrors while he worked at the Wiltwyck School for Boys during the late fifties and sixties. He and his colleagues deemphasized insight, like other contemporary family therapists, and developed a highly structured approach to family therapy that focused on communication, generational patterns of organization, and affect.[25] When Minuchin left Wiltwyck in 1965 for the Philadelphia Child Guidance Clinic, he brought his burgeoning approach to family therapy and his investment in one-way mirrors with him. A 1978 *New Yorker* article by Janet Malcolm on family therapy begins with a vivid description of her experience behind the mirror with Minuchin. Malcolm recounts how he repeatedly interrupted and redirected a therapy session conducted by a graduate student with a family in which the daughter had anorexia. Minuchin called the student on a phone in the therapy room to give her instructions on how to proceed, and he entered the room himself on several occasions to make a statement before hastily withdrawing again behind the mirror.[26]

This episode highlights a key feature of family therapists' use of one-way mirrors. The mirror enabled them to watch a therapy session without being present in the room, but it was a breakable boundary. Because therapists (whether supervisors or students) were watching in real time, they could interact with the session's participants. During the 1970s, a group of therapists in Milan developed a distinctive and influential approach to family treatment that routinized their use of the one-way mirror as an interactive threshold. In their model of systemic therapy, they conducted sessions with two therapists in the room with a family and two other therapists behind a one-way screen. The therapists who watched unseen from behind the screen could intervene by calling the other therapists out of the room to request information or make recommendations. All four therapists conferred at the end of the session in order to share opinions and make a collective intervention or assignment for the family.[27]

Thus while films and later videotapes had certain advantages over one-way mirrors (they could be viewed at a time other than the actual therapy session, edited, interspersed with explanatory intertitles, copied, sold, and played repeatedly), mirrors had the potential for live interaction between those being seen and those doing the seeing. Family therapists used one-way mirrors as a technology of perception by structuring the relationship between observer and subject in ways that invoked an ideal of objectivity grounded in nonintervention but retained the possibility for breaking the barrier between those on opposite sides of the mirror.

In contrast, films gave family therapists a different level of control from that possible in demonstration interviews and one-way mirrors. Although they all allowed observers to watch therapy in action, with

film the therapists could edit scenes, splice multiple sessions together, and include explanatory text. For example, in the film *In and Out
of Psychosis*, Nathan Ackerman presented excerpts from his consultations with one family over the course of fifteen months, beginning in
November 1959.[28] The film opened with white-on-black text that introduced the participants as a sixteen-year-old daughter who had been having hallucinatory communication with a kingdom named Queendom,
her mother and father, and her maternal grandmother. One of the intertitles explained, "The focus of these interviews is the emotional link
between the disorder of family relationships and the girl's breakdown."
The room arrangement consisted of a half-circle of chairs behind a low
table with several microphones on it, facing the fixed position of the
camera.

The bulk of the film came from Ackerman's second meeting with
this family, in which he explored the alignment between daughter and
father, the lack of open discussion about sex in the family, and the intru-
sive, domineering presence of the grandmother. The film also included
scenes from sessions one month and fifteen months later. Explanatory
text appeared at regular intervals to guide the viewer by providing
commentary on family dynamics, nonverbal behavior including bodily
positions, and Ackerman's interventions. The film concluded with an
optimistic statement that claimed, "The progress of the psychotherapy
of this patient and her family is good. There is a substantial change
for the better in [the daughter]. There is also a shift toward health in
the parental relationships, both in terms of improved marital adaptation
and improved child care. . . . The overall picture is one of impressive
change in the direction of re-adaptation toward health." The film operates in what film scholars have called the expository mode of documentary because it addresses the viewer directly through its commentary,
its "voice of authority" lies in the film itself rather than in someone in
the film, and it is structured around meeting the need for a solution to a
problem.[29]

The presumption of documentary realism functioned in Ackerman's
films to offer seemingly unimpeded access to the therapeutic process.[30]
Indeed, in a 1969 article on types of family therapy approaches, Christian Beels and Andrew Ferber characterized watching therapy films and
videos, along with listening to audiotapes, as a kind of "direct experience" akin to observing demonstration interviews or ongoing therapy.[31]
However, decisions about camera placement, film quality, lighting, editing, and the content of intertitles shaped what and how a viewer could

see, thereby undercutting the alleged directness of the film. Although the film did not acknowledge the interpretative work being done by these elements, they functioned to guide the viewer, presumably a family therapist-in-training, into seeing certain aspects of family life as pathological and ultimately treatable.

In his use of films as pedagogical and therapeutic tools, Ackerman was not alone among family therapists or psychiatrists in general. Four prominent family therapists (Ackerman, Bowen, Jackson, and Carl Whitaker) conducted an interview with the same family in a 1964 instructional film series.[32] Following each session, the given therapist talked with the family's long-term therapist about his understanding of the family and gave an explanation of his interactions with them, which were not automatically apparent from viewing the therapy session. These didactic conversations served a function similar to that of the intertitles in Ackerman's films by guiding viewers' interpretation of the films. As Alison Winter has shown, other midcentury psychiatric researchers turned to film as a technology of authenticity in their studies of memory in ways that shaped the history of modern selfhood.[33]

Some family therapists used also film or video in order to enable family members to observe their own patterns of interaction, as well as their change over time.[34] In a uniquely longitudinal arrangement, Murray Bowen videotaped his monthly psychotherapy sessions with two separate couples over fifteen years, beginning in 1968. Students and other professionals watched the sessions over closed-circuit television in an adjoining amphitheater at the Medical College of Virginia in Richmond, and then the couple joined the observers and interacted with them at the end of the sessions. As part of a research project, Bowen showed the couples clips from earlier sessions and used their responses as part of the ongoing therapy.[35] This kind of therapeutically justified interaction between observer and observed stood in contrast to the noninterventionist ideal of naturalistic observation animating his 1950s research at NIMH, on which Bowen had based his claims to knowledge of family life.

The use of film and video by early family therapists highlights some of the salient features of those media for clinical and pedagogical purposes: their reproducibility, ability to be stored and replayed at a later time, and capacity for modification and arrangement.[36] Although the temporal implications of reproduction, archiving, and editing set film apart from one-way mirrors, both types of visual technologies underscored the importance of observation in the clinical practices, research methodologies, and pedagogical strategies of early family therapists.

In training a new kind of therapist through their use of visual technologies, Ackerman and other early family therapists also helped to define a new therapeutic subject. Wendy Kozol has argued that "postwar mass media fashioned a cultural ideal of family through stories and pictures about a world of middle-class domesticity."[37] Family therapy training films similarly drew on and contributed to postwar cultural and social scientific ideals of family through a "visual portrait of domesticity,"[38] framed in this case in therapeutic terms. In addition, the one-way mirror and films made possible a type of clinical spectatorship that fostered a new kind of practitioner, the family therapist, and a new kind of therapeutic subject, the observable family.[39]

Spectatorship and the Family in Popular Culture

Beyond the context of training programs, the interdependency among visual technologies, therapeutic practices, and conceptions of pathology or deviance was also apparent in family therapists' approach to popular culture. Some therapists harnessed their emphasis on the visual to popular concerns about family life by participating in public forums, such as a 1961 conference in California organized to address the question, "What is happening to the family in suburbia?" There, John Weakland discussed the Palo Alto group's ongoing research project on families, schizophrenia, and communication. He concluded his talk by drawing connections between his group's research on schizophrenia and the broader concerns of the conference by commenting on what he called "compulsory utopias and their treatment." Weakland asked, " 'How can difficulties of the sort we see in schizophrenic patients occur in such nice settings as we often see them in pleasant families and suburbia?' Maybe it's a lead into that question to suggest that maybe things can be too nice. . . . You see, one problem these families have is not just certain things *are* nice, but that things *have to* be nice. They're supposed to be nice and they're supposed so strongly, you might even say forcefully, that they darned well better be; so if someone indicates that they're not, you're in trouble."[40] These comments pointed to the underbelly of the suburban ideal of the postwar period, which also concerned contemporary cultural critics of the conformity of suburbia and mass society such as William Whyte and David Reisman, whom Ackerman and others explicitly referenced in their work.[41]

The optimistic view of expert therapeutic solutions, the tenuousness of mental health, and the extensive concerns about the hazards of family life were all on display in the 1959 television program *The Fine Line*, discussed in the introduction. In the opening sequences, the show's narrator urged viewers to keep watching because "seeds of insanity might be lurking in your own home."[42] The show illustrated that even the proverbial man on the street had anxieties and obsessive thoughts that emerged once he was on the psychoanalytic couch. The show also asked how one could avoid crossing that fine line between sanity and insanity.

In answer, the narrator turned to the family. Actors performed two breakfast scenes in which a mother and father talked to their young-adult daughter about her activities the night before. As Salvador Minuchin remarked in a different context, such quotidian interactions were the "warp and woof, the very fabric of our raw material."[43] In one scene, the family became embroiled in a series of double binds, while in the other they did not. With Gregory Bateson and Don Jackson serving as the experts, the show discussed how double binds affected the mental instability of those long caught in them. They thus used the program as a means for conveying their theory about family communication and schizophrenia to a broader popular audience through a visual medium.

Family therapists further bolstered their claims by analyzing the pathological interactions of fictional families represented in plays and television shows. For example, Ibsen's plays were a recurring target of analysis during the first decade of publication of *Family Process*.[44] The journal similarly published articles on T. S. Eliot's play *The Cocktail Party* and on Brechtian theater as a model for family therapy. It also published an article on the television series *All in the Family*, which framed the series as a mirror of American culture and a dramatization of the theories of some therapists regarding the family as a homeostatic system.[45] Outside the pages of *Family Process*, Don Jackson found parallels between his research on marriage and the representation of the problematic interactions between the two central characters in Mike Nichols's Broadway production of Neil Simon's play, *The Odd Couple*. In 1965 Jackson wrote to Nichols to praise him for his comedic work with Elaine May and to note the similarities between Jackson's work and *The Odd Couple*. He described his own account of marriage in a forthcoming article in the *Archives of General Psychiatry* as "curiously like the write-ups I have read of 'The Odd Couple,'" despite the fact that the play's characters were unmarried roommates rather than a husband and wife. In a comment that summed up his sympathetic reading of cultural productions, Jackson noted that he and other behavioral scientists "have a great deal to learn from artists."[46]

By applying their family systems framework to popular culture, family therapists promoted the relevance of their field beyond the walls of the therapy room. In turn, their clinical interventions with the individual families under their care perpetuated the visions of family life represented in postwar American culture. During the 1950s and 1960s, family dramas played out in therapy sessions with families who were not composed of actors and who worked without a script. Such dramas were directed by family therapists, who often used the language of theater and drama both to describe families as units that performed their patterns of interactions and structural tensions and to portray their own therapeutic roles and interventions as performance.

The Politics of Performance in Family Research

By the 1960s, family therapists had expanded their visually oriented methodologies in their research practices as well as their clinical and pedagogical work. They went beyond the naturalistic observation of schizophrenic families, as discussed in chapter 4, in order to study a growing number of problems, including delinquency. The following case study of a research project on families and delinquency highlights the close ties of research techniques to visual technologies, as well as to normative models of family life.

In 1967, Salvador Minuchin and four colleagues published *Families of the Slums: An Exploration of Their Structure and Treatment* based on the findings of their NIMH-funded project on family therapy at the Wiltwyck School for Boys.[47] The project was significant not only for its invocation of the culture concept, as discussed in chapter 3, but also for the visual orientation of its novel assessment tools and therapeutic techniques. Research and treatment went hand in hand in the project, as did conceptions of pathological and normal families. The Wiltwyck project also reflected the renewed interest in the late 1950s and 1960s in the role of family in the creation of delinquency.[48] Much of that attention addressed the role of poverty in family environments that fostered delinquency, just as *Families of the Slums* did, but popular postwar concerns about delinquency and family also extended to white, middle-class adolescents.[49] Such concerns were exemplified by the families of the teenage characters in *Rebel Without a Cause*, including James Dean's overbearing mother and apron-wearing father, as well as the 1954 congressional hearings on the deleterious effects of comic books, radio, and TV on children.

The reformatory context of the Wiltwyck project differentiated it from most family therapy research or clinical projects and directly shaped its course. According to the researchers' stated goals, "We wanted to study the structure and process of disorganized, low socioeconomic families that had each produced more than one acting-out (delinquent) child; and we hoped to experiment with and develop further therapeutic approaches designed for such families."[50] Boys came to Wiltwyck through the juvenile court system, as they did for the few other clinicians who began conducting family therapy with delinquent patients. One of these was Charles Fulweiler, who worked for a period with the guidance clinic of the Alameda County Probation Department and received referrals from probation officers.[51] In contrast, most family therapists were child psychiatrists or worked with patients with schizophrenia or other psychiatric problems, and they typically drew their patients through referrals from physician colleagues, hospitals or institutions in which patients had sought some form of treatment and happened to get family therapy, or research subject recruitment efforts.

The Wiltwyck team's claim for the significance of its scholarship had at least two components: expanding on existing research techniques and providing psychotherapy to previously underserved populations. The researchers wrote that their areas of interest were "largely uncharted. . . . The reader will note that ours is not a 'typical' clinical study. We did not utilize traditional diagnostic categories or employ traditional tests such as intelligence tests; nor were we concerned with individual personality appraisals. . . . The development of special psychotherapeutic techniques for this segment of the population was delayed because conceptualizations about treatment are dependent on the social and scientific setting of the theoretician and the population he studies."[52] Moreover, the project's novel research procedures and clinical techniques operated explicitly in a visual and performative register that the Wiltwyck team justified based on the needs of the population under study.

Minuchin and his coauthors—Braulio Montalvo, Bernard Guerney Jr., Bernice Rosman, and Florence Schumer—characterized the Wiltwyck boys' lives and prospects in bleak terms:

These children live in dire poverty; they have seen alcoholism, homosexuality, addiction, promiscuity, prostitution and mental illness. Much is in their own families. Pathology and poverty have seeped into their lives with such a pervasive, dark insistence that many of them know of no other existence or reality. . . . These are the children who have challenged us. Their families are impoverished, disadvantaged, unstable, "hard-core" families. They are mostly from minority ethnic backgrounds (Negro and Puerto Rican), and they dwell in the congested, rat-infested ghettos and slums of New York City.[53]

The research in *Families of the Slums* drew on family therapy sessions, as well as the results of behavioral and psychological projection tests. The project's staff claimed that their own backgrounds made them particularly well suited for working with the linguistic, racial, and economic backgrounds of the families under study. The project included three psychiatrists, two psychologists, and two social workers. This group contained two fluent Spanish speakers (one from Argentina, one from Puerto Rico), one African American, three therapists with psychoanalytic training, and five professionals who had extensive experience working with children designated, in their terms, delinquent, underprivileged, and/or minority.

To characterize the families more precisely, the researchers at Wiltwyck employed two assessment procedures that they developed specifically for their own study. The first was designed "to elucidate some of the structural and dynamic features of our delinquent-producing families" by observing how family members interacted as they discussed a set of five questions and performed several tasks together.[54] The Family Task procedure, as it was called, lasted about forty-five minutes and was designed as an assessment tool that enabled families to perform their typical patterns of interaction. The Family Task assignments were prerecorded to avoid giving a central role to those family members who could read. Questions included asking the family to plan a meal, decide how to spend $10, and identify who in their family was the most bossy, was the biggest troublemaker, got away with murder, had the most fights, or was the biggest crybaby. One of the tasks was to use blocks to build a copy of a premade structure that was sitting on a table.[55] Each assessment session took place in a room with sofa and chairs arranged in a semicircle facing a one-way mirror, and they were all audio-recorded and then transcribed. Behind the mirror, one observer listened to the family's conversation and recorded who was speaking, while a second observer, who could not hear the conversation, wrote a running commentary on the nonverbal interactions and activities in the room.

Minuchin and his colleagues thereby combined the use of audio technology, which recorded sound but not visual information, with notes on posture, facial expression, bodily proximity, gesture, and other nonverbal forms of interaction and activity. They analyzed the Family Task procedure by counting the number of "verbalizations" and the target of those verbalizations (e.g., mother, young children); by scoring verbal statements according to categories designed to describe family members' interactions (e.g., leadership, behavior control, guidance, agreement) rather than the content of the statements; and by qualitatively addressing the content of the families' responses.[56]

In addition to the Family Task, the Wiltwyck team designed a pictorial apperceptive projective instrument named the Wiltwyck Family Interaction Apperception Technique (FIAT; see fig. 8), which they based on a modification of the Thematic Apperception Test (TAT). Developed by the American psychologists Henry A. Murray and Christiana Morgan in the mid-1930s, the TAT was initially a tool for clinical assessment based on stories told about a series of pictorial images. By the 1940s, it had also increasingly become an instrument for psychological research on personality.[57] The FIAT differed from the TAT in several ways. It featured images of multiple people in order to concentrate on issues relevant for the Wiltwyck study, and the instructions specifically called for coding the research subjects' stories for their comments about family interactions, by contrast with the TAT which assessed intrapsychic, psychodynamic phenomena. For instance, the scoring system to code the stories about the FIAT images focused on eight variables: "control, guidance, acceptance of responsibility, nurturance, affection, cooperation, aggression, and family harmony."[58] Just as other projective techniques, such as the Rorschach inkblot test, aligned with specific concepts of the self, so too the FIAT worked in tandem with an understanding of its research subject, the structured and interactive family.[59] The transition to a family perspective was thus embedded in this assessment instrument at the level of reframing what a projective apperceptive instrument could assess, namely, family patterns rather than personality, as well as in the iconography of families in the FIAT pictures themselves.

The developers of the FIAT claimed that "this instrument took into consideration a number of problems faced by those using projective techniques with respect to eliciting maximum productivity from

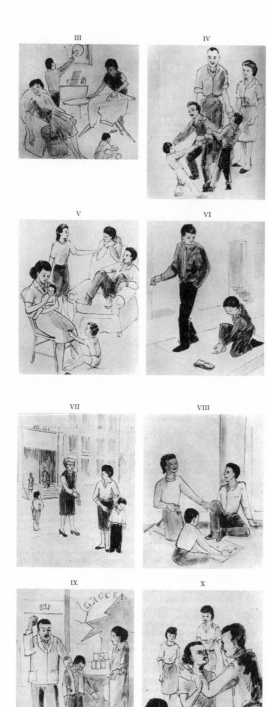

Figure 8. The Wiltwyck Family Interaction Apperception Technique (FIAT). From Salvador Minuchin, Braulio Montalvo, Bernard G. Guerney, Bernice L. Rosman, and Florence Schumer, *Families of the Slums: An Exploration of the Structure and Treatment* (New York, 1967), Appendix D, 438–439. Copyright © 1967 Salvador Minuchin. Reprinted by permission of Basic Books, a member of the Perseus Book Group.

various populations."[60] To this end, the researchers designed the scenes to be familiar and recognizable to the population under study, unlike most standard projective tools, which Minuchin and his colleagues criticized as ineffective for people with diverse educational or cultural backgrounds. The situations portrayed were supposed to be simple and concrete so that children as well as adults could respond. In addition, the figures were drawn with racial characteristics that were "deliberately indeterminate" to make the test appropriate for administering to multi-racial groups.[61] The FIAT images visually invoked race by refusing to specify it, and this became the very grounds on which the researchers legitimated the results of their study with racially mixed research subjects.

The Wiltwyck team justified the design of the FIAT on the basis of the racial, economic, and cultural variability of the research subjects, but its images were not about race per se. That is, Minuchin and his colleagues did not use the images in the FIAT to make claims about racial categories themselves. By contrast, nineteenth- and twentieth-century comparative illustrations and collections of photographs highlighted differences in skin tone either to argue for the fixity of racial types or to challenge that alleged fixity, as W. E. B. DuBois did in his 1906 sociological and photographic study of race mixing.[62]

The FIAT cards also illustrated the continued importance of the visual in American concepts of race even in the context of the postwar ascendance of cultural and environmental rather than biological theories of human variation. Postwar theories of race entailed a shift among anthropologists and biologists from studying morphologically based racial differences, such as cranial size, to researching genetic variability in populations and giving renewed attention to cultural differences. In part a repudiation of the Nazis' use of biological justifications of racial inferiority to rationalize the Holocaust, the postwar emphasis on cultural and environmental explanations for group differences was indebted to the anthropologists Franz Boas and Ashley Montagu, and it received its iconic articulation in the 1950 statement *The Race Question* by the United Nations Educational, Scientific and Cultural Organization (UNESCO).[63]

Although they modified the images in their projective instrument to accord with their understandings of the distinctive social experiences of their research subjects, Minuchin and his colleagues retained a more conventional nuclear family structure as their model of healthy family functioning. They explicitly defined their baseline family structure in terms described by the sociologist Talcott Parsons. According to their reading of Parsons, the structure of the nuclear family derived from differentiation on two axes: hierarchy, associated with generational differences between parents and children, and instrumental versus expressive function, associated with respective gender roles of husbands and wives as well as sons and daughters.[64] In this model, proper maintenance of roles was integral to a healthy family.

In contrast to the clearly defined generational and gender roles in Parsons's model, the Wiltwyck team argued that its research families were distinguished by a series of unstable father figures; an unpredictable pattern of parental authority in which parents were at times in absolute, autocratic control and at other times completely helpless; and a breakdown in communication between parents and children, with increased solidarity among siblings and opposition to parents.[65]

> From the beginning we were impressed by the striking fact that more than three-fourths of the families to which we had been exposed had no father or stable father figure. . . . For her part, the mother seemed able to respond to and interact with the children only when they were submissive or requesting some infantile basic need be met. . . . The mothers seemed to see themselves as powerless, helpless, and overwhelmed by the children's demands. . . . When a child asked for parental guidance, the mother would respond with a counter-demand for the child's autonomy: "You should know"; or she would relinquish authority to a sibling.[66]

Basing its findings on the research subjects' performances on the Family Tasks and their projective responses to the FIAT, *Families of the Slums* painted a picture of an erratic family existence in which children lacked stability and clear guidance. Coupling therapeutic recommendations with recognition of the importance of social programs and structural change in employment for improving their patients' lives, the study returned in its analysis to the "tangle of pathology," to use Daniel Patrick Moynihan's words, of the low-income, black matriarchal family. On this point, the Wiltwyck study was explicitly in conversation with social science research of the 1930s to 1960s, including work by Oscar Lewis, Thomas Pettigrew and Kenneth Clark. Such scholars developed theories regarding the culture of poverty and damaged black psyche, and they portrayed the black family in particular as a pathological matriarchy with roots in the social conditions of slavery.[67]

As for the therapist's role in the project, the authors of *Families of the Slums* characterized it as unusual in that it combined traditional psychodynamic elements, such as "interpreting underlying dynamics," with nontraditional elements, such as assigning tasks and directing the family drama on either side of the mirror: "At times he is like the director of a play, suggesting that the family members try to comply, pressuring them into seeking new methods of interacting, and demanding that they fulfill his expectations."[68] Through the play analogy, Minuchin and his colleagues echoed the dramatic associations used by other family therapists in their characterizations of family problems and their depictions of therapists as theatrical directors.

Minuchin thus emphasized the performative dimensions of the pathology of the families themselves and of his therapeutic interventions. The Wiltwyck team members complemented their research-oriented use of the one-way mirror in the Family Task procedure with a therapeutic use of the one-way mirror that instantiated their emphasis on performance. In one case, a father regularly criticized his older son yet seemed to want to help him, while the son appeared to want parental acceptance yet regularly provoked his father, which intensified his father's criticisms. The therapist directed the father to highlight positive aspects of his son and the son to avoid antagonizing his father in order to stop blocking his father's support. Behind a one-way screen, a second therapist observed with the mother and a second son. The mother expressed her discontent with her husband's "preaching" and her desire to protect her son, to which the therapist responded that the wife and her husband were fighting through their son, which prevented father and son from developing an independent relationship. The therapist further tried to restructure the family's pattern of interacting with the following observation and instruction:

> The therapist . . . noted that her tendency was to empathize with the attacked child, label her husband the aggressor, and intervene in such a way that she and her husband soon became involved in a heated argument which "freed," and at the same time isolated, the son. The therapist suggested to the wife that she should now go into the other room and try to help the husband support the son. His suggestion clearly challenged the automatic pathway of mother-to-son-to-father, calling into play the heretofore nonexistent cooperative pathway of wife-to-husband-to-son.[69]

Minuchin analyzed this sequence and others like it by considering the roles of the observer, the participants in the task, and the therapist. The Wiltwyck group aimed to shift the reaction of the observer, the mother, from quickly engaging in established patterns of interaction, even from behind the mirror, to identifying with the therapist in his management of family conflicts. For the participants, the therapists aimed to disrupt a routinized sequence of automatic responses through the assigned task.

They also noted the impact on participants of working on a task in front of observing family members: "The consciousness of being observed is an intermediate step in the process of introspection. *The participant observed in himself what he assumes the unseen observer is focusing on.* This sense of being observed indirectly brings the observer's role to the participating members as well."[70] The Wiltwyck team framed this internalization of the unseen observer as a part of the therapeutic process that produced a form of self-disciplining in which family members modified their own behavior according to their presumptions about the focus of the observers, unseen behind the one-way mirror.[71]

Overall, the project entailed a reassessment of several aspects of apperceptive testing and psychotherapy, and visually oriented techniques played a central role on all fronts. As explanation for their development of new tools and techniques, the study's authors explicitly discussed the challenges and hazards of using more standard psychodynamic psychotherapy with their population: "The range and content of their life experiences and value systems are in sharp contrast to those of the middle-class professional. Their lack of verbal and conceptual skills, special linguistic code, motoric 'acting-out' orientation, nonintrospective approach, and the communicational difficulties between therapist and patient contribute to the serious limitations of the 'talking therapies' in general."[72] The researchers also positioned their project in contrast to the still-young field of family therapy. "The conceptual models in the growing literature on family systems are not fully applicable to our group. These are models of the American middle-class family (or sometimes the stable working-class family); they focus on intimate interspouse communication and on the socialization process of the child in a child-centered family."[73] Claiming that their techniques marked a change from psychodynamic therapy and the burgeoning practices of family therapy, Minuchin and his colleagues framed them as a necessary adaptation to the unique demands of the families being targeted.

In an afterword, the authors of *Families of the Slums* commented on the project's success. They based their assessment on clinical outcome, as well as an experimental research design involving twelve experimental families and ten control families. They considered seven of the experimental families to have been successfully treated. The criteria were not tied to an improvement in economic status or a decline in delinquent behaviors but rather to the modes of communication and generational lines established. Minuchin and his colleagues also framed the project as a reform-minded expansion of therapy services to a population that psychotherapy generally had not reached. This framing was apropos of the populations generally served by family therapists and psychoanalysts in the United States during the 1950s, although it elided the longer history of psychotherapeutic interventions with delinquents in the child guidance movement as well as the tradition of social justice and free clinics among early twentieth-century Austrian and German analysts.[74]

Ironically, the "special case" or unique status of the poor families treated at Wiltwyck later came undone when Minuchin expanded his use of the techniques developed particularly for families of the slums. For example, he identified the problem of "affective suction" at Wiltwyck: "The therapeutic problem, then, is how to enter into a family system in order to challenge it while avoiding, at the same time, the power of that system to induct the therapist into the patterns of interaction that maintain current homeostasis."[75] This would become a challenge for the whole field of family therapy. Minuchin himself applied his theory of enmeshed families, his assessment technique of the Family Task, and his clinical methods of structural family therapy, which he developed with delinquent sons, to his well-known later work on anorexic daughters.[76]

Beyond Minuchin's justification for his work at Wiltwyck on the political grounds of helping a disadvantaged population, other family therapists made explicit claims for the politics of their therapeutic practices on the basis of their emphasis on the visual. By the late 1960s, one family therapist insisted that the "visibility and openness" encouraged through family therapy

> may be instrumental to a search for equality and common purpose among people, [since] the tyrannies of groups over individuals, and the conspiracies of individuals against themselves, and even the maintenance of incompetence and inaction, are dependent on secrecy . . . . We are, families and therapists, in pursuit of the moment, in pursuit of confrontation and embrace and dialogue in the clarion, crisp now. We suspect the unseen, the unseeable: psychoanalysis' reverence for the past and for the metaphysics of internal dialogue fades; families and therapists meet together and discover hopefulness in understanding and experiencing the present.[77]

Thus the emphasis on the visible was re-framed as "openness" and given political momentum and weight that resonated with the "clarion, crisp now" of the late sixties. Nathan Ackerman echoed this characterization when he wrote in 1970, "It is hardly an accident of history that this last decade—luridly identified as the 'wild and explosive sixties,' 'the unbelievable sixties'—has ushered in a radical shift in our perspectives on human nature, interpersonal relationships, social values, individual and family breakdown, and the theory of healing."[78] Such depictions of the political resonances of family therapy highlighted the liberating potential of family therapists' visual orientation, but they also disavowed their own techniques for disciplining observation in their claims of openness.

Even as they praised the virtues of visibility and openness, early family therapists were more circumspect about issues of power and clinical spectatorship that subtly shaped the relationship between those being observed and those doing the observing. Films and transcripts of therapy sessions reproduced family members' words, in contrast to clinician-written case summaries that spoke solely in the voice of the therapist. However, the films and transcripts did not speak for or represent the families in an unmediated way, and the therapy setting and therapists' interventions organized and gave meaning to the families' presence and actions. Such issues came to the fore in a controversy in the late 1960s involving the Philadelphia Child Guidance Clinic (PCGC), where Minuchin served as director after leaving Wiltwyck in 1965. Braulio Montalvo, who left Wiltwyck with Minuchin, and Jay Haley, who had left the MRI in Palo Alto, were also part of the clinical staff of the PCGC. As part of a community initiative with the poor, predominately African American and Puerto Rican community in which it was located, PCGC sponsored a project in which a small group of teenage girls made a film about their families. The clinicians thereby gave a camera to individuals who were typically in front of the camera lens or one-way mirror in family therapy rather than behind it.[79] The girls' film, which did not consistently portray their families in an idealized light, sparked a controversy in which community leaders demanded that PCGC destroy or turn over the film, but Minuchin, Haley, and others at PCGC refused.[80] The controversy not only spoke to the politics of observation and representation in ways that echoed the ideological struggles over cross-cultural representation between ethnographers and ethnographic research subjects but also implicated the politically charged relations between a clinical institution and its surrounding community.

The media of film and television became important vehicles not only for conveying popular representations of family life in the 1950s but also for iterating the interpersonal patterns that constituted the target of family therapists' interventions. The postwar shift from treating individual patients to treating whole families entailed new attention to observable interactions among family members, as opposed to the psychoanalytic examination of unresolved internal conflicts. The visual framework guiding family therapists' use of film, closed-circuit television, and one-way mirrors in education, research, and therapeutic interventions underscored the field's orientation toward observable interactions rather than intrapsychic problems.

However, the visual technologies of family therapy education were not inherently self-explanatory, despite therapists' praise for their objectivity and transparency. In the case of both Ackerman and the MRI staff, educators were teaching new family therapists *how* to observe and thereby understand particular types of family interaction and therapist interventions. Once appropriately trained, the therapists came to the films, one-way mirrors, demonstration sessions, and transcripts prepared to watch them for particular types of interactions. Though glossed as self-evident means of capturing reality, the recording technologies in particular served a mediating function by positioning the observer as an omniscient, nonintervening fly on the wall yet nevertheless provided a means for the therapist to edit and frame the films or audiotapes of therapy sessions. The intertitles and editing choices in Ackerman's films guided viewers to certain conclusions, as did the Structured Interview and the theoretical orientation toward seeing family homeostasis at the MRI and the structural use of family subunits, one-way mirrors, and dramatic interventions by Minuchin at Wiltwyck and the Philadelphia Child Guidance Clinic.

In all these cases, family therapists opened up the process of therapy for viewing but then worked to stabilize viewers' interpretation. They thus educated other members of their field to become observers who were oriented toward seeing the family as a homeostatic system and therefore intervened to disrupt and then rearrange families' cyclical patterns. Furthermore, their educational, therapeutic, and research practices contributed to the production of a new therapeutic subject, the family system, which was in contrast to the psychoanalytic subject. The use of visual technologies such as films and one-way mirrors was central to this process.

EPILOGUE

In 1971, filmmaker Craig Gilbert and his documentary film crew spent seven months recording the everyday exploits of a white California family, the Louds, for the series *An American Family*, which PBS broadcast in 1973. The camera captured Pat Loud asking her husband for a divorce, the participation of the Louds' oldest son Lance in the gay community in New York City's Chelsea district, and other, more mundane matters, such as the morning breakfast routine. When *An American Family* aired in 1973, it drew widespread attention, including a cover story in *Newsweek* and a feature in the *New York Times Magazine*.[1] The prominent coverage of the series underscored the broad-based interest in the state of the family at that time.

A product of the early 1970s, *An American Family* registered in a different idiom than did *Rebel Without a Cause*. It was a documentary in the experimental style of cinema verité rather than a Hollywood studio movie; it was more in tune with the humanistic psychology of the 1960s and early 1970s than the authoritative psychiatric expert of the 1950s; and it focused on divorce rather than delinquency. Such differences were also symptomatic of broader changes in family and political life during the period. As Steven Mintz and Susan Kellogg have argued, "The dramatic social transformations taking place in sexual values and in women's and young people's lives would, in the 1960s and 1970s, undermine the patterns of early marriage, large families, and stable divorce rates characteristic of the postwar era."[2] By the early 1970s, anxieties about family decline multiplied in the face of increasing rates of divorce, single parenthood, and mothers' participation in the labor force. Such anxieties were further intertwined with fears about national decline epitomized by the failures of the Vietnam War and the OPEC oil embargo of 1973–74.[3] Tellingly, the 1973 *Newsweek* issue with the Loud family on the cover, accompanied by the banner "The Broken Family," fell between other cover stories that year on Watergate, Vietnam, and the energy crisis. A growing focus on divorce and other transitions in a family's life cycle was similarly an important transition in the target of family therapists' attention by the 1970s.

Despite these important differences and the social and political upheavals separating the 1950s from the early 1970s, *Rebel Without a Cause* and *An American Family* shared an implicit association between family and therapeutic culture that only grew after *Rebel*'s release in 1955. In the media blitz that followed *An American Family*, Pat Loud explained the family's rationale for participating in Gilbert's project in terms that resonated with the strengthening intersections between the familial and the therapeutic domains in the decades leading up to the show: "We really believed, so help me, that by letting all of us hang out, we might help to free some pent-up soul out there."[4] Although the Loud family did not undergo family therapy on TV, the series illustrates the significant role of observation and performance in the cultural consolidation of family life, psychological explanations, and therapeutic intervention. This consolidation became almost commonsensical in the decades after World War II, and it was exemplified in the emergence of the clinical field of family therapy.[5]

The PBS series is also a fitting conclusion to a history of family therapy because it raises questions about the production of knowledge about families. In her analysis of *An American Family*, Paula Rabinowitz describes the series' representational approach of cinema verité as one that "depicts history and subjectivity through vignettes of intimate life."[6] Similar vignettes were central to the research, clinical, and pedagogical practices of postwar family therapists who employed them as evidence in their development of theories of the family oriented toward observable interpersonal interactions.

The Pathological Family has examined the making of family therapy by training a close eye on the target of the field's therapeutic interventions, the family. During the decades after World War II, family therapists and researchers developed a heterogeneous array of theories and practices that engaged with contemporary visions of family life and changing understandings of pathology. The field's development entailed refiguring the family into the primary unit of disease and treatment, thereby transforming it into a therapeutic subject. Clinicians and researchers in the new field fostered normative visions of family life through the standards, explicit or implicit, against which patients were held and through the metaphors, such as homeostasis and ecology, that structured their conceptions of family pathology and their therapeutic practices. In their approach to families as therapeutic subjects, these therapists also refigured the meaning of disease. Schizophrenia and delinquency, the hallmark problems of the field's first decades, came to be seen as disorders of the family, rather than the moral failings, psychological conflicts, or the biological makeup of an individual. The therapists located the solution to schizophrenia and delinquency in therapeutic interventions into families' recurrent patterns of interaction and structure. Embedded in the circular patterns of a family system, pathology became understandable and treatable through observing and intervening in interactions among family members, as opposed to other methods such as accessing the unconscious or ordering biochemical assays. No longer merely the source of psychopathology, the family itself became the patient.

The ways in which family therapists made the family into a therapeutic subject were not easily realized, nor was success inevitable. Rather, it took much work (logistical, professional, conceptual, material) to effect a change from an individual to a family orientation. In addition, even though family therapists arrayed themselves (albeit to varying degrees) against psychoanalysis and an emphasis on the individuated psyche, they shared with their rivals the post-war "romance of American psychology," which entailed an expansion in psychological experts, psychopathological explanations for problems like delinquency and racial inequality, and psychotherapeutic solutions. The history of family therapy thus illuminates some of the complex heterogeneity of the therapeutic orientation of the twentieth century.

In developing their own approach as a counterpoint to the then-dominant psychoanalytic orientation of psychiatry, family therapists regularly discussed the importance of observing families and family therapy in action for the diverse purposes of assessment, research, training, and treatment. Like cinema verité, family therapists' epistemology of observing and documenting family life presumed that meaningful patterns became apparent in small exchanges and the little moments of daily life and that watching and recording provided a more objective view of family dynamics and the therapy process than family histories or narrative case reports could. They explicitly framed their willingness to put their therapy on display—whether in transcripts, before the camera, on stage, or in front of the one-way mirror—in terms of a politics of openness, which they counterpoised to the confidentiality of psychoanalysis.

The interdisciplinarity that threaded through the history of family therapy also had political resonances in the decades after World War II. Family therapists self-consciously drew on nonclinical fields such as cybernetics, anthropology, and sociology. They claimed that their turn from the individual to the family entailed recognition of the context of disease or deviance and that once they had recognized the crucial role of the family context, it was a small step to move beyond the family to the larger social context. In so doing, they contributed to contemporary socioenvironmental approaches to pathology. In the postwar years, social psychiatry and social medicine, like family therapy, were informed by the social and behavioral sciences, and they represented the environmentally oriented, activist wing of clinical practitioners. Beyond the realms of medicine and psychotherapy, interdisciplinarity itself became associated with the values of democracy and openness in the sciences and social sciences, as historians such as Jamie Cohen-Cole, Peter Galison, and David Hollinger have shown.[7]

By the 1970s, the changing contours of the field had resulted in an expansion in the kinds of problems seen as amenable to treatment as well as recognition of shifting family demographics. Clinicians made claims for the viability of treating a widening array of issues at the level of the family, from eating disorders to life cycle transitions to sexual violence. Demographic changes such as the rising divorce rates of the 1970s and the growing number of single-parent households and same-sex parents by the turn of the twenty-first century also affected the clinical field by altering the prevalence of different familial configurations. The advent of in vitro fertilization in the late 1970s, along with the development of other forms of assisted reproduction such as egg donation and surrogacy, contributed to the proliferation of types of kinship that did not fit into the normative model of a biological nuclear family. From the demise of miscegenation laws following the Supreme Court ruling in *Loving v. Virginia* in 1967 to the legalization of gay marriage in Massachusetts in 2004 following *Goodridge v. Department of Public Health*, changes in marriage and family law further upended the totemic 1950s sitcom version of family life. By the late twentieth century, many family therapists embraced this growing variability in the meanings and forms of family in their practices.

As some family therapists turned their therapeutic lens to more expansive contexts and problems, they faced a dilemma: were their therapeutic interventions promoting adjustment to the social and political circumstances in which families found themselves, or were they engaged in a more transformative process of social change, family by family? The therapists neither framed nor answered this question in uniform ways. Moreover, those who identified their therapeutic efforts as challenges to social injustice grappled explicitly with this tension. In 1967, Minuchin and his colleagues at Wiltwyck characterized the contrast between large-scale, social changes and psychotherapeutic changes as a "false dichotomy," given "the need for multiple levels of intervention" to alleviate problems of poverty and delinquency.[8] In later years, Minuchin wrote of the limits to addressing problems such as poverty through therapeutic interventions and of not having done enough at Wiltwyck to challenge the inequities of larger social systems.[9]

This complex dialectic between the therapeutic and the political was at the heart of the psychological orientation of postwar America, according to which individual mental health became both the root and the reflection of the health of the social and political economy. As Ellen Herman has compellingly argued, "For better or worse, psychology's rise to power during the post-war decades changed ordinary Americans' expectations of their lives by publicizing the pertinence of emotion, the virtues of insight, and the unavoidability of subjectivity in the conduct of private and public affairs. . . . The real threats to global peace and national security, [behavioral experts] believed, were epidemics of irrational emotion and flawed national characters in need of containment and reconstruction."[10] In the clinical realm, the complex relationship between the therapeutic and the political motivated the radical therapy movement of the late 1960s and 1970s, whose motto was "change, not adjustment."[11] It also animated the antipsychiatry movement, particularly the work of R. D. Laing in London during the sixties. Laing developed a critique of society and the nuclear family through his view of schizophrenia as a label given by a sick society to those who did not conform to its mad ways, and he celebrated the schizophrenic experience as a heroic journey.[12]

The paradoxical intersections of the therapeutic and the political also informed conflicting currents in second-wave feminism. During the 1960s and 1970s, some feminists critiqued psychoanalysis for attributing women's problems to psychic pathology rather than structural inequalities. Such critiques sat uneasily alongside the psychologically inflected framework of "the personal is political" in consciousness-raising groups and the "therapeutic politics" of activism against child sexual abuse in which altering emotions and one's sense of self were as important for social change as institutional and state-based interventions.[13]

Drawing on the women's movement of the 1960s and 1970s, a feminist critique emerged within family therapy by the late 1970s and 1980s. Family therapists such as Rachel Hare-Mustin, Marianne Walters, Betty Carter, Peggy Papp, Olga Silverstein, Deborah Luepnitz, Lois Braverman, and Marion Lindblad-Goldberg challenged the gendered assumptions and unequal power dynamics within both the profession of family therapy and the field's theories of family functioning. Most of the female family therapists had been trained as social workers, unlike many of their male colleagues, who had medical backgrounds and assumed founding leadership roles in their new field. This pattern replicated the historical asymmetry in the relative status of social work and medicine.[14]

One crucial target of critique was family therapists' emphasis on the circular causality of a family system. This approach, feminist family therapists charged, did not address power and gender differentials in the larger society in general and family relations in particular, nor did it provide a satisfactory way of addressing family violence since it removed responsibility for violence from the typically male abuser. Furthermore, feminists identified the traditional, patriarchal nuclear family as the normative model implicitly operating in many schools of family therapy. For example, despite the guise of avoiding blame in a circular system, some approaches to family therapy covertly continued to blame dominant mothers and offer interventions based on the presumption that strengthening the father's role and reducing the mother's control over the family would be therapeutic.[15]

In addition to critiques of gender, during the 1980s and 1990s some family therapists challenged the ways in which their field had addressed sexuality, ethnicity, and other forms of difference.[16] As the preface to *Re-Visioning Family Therapy: Race, Culture, and Gender in Clinical Practice*, framed its charge, "This book grew out of our increasing need as family therapists to break out of the constraints of our traditional monocular vision of families as white, heterosexual, and middle-class, and to redefine the boundaries of our field. . . . Over the past few years, we have been struggling to envision theory and practice that will begin to transform our field so that we can see ourselves and our clients more clearly, and can provide services that will be more healing and will offer a sense of hope and belonging for all who seek our help."[17] These remarks were indicative of more widespread concerns in the field about the impact of social inequities on the therapeutic process during the 1990s. The contemporaneous rise of narrative therapy drew on these concerns by framing its clinical approach as one that attended to the damaging effects of cultural norms and structural inequalities in the stories that people told themselves about the nature of their problems, as well as in the power dynamics between patient and therapist.[18] Even as it represented a challenge to social and cultural hierarchies, narrative therapy also entailed reinvestment in both therapy as a suitable practice and family as a suitable locus for intervention in alleviating suffering and producing social change.

The family therapist Richard Simon reflected on the early years of his field in a *Family Therapy Networker* article that evocatively framed the tension between the therapeutic and the political:

> Drawing on the social ferment of the 1960s and the community psychiatry movement, we [family therapists] took a broad view of the influence of social context on individual difficulties. I fully expected that, over time, family systems work would consign all other therapeutic approaches to the realm of musty antiques. Once we left pathologizing diagnoses and emotional archaeology behind, there were no limits to what might be accomplished: our work might even trump the culture of poverty and cure schizophrenia! But that optimism wasn't the product of an ivory tower intellectuality: it emerged from the dramas that unfolded daily in therapy rooms, before one-way mirrors, and on training videotapes. . . . [By the 1990s] we became less sanguine about the ability of family therapy—or any kind of therapy—to trump enormous cultural and economic pressures, even among well-educated, middle-class clients. . . . Family therapy, that once confident iconoclastic movement, is no longer poised on the threshold of sweeping every other approach away.[19]

Simon thus situates the origins of family therapy in the seemingly more appealing context of the activist sixties rather than the conformist fifties, despite the field's emergence during the latter decade. He also emphasizes the therapeutic optimism of the field's early years, which he ties to the use of visual technologies and the performative dimensions of therapy. Ultimately, his characterization of the 1990s highlights family therapists' own self-reflexive critique of the relationship between the therapeutic and the political, which was also manifest in the field's turn to narrative and discursive approaches to therapy.

Although Simon notes the dimming of family therapy's early ambitions, one might also cast its subsequent history as one of diffusion through institutionalization, which is not a novel phenomenon. The field grew rapidly in the 1970s and 1980s and has become part of the recognized psychotherapeutic repertoire, though by the 1990s it was also forced to evolve in the face of the changing landscape of managed care reimbursement and the explosive growth of psychopharmacology. No longer the radical outsider and upstart, family therapy is now an established mode of psychotherapy, regularly taught in clinical social work, psychology, and psychiatry programs and included in textbooks with other approaches, such as cognitive, gestalt, behavior, and psychodynamic therapies.[20] Membership in the AAMFT grew from 973 in 1970 to 7,565 in 1979 to over 24,000 in 2010.[21] According to a 1996 report from the U.S. Public Health Service, 11 percent of clinically trained mental health personnel identified themselves as marriage and family therapists (compared with 22 percent social work, 16 percent psychology, 8 percent psychiatry, and 43 percent other fields such as psychiatric nursing and counseling).[22] The field has also expanded to help families address a wider array of issues such as child and adolescent school problems, divorce, remarriage, chronic medical diseases, substance abuse, eating disorders, bereavement, and family violence.

Beyond the clinical realm, the synergy between family and therapy has influenced contemporary cultural forums ranging from talk show treatments of dysfunctional families to televised confessions of disgraced politicians who invoke family as a therapeutic fix for their political problems and therapy as a political fix for their family problems. As Mimi White has argued, modern television programs "feature the simultaneous deployment of discourses on the family, the media, consumer culture, and therapeutic and confessional relations."[23] In the early twenty-first century, the configurations of kinship appear ever more variable, from the triptych of marital and parental arrangements represented in the television program *Modern Family* to newspaper articles about the impact of reproductive technology on understandings of genealogy and intimacy to the tableau of a female vice-presidential candidate with her husband, her children, and her unmarried teenaged daughter's boyfriend and baby.[24] Whether celebrated or denounced, these representations of modern American families underscore the mutually constitutive relationship between family life and therapeutic culture in what Lauren Berlant has called "the intimate public sphere," in which emotional contact and familial pursuits become a kind of political engagement.[25]

During the 1950s and 1960s, family therapists still retained the characteristic optimism and pessimism of the postwar period: optimism about the extent of change they could induce through therapeutic intervention but pessimism about the extent of the problems—including prejudice, schizophrenia, and delinquency—that lay embedded in family systems. They also theorized a pivotal role for the family in the relationship between social order and individual disorder, such that therapeutically intervening in the family had implications for both societal and personal well-being. Early family therapists' revolutionary aspirations for their field and their midcentury assumptions about pathological families have since been tempered, but the ties between the familial and the therapeutic remain. We only have to look at the enduring power of the discourse of "family values" to see that the popular notion of the family as the locus where everything can go right or wrong is still with us—and still contested.

NOTES

Introduction

1. *The Fine Line*, 1959, videotape, Don D. Jackson Archive (Mental Research Institute, Palo Alto, CA), Marriage and Family Therapy Program, University of Louisiana at Monroe (hereafter Jackson Archive).

2. Influential works from a much larger literature include Stephanie Coontz, *The Way We Never Were: American Families and the Nostalgia Trap* (New York, 1992); Elaine Tyler May, *Homeward Bound: American Families in the Cold War Era* (New York, 1988); and Joanne Meyerowitz, ed., *Not June Cleaver: Women and Gender in Postwar America, 1945–1960* (Philadelphia, 1994).

3. "The value of health relates to the good life in strange ways," wrote Nathan W. Ackerman in *Treating the Troubled Family* (New York, 1966), 50.

4. On the distinctions between norm, normal, and health and on the changing historical relationship between the normal and the pathological, see the classic articulation in Georges Canguilhem, *The Normal and the Pathological* (1966; repr., New York, 1991). On the historical analysis of difference, particularly binary oppositions, I have found Joan Scott's methodological comments on gender as an analytic category to be particularly helpful. Scott's essay "Gender: A Useful Category of Historical Analysis" and related essays are collected in Joan Wallach Scott, *Gender and the Politics of History* (New York, 1988).

5. Don D. Jackson, "Psychotherapy: Note on Concept of 'Growth' in Terms of Culture," no date, folder "Psychotherapy Book, Folder 2," Jackson Archive.

6. Key sources in a substantial literature too large to cite in full include Ellen Herman, *The Romance of American Psychology: Political Culture in the Age of Experts* (Berkeley, 1995); T. J. Jackson Lears, "From Salvation to Self-Realization: Advertising and the Therapeutic Roots of the Consumer Culture, 1880–1930," in *The Culture of Consumption: Critical Essays in American History, 1880–1980*, ed. Richard Wrightman Fox and T. J. Jackson Lears (New York, 1983), 1–38; Eva S. Moskowitz, *In Therapy We Trust: America's Obsession with Self-Fulfillment* (Baltimore, 2001); Joel Pfister and Nancy Schnog, eds., *Inventing the Psychological: Toward a Cultural History of Emotional Life in America* (New Haven, 1997); and Nikolas Rose, *Governing the Soul: The Shaping of the Private Self* (London, 1989).

7. In her account of Cold War American families and the ideology of domestic containment, Elaine Tyler May describes what she calls the "near deification of postwar

professionals," including psychiatrists and other psychological experts, in May, *Homeward Bound*, 187 and passim. See also Herman, *Romance of American Psychology*, 238–275, on postwar psychological experts and healers as part of a "growth industry" driven by state-supported measures, clinicians' expansive aims, and an expanding consumer market for psychotherapy.

8. Beth Bailey, *Sex in the Heartland* (Cambridge, MA, 2002); Ruth Feldstein, *Mother-hood in Black and White: Race and Sex in American Liberalism, 1930–1965* (Ithaca, 2000); Da-ryl Michael Scott, *Contempt and Pity: Social Policy and the Image of the Damaged Black Psyche* (Chapel Hill, NC, 1997); Lori Rotskoff, *Love on the Rocks: Men, Women, and Alcohol in Post–World War II America* (Chapel Hill, 2002); and Ellen Herman, *Kinship by Design: A History of Adoption in the Modern United States* (Chicago, 2008).

9. On the relationship of the group more broadly to the history of therapeutic cul-ture and individualism, see Peter Phillips Sheehy, "The Triumph of Group Therapeutics: Therapy, the Social Self, and Liberalism in America, 1910–1960" (PhD diss., University of Virginia, 2002).

10. The classic articulation of the postwar ideology of domestic containment is May, *Homeward Bound*. See also Mary Beth Haralovich, "Sitcoms and Suburbs: Positioning the 1950s Homemaker," *Quarterly Review of Film and Video* 11 (1989): 61–83; Wendy Kozol, *Life's America: Family and Nation in Postwar Photojournalism* (Philadelphia, 1994); Lynn Spigel, *Wel-come to the Dreamhouse: Popular Media and Postwar Suburbs* (Durham, NC, 2001); Judith E. Smith, *Visions of Belonging: Family Stories, Popular Culture, and Postwar Democracy, 1940–1960* (New York, 2006); and Jessica Weiss, *To Have and To Hold: Marriage, the Baby Boom and Social Change* (Chicago, 2000).

11. For perspectives on these multifaceted changes, see Andrew J. Cherlin, *Marriage, Divorce, Remarriage*, 2nd ed. (Cambridge, MA, 1992); Paula S. Fass, "The Child-Centered Family? New Rules in Postwar America," in *Reinventing Childhood after World War II*, ed. Paula S. Fass and Michael Grossberg (Philadelphia, 2012), 1–18; Steven Mintz and Susan Kellogg, *Domestic Revolutions: A Social History of American Family Life* (New York, 1988); and a thoughtful review that highlights the historical literature on postwar African American family life, Stephen Lassonde, "Family and Demography in Postwar America: A Hazard of New Fortunes?" in *A Companion to Post-1945 America*, ed. Jean-Christophe Agnew and Roy Rosenzweig (Malden, MA, 2002), 3–19. Historians of women's labor have challenged facile generalizations that women did not work outside the home until World War II "Rosie the Riveters" entered the factory. Such scholarship discusses working-class women and women of color who had long worked outside the home and who faced different employment conditions during and after the war from their white, middle-class counterparts. E.g., Susan Hartmann, "Women's Employment and the Domestic Ideal in the Early Cold War Years," in Meyerowitz, *Not June Cleaver*, 84–100; Maureen Honey, "The Working-Class Woman and Recruitment Propaganda During World War II: Class Differences in the Portrayal of War Work," *Signs* 8 (Summer 1983): 672–687; Jacqueline Jones, *Labor of Love, Labor of Sorrow: Black Women, Work, and the Family from Slavery to the Present* (New York, 1985); and Alice Kessler-Harris, *Out to Work: A History of Wage-Earning Women in the United States* (New York, 1982).

12. Joanne Meyerowitz, "'How Common Culture Shapes the Separate Lives': Sexuality, Race, and Mid-Twentieth-Century Social Constructionist Thought," *Journal of American History* 96 (2010): 1059.

13. The associations between motherhood, the domestic sphere, and the production of good citizens have a much longer history. E.g. Linda K. Kerber, *Women of the Republic: Intel-lect and Ideology in Revolutionary America* (Chapel Hill, NC, 1980); and Mary P. Ryan, *Cradle of the Middle Class: The Family in Oneida County, New York, 1790–1865* (Cambridge, UK, 1981). However, the line between colonial Republican motherhood and the ideals of parent-ing embodied in family therapy was not an entirely straight one. For example, Rebecca Plant argues that the interwar period saw a decline in sentimental maternalism, with its attendant romanticization of mother love as civic duty, which was superseded by the postwar rise of a

more narrow, psychological view of motherhood that nonetheless continued to have political implications. Rebecca Plant, *Mom: The Transformation of Motherhood in Modern America* (Chicago, 2010).

14. Publications by Philip Wylie, David Levy, Edward Stecker, Frieda Fromm-Reichmann, and studies on culture and personality, authoritarianism, and prejudice contributed to this perception. Important secondary literature on family and delinquency in the 1950s includes Wini Breines, *Young, White, and Miserable: Growing Up Female in the Fifties* (Boston, 1992); and James Gilbert, *A Cycle of Outrage: America's Reaction to the Juvenile Delinquent in the 1950s* (New York, 1986). For thoughtful articulations of the simultaneously optimistic and despairing attitudes of Americans toward the family from the 1940s to the 1960s, see James Gilbert, *Another Chance: Postwar America, 1945–1968* (Philadelphia, 1981), 54–75; and Warren Susman, "Did Success Spoil the United States? Dual Representations in Postwar America," in *Recasting America: Culture and Politics in the Age of the Cold War*, ed. Lary May (Chicago, 1989), 19–37.

15. Cf. Lizabeth Cohen, *A Consumers' Republic: The Politics of Mass Consumption in Postwar America* (New York, 2003).

16. "The transitory shifts of mood, the fleeting, subtle exchanges and interchanges, the dramatic confrontations and insights, and the humdrum, prosaic, apathetic interactions in which nothing, it would seem, is happening—these are the warp and the woof, the very fabric of our raw material." Salvador Minuchin et al., *Families of the Slums: An Exploration of Their Structure and Treatment* (New York, 1967), 43.

17. Ackerman, *Treating the Troubled Family*, 50.

18. According to Murray Bowen, "Psychotherapeutically, the family is treated as if it were a single organism." Murray Bowen, with Robert H. Dysinger, MD and Betty Basamania, MSW, "The Role of the Father in Families with a Schizophrenic Patient," *American Journal of Psychiatry* 155 (1959): 1017–1020, reprinted in Murray Bowen, *Family Therapy in Clinical Practice* (New York, 1978), 17. Bowen initially presented this material at the Annual Meeting of the American Orthopsychiatric Association in May 1958.

19. My framing of the postwar period through the end of the 1960s avoids drawing a stark contrast between the allegedly conformist 1950s and rebellious 1960s. For a useful historiographic review of related issues, see Thomas J. Sugrue, "Reassessing the History of Postwar America," *Prospects* 20 (1995): 493–509, as well as articles by others in a special section of *Prospects*, "The Politics of Cold War America."

20. Cited in *Oxford English Dictionary*, 2nd ed., s.v. "nuclear."

21. Susan Leigh Star and James R. Griesemer, "Institutional Ecology, 'Translations' and Boundary Objects: Amateurs and Professionals in Berkeley's Museum of Vertebrate Zoology, 1907–39," *Social Studies of Science* 19, no. 3 (August 1989): 393.

22. On the phenomenon of simultaneous discovery, see Robert K. Merton, *The Sociology of Science: Theoretical and Empirical Investigations* (Chicago, 1973).

23. Though family therapists' accounts for the origins of their field vary in emphasis and some details, the general outline described here follows their literature. See, e.g., Herbert Goldenberg and Irene Goldenberg, *Family Therapy: An Overview*, 7th ed. (Belmont, CA, 2008); Philip J. Guerin, ed., *Family Therapy: Theory and Practice* (New York, 1976); Jay Haley, ed., *Changing Families: A Family Therapy Reader* (New York, 1971); and Lynn Hoffman, *Foundations of Family Therapy: A Conceptual Framework for Systems Change* (New York, 1981). *The Pathological Family* is not a comprehensive survey of the many schools and approaches to family therapy. For such a survey, see Goldenberg and Goldenberg, *Family Therapy*.

24. Murray Bowen, "Family Psychotherapy," *American Journal of Orthopsychiatry* 31 (January 1961): 40–60, reprinted in Bowen, *Family Therapy in Clinical Practice*, 77. Bowen first presented the paper at a 1959 workshop chaired by Stephen Fleck titled "The Family as the Unit of Study and Treatment."

25. On the history of child care in the twentieth-century United States, particularly regarding debates about child care as "mother care" and provision of care for the children

of working women, see Sonya Michel, *Children's Interests/Mothers' Rights: The Shaping of America's Child Care Policy* (New Haven, 1999); and Elizabeth Rose, *A Mother's Job: The History of Day Care, 1890–1960* (New York, 1999).

26. On humanistic psychology, see Ellen Herman, *The Romance of American Psychology: Political Culture in the Age of Experts* (Berkeley, 1995), 264–275; and Laura N. Rice and Leslie S. Greenberg, "Humanistic Approaches to Psychotherapy," in *History of Psychotherapy: A Century of Change*, ed. Donald K. Freedheim (Washington, D.C., 1992), 197–224.

27. James Framo, ed., *Family Interaction: A Dialogue between Family Researchers and Family Therapists* (New York, 1972), 6.

28. Ibid., 1. A Kuhnian framework has continued to structure subsequent accounts of the history of family therapy, whether these accounts favor or debunk the therapy's revolutionary status. E.g., Adele M. Brodkin, "Family Therapy: The Making of a Mental Health Movement," *American Journal of Orthopsychiatry* 50 (January, 1980): 4–17; and Florence W. Kaslow, "Marital and Family Therapy," in *Handbook of Marriage and the Family*, ed. Marvin B Sussman and Suzanne K. Steinmetz (New York, 1987), 837.

29. Jay Haley, "Critical Overview," in Framo, ed., *Family Interaction*, 14–15.

30. Ibid.

31. Jules Riskin, "Family Data Sheets—H. Family," November 8, 1960, Jackson Archive., Monroe, LA.

32. See, e.g., Julia Grant, *Raising Baby by the Book: The Education of American Mothers* (New Haven, 1998); Margo Horn, *Before It's Too Late: The Child Guidance Movement in the United States, 1922–1945* (Philadelphia, 1989); Kathleen W. Jones, *Taming the Troublesome Child: American Families, Child Guidance, and the Limits of Psychiatric Authority* (Cambridge, MA, 1999); Fred Matthews, "The Utopia of Human Relations: The Conflict-Free Family in American Social Thought, 1930–1960," *Journal of the History of the Behavioral Sciences* 24 (1988): 343–362; and Theresa R. Richardson, *The Century of the Child: The Mental Hygiene Movement and Social Policy in the United States and Canada* (Albany, 1989).

33. Kristin Celello, *Making Marriage Work: A History of Marriage and Divorce in the Twentieth-Century United States* (Chapel Hill, NC, 2009); Rebecca L. Davis, *More Perfect Unions: The American Search for Marital Bliss* (Cambridge, MA, 2010); and Christina Simmons, *Making Marriage Modern: Women's Sexuality from the Progressive Era to World War II* (New York, 2009).

1. Personality Factories

1. Margaret Mead, "What's the Matter with the Family?," *Harper's*, April 1945, 393–399; Reuben Hill, "The American Family: Problem or Solution?," *American Journal of Sociology* 53 (September 1947): 125–130; Della D. Cyrus, "What's Wrong with the Family?," *Atlantic Monthly*, November 1946, 67–73; and "The American Family in Trouble," *Life*, July 26, 1948, 83–96.

2. Talcott Parsons and Robert F. Bales, *Family, Socialization and Interaction Process* (Glencoe, IL, 1955), 16.

3. Philip Wylie, *Generation of Vipers* (1942; repr., New York, 1955). On the history of momism and its relationship to the history of psychiatry, see Mari Jo Buhle, *Feminism and Its Discontents: A Century of Struggle with Psychoanalysis* (Cambridge, MA, 1998); Ruth Feldstein, *Motherhood in Black and White: Race and Sex in American Liberalism, 1930–1965* (Ithaca, 2000); and Rebecca Jo Plant, *Mom: The Transformation of Motherhood in Modern America* (Chicago, 2010).

4. See Kristin Celello, *Making Marriage Work: A History of Marriage and Divorce in the Twentieth-Century United States* (Chapel Hill, NC, 2009); Rebecca L. Davis, *More Perfect Unions: The American Search for Marital Bliss* (Cambridge, MA, 2010); and Christina Simmons, *Making Marriage Modern: Women's Sexuality from the Progressive Era to World War I* (New York, 2009).

5. Beth L. Bailey, *From Front Porch to Back Seat: Courtship in Twentieth-Century America* (Baltimore, 1988), 119–140.

6. Nancy F. Cott, *Public Vows: A History of Marriage and the Nation* (Cambridge, MA, 2000), 156–199; John D'Emilio and Estelle B. Freedman, *Intimate Matters: A History of Sexuality in America* (New York, 1988), 265–273; and Simmons, *Making Marriage Modern*, 105–137.

7. Jane Gerhard, *Desiring Revolution: Second-Wave Feminism and the Rewriting of American Sexual Thought, 1920–1982* (New York, 2001), 13–49. See also Steven Seldman, *Romantic Longings: Love in America, 1830–1989* (New York, 1992).

8. On the history of marriage counseling, see Davis, *More Perfect Unions*; and Eva S. Moskowitz, *In Therapy We Trust: America's Obsession with Self-Fulfillment* (Baltimore, 2001), 70–99. On early twentieth-century approaches to marriage and gender, see Elizabeth Lunbeck, *The Psychiatric Persuasion: Knowledge, Gender, and Power in Modern America* (Princeton, 1994).

9. Carlfred B. Broderick and Sandra S. Schrader, "The History of Professional Marriage and Family Therapy," in *Handbook of Family Therapy*, ed. Alan S. Gurman and David P. Kniskern (New York, 1981), 26–27.

10. Moskowitz, *In Therapy We Trust*, 75. On Popenoe, eugenics, and marriage counseling, see Davis, *More Perfect Unions*, 33–38, 121–124; Wendy Kline, *Building a Better Race: Gender, Sexuality, and Eugenics from the Turn of the Century to the Baby Boom* (Berkeley, 2001); and Alexandra Minna Stern, *Eugenic Nation: Faults and Frontiers of Better Breeding in Modern America* (Berkeley, 2005), chap. 5.

11. Davis, *More Perfect Unions*, 121, 124–131; and Celello, *Making Marriage Work*, 37–40, 72–102.

12. Moskowitz, *In Therapy We Trust*, 76; and Stern, *Eugenic Nation*, 161. For a related discussion of eugenics in pronatalist and infant-health movements of the early twentieth century, see Alisa C. Klaus, *Every Child a Lion: The Origins of Maternal and Infant Health Policy in the United States and France, 1890–1920* (Ithaca, 1993); Laura L. Lovett, *Conceiving the Future: Pronatalism, Reproduction, and the Family in the United States, 1890–1938* (Chapel Hill, NC, 2007); and Richard A. Meckel, *Save the Babies: American Public Health Reform and the Prevention of Infant Mortality, 1850–1929* (Baltimore, 1990).

13. Atina Grossmann, *Reforming Sex: The German Movement for Birth Control and Abortion Reform, 1920–1950* (New York, 1995), 9–11 and chap. 3; Eli Zaretsky, *Secrets of the Soul: A Social and Cultural History of Psychoanalysis* (New York, 2004), 222.

14. David Mace, "The Marriage Guidance Council," *Probation*, January–February 1947, 86.

15. "Marriage Counseling," *Marriage and Family Living* 11 (1949): 5, cited in Broderick and Schrader, "History of Professional Marriage and Family Therapy," 14.

16. Sharp articulations of the relationship between psychology and politics from the 1930s include the American political scientist Harold D. Lasswell, *Psychopathology and Politics* (Chicago, 1930) and the Austrian psychoanalyst Wilhelm Reich, *The Mass Psychology of Fascism* (1933; repr., New York, 1970). Though distinct in many ways, both books emphasized the role of family upbringing in the formation of political culture. On the twentieth-century psychologization of motherhood, see Rebecca Jo Plant, *Mom: The Transformation of Motherhood in Modern America* (Chicago, 2010). On the parallel psychologization of fatherhood, see Robert L. Griswold, *Fatherhood in America: A History* (New York, 1993).

17. The relevant literature on the extended, complex historical relation between child rearing and the production of democratic citizens, particularly in relation to the history of industrialization and capitalism, is too large to cite in full, but influential sources include Leonore Davidoff and Catherine Hall, *Family Fortunes: Men and Women of the English Middle Class, 1780–1850* (Chicago, 1987); Linda K. Kerber, *Women of the Republic: Intellect and Ideology in Revolutionary America* (Chapel Hill, NC, 1980); Stephanie Coontz, *The Social Origins of Private Life: A History of American Families, 1600–1900* (London, 1988); and Mary P. Ryan, *Cradle of the Middle Class: The Family in Oneida County, New York, 1790–1865* (Cambridge, UK, 1981).

18. Julia Grant, *Raising Baby by the Book: The Education of American Mothers* (New Haven, 1998), 9. In a related vein, essays in *Mothers of a New World* examine the intertwined emergence of women's social movements and welfare states at the turn of the twentieth century, showing how women reformers and activists refigured their private, maternal responsibilities for child rearing into public programs and policies. Seth Koven and Sonya Michel, eds., *Mothers of a New World: Maternalist Politics and the Origins of Welfare States* (New York, 1993).

19. Rima D. Apple, *Perfect Motherhood: Science and Childrearing in America* (New Brunswick, NJ, 2006); and Grant, *Raising Baby by the Book*, 41.

20. Paula Fass, *The Damned and the Beautiful* (New York, 1977), 95–118; Howard J. Faulkner and Virginia D. Pruitt, eds., *Dear Dr. Menninger: Women's Voices from the Thirties* (Columbia, MO, 1997); Grant, *Raising Baby by the Book*; Fred Matthews, "The Utopia of Human Relations: The Conflict-Free Family in American Social Thought, 1930–1960," *Journal of the History of the Behavioral Sciences* 24 (October 1988): 343–362; and Sonya Michel, "American Women and the Discourse of the Democratic Family in World War II," in *Behind the Lines: Gender and the Two World Wars*, ed. Margaret Randolph Higonnet, Jane Jenson, Sonya Michel, and Margaret Collins Weitz (New Haven, 1987).

21. Meghan Crnic, "Better Babies: Social Engineering for 'a Better Nation, a Better World,'" *Endeavour* 33 (2009): 13–18; Klaus, *Every Child a Lion*; and Alexandra Minna Stern, "Better Baby Contests at the Indiana State Fair: Child Health, Scientific Motherhood and Eugenics in the Midwest," in *Formative Years: Children's Health in the United States, 1880–2000*, ed. Alexandra Minna Stern and Howard Markel (Ann Arbor, 2002), 121–152.

22. William A. White, "Childhood: The Golden Period for Mental Hygiene," *Mental Hygiene* 4 (1920): 259, 267, quoted in Kathleen W. Jones, *Taming the Troublesome Child: American Families, Child Guidance, and the Limits of Psychiatric Authority* (Cambridge, MA, 1999), 54.

23. My brief discussion of mental hygiene draws on Gerald N. Grob, *Mental Illness and American Society, 1875–1940* (Princeton, 1983); Jones, *Taming the Troublesome Child*; Fred Matthews, "In Defense of Common Sense: Mental Hygiene as Ideology and Mentality in Twentieth-Century America," *Prospects* 4 (1979): 459–516; and Theresa R. Richardson, *The Century of the Child: The Mental Hygiene Movement and Social Policy in the United States and Canada* (Albany, 1989). For an international perspective, see Mathew Thomson, "Mental Hygiene as an International Movement," in *International Health Organisations and Movements, 1918–1939*, ed. Paul Weindling (Cambridge, UK, 1995), 283–304.

24. Jones, *Taming the Troublesome Child*.

25. My argument here follows Jones. See also Horn, *Before It's Too Late*. On the history of the child guidance movement in Britain, including the role of the Commonweath Fund and other internationally oriented interwar American foundations, see John Stewart, "The Scientific Claims of British Child Guidance, 1918–1945," *British Journal for the History of Science* 42, no. 3 (September 2009): 407–432.

26. Jones, *Taming the Troublesome Child*, 177. For more on mother blaming, see the essays in Molly Ladd-Taylor and Lauri Umansky, eds., *"Bad" Mothers: The Politics of Blame in Twentieth-Century America* (New York, 1998).

27. Grant, *Raising Baby by the Book*, esp. chap. 5. Jones connects her argument about mothers seeking out advice with patient-perspective historiography in the history of medicine, as well as work in women's history on the agency of people subjected to the interventions of helping professionals. Jones, *Taming the Troublesome Child*, 5. On the history of modern child-rearing advice, see Ann Hulbert, *Raising America: Experts, Parents, and a Century of Advice about Children* (New York, 2003); and Peter N. Stearns, *Anxious Parents: A History of Modern Childrearing in America* (New York, 2003).

28. Michel, "Discourse of the Democratic Family."

29. Lawrence Frank, quoted in Griswold, *Fatherhood*, 100–101. See also Dennis Bryson, "Lawrence K. Frank, Knowledge, and the Production of the 'Social,'" *Poetics Today* 19, no. 3 (Autumn 1998): 401–21.

30. Lawrence Frank, quoted in Griswold, *Fatherhood*, 100–101.

31. Griswold, *Fatherhood*, 101, 162–184. According to the Groveses, "In many cases where we say the child has been spoiled by too much mother, the actual fact is not that the child has been hurt by the over-abundant love of the mother, but by too little affection from the father." Quoted in Griswold, *Fatherhood*, 101. On the broader history of fatherhood and masculinity in twentieth-century America, see also Gail Bederman, *Manliness and Civilization: A Cultural History of Gender and Race in the United States, 1880–1917* (Chicago, 1995); James Gilbert, *Men in the Middle: Searching for Masculinity in the 1950s* (Chicago, 2005); Michael Kimmel, *Manhood in America: A Cultural History* (New York, 1996); and Ralph LaRossa, *Of War and Men: World War II in the Lives of Fathers and Their Families* (Chicago, 2011).

32. Roy R. Grinker and John P. Spiegel, *Men under Stress* (Philadelphia, 1945).

33. Edward Strecker, *Their Mothers' Sons* (New York, 1946), 13.

34. On the history of the Tavistock Clinic and Institute, including their interactions with similar institutes in the United States such as the Institute of Human Relations at Yale, see Peter Miller and Nikolas Rose, "On Therapeutic Authority: Psychoanalytic Expertise under Advanced Liberalism," *History of the Human Sciences* 7, no. 3 (1994): 32–34.

35. Tom Harrison, *Bion, Rickman, Foulkes and the Northfield Experiments: Advancing on a Different Front* (London, 2000). On the link between Bion's wartime work on "the group" and psychoanalytic attention to the mother and infant, see Zaretsky, *Secrets of the Soul*, 269–270. On the history of group psychotherapy in England, see Miller and Rose, "On Therapeutic Authority," 38–51; and in the United States, Peter Phillips Sheehy, "The Triumph of Group Therapeutics: Therapy, the Social Self, and Liberalism in America, 1919–1960" (PhD diss., University of Virginia, 2002).

36. Zaretsky, *Secrets of the Soul*, 249–275; Denise Riley, *War in the Nursery: Theories of the Child and Mother* (London, 1983); Marga Vicedo, "The Social Nature of the Mother's Tie to Her Child: John Bowlby's Theory of Attachment in Post-War America," *British Journal of the History of Science* 44, no. 3 (2011): 1–26; and Lisa Cartwright, "'Emergencies of Survival': Moral Spectatorship and the 'New Vision of the Child' in Postwar Child Psychoanalysis," *Journal of Visual Culture* 3 (2004): 35–49.

37. C. Christian Beels, "Notes for a Cultural History of Family Therapy," *Family Process* 41 (2002): 67–82; John Byng-Hall, "An Appreciation of John Bowlby: His Significance for Family Therapy," *Journal of Family Therapy* 13 (1991): 5–16. On marriage counseling and the Balint technique, see Miller and Rose, "On Therapeutic Authority," 51–58. See also Broderick and Schrader, "History of Professional Marriage and Family Therapy," 13, 17.

38. Ellen Herman, *The Romance of American Psychology: Political Culture in the Age of Experts* (Berkeley, 1995), 3.

39. On being "nervous in the service" during World War II (to quote Herman) and the "lessons of war" (to quote Grob), see Herman, *Romance of American Psychology*, 82–123; Gerald Grob, *From Asylum to Community: Mental Health Policy in Modern America* (Princeton, 1991), 5–23; and Nathan Hale, *The Rise and Crisis of Psychoanalysis in the United States: Freud and the Americans, 1917–1985* (New York, 1995), 187–210. On the demand for psychiatric and psychological clinicians at VA hospitals, see Herman, *Romance of American Psychology*, 242–245; and James H. Capshew, *Psychologists on the March: Science, Practice, and Professional Identity in America, 1929–1969* (Cambridge, UK, 1999), 171–174.

40. On the history of the impact of World War II on the establishment of NIMH and its rapid expansion, see Grob, *From Asylum to Community*, 44–69; and Herman, *Romance of American Psychology*, 245–249.

41. Joint Commission on Mental Illness and Health, *Action for Mental Health: Final Report of the Joint Commission on Mental Illness and Health* (New York, 1961); Gerald Gurin, *Americans View Their Mental Health: A Nationwide Interview Survey; A Report to the Staff Director, Jack R. Ewalt*, Joint Commission on Mental Health Monograph Series, no. 4 (New York, 1960); and Leo Srole et al., *Mental Health in the Metropolis: The Midtown Manhattan Study*, rev. and enl. ed. (1962; repr., New York, 1975).

42. On postwar psychoanalysis and the popularization of psychoanalysis in the United States, see e.g., Jonathan Freedman, "From *Spellbound* to *Vertigo*: Alfred Hitchcock and

Therapeutic Culture in America," in *Hitchcock's America*, ed. Jonathan Freedman and Richard Millington (New York, 1999); Hale, *Rise and Crisis of Psychoanalysis*; and A. Michael Sulman, "The Humanization of the American Child: Benjamin Spock as a Popularizer of Psychoanalytic Thought," *Journal of the History of the Behavioral Sciences* 9 (1973): 258–65.

43. James Gilbert, *Another Chance: Postwar America, 1945–1968* (Philadelphia, 1981), 55. For a useful analysis suggesting that postwar America continued through the 1960s rather than drawing a stark contrast between the allegedly conformist 1950s and rebellious 1960s, see Thomas J. Sugrue, "Reassessing the History of Postwar America," *Prospects* 20 (1995): 493–509, as well as other articles in a special section of *Prospects*, "The Politics of Culture in Cold War America."

44. E.g., Jane F. Levey, "Imagining the Family in Postwar Popular Culture: The Case of *The Egg and I* and *Cheaper by the Dozen*," *Journal of Women's History* 13, no. 3 (Autumn 2001): 125–150; Elaine Tyler May, *Homeward Bound: American Families in the Cold War Era* (New York, 1988); and William Graebner, *The Age of Doubt: American Thought and Culture in the 1940s* (Boston, 1991). Similarly, Steven Mintz has argued, "The 1950s was a period of outward optimism but inward anxiety and fear. . . . We may recall the 1950s as a time of unlocked doors and stable nuclear families, but the decade of Ozzie and Harriet was also a period of intense anxiety over juvenile delinquency and gangs." Steven Mintz, *Huck's Raft: A History of American Childhood* (Cambridge, MA, 2006), 293.

45. Jamie Cohen-Cole, *The Open Mind: Cold War Politics and the Sciences of Human Nature* (Chicago, forthcoming); and Jill G. Morawski, "Organizing Knowledge and Behavior at Yale's Institute of Human Relations," *Isis* 77, no. 2 (1986): 219–242.

46. Parsons and Bales, *Family, Socialization and Interaction Process*, 16.

47. Helen Leland Witmer and Ruth Kotinsky, eds., *Personality in the Making: The Fact-Finding Report of the Midcentury White House Conference on Children and Youth* (New York, 1952), xviii. This conference was the fifth in a series of decennial conferences begun in 1909. The earlier four conferences focused on the problems of socially disadvantaged children or on social and economic aspects of the welfare of all American children. In contrast, the midcentury conference was explicitly oriented toward a psychological assessment of children's needs and societal ills. Ibid., xv.

48. Ibid., 435.

49. T. W. Adorno et al., *The Authoritarian Personality* (New York, 1950); Bruno Bettelheim and Morris Janowitz, *Dynamics of Prejudice: A Psychological and Sociological Study of Veterans* (New York, 1950); and Bruno Bettleheim, *The Empty Fortress* (New York, 1967). For discussion of these issues and references to a much larger literature, see Herman, *Romance of American Psychology*, 48–123, 174–207; Ruth Feldstein, "Antiracism and Maternal Failure in the 1940s and 1950s," in Ladd-Taylor and Umansky, *"Bad" Mothers*, 145–168; Joanne Meyerowitz, "How Common Culture Shapes the Separate Lives: Sexuality, Race, and Mid-Twentieth-Century Social Constructionist Thought," *Journal of American History* 96 (2010): 1057–1084; Jennifer Terry, "'Momism' and the Making of Treasonous Homosexuals," in Ladd-Taylor and Umansky, *"Bad" Mothers*, 169–190; and Elisabeth Young-Bruehl, *The Anatomy of Prejudices* (Cambridge, 1996).

50. Adorno et al., *The Authoritarian Personality*; Gunnar Myrdal, *An American Dilemma* (New York, 1944); and Abram Kardiner and Lionel Ovesey, *The Mark of Oppression: Explorations in the Personality of the American Negro* (Cleveland, 1951).

51. On governmentality at midcentury, see Anna McCarthy, *The Citizen Machine: Governing by Television in 1950s America* (New York, 2010); and Nikolas Rose and Peter Miller, *Governing the Present: Administering Economic, Social and Personal Life* (Cambridge, 2008).

52. Though family therapists' accounts for the origins of their field vary in emphasis and some details, this general outline is pervasive in the family therapy literature. See, e.g., Irene Goldenberg and Herbert Goldenberg, *Family Therapy: An Overview*, 7th ed. (Belmont, CA, 2008); Philip J. Guerin, ed., *Family Therapy: Theory and Practice* (New York, 1976); Jay Haley, ed., *Changing Families: A Family Therapy Reader* (New York, 1971); and Lynn Hoffman, *Foundations of Family Therapy: A Conceptual Framework for Systems Change* (New York, 1981).

53. There were many others who played an early role in the development of family therapy, including (but not limited to) John Bell, Normal Bell, Ivan Boszormenyi-Nagy, Nathan Epstein, Stephen Fleck, James Framo, Theodore Lidz, Robert MacGregor, Christian Midelfort, Peggy Papp, Normal Paul, Albert Scheflen, Carlos Sluzki, Virginia Satir, John Spiegel, Carl Whitaker, and Lyman Wynne. The members of the Palo Alto research group (Gregory Bateson, Jay Haley, Don D. Jackson, Paul Watzlawick, and John Weakland) are discussed in chapter 2.

54. Nathan W. Ackerman, "Adolescent Problems: A Symptom of Family Disorder," *Family Process* 1, no. 2 (September 1962): 202, 205.

55. Ibid., 205.

56. Ibid., 202.

57. For more on postwar studies and Hollywood representations of juvenile delinquency, see James Gilbert, *A Cycle of Outrage: America's Reaction to the Juvenile Delinquent in the 1950s* (Oxford, 1986).

58. "This book is dedicated to Nathan W. Ackerman, the 'grandfather' of family therapy and my friend, who died just before publication of these proceedings." James Framo, ed., *Family Interaction: A Dialogue between Family Researchers and Family Therapists* (New York, 1972).

59. Nathan W. Ackerman, "The Unity of the Family," *Archives of Pediatrics* 55 (1938): 51–62; and Nathan W. Ackerman, "The Family as a Social and Emotional Unit," *Bulletin of the Kansas Mental Hygiene Society* 12 (1937): 2.

60. Donald Bloch and Robert Simon, eds., *The Strength of Family Therapy: Selected Papers of Nathan W. Ackerman* (New York, 1982), xvi.

61. Nathan Ackerman, "The Future of Family Psychotherapy," in *Expanding Theory and Practice in Family Therapy*, ed. Nathan W. Ackerman, Frances L. Beatman, and Sanford N. Sherman (New York, 1967), 15. See Nathan W. Ackerman, *The Psychodynamics of Family Life: Diagnosis and Treatment of Family Relationships* (New York, 1958) for Ackerman's take on Freud and the family.

62. Nathan W. Ackerman, "The Family as a Psychosocial Entity," in *Treating the Troubled Family* (New York, 1966), 58.

63. Ibid., 59. Analogizing a family to an organism not only underscored the reproductive aspects of family life but also promoted a conception of the family as natural, with an internally consistent organization.

64. Nathan W. Ackerman, introduction to *Family Process*, ed. Nathan W. Ackerman (New York, 1970), xi.

65. Ackerman, "Family Psychotherapy and Psychoanalysis: The Implications of Difference," in Ackerman, *Family Process*, 6.

66. Ackerman, *Family Process*, xiii.

67. Murray Bowen, *Family Therapy in Clinical Practice* (New York, 1978), 287.

68. Frieda Fromm-Reichmann, "Notes on the Development of Treatment of Schizophrenics by Psychoanalytic Psychotherapy," *Psychiatry* 11, no. 3 (August 1948): 265. See Gail A. Hornstein, *To Redeem One Person Is to Redeem the World: The Life of Frieda Fromm-Reichmann* (New York, 2000).

69. Quoted in Carol Eadie Hartwell, "The Schizophrenogenic Mother Concept in American Psychiatry," *Psychiatry: Interpersonal and Biological Processes* 59 (Fall 1996): 282.

70. Theodore Lidz, Stephen Fleck, and Alice R. Cornelison, *Schizophrenia and the Family* (New York, 1965); John Rosen, *Direct Analysis: Selected Papers* (New York, 1953); Frances D. Horowitz and Lloyd L. Lovell, "Attitudes of Mothers of Female Schizophrenics," *Child Development* 31 (June 1960): 299–305. See also Sander L. Gilman, "Constructing Schizophrenia as a Category of Mental Illness," in *Disease and Representation: Images of Illness from Madness to AIDS* (Ithaca, 1988), 202–230.

71. Herbert Goldenberg and Irene Goldenberg, *Family Therapy: An Overview*, 7th ed. (Belmont, CA, 2008), 176.

72. Bowen, *Family Therapy in Clinical Practice*, xiv.

73. Murray Bowen to Robert C. Burnham, Chairman of the Students' Advisory Committee of the Washington Psychoanalytic Institute, February 10, 1963, drawer 5, folder "Misc.," Bowen Archive, Bowen Center for the Study of the Family, Washington, DC (hereafter Bowen Archive).

74. [Murray Bowen], "Toward the Differentiation of a Self in One's Own Family," in Framo, *Family Interaction*, 111–166. The editor of the conference proceedings published Bowen's talk anonymously because of the "legal and ethical problems" and "sticky issues" involved in publishing a paper that revealed Bowen's personal family situation (p. xviii), but the paper is easily identifiable as Bowen's, both because of its unique theoretical framework and because of Bowen's own later references to his work with his extended family.

75. Bowen, *Family Therapy in Clinical Practice*, 185.

76. Thanks to family therapist Fred Sander for suggesting this phrase. See also the banter between Murray Bowen, Nathan Ackerman, and Carl Whitaker regarding the "family" of family therapy and being one another's brothers in the proceedings from a 1967 conference, in Framo, *Family Interaction*, 165, 169, 173.

77. Sigmund Freud, *Totem and Taboo: Some Points of Agreement between the Mental Lives of Savages and Neurotics*, trans. James Strachey (1913; repr., London, 1950), 155.

78. Olga Silverstein, one of the four founders of the influential Women's Project in Family Therapy in 1977, described the field in a 1991 interview in the following way: "The field, like every field, was run by men and worked by women. It was a pyramid in which the men were the so-called thinkers, the theoreticians, and the women were the executioners or actors, so that the men would build their reputations and have big armies of working ants on the bottom which were the social workers who were largely women. The men were the doctors." Quoted in Sukie Magraw, "Feminism and Family Therapy: An Oral History" (PhD diss., California School of Professional Psychology at Berkeley/Alameda, 1992), 115.

79. J. C. Flugel, *The Psycho-analytic Study of the Family* (London, 1921).

80. Bowen, *Family Therapy in Clinical Practice*, 184.

81. "[Psychoanalysis] gained increasing acceptance in psychiatry during the 1930s, provided concepts for mass use during World War II, and then contributed to the popularity of psychiatry as a specialty after the war. . . . Hundreds of eager psychiatrists began experimenting with modifications of psychoanalytic treatment for the more difficult problems. Those who began family research appear to have been motivated by a search for more effective treatment methods. The strict admonition against contaminating the transference relationship may have accounted for the isolation of the early work and the slowness to report this supposedly unacceptable practice in the literature." Ibid., 186.

82. Ibid.

83. Don D. Jackson to Salvador Minuchin, March 7, 1962, folder "Variety of Materials from Jules Riskin's Files," Jackson Archive.

84. Salvador Minuchin and Michael P. Nichols, *Family Healing: Tales of Hope and Renewal from Family Therapy* (New York, 1993), 3–47.

85. Salvador Minuchin, foreword to *Family Therapy: Concepts and Methods*, 4th ed., by Michael P. Nichols and Richard C. Schwartz (Boston, 1998), xiii.

86. My thanks to Robert Self for helping me articulate these connections.

87. Virginia Satir, *Conjoint Family Therapy: A Guide to Theory and Technique*, 2nd ed. (1964; repr., Palo Alto, 1967), chap. 12.

88. Ackerman wrote, "In a first contact with a troubled family, a formal procedure for intake and diagnosis is disadvantageous. It is preferable to initiate the process in a fresh, unprejudiced way, without historical data obtained separately and at different times from one or another member of the family. . . . For the clinician the live, pungent and dramatic quality of spontaneous historical disclosures is a convincing experience. After all, history, in the best sense, is contemporary. Its importance and relevance hinge on its being a vital part of the here and now." *Treating the Troubled Family*, 93. Jay Haley concurred with Ackerman's position on taking a history, though he espoused a different model of family therapy. In 1970 Haley wrote, "When a family therapist interviews, he wishes to find out what is happening in people's lives right now. . . . When gathering information, he wants to observe the family

members dealing with one another. Even if he does not regularly treat the family together as a group, he prefers at least one session so he can observe their interaction. Because of his interest in sequences and patterns of behavior in the family, he would rather observe than listen to a person's report about his family. What someone says might or might not be related to what is actually happening and often provides little information for designing a therapeutic intervention." "Family Therapy: A Radical Change," in *Changing Families: A Family Therapy Reader*, ed. Jay Haley (New York, 1971), 280–281.

89. Ackerman, *Treating the Troubled Family*, 94. The editors of Ackerman's collected papers provide a less standardized account in their description of patients coming and going at irregular intervals and sessions lasting from fifteen minutes to well over two hours. Donald Bloch and Robert Simon, eds., *The Strength of Family Therapy: Selected Papers of Nathan W. Ackerman* (New York, 1982), xvi.

90. Robert MacGregor, "Multiple Impact Psychotherapy with Families," *Family Process* 1 (March 1962): 15–29.

91. As family therapist Donald Bloch observed in 1976, "Attention to the membership to be included in the actual therapy sessions has been an early and persistent concern of family therapists." "Including the Children in Family Therapy," in *Family Therapy: Theory and Practice*, ed. Philip J. Guerin (New York, 1976), 169.

92. Don D. Jackson, "The Eternal Triangle: An Interview with Don D. Jackson, M.D.," in Jay Haley and Lynn Hoffman, *Techniques of Family Therapy* (New York, 1967), 190.

93. Don Jackson, "Family Data Sheets—K. Family," July 1962, Jackson Archive.

94. Jackson, "Eternal Triangle," 190. See also Paul Watzlawick, Janet Beavin, and Don D. Jackson, *Pragmatics of Human Communication: A Study of Interactional Patterns, Pathologies, and Paradoxes* (New York, 1967), 236–253.

95. Jackson, "Eternal Triangle," 227.

96. Ibid.

97. Don D. Jackson, "The Question of Family Homeostasis," *Psychiatric Quarterly Supplement* 31 (1957): 79–90.

98. Carl Whitaker, "My Philosophy of Psychotherapy," *Journal of Contemporary Psychotherapy* 6(1973): 49–52, reprinted in *From Psyche to System: The Evolving Theory of Carl Whitaker*, ed. John R. Neill and David P. Kniskern (New York, 1982), 33–34.

99. Salvador Minuchin and Avner Barcai, "Therapeutically Induced Family Crisis," in *Science and Psychoanalysis: Childhood and Adolescence*, ed. Jules H. Masserman, vol. 14 (New York, 1969), 204.

100. Ibid., 202.

101. At the four-and-a-half-hour emergency family therapy session that evening, the therapist focused on having the parents negotiate their conflict without the intervention of the children. After several additional months of therapy, the daughter was attending school, which she had previously not been able to do, and had been hospitalized only twice for her medical condition, acidosis.

102. Jay Haley, "Approaches to Family Therapy," *International Journal of Psychiatry* 9 (1970): 233–242, reprinted in Haley, *Changing Families*, 227–236; Murray H. Sherman et al., "Non-Verbal Cues and Reenactment of Conflict in Family Therapy," *Family Process* 4 (March 1965); and Gerald Zuk, "Family Therapy," *Archives of General Psychiatry* 16 (1967): 71–79.

103. George H. Grosser and Norman L. Paul addressed ethical objections to family therapy regarding the management of hostility in family therapy sessions, concerns about harm to the family unit and parents' authority or self-esteem, and professional standards of patient confidentiality in "Ethical Issues in Family Group Therapy," *American Journal of Orthopsychiatry* 34 (1964): 875–885. For an alternative defense of family therapy against charges of manipulation or unethical practices, see Jay Haley, *Problem-Solving Therapy: New Strategies for Effective Family Therapy* (San Francisco, 1976), 195–221. Athena McLean discusses her own ethical concerns about the impact of disrupting family patterns in one-time demonstration interviews that provide little follow-up care for families in "Family Therapy Workshops in the United States: Potential Abuses in the Production of Therapy in an Advanced Capitalist Society," *Social Science and Medicine* 23 (1986): 179–190.

104. Christian Beels and Andrew Ferber described the tasks of Satir and Bowen in "Family Therapy: A View," *Family Process* 8 (September 1969): 306.

105. For an example of such debates on insight and their connection to schisms in the field between psychodynamically inclined and more systems-oriented therapists, see Beels and Ferber, "Family Therapy: A View," 280–318, and the ensuing discussion comments by James Framo and Gerald Zuk.

106. E.g., Haley asserted, "When the unit with the problem is defined as two or more people, inevitably therapy has as its goal a change in the ways people deal with one another. The communicative sequence between intimates is the focus of change. With this focus, ideas about lifting repression, expressing emotion when alone with a therapist, or becoming aware of how one deals with other people are peripheral matters. The cause of change centers in the way the therapist intervenes in the family and requires a different sequence of behavior among the members. . . . Typically the family therapist talks to family members about understanding each other because they expect this, but he does not necessarily assume that this will cause them to change." "Family Therapy: A Radical Change," 282–283. Haley's approach stood in contrast to that of clinicians such as Nathan Ackerman and Murray Bowen, who retained some role for insight in the therapeutic process. See also Gerald Zuk, "Family Therapy," in Haley, *Changing Families*, 212–226. Zuk discusses insight and the importance of the expression of conflict for generating change in families and the role of the therapist in defining areas of conflict and then acting as a go-between or broker.

107. Murray Bowen, "The Use of Family Theory in Clinical Practice," *Comprehensive Psychiatry* 7 (1966): 345–374, reprinted in Haley, *Changing Families*, 168.

108. Lynn Hoffman, *Foundations of Family Therapy: A Conceptual Framework for Systems Change* (New York, 1981), 77.

109. In a panel at a 1965 conference on family therapy sponsored by Jewish Family Service of New York, Don D. Jackson claimed, "It has turned out that if normal families—by which I mean simply families that will volunteer, people who have never seen a therapist and never been arrested—are contrasted with families that come for help because somebody in the family has been identified as a patient—either delinquent, schizophrenic, or an underachiever—considerable differences will be found between these two groups of families in certain measurements. How well these data will hold up in repeated testing still remains an open question." From "Differences between 'Normal' and 'Abnormal' Families," in Ackerman, Beatman, and Sherman, *Expanding Theory and Practice*, 99–100.

110. On the mutually constitutive relationship between the normal and the pathological, see Georges Canguilhem, *The Normal and the Pathological* (1966; repr., New York, 1991).

111. Satir, *Conjoint Family Therapy*.

112. Haley, "Family Therapy: A Radical Change," 281.

113. Ibid.

114. Ibid.

115. Films and one-way mirrors were also used for supervision and teaching, even among therapists who did not use the technologies as part of their clinical repertoire.

116. For example, Norman Paul, "Effects of Playback on Family Members of Their Own Previously Recorded Conjoint Therapy Material," *Psychiatric Research Report* 20 (1966): 175–187; and Ian Alger and Peter Hogan, "Enduring Effects of Videotape Playback Experience on Family and Marital Relationships," *American Journal of Orthopsychiatry* 39 (1969): 86–94.

117. Salvador Minuchin et al., *Families of the Slums: An Exploration of Their Structure and Treatment* (New York, 1967).

118. Haley and Hoffman, *Techniques of Family Therapy*, ix–x (emphasis added).

119. A few family therapists advocated home visits or even home-based therapy, which drew on a long tradition of home visits in social work. On the history of psychiatric social work and home visits, see Lunbeck, *Psychiatric Persuasion*. Examples in family therapy include Alfred S. Friedman, "Family Therapy as Conducted in the Home," *Family Process* 1 (March 1962): 132–140; Richard Fisch, "Home Visits in a Private Psychiatric Practice," *Family Process*

3 (March 1964): 114–126; Israel Zwerling and Marilyn Mendelsohn, "Initial Family Reactions to Day Hospitalization," *Family Process* 4 (March 1965): 50–63; and Constance Hanson, "An Extended Home Visit with Conjoint Family Therapy," *Family Process* 7 (March 1968): 67–87. On patient-perspective history of medicine, see Arthur Kleinman, *The Illness Narratives: Suffering, Healing and the Human Condition* (New York, 1988); and Roy Porter, "The Patient's View: Doing Medical History from Below," *Theory and Society* 14 (1985): 175–198.

120. Audiotape, "Life and Work of Nathan Ackerman by the Historic Committee of the AAPsa (American Academy of Psychoanalysis), November 29, 1979, at the Semiannual Meeting at the Waldorf Astoria," box 4, folder 3, American Academy of Psychoanalysis collection, Oskar Diethelm Library for the History of Psychiatry, New York Hospital-Cornell Medical Center, New York.

121. Milton and Margaret Silverman, "Psychiatry inside the Family Circle," *Saturday Evening Post*, July 28–August 4, 1962, 51.

122. Lynn Spigel, *Welcome to the Dreamhouse: Popular Media and Postwar Suburbs* (Durham, NC, 2001), 2. Spigel analyzes architecture, television, and other media in order to "examine how middle-class ideas about family life—and the perceived divisions between private and public worlds—helped shape the visual forms, storytelling practices, and reception contexts of postwar media and consumer culture" (p. 3). A critique of the lack of distinction between public and private is at the heart of Christopher Lasch, *Haven in a Heartless World: The Family Besieged* (New York, 1977), xvii–xviii: "Most of the writing on the modern family takes for granted the 'isolation' of the nuclear family not only from the kinship system but from the world of work. It assumes this isolation makes the family impervious to outside influences. In reality, the modern world intrudes at every point and obliterates its privacy. The sanctity of the home is a sham in a world dominated by giant corporations and by the apparatus of mass promotion. . . . The same historical developments which have made it necessary to set up private life—the family in particular—as a refuge from the cruel world of politics and work, an emotional sanctuary, have invaded this sanctuary and subjected it to outside control." For additional historical analyses of separate spheres and the public and the private, see Laura McCall and Donald Yacavone, eds., *A Shared Experience: Men, Women, and the History of Gender* (New York, 1998); and Dorothy O. Helly and Susan Reverby, eds., *Gendered Domains: Rethinking Public and Private in Women's History: Essays from the Seventh Berkshire Conference on the History of Women* (Ithaca, 1992).

123. Robert MacGregor, "Communicating Values in Family Therapy," in *Family Therapy and Disturbed Families*, ed. Gerald Zuk and Ivan Boszormenyi Nagy (Palo Alto, 1967), 178–185.

124. In his response to Christian Beels and Andrew Ferber's article on types of family therapists, Lyman Wynne wrote, "I am aware of not being the same therapist (a) when I am seeing an upper-middle class urban Jewish couple and their drug-taking college dropout son and (b) when I am meeting with a lower class Southern Protestant family with two hebephrenic children." "Discussion: Comments by Lyman C. Wynne," *Family Process* 8 (September 1969): 327.

125. E.g., Gerald Handel, "Prologue: Views of a Changing Interior," in *The Psychosocial Interior of the Family: A Sourcebook for the Study of Whole Families*, ed. Gerald Handel, 2nd ed. (1967; repr., Chicago, 1972), v–xix.

126. Haley and Hoffman, *Techniques of Family Therapy*, v.

127. Murray Bowen, "The Use of Family Theory in Clinical Practice," *Comprehensive Psychiatry* 7 (1966): 345–374, reprinted in Haley, *Changing Families*, 169 (emphasis in original).

2. "Systems Everywhere"

1. Gregory Bateson, Don D. Jackson, Jay Haley, and John Weakland, "Toward a Theory of Schizophrenia," *Behavioral Science* 1 (1956): 251–264, reprinted in Gregory Bateson, *Steps to an Ecology of Mind: Collected Essays in Anthropology, Psychiatry, Evolution and Epistemology* (New York, 1972), 201–227.

2. Ibid., 217–218. Jackson described this case to the group in one of its weekly meetings. In response to his recounting of the hospital exchange between mother and son, John Weakland commented, "She's a fast mover." Jackson replied, "Yeah, she keeps him coming and going," and Bateson added, "Yeah, these things happen damn fast I suspect." Jackson Conference Transcript (hereafter *JCT*), December 8, 1955, Jackson Archive. In using the phrase "Jackson Conference" to identify the Palo Alto group's weekly meetings, I am following the nomenclature employed at the Jackson Archive, which houses the recordings and transcriptions of the meetings.

3. Luc Ciompi, *The Psyche and Schizophrenia: The Bond between Affect and Logic*, trans. Deborah Lucas Schneider (Cambridge, MA, 1988), 126, cited in Edward Dolnick, *Madness on the Couch: Blaming the Victim in the Heyday of Psychoanalysis* (New York, 1998), 117. On criticisms of the double bind, see Paul Watzlawick, "A Review of the Double Bind Theory," *Family Process* 2 (March 1963): 132–153; and Carlos E. Sluzki and Donald C. Ransom, eds., *Double Bind: The Foundation of the Communicational Approach to the Family* (New York, 1976).

4. Ludwig von Bertalanffy's introduction to *General System Theory* includes a section titled "Systems Everywhere" in which he discusses the diffusion of systems thinking through different scientific fields, popular thought, and mass media. *General System Theory: Foundations, Developments, Applications* (New York, 1968), 3–10.

5. This list draws together a diverse array of fields among which there were also important distinctions. For example, Evelyn Fox Keller differentiates between the quantitative, content-neutral use of "information" in cybernetics and Claude Shannon's information theory on the one hand and the use of "information" as a more particular kind of unidirectional instruction by molecular biologists on the other, in *Refiguring Life: Metaphors of Twentieth-Century Biology* (New York, 1995), 89–99. While these kinds of differences suggest the diverse implementations of systems theory and cybernetics, there were also historical actors (including von Bertalanffy and Norbert Wiener) who were committed to using systems theory and cybernetics to unify the sciences. On postwar attempts to build a unified theory of science that bore a markedly American stamp, see Peter Galison, "The Americanization of Unity," *Daedalus* 127 (Winter 1998): 45–71.

6. Cf. Ludmilla Jordanova, "Naturalizing the Family: Literature and the Bio-Medical Sciences in the Late Eighteenth Century," in *Languages of Nature: Critical Essays on Science and Literature*, ed. Ludmilla Jordanova (London, 1986), 86–116; Judith Butler, "Is Kinship Always Already Heterosexual?," *differences* 13 (2002): 14–44; Ellen Herman, *Kinship by Design: A History of Adoption in the Modern United States* (Chicago, 2008); and Sarah Franklin and Susan McKinnon, eds., *Relative Values: Reconfiguring Kinship Studies* (Durham, NC, 2001).

7. "The Role the Paradoxes of Abstraction in Communication," undated draft of a grant application (1954?), folder "Bateson Archive Materials/Related Files," 9, Jackson Archive.

8. Ibid., 1.

9. Ibid., 10.

10. Eugen Bleuler, "The Fundamental Symptoms of Dementia Praecox or the Group of Schizophrenia (1911)," in *The Origins of Modern Psychiatry*, ed. C. Thompson (Chichester, UK, 1987), 165–209; and J. S. Kasanin, ed., *Language and Thought in Schizophrenia* (New York, 1964). See also Sander L. Gilman, "Constructing Schizophrenia as a Category of Mental Illness," in *Disease and Representation: Images of Illness from Madness to AIDS* (Ithaca, 1988), 213–222, on the central place of language in the conceptions of schizophrenia espoused by psychiatrists.

11. For more on the Macy meetings, see Steve Joshua Heims, *Constructing a Social Science for Postwar America: The Cybernetics Group, 1946–1953* (Cambridge, MA, 1993).

12. Norbert Wiener, *Cybernetics, or Control and Communication in the Animal and the Machine*, 2nd ed. (1948; repr., New York, 1961), 11–12.

13. See Peter Galison, "The Ontology of the Enemy: Norbert Wiener and the Cybernetic Vision," *Critical Inquiry* 21 (Autumn 1994): 228–266.

14. Wiener, *Cybernetics*, 8.

15. Ibid., 42.

16. N. Katherine Hayles, "Designs on the Body: Norbert Wiener, Cybernetics, and the Play of Metaphor," *History of the Human Sciences* 3 (1990): 215.

17. See, e.g., Paul Watzlawick, Janet Beavin, and Don D. Jackson, *Pragmatics of Human Communication: A Study of Interactional Patterns, Pathologies, and Paradoxes* (New York, 1967), 28–30.

18. Tara Abraham, "(Physio)logical Circuits: The Intellectual Origins of the McCulloch-Pitts Neural Networks," *Journal of the History of the Behavioral Sciences* 38 (2002): 3–25; Paul N. Edwards, *The Closed World: Computers and the Politics of Discourse in Cold War America* (Cambridge, MA, 1996); Galison, "Ontology of the Enemy"; Slava Gerovitch, *From Newspeak to Cyberspeak: A History of Soviet Cybernetics* (Cambridge, 2002); Orit Halpern, "Dreams for Our Perceptual Present: Temporality, Storage, and Interactivity in Cybernetics," *Configurations* 13, no. 2 (2005): 283–319; Donna Haraway, "The High Cost of Information in Post–World War II Evolutionary Biology: Ergonomics, Semiotics, and the Sociobiology of Communication Systems," *Philosophical Forum* 13 (1981–82): 244–278; N. Katherine Hayles, *How We Became Posthuman: Virtual Bodies in Cybernetics, Literature, and Informatics* (Chicago, 1999); Thomas P. Hughes, "Spread of the Systems Approach," *Rescuing Prometheus* (New York, 1998), 141–195; Lily E. Kay, "Cybernetics, Information, Life: The Emergence of Scriptural Representations of Heredity," *Configurations* 5 (1997): 23–91; Jennifer S. Light, *From Warfare to Welfare: Defense Intellectuals and the War on American City Problems* (Baltimore, 2003); Andrew Pickering, *The Cybernetic Brain: Sketches of Another Future* (Chicago, 2010); Peter J. Taylor, "Technocratic Optimism, H. T. Odum, and the Partial Transformation of Ecological Metaphor after World War II," *Journal of the History of Biology* 21 (Summer 1988): 213–244; and JoAnne Yates, *Control through Communication: The Rise of System in American Management* (Baltimore, 1989).

19. Wiener, *Cybernetics*, 28–29. On Wiener's moral ambivalence about cybernetics and his liberal humanistic values, see Hayles, *How We Became Posthuman*, chap. 4.

20. My overview of the Macy meetings draws on Heims, *Constructing a Social Science*, and Heinz von Foerster, ed., *Cybernetics: Circular Causal and Feedback Mechanisms in Biological and Social Systems (Transactions of the Sixth–Tenth Conferences)* (New York, 1949–53).

21. E.g., Jay Haley, *Strategies of Psychotherapy* (New York, 1963), 21–59; and Haley, *Uncommon Therapy: The Psychiatric Techniques of Milton Erickson, M.D.* (New York, 1973).

22. Arturo Rosenblueth, Norbert Wiener, and Julian Bigelow, "Behavior, Purpose, and Teleology," *Philosophy of Science* 10 (1943): 18–24.

23. Walter B. Cannon, *The Wisdom of the Body* (New York, 1932). For secondary literature on Cannon and homeostasis, including affinities with the nineteenth-century French physiologist Claude Bernard and sociopolitical applications of homeostasis, see Georges Canguilhem, *The Normal and the Pathological* (1966; repr., New York, 1991 (1966)); Cross and Albury, "Walter B. Cannon, L. J. Henderson, and the Organic Analogy"; and Donald Fleming, "Walter B. Cannon and Homeostasis," *Social Research* 51 (Autumn 1984): 609–640.

24. Heims, *Constructing a Social Science*, 14–17.

25. von Foerster, *Cybernetics*, 8:20.

26. Hayles, *How We Became Posthuman*, 8.

27. Heims, *Constructing a Social Science*, 17.

28. "Introductory Discussion," in *Cybernetics: Circular Causal and Feedback Mechanisms in Biological and Social Systems (Transactions of the Sixth Conference, March 24–25, 1949, New York, NY)*, ed. Heinz von Foerster (New York, 1950), 9.

29. Cited in David Lipset, *Gregory Bateson: The Legacy of a Scientist* (Englewood Cliffs, NJ, 1980), 180.

30. See ibid., 172–174. In Haley's history of the Palo Alto group, written as the project was ending in 1961, he provided this illustration of deutero-learning: "For example, the dog in the Pavlovian experiment not only learns to salivate when the bell rings, but at another level he learns to see the world to be a place where you passively wait for reward and do not

actively seek it." Jay Haley, "The Development of a Theory: The Rise and Demise of a Research Project," 1961, 2, Jackson Archive, published with minor revisions plus commentary from Gregory Bateson and John Weakland in Jay Haley, "Development of a Research Project," in Sluzki and Ransom, *Double Bind*, 59–104.

31. Gregory Bateson, *Naven: A Survey of Problems Suggested by a Composite Picture of the Culture of a New Guinea Tribe Drawn from Three Points of View* (Stanford, 1936).

32. Bateson became disgruntled with his war work for the Office of Strategic Services, which employed many anthropologists in the early 1940s, and held several temporary teaching positions before making his way to California. Lipset, *Gregory Bateson*, 174–178.

33. Jurgen Ruesch and Gregory Bateson, *Communication: The Social Matrix of Psychiatry* (New York, 1951).

34. This point is discussed in Lipset, *Gregory Bateson*, 188, and Steve P. Heims, "Gregory Bateson and the Mathematicians: From Interdisciplinary Interaction to Societal Functions," *Journal of the History of the Behavioral Sciences* 13 (1977): 150.

35. Ruesch and Bateson, *Communication*, 168. On McCulloch and Pitts, see Abraham, "(Physio)logical Circuits"; and Heims, *Constructing a Social Science*.

36. Lipset, *Gregory Bateson*, 206.

37. Gregory Bateson, principal investigator, "Schizophrenic Communication: Application for Research Grant, Public Health Service, National Institutes of Health," June 23, 1954, unlabeled folder, Jackson Archive.

38. Ibid., 7.

39. Gregory Bateson to Norbert Wiener, c. April 1954, COR box 37, folder 1496, Gregory Bateson papers, MS 98, Special Collections and Archives, University Library, University of California, Santa Cruz.

40. When the Palo Alto group began to discuss writing a collaborative article on the double bind in February 1956, Bateson told Haley, Jackson, and Weakland, "The invention of the double bind was between the Rockefeller and the Macy [foundation grants]. It arose from my conversation with Wiener when I went East to sell the Rockefeller on a renewal and they didn't buy it." *JCT*, February 21, 1956.

41. Bateson, "Schizophrenic Communication," 8.

42. The literature on motherhood, maternalism, and mother love is vast. For useful sources on the midcentury American psychologization of motherhood, including thoughtful discussions of Wylie's momism, see Rebecca Plant, *Mom: The Transformation of Motherhood in Modern America* (Chicago, 2010); Mari Jo Buhle, *Feminism and Its Discontents: A Century of Struggle with Psychoanalysis* (Cambridge, MA, 1998), 125–164; and Ruth Feldstein, *Motherhood in Black and White: Race and Sex in American Liberalism, 1930–1965* (Ithaca, 2000).

43. Gerald N. Grob, *From Asylum to Community: Mental Health Policy in Modern America* (Princeton, 1991), 97. See also Gerald N. Grob, "Origins of DSM-I: A Study in Appearance and Reality," *American Journal of Psychiatry* 148 (1991): 421–431.

44. American Psychiatric Association, *Diagnostic and Statistical Manual: Mental Disorders* (Washington, DC, 1952), 5.

45. Emil Kraepelin, *Lectures on Clinical Psychiatry*, authorized trans. from the 2nd German ed., rev. and ed. T. Johnstone (London, 1906); and Emil Kraepelin, "Dementia Praecox and Paraphrenia (1919) and Introductory Lectures on Clinical Psychiatry (1906) III Dementia Praecox," in Thompson, *Origins of Modern Psychiatry*, 225–243.

46. Bleuler, "The Fundamental Symptoms of Dementia Praecox or the Group of Schizophrenia (1911)," in *The Origins of Modern Psychiatry*, 165–209. See Richard Noll, *American Madness: The Rise and Fall of Dementia Praecox* (Cambridge, MA, 2011).

47. My discussion draws on Gilman, "Constructing Schizophrenia," and Harry Stack Sullivan, *Schizophrenia as a Human Process* (New York, 1962).

48. Joel Braslow, *Mental Ills and Bodily Cures: Psychiatric Treatment in the First Half of the Twentieth Century* (Berkeley, 1997); and Jack David Pressman, *Last Resort: Psychosurgery and the Limits of Medicine* (Cambridge, UK, 1998).

49. On the history of chlorpromazine and the psychiatric profession's management of side effects, efficacy questions, legal challenges, and patient's rights, see Sheldon Gelman, *Medicating Schizophrenia: A History* (New Brunswick, NJ, 1999). See also Jonathan Metzl, *The Protest Psychosis: How Schizophrenia Became a Black Disease* (Boston, 2009).

50. Braslow, *Mental Ills and Bodily Cures*, 104.

51. Mortimer Ostow, "The New Drugs," *Atlantic Monthly*, July 1961, 92–96; and Gelman, *Medicating Schizophrenia*, 27–28. For a reassessment of the historical presumption of a clear distinction between biological and psychoanalytic psychiatry, see Jonathan Metzl, *Prozac on the Couch: Prescribing Gender in the Era of Wonder Drugs* (Durham, NC, 2003). The Palo Alto research group members also discussed the use of psychotropic drugs such as Serpasil as a means of lowering patients' anxiety defenses so that psychotherapy could proceed. *JCT*, February 23, 1955.

52. For a sample of this diversity, see the essays in Alfred Auerback, ed., *Schizophrenia: An Integrated Approach* (New York, 1959); and Don D. Jackson, ed., *The Etiology of Schizophrenia* (New York, 1960). For a slightly later period, see John Romano, ed., *The Origins of Schizophrenia* (Amsterdam, 1967); David Rosenthal and Seymour Kety, eds., *The Transmission of Schizophrenia* (Oxford, 1968); and Lyman C. Wynne, Rue L. Cromwell, and Steven Matthysse, eds., *The Nature of Schizophrenia: New Approaches to Research and Treatment* (New York, 1978).

53. This brief overview emphasizes common themes, but there were also significant points of disagreement among analysts' views of the cause, nature, and appropriate treatment of schizophrenia—for example, regarding the potential for transference by a schizophrenic patient.

54. For example, in a 1954 grant application, they wrote, "The proposed research will focus upon an entirely different aspect of schizophrenic communication (from an approach in terms of symbols, delusional content, condensation, displacement, projection, etc.). It is generally agreed that schizophrenics have difficulty in discriminating between 'reality' and fantasy; and also that they have difficulty in the use of non-verbal and implicit signals. . . . The research, starting from these two generalizations, will study the schizophrenic's use of that particular category of non-verbal and implicit signals which indicate whether a given utterance is literal or metaphoric, jocular or serious, sincere or histrionic, etc. This class of signals we call 'reality-qualifiers.' " Cited in Haley, "Development of a Theory," 10.

55. Theodore Lidz, "The Intrafamilial Environment of Schizophrenic Patients: II. Marital Schism and Marital Skew," *American Journal of Psychiatry* 114 (1957): 241–248; Theodore Lidz, Stephen Fleck, and A. R. Cornelison, *Schizophrenia and the Family* (New York, 1965); Lyman C. Wynne, Irving M. Rychoff, Juliana Day, and Stanley I. Hirsch, "Pseudo-Mutuality in the Family Relations of Schizophrenics," *Psychiatry* 21 (May 1958): 205–220; and Murray Bowen, *Family Therapy in Clinical Practice* (New York, 1978).

56. Frieda Fromm-Reichmann, *Psychoanalysis and Psychotherapy: Selected Papers* (Chicago, 1959); Harry Stack Sullivan, *Collected Works* (New York, 1953); Dolnick, *Madness on the Couch*, 84–166; and Nathan G. Hale Jr., *The Rise and Crisis of Psychoanalysis in the United States: Freud and the Americans, 1917–1985* (New York, 1995), 264–270. For biographical studies of Fromm-Reichmann and Sullivan, see Gail A. Hornstein, *To Redeem One Person Is to Redeem the World: The Life of Frieda Fromm-Reichmann* (New York, 2000); and Helen Swick Perry, *Psychiatrist of America: The Life of Harry Stack Sullivan* (Cambridge, MA, 1982).

57. Bateson, "Schizophrenic Communication," 10.

58. E.g., *JCT*, September 28, 1955; November 2, 1955; November 19, 1955; and February 14, 1956. They discussed Sullivan on February 21, 1956, and references to his work peppered their weekly conversations.

59. The reference to visual anthropology is more than one of passing resemblance. Bateson's work with Margaret Mead in Bali during the 1930s produced some of the classic film footage and photography of visual anthropology. Gregory Bateson and Margaret Mead, *Balinese Character: A Photographic Analysis* (New York, 1942), and the films *First Days in the Life of a New Guinea Baby* (1951), *Childhood Rivalry in Bali and New Guinea* (1952), and *Trance and*

Dance in Bali (1952). Bateson and Mead discussed the differences in their views of the role of the camera in research in "Margaret Mead and Gregory Bateson on the Use of the Camera in Anthropology," *Studies in the Anthropology of Visual Communication* 4 (1977): 78–80. See chapter 5 for further discussion of visual anthropology and family therapy training films.

60. "Tentative Outline for a Six-Year Research Project on Psychotherapy," c. 1951, folder "Tentative Outline for a Six-Year Research Project on Psychotherapy," Jackson Archive.

61. Don D. Jackson, "Family Therapy in the Family of the Schizophrenic," in *Contemporary Psychotherapies*, ed. Morris I. Stein (New York, 1961), 272.

62. Don D. Jackson, "The Question of Family Homeostasis," *Psychiatric Quarterly Supplement* 31 (1957): 79–90. Jackson initially presented this material at the Palo Alto VA and the 1954 APA meeting in St. Louis.

63. Don D. Jackson, "The Study of the Family," *Family Process* 4 (March 1965): 6.

64. Ibid., 11.

65. He later published on marital rules and quid pro quo in Don D. Jackson, "Family Rules: Marital Quid Pro Quo," *Archives of General Psychiatry* 12 (1965): 589–594.

66. Jackson, "Question of Family Homeostasis," 1–2.

67. Grob, *From Asylum to Community*, 63–67, 100–102; and Committee on the Family, "Integration and Conflict in Family Behavior," GAP Report No. 27, August 1954.

68. Haley, "Development of a Theory." See also Dolnick, *Madness on the Couch*, 122; and Lipset, *Gregory Bateson*, 206.

69. The reel-to-reel audio recordings of these meetings are extant and available at the Don D. Jackson Archive in Monroe, Louisiana. The Jackson Archive director, Wendel Ray, and his family therapy students have transcribed many of the meetings. I thank him for sharing his unpublished transcriptions with me.

70. *JCT*, September 14, 1955; November 17, 1955; November 28, 1955.

71. *JCT*, August 31, 1955.

72. Ibid. Jackson also refers to Fairbairn on March 6, 1956, in a discussion of the meaning of "interpersonal."

73. *JCT*, December 8, 1955.

74. *JCT*, February 23, 1955.

75. *JCT*, February 16, 1955.

76. *JCT*, December 8 and 29, 1955, and March 19, 1957.

77. E.g., *JCT*, December 15, 1955.

78. *JCT*, February 16, 1955, and April 27, 1955.

79. *JCT*, February 23, 1955.

80. E.g., *JCT*, August 31, 1955; November 28, 1955; December 15, 1955; and February 26, 1957. Though they generally focused on mother-child interactions during the mid-1950s, they occasionally discussed the role of fathers and the larger family unit of mother-father-child, e.g., April 27, 1955.

81. *JCT*, December 15, 1955.

82. *JCT*, August 31, 1955.

83. E.g., *JCT*, November 28, 1955; December 8, 1955; December 15, 1955; and December 29, 1955.

84. In the group meeting on November 23, 1955, Jackson and Haley had the following conversation, which brought together Bateson's approach to Logical Types and ego psychology:

> **H:** He can then say "Well I'll stay home because you want me to stay home," but if she does it indirectly, then I suspect that something like the "flavor" of a double bind arises. When she says "you don't love me." What I would like to see is this clearly written out. How he's caught if he stays home, caught if he doesn't stay home.
>
> **J:** Okay, and I think it can be done, particularly two ways. One way that I've become very fond of is Greg's logical types. I think this is a very good analogy, although I think it's an analogy. I think the other way it could be done is by using the data

that is already known about how a child begins to differentiate itself into a person, how the ego forms. I think that a little bit is known about that. I think it fits in clearly with the double bind, but of the early difficulty of knowing what's her and what's me. And that one gradually learns to make the distinction first between self and part objects and then whole objects. And that the ability to finally achieve the feeling of this is me, you know, is related to mental health. Whereas if mother puts it so that it is not her that is saying it, but she works on something in you so that you say it, it keeps this boundary between you and her and therefore the rest of the world fuzzy.

H: Okay, that would be another analogy.

J: But I think this could be developed in some detail which I'm not doing.

H: I think it could be but I don't know whether you could go to a specific piece of data and diagram that out of it, unless you had a level of discourse a little different from that kind of discourse. I think the logical type level you could diagram. I can diagram the Erickson 'stay awake' one, but we have a project on schizophrenia, we assume that the double bind is the precipitating factor and so many other things, we should be able to diagram this from schizophrenic data.

85. For an influential anthology on the relevant issues, see Michael Lynch and Steve Woolgar, eds., *Representation in Scientific Practice* (Cambridge, MA, 1990). An excellent sample from a substantial literature is David Kaiser, *Drawing Theories Apart: The Dispersion of Feynman Diagrams in Postwar Physics* (Chicago, 2005).

86. In the middle of their meeting, Jackson said, "We're just going from hypothesis to wild speculation." *JCT*, December 15, 1955.

87. Ibid.

88. "A free-wheeling interview often ended up with little information and the patient thoroughly on the spot. When we turned to sound movies, which could only be one-half hour in length, the need for structure was even more acute." From "The Structured Interview," c. 1962, unlabeled folder, 1, Jackson Archive.

89. Ibid.

90. Transcripts of initial family interviews, 1957–59, Jackson Archive.

91. John Weakland, "Family Filming Sessions—Revised Script Outline," June 19, 1959, folder "Family Therapy in Schizophrenia," 1, Jackson Archive. Weakland began the outline by explaining, "This outline attempts to summarize what we currently think a family filming should cover, in terms of a list of broadly labeled scenes, in sequence, together with some indication of the framing remarks setting up these scenes, and of the aspects of family interaction they are primarily or secondarily expected to illuminate." The first such scene was titled "Unstructured Interaction." It came with these instructions: "Framing—'Please sit down; everything will be ready in a minute or two and I'll be back with you then.' Focus—Family interaction, especially their qualifications and disqualifications of others and self with outside influence minimized." The second scene was based on "cooperative planning," with the family asked to "spend a few minutes planning something you'd like to do together as a family" and a focus on "leadership and agreement or disagreement. Secondarily, data should be available on potential coalitions and relations of third parties to them—e.g., do third parties break up, if any begin to form." The outline included four additional scenes, but these two illustrate the orientation of the interview.

92. Information on referral sources was recorded on "Family Data Sheets," many of which are available at the Jackson Archive. Recruitment letters can be found in the folder "Family Search—Outline" at the Jackson Archive.

93. Dr. Jules Riskin, "Family Data Sheet," November 8, 1960, Jackson Archive.

94. Gregory Bateson and John Weakland, "Final Report on Mental Health Project Grant OM-324 C2, National Institute of Mental Health: Family Therapy in Schizophrenia," November 20, 1962, folder "Final Report to NIMH," Appendix II, Jackson Archive.

95. Ibid. The miscellaneous families included one with "shut-ins," another with a schizophrenic husband rather than a schizophrenic child, and one with family problems but no schizophrenia.

96. Bateson et al., "Toward a Theory of Schizophrenia," 206–207.

97. Bateson, Jackson, Haley, and Weakland corresponded with other researchers studying schizophrenia and the family, such as Murray Bowen, Elliot Mishler and Nancy Waxler, R. D. Laing, Nathan Epstein, and Stephen Fleck. For one review of differences among family therapists' approaches to family systems and schizophrenia, with responses from the clinicians and theorists whose work was included in the review, see Elliot G. Mishler and Nancy E. Waxler, *Family Processes and Schizophrenia* (New York, 1968).

98. For useful albeit opinionated reviews of responses to "Toward a Theory of Schizophrenia," see Paul Watzlawick, "A Review of the Double Bind Theory," *Family Process* 2 (March 1963): 132–153; and Gina Abeles, "Researching the Unresearchable: Experimentation on the Double Bind," and Carlos E. Sluzki and Donald C. Ransom, "Comment on Gina Abeles' Review," in Sluzki and Ransom, *Double Bind*, 113–163. The "pseudo-psychologizing" critique came from Mortimer Ostow, "Discussion of Arieti's 'Recent Conceptions and Misconceptions of Schizophrenia," *American Journal of Psychotherapy* 14 (1960): 23–29, quoted in Watzlawick, "Review of the Double Bind Theory," 135.

99. In the preface to *Double Bind*, Sluzki and Ransom combine a critique of the original statement of the double bind theory with an embrace (affective connotation intended) of its continued utility:

Over the years, the logical beauty of the concept has created an illusion of concreteness: it gives the impression of being a handy notion that can be plugged into many different models. But this misunderstanding has led to many intellectual dead ends. Double Bind contains a general theory in its own right, and let the reader be forewarned that he or she is dealing with a powerful idea that, when apprehended, cannot help but change his or her view of human behavior. Considering the passion that it has evoked, the notion of the double bind should be approached with scientific rigor as well as tenderness. In that way, a long lasting, loving relationship will likely be established between the idea and the reader . . . if it does not exist already. (P. vii)

100. Gregory Bateson to Paul Watzlawick, May 13, 1966, COR box 36, folder 1463, Gregory Bateson Archive, Santa Cruz, California.

101. Cited in Sluzki and Ransom, "Comment on Abeles' Review," 161.

102. Haley, "Development of a Theory," 29–46. The array of projects was also apparent in grant applications and publications from that time.

103. Ibid., 52.

104. Quoted in Lipset, *Gregory Bateson*, 237.

105. Ibid., 236–237.

106. Galison further argues,

In principle, can the cultural meanings of feedback systems be dissociated from the origins of the technology? Of course. . . . Of interest is not the mere identification of associations, but the cultural historical account of their assembly, persistence, and deconstruction. Cultural meaning is neither aleatory nor eternal. We are not free by fiat alone to dismiss the chain of associations that was forged over decades in the laboratory, on the battlefield, in the social sciences, and in the philosophy of cybernetics. . . . What we *do* have to acknowledge is the power of a half-century in which these and other associations have been reinstantiated at every turn, in which opposition is seen to lie at the core of every human contact with the outside world. ("Ontology of the Enemy," 264–265)

107. The pervasiveness of metaphor not only in literature and everyday life but also in scientific discourse challenges traditional views of scientific language by showing that language is

not a transparent medium for transporting knowledge or an unmediated window onto nature. For more extended analyses of metaphor and science, many of which address holism, homeostasis, systems, and cybernetics, see James L. Bono, "Science, Discourse, and Literature: The Role/Rule of Metaphor in Science," in *Literature and Science: Theory & Practice*, ed. Stuart Peterfreund (Boston, 1990), 59–89; Stephen J. Cross and William R. Albury, "Walter B. Cannon, L. J. Henderson, and the Organic Analogy," *Osiris* 3 (1987): 165–192; Edwards, *Closed World*; Anne Harrington, *Reenchanted Science: Holism in German Culture from Whilhem II to Hitler* (Princeton, 1996); Hayles, "Designs on the Body"; Mary Hesse, *Revolutions and Reconstructions in the Philosophy of Science* (Brighton, UK, 1980); Kay, "Cybernetics, Information, Life"; Evelyn Fox Keller, *Making Sense of Life: Explaining Biological Development with Models, Metaphors, and Machines* (Cambridge, MA, 2002); and Taylor, "Technocratic Optimism."

108. Jackson, "Question of Family Homeostasis," 79.

109. Taylor, "Technocratic Optimism," 215–223.

110. Cited in Michael G. Barbour, "Ecological Fragmentation in the Fifties," in *Uncommon Ground: Rethinking the Human Place in Nature*, ed. William Cronon (New York, 1995), 233.

111. For more on the twentieth-century history of the science of ecology in the United States, see Barbour, "Ecological Fragmentation in the Fifties"; Sharon E. Kingsland, *Modeling Nature: Episodes in the History of Population Ecology* (Chicago, 1985); Gregg Mitman, *The State of Nature: Ecology, Community, and American Social Thought, 1900–1950* (Chicago, 1992); and Taylor, "Technocratic Optimism."

112. Cf. Gerald Markowitz and David Rosner, *Children, Race, and Power: Kenneth and Mamie Clark's Northside Center* (Charlottesville, VA, 1996).

113. Edgar H. Auerswald, "Interdisciplinary versus Ecological Approach," in *Family Process*, ed. Nathan W. Ackerman (New York, 1970), 235.

114. Ibid., 236.

115. For a classic articulation of sociological labeling theory, see Thomas J. Scheff, *Being Mentally Ill: A Sociological Theory* (Chicago, 1966). See also Erving Goffman, *Asylums: Essays on the Social Situation of Mental Patients and Other Inmates* (Garden City, NY, 1961).

116. See also Lynn Hoffman, "Deviation-Amplifying Processes in Natural Groups," in *Changing Families: A Family Therapy Reader*, ed. Jay Haley (New York, 1971), 285–311, for a discussion relating cybernetics-based family therapy and the sociology of deviance.

117. Jerome Agel, ed., *Radical Therapist: The Radical Therapist Collective* (New York, 1971), cover.

118. Lyman Wynne, "Problems to Be Investigated," in *Family Interaction: A Dialogue Between Family Researchers and Family Therapists*, ed. James Framo (New York, 1972), 89.

119. Subsequent nonequilibrium family therapists such as Paul Dell and Mony Elkaim developed family life cycle, developmental, and evolutionary models of family life. For a useful summary, see Lynn Hoffman, *Foundations of Family Therapy: A Conceptual Framework for Systems Change* (New York, 1981), 156–176, 339–349.

120. Harrington, *Reenchanted Science*, xxiii.

121. Cross and Albury, "Walter B. Cannon, L. J. Henderson, and the Organic Analogy"; and Harrington, *Reenchanted Science*.

122. Edwards, *Closed World*, 114.

123. Wynne, "Problems to Be Investigated," 89–91.

124. Howard Brick, *The Age of Contradiction: American Thought and Culture in the 1960s* (New York, 1998), 124.

125. Lipset, *Gregory Bateson*, 201.

126. *JCT*, February 21, 1956.

127. Jules Henry to John Weakland, January 23, 1961, Jackson Archive. Group members also discussed the double bind in correspondence with prominent psychiatrists and scholars such as Wiener, Bertalanffy, Erving Goffman, Thomas Szasz, R. D. Laing, and W. R. D. Fairbairn.

128. R. D. Laing, *Knots* (London, 1970). Laing refers to the double bind and related work by members of the Palo Alto group in *The Self and Others: Further Studies in Sanity and*

Madness (London, 1961); R. D. Laing, "Mystification, Confusion, and Conflict," in *Intensive Family Therapy*, ed. Ivan Boszormenyi-Nagy and James L. Framo (New York, 1965), 353; R. D. Laing, *The Politics of the Family, and Other Essays* (New York, 1969), 52, 110; and R. D. Laing and Aaron Esterson, *Sanity, Madness, and the Family: Families of Schizophrenics*, 2nd ed. (1964; repr., London, 1970), xii.

129. Mara Selvini Palazzoli et al., *Paradox and Counterparadox* (New York, 1978).

130. Milton Berger, ed., *Beyond the Double Bind: Communication and Family Systems, Theories and Techniques with Schizophrenics* (New York, 1978), xi.

131. Gregory Bateson, Don D. Jackson, Jay Haley, and John H. Weakland, "A Note on the Double Bind—1962," *Family Process* 2 (March 1963): 154–161.

132. Ibid., 157.

133. John Weakland, "The 'Double Bind' Hypothesis of Schizophrenia and Three-Party Interaction," in *The Etiology of Schizophrenia*, ed. Don D. Jackson (New York, 1960), 373–388. Reprinted in Sluzki and Ransom, eds., *Double Bind*, 23–37.

134. Fred Ford to MRI Staff, "Family Therapy Theory," March 30, 1966, 1, Jackson Archive.

135. Watzlawick, "A Review of the Double Bind Theory," 140 (emphasis in original).

136. Milton and Margaret Silverman, "Psychiatry inside the Family Circle," *Saturday Evening Post*, July 28–August 4, 1962, 46–51.

137. Janet Malcolm, "The One-Way Mirror," *New Yorker*, May 15, 1978, 39–114.

138. Christopher Lasch, *Haven in a Heartless World: The Family Besieged* (New York, 1977), 153–155; Mark Poster, *Critical Theory of the Family* (New York, 1978), 111–120; and Dolnick, *Madness on the Couch*, 117–123.

139. Paolo Bertrando, "The Evolution of Family Interventions for Schizophrenia: A Tribute to Gianfranco Cecchin," *Journal of Family Therapy* 28 (2006): 4–22.

140. Gregory Bateson to Norbert Wiener, November 23, 1959, COR box 37, Folder 1496, Bateson papers.

3. The Culture Concept at Work

1. A. L. Kroeber and Clyde Kluckhohn, *Culture: A Critical Review of Concepts and Definitions* (Cambridge, MA, 1952).

2. Several scholars have discussed the historical overlap between humanistic and anthropological notions of culture, despite Kroeber and Kluckhohn's claims for their distinctness. E.g., Susan Hegeman, *Patterns for America: Modernism and the Concept of Culture* (Princeton, 1999); George Stocking, *Race, Culture and Evolution: Essays in the History of Anthropology* (New York, 1968), 69–90; and Raymond Williams, *Keywords: A Vocabulary of Culture and Society* (1976; repr., New York, 1985).

3. On the prewar popularization of the culture concept, see John S. Gilkeson Jr., "The Domestication of 'Culture' in Interwar America, 1919–1941," in *The Estate of Social Knowledge*, ed. Joanne Brown and David K. Van Keuren (Baltimore, 1991), 153–174; and Marc Manganaro, *Culture, 1922: The Emergence of a Concept* (Princeton, 2002).

4. On scientific objects as variably salient, emergent, and productive at different times, see Lorraine Daston, "The Coming into Being of Scientific Objects," in *Biographies of Scientific Objects*, ed. Lorraine Daston (Chicago, 2000), 1–14. Two essays are particularly relevant to this chapter: Peter Wagner, "'An Entirely New Object of Consciousness, of Volition, of Thought:' The Coming into Being and (Almost) Passing Away of 'Society' as a Scientific Object," 132–157, and Marshall Sahlins, "'Sentimental Pessimism' and Ethnographic Experience, or, Why Culture Is Not a Disappearing 'Object,'" 158–202.

5. Committee on the Family, "Integration and Conflict in Family Behavior," GAP Report No. 27, August 1954, 1, 2, 3.

6. On the history of GAP, see Gerald N. Grob, *From Asylum to Community: Mental Health Policy in Modern America* (Princeton, 1991), 29–43; and Ellen Herman, *The Romance of American Psychiatry* (Berkeley, 1995), 247–253.

7. On the history of the impact of World War II on psychiatry, see Grob, *From Asylum to Community*, 5–43; Herman, *Romance of American Psychiatry*, 17–123; and Nathan Hale, *The Rise and Crisis of Psychoanalysis in the United States* (New York, 1995), 187–210.

8. Grob, *From Asylum to Community*, 30.

9. Gerald N. Grob, "Psychiatry and Social Activism: The Politics of a Specialty in Postwar America," *Bulletin of the History of Medicine* 60 (Winter 1986): 477–501; and Herman, *The Romance of American Psychiatry*, 250–251.

10. See Johannes C. Pols, "Managing the Mind: The Culture of American Mental Hygiene, 1910–1950," (PhD diss., University of Pennsylvania, 1997); Kathleen Jones, *Taming the Troublesome Child: American Families, Child Guidance, and the Limits of Psychiatric Authority* (Cambridge, MA, 1999); Elizabeth Lunbeck, *The Psychiatric Persuasion: Knowledge, Gender, and Power in Modern America* (Princeton, 1994); Margo Horn, *Before It's Too Late: The Child Guidance Movement in the United States, 1922–1945* (Philadelphia, 1989); and Theresa Richardson, *The Century of the Child: The Mental Hygiene Movement and Social Policy in the United States and Canada* (Albany, 1989).

11. Committee on the Family, "Integration and Conflict," 1.

12. One family therapist, Nathan Ackerman, was a founding member of GAP but he served on the Committee on Social Issues rather than the Committee on the Family.

13. Grob, *From Asylum to Community*, 54.

14. Ibid., 61–66.

15. David A. Hollinger, "Science as a Weapon in *Kulturkampfe* in the United States during and after World War II," *Isis* 86 (1995): 440–454; and Jamie Cohen-Cole, *The Open Mind: Cold War Politics and the Sciences of Human Nature* (Chicago, forthcoming).

16. Committee on the Family, "Integration and Conflict," 1.

17. Ibid.

18. Ibid., 3.

19. Ibid., 4.

20. Ibid.

21. Ibid., 22.

22. For more on culture and personality studies, see edited collections such as Clyde Kluckhohn and Henry A. Murray, eds., *Personality in Nature, Society, and Culture* (New York, 1948); Douglas G. Haring, ed., *Personal Character and Cultural Milieu* (Syracuse, 1948); and Kaplan, ed., *Studying Personality Cross-Culturally*; individual works by scholars including, among many, Edward Sapir, Ralph Linton, Abram Kardiner, Margaret Mead, Ruth Benedict, Clyde Kluckhohn, Geoffrey Gorer, A. Irving Hallowell, and Weston La Barre; and secondary sources including Mari Jo Buhle, *Feminism and Its Discontents: A Century of Struggle with Psychoanalysis* (Cambridge, MA, 1998); William C. Manson, *The Psychodynamics of Culture: Abram Kardiner and Neo-Freudian Anthropology* (New York, 1988); Joanne Meyerowitz, "'How Common Culture Shapes the Separate Lives': Sexuality, Race, and Mid-Twentieth-Century Social Constructionist Thought," *Journal of American History* 96 (2010): 1057–1084; Graham Richards, *"Race," Racism and Psychology: Towards a Reflexive History* (London, 1997); and George W. Stocking Jr., ed., *Malinowski, Rivers, Benedict and Others: Essays on Culture and Personality* (Madison, WI, 1986).

23. See Buhle, *Feminism and Its Discontents*, 99–124, on anthropologists' negative reactions to Freud's own anthropologically informed books and their opposition to the universality of the Oedipus complex.

24. Milton Singer, "A Survey of Culture and Personality Theory and Research," in *Studying Personality Cross-Culturally*, ed. Bert Kaplan (New York, 1961), 15.

25. Kluckhohn and Murray, eds., *Personality in Nature, Society, and Culture*, 35.

26. Committee on the Family, "Integration and Conflict," 8.

27. Ibid., 12.

28. This account of the simultaneous invention of family therapy in scattered locations and practitioners' subsequent discovery of one another in the mid- to late 1950s is the standard narrative in family therapists' own historical accounts, as chapter 1 discusses.

29. Family therapists' own historical accounts commonly refer to the inauguration of *Family Process* as a touchstone in the development of their field. However, the journal's creation did not signal unified agreement about family therapy. Contentious debates erupted among editorial board members and between the two institutions cosponsoring the journal, as well as among the journal's readers.

30. "Family: Journal for the Study and Treatment of Group Interaction," no date, folder "Proposal for New Journal: Family Process," Jackson Archive.

31. Ibid., 2–3.

32. Ibid.

33. Ibid.

34. Ibid., 3–4.

35. Ibid., 4.

36. E.g., Nancy Tomes, *A Generous Confidence: Thomas Story Kirkbride and the Art of Asylum-Keeping, 1840–1883* (Cambridge, UK, 1984); and Anne Digby, *Madness, Morality, and Medicine: A Study of the York Retreat, 1796–1914* (Cambridge, MA, 1985). For a contemporaneous critique of the family model in mental hospital life, see Erving Goffman, *Asylums: Essays on the Social Situation of Mental Patients and Other Inmates* (Garden City, NY, 1961).

37. "Introduction to *Family Process*," *Family Process* 1 (March 1962): 2.

38. Ibid.

39. T. W. Adorno et al., *The Authoritarian Personality*, Studies in Prejudice, ed. Max Horkheimer (New York, 1950). Other significant postwar studies on prejudice included Bruno Bettelheim and Morris Janowitz, *Dynamics of Prejudice: A Psychological and Sociological Study of Veterans*, Studies in Prejudice, ed. Max Horkheimer and Samuel H. Fowerman (New York, 1950); Gordon Allport, *The Nature of Prejudice* (Reading, MA, 1954); and Gunnar Myrdal, *An American Dilemma: The Negro Problem and Modern Democracy* (New York, 1944).

40. Nathan W. Ackerman and Marie Jahoda, *Anti-Semitism and Emotional Disorder*, Studies in Prejudice, ed. Max Horkheimer (New York, 1950), 2.

41. Ibid., 84.

42. Ackerman and Jahoda explicitly addressed the limits of their data set and patient population in a discussion of methodology. Ibid., 17–24.

43. Ibid., 45.

44. E.g., Jennifer Terry, "'Momism' and the Making of Treasonous Homosexuals," in *"Bad" Mothers: The Politcs of Blame in Twentieth-Century America*, ed. Molly Ladd-Taylor and Lauri Umansky (New York, 1998), 169–190.

45. Ackerman and Jahoda, *Anti-Semitism and Emotional Disorder*, 9.

46. Ibid., 93.

47. Donald Bloch and Robert Simon, eds., *The Strength of Family Therapy: Selected Papers of Nathan W. Ackerman* (New York, 1982), 119.

48. Nathan W. Ackerman, *The Psychodynamics of Family Life: Diagnosis and Treatment of Family Relationships* (New York, 1958), 15.

49. Nathan W. Ackerman, *Treating the Troubled Family* (New York, 1966), 62.

50. E.g., Ackerman, *Treating the Troubled Family*, 61; and *Psychodynamics of Family Life*, 100.

51. E.g., Ackerman, *Treating the Troubled Family*, 42–44, 53, 77.

52. Ackerman, *Psychodynamics of Family Life*, 18.

53. Ibid., 334.

54. Michael Harrington, *The Other America: Poverty in the United States* (New York, 1962), 16–17. See also Oscar Lewis, *Five Families* (New York, 1959). There is an extensive literature on the history of Harrington's work on the culture of poverty and its relationship to President Lyndon Johnson's War on Poverty. Helpful historical accounts include Alice O'Connor, *Poverty Knowledge: Social Science, Social Policy, and the Poor in Twentieth-Century US History* (Princeton, 2001), chap. 4; and James T. Patterson, *America's Struggle against Poverty, 1900–1994*, enlarged ed. (Cambridge, MA, 1994), 91–154.

55. Harrington, *The Other America*, 126 and passim in chap. 7, 121–138. An important contemporary study that documented a higher incidence of mental illness among poor people was A. B. Hollingshead and R. C. Redlich, *Social Class and Mental Illness* (New York, 1958).

56. Phebe Sessions, "Family Therapy and Urban Poverty: Structural Family Therapy in Context" (PhD diss., Brandeis University, 1991), 17, 46.

57. On other contemporary, psychiatrically oriented services for troubled youth in postwar Harlem, see Gerald Markowitz and David Rosner, *Children, Race, and Power: Kenneth and Mamie Clark's Northside Center* (Charlottesville, VA, 1996). Markowitz and Rosner based their thoughtful account on interviews and research in an impressively extensive range of archival collections.

58. Salvador Minuchin et al., *Families of the Slums: An Exploration of Their Structure and Treatment* (New York, 1967), 22, 24.

59. Ibid., 22–30.

60. Ibid., 22–23. I found James Patterson's discussion helpful in crystallizing the importance of these two facets of the culture-of-poverty argument and in drawing attention to the hereditary, quasi-eugenic overtones of this literature. Patterson, *America's Struggle against Poverty*, 119–120.

61. Minuchin et al., *Families of the Slums*, 22.

62. Ibid., 30.

63. Ibid., 24.

64. Ibid., 25.

65. Ibid., 28.

66. Ibid., 28–30.

67. James Patterson makes a similar critique regarding the popular, unqualified statements about a culture of poverty by Harrington and others: "Some, including Harrington, used the term [culture of poverty] carelessly, to promote active public measures against poverty. Others, such as the conservative *Saturday Evening Post*, employed it to confirm crude and unflattering stereotypes about the poor and to excuse a policy of neglect. . . . Like the metaphor of contagion as applied to the urban slums of 1900, the stereotype enabled more fortunate Americans to relieve themselves of guilt and anxiety." *America's Struggle against Poverty*, 124.

68. Chapter 5 of *Families of the Slums* is titled "The Disorganized and Disadvantaged Family: Structure and Process."

69. Minuchin et al., *Families of the Slums*, 193–196. Minuchin and his colleagues argued,

The stereotyped way in which our children relate to the surrounding world reflects a quality of experience that seems to be comprised of several factors: a sense that 'the world stimulates me and I am only a passive recipient of stimuli'; an either/or experience of aggression without the ability to tune in nuances of affective experience; an accompanying lack of flexibility within an extremely narrow range of verbal response; and a concomitant inability to focus on an event in such a way as to be able to store, or, later on, recover the experience. This cluster of features reflects a style of experiencing life in the midst of the family and the home, for it is here that much basic learning takes place. We have been impressed by certain qualities of the physical and social environment of our children and by the reaction patterns which they seem to foster. One essential feature of the family and home environment is its impermanence and unpredictability. These characteristics make it difficult for the growing child to define himself in relation to his world. . . . Multiple, erratic nurturing figures can increase the child's sense of an unstable world and hinder his movement from a diffuse to a more focused sense of self. In the socialization of the child, these families seem to be characterized by two major features: parents' responses to children's behavior are relatively random and therefore deficient in the qualities that convey rules which can be internalized; and the parental emphasis is on the control and inhibition of behavior rather than on guidance. . . .[An] overtaxed mother responds erratically to a confused child who behaves in ways that will assure him of continuous contact with an outside controlling figure.

70. Sheldon Glueck and Eleanor T. Glueck, *Delinquents in the Making: Paths to Prevention* (New York, 1952); Albert K. Cohen, *Delinquent Boys: The Culture of the Gang* (Glencoe, IL, 1955); and Richard A. Cloward and Lloyd E. Ohlin, *Delinquency and Opportunity: A Theory of Delinquent Gangs* (Glencoe, IL, 1960).

71. See James Gilbert, *A Cycle of Outrage: America's Reaction to the Juvenile Delinquent in the 1950s* (New York, 1986), 136–137; and Patterson, *America's Struggle against Poverty*, 116–118.

72. Patterson, *America's Struggle against Poverty*, 103.

73. Ibid., 121–124.

74. Minuchin et al., *Families of the Slums*, 237.

75. O'Connor, *Poverty Knowledge*, 10.

76. Daryl Michael Scott, *Contempt and Pity: Social Policy and the Image of the Damaged Black Psyche* (Chapel Hill, NC, 1997).

77. Daniel Patrick Moynihan, *The Negro Family: The Case for National Action* (Office of Policy Planning and Research, U.S. Department of Labor, March 1965), reprinted in Lee Rainwater and William L. Yancey, *The Moynihan Report and the Politics of Controversy, Including the Full Text of* The Negro Family: The Case for National Action, *by Daniel Patrick Moynihan* (Cambridge, MA, 1967), 51.

78. Ibid., chap. 3, "The Roots of the Problem," and chap. 4, "The Tangle of Pathology."

79. Minuchin et al., *Families of the Slums*, 370–371. Their citations included Thomas F. Pettigrew, *A Profile of the Negro American* (Princeton, 1964); and Kenneth Clark, *Dark Ghetto: Dilemmas of Social Power* (New York, 1965).

80. *New York Times*, November 28, 1965, sec. 7, p. 60.

81. Minuchin et al., *Families of the Slums*, 234. Such concerns were rooted in a psychoanalytic concern for sexual identity formation. See also Herman, *Romance of American Psychology*, 205.

82. Minuchin et al., *Families of the Slums*, 260.

83. Ibid., 261.

84. Ibid., 218–219.

85. Rainwater and Yancey, *Moynihan Report and the Politics of Controversy*, 51. There is an extensive literature on the Moynihan Report. An excellent starting point is the Rainwater and Yancey volume, which includes the full text of the report, reprints many of the key articles and reports written in response, provides background to the production of the report, and summarizes the main critiques made at that time. Historians, notably Herbert Gutman, launched an attack on Moynihan's historical characterization of the black family by documenting the persistence of organized, two-parent families during slavery. Herbert G. Gutman, *The Black Family in Slavery and Freedom, 1750–1925* (New York, 1976). Feminist activists and scholars have since challenged the portrayal of female-headed households as inherently pathological. On the historical construction in social scientific studies of the African American family as a pathological matriarchy, see Ruth Feldstein, *Motherhood in Black and White: Race and Sex in American Liberalism, 1930–1965* (Ithaca, 2000), 139–164; Herman, *Romance of American Psychology*, 174–207; Patricia Morton, *Disfigured Images: The Historical Assault on Afro-American Women* (New York, 1991), 67–97; O'Connor, *Poverty Knowledge*, 74–136, 196–210; and Scott, *Contempt and Pity*. For a more recent reappraisal, see James T. Patterson, *Freedom Is Not Enough: The Moynihan Report and America's Struggle over Black Family Life* (New York, 2010).

86. Daryl Michael Scott discusses challenges to cultural assimilation in *Contempt and Pity*, 161–185.

87. Herman, *Romance of American Psychology*, 203–204. For a survey of historical scholarship on African American family life, including responses to the Moynihan Report, see Stephen Lassonde, "Family and Demography in Postwar America: A Hazard of New Fortunes?," in *A Companion to Post-1945 America*, ed. Jean-Christophe Agnew and Roy Rosenzweig (Malden, MA, 2002), 3–19. See also Miriam Lynnell Harris, "From Kennedy to Combahee: Black Feminist Activism from 1960 to 1980" (PhD, University of Minnesota, 1997); and Patricia Morton, *Disfigured Images: The Historical Assault on Afro-American Women* (New York, 1991).

88. Salvador Minuchin, *Families and Family Therapy* (Cambridge, MA, 1974), 95.

89. Harrington, *The Other America*, 159–60.

90. Minuchin et al., *Families of the Slums*, 368–378.

91. Ibid., 371–372.

92. I selected these particular articles by searching *Family Process* on CD-ROM for articles from the first decade of the journal (1962–72) with multiple references to "culture." D. Narain, "Growing Up in India," *Family Process* 3 (March 1964): 127–154; Erik Grönseth, "Research on Socialization in Norway," *Family Process* 3 (September 1964): 302–322; Constantina Safilios-Rothschild, "Deviance and Mental Illness in the Greek Family," *Family Process* 7 (March 1968): 100–117; Carroll M. Brodsky, "The Social Recovery of Mentally Ill Housewives," *Family Process* 7 (September 1968): 170–183; Carolyn L. Attneave, "Therapy in Tribal Settings and Urban Network Intervention," *Family Process* 8 (September 1969): 192–210; Richard A. Gardner, "A Four-Day Diagnostic-Therapeutic Home Visit in Turkey," *Family Process* 9 (September 1970): 301–330; Albert E. Scheflen, "Living Space in an Urban Ghetto," *Family Process* 10 (December 1971): 429–450; David Kinzie, P. C. Sushama, and Mary Lee, "Cross-Cultural Family Therapy—A Malaysian Experience," *Family Process* 11 (March 1972): 59–67; and Mordecai Kaffman, "Family Conflict in the Psychopathology of the Kibbutz Child," *Family Process* 11 (June 1972): 171–189.

93. See Edward Said, *Orientalism* (New York, 1978), and James Clifford's discussion of Said's work in "On *Orientalism*," in *The Predicament of Culture: Twentieth-Century Ethnography, Literature and Art* (Cambridge, MA, 1988), 255–276.

94. Marvin K. Opler, "Social and Cultural Influences on the Psychopathology of Family Groups," in *Family Therapy and Disturbed Families*, ed. Gerald Zuk and Ivan Boszormenyi-Nagy (Palo Alto, 1967), 133–158. "Despite the label of 'family,' anthropologists know that this unit of social organization varies notoriously in size, in extent of kinship, in locale, and in functional relationships both within the unit and with other social units. Its economy, its degree of autonomy from other elements in social structure, its religion or patterns of belief, even its modes of marital and sexual regulation and its recreational forms are matters that are not self-defined nor internally arrived at by some process of reasoning" (p. 133).

95. Wynne wrote, "More conceptualisation and hypothesis-formation is needed (and will soon be forthcoming) on the problem of boundaries between nuclear family units and the extended family, community, and broader culture and social structure. . . . In our NIMH work, we are greatly interested in considering modifications of theory that may be necessary for families of different kinds and in studying families of schizophrenics using a cross-cultural and cross-class frame of reference." Lyman C. Wynne, "Responses of the Theorists," in *Family Processes and Schizophrenia*, ed. Elliot G. Mishler and Nancy E. Waxler (New York, 1968), 283–284. See also Gregory Bateson, "Cultural Problems Posed by a Study of Schizophrenic Process," in *Schizophrenia: An Integrated Approach*, ed. Alfred Auerback (New York, 1959), 141–143.

96. Kinzie, Sushama, and Lee, "Cross-Cultural Family Therapy," 59–60.

97. Don D. Jackson, "Psychotherapy: Note on Concept of 'Growth' in Terms of Culture," no date, folder "Psychotherapy Book, Folder 2," Jackson Archive.

98. Ibid.

99. R. D. Laing, *The Politics of the Family, and Other Essays* (New York, 1969); and Jerome Agel, ed., *Radical Therapist: The Radical Therapist Collective* (New York, 1971).

100. O'Connor, *Poverty Knowledge*, 9. See also Herman, *Romance of American Psychology*; Hale, *Rise and Crisis of Psychoanalysis*; Scott, *Contempt and Pity*; Joel Pfister and Nancy Schnog, eds., *Inventing the Psychological: Toward a Cultural History of Emotional Life in America* (New Haven, 1997). Cultural critics of the 1950s such as David Reisman and C. Wright Mills were particularly concerned about the culture of conformity promulgated by mass society in the postwar years. Later American social critics—notably Philip Rieff in *The Triumph of the Therapeutic* (Chicago, 1966) and Christopher Lasch in *The Culture of Narcissism* (New York, 1979)—similarly derided the twentieth-century psychologization of American culture, politics, and social sciences.

101. Robert MacGregor, "Communicating Values in Family Therapy," in Zuk and Nagy, *Family Therapy and Disturbed Families*, 178.

102. Note that in the quoted phrase, "value system" and "family" are singular, which implies a single set of values for *the* middle-class family in the United States. Ibid., 178.

103. Ibid., 179.

104. Ibid., 180.

105. Scheflen, "Living Space in an Urban Ghetto," 429–430.

106. Ibid., 450.

107. Ibid.

108. George E. Marcus and Michael M. J. Fischer, *Anthropology as Cultural Critique: An Experimental Moment in the Human Sciences* (Chicago, 1986).

4. Observational Practices and Natural Habitats

1. The family studies literature from this period is extensive. For significant examples, see work by William J. Goode, Talcott Parsons, Alex Bavales, Carle Zimmerman, Margaret Mead, William Ogburn, Ernst Burgess, Else Frenkel-Brunswik, Oscar Lewis, Lee Rainwater, Fred Strobtbeck, Sheldon and Eleanor T. Glueck, Reuben Hill, E. Franklin Frazier, Lionel Ovesey, and Abram Kardiner. Useful contemporary anthologies, with various discussions of methodology, include Norman W. Bell and E. F. Vogel, eds., *A Modern Introduction to the Family* (1960); H. T. Christensen, ed., *Handbook of Marriage and the Family* (Chicago, 1964); James Framo, ed., *Family Interaction: A Dialogue between Family Researchers and Family Therapists* (New York, 1972); Iago Galdston, ed., *The Family in Contemporary Society* (New York, 1958); and Gerald Handel, ed., *The Psychosocial Interior of the Family: A Sourcebook for the Study of Whole Families*, 2nd ed. (1967; repr., Chicago, 1972).

2. Lorraine Daston and Elizabeth Lunbeck, eds., *Histories of Scientific Observation* (Chicago, 2011), 2.

3. There is a robust literature on the importance of place in scientific research and practice. See Adi Ophir and Steven Shapin, "The Place of Knowledge: A Methodological Survey," *Science in Context* 4 (1991): 3–21, and other essays in the same issue of *Science in Context* organized around the theme "The Place of Knowledge: The Spatial Setting and Its Relation to the Production of Knowledge."

4. Notable sources include Robert E. Kohler, *Landscapes and Labscapes: Exploring the Lab-Field Border in Biology* (Chicago, 2002); and Henrika Kuklick and Robert E. Kohler, eds., *Science in the Field*, Osiris, 2nd ser., vol. 11 (Chicago, 1996).

5. Jules Henry, *Pathways to Madness* (New York, 1965); and David Kantor and William Lehr, *Inside the Family: Toward a Theory of Family Process* (San Francisco, 1975).

6. Henry, *Pathways to Madness*, 439.

7. Since the 1970s, science studies scholars have examined science as practice, in contrast to an older approach to science as ideas. A parallel trend among historians of medicine focused attention on the history of therapeutic practices, not just on the development of medical theories.

8. Eliot Weinberger, "The Camera People," in *Visualizing Theory: Selected Essays from V.A.R., 1990–1994*, ed. Lucien Taylor (New York, 1994), 15. The following sources are also

useful points of entry into the extensive literatures on documentary film and visual anthropology: Marcus Banks and Howard Morphy, *Rethinking Visual Anthropology* (New Haven, 1997); Jonathan Kahana, *Intelligence Work: The Politics of American Documentary* (New York, 2008); Bill Nichols, *Representing Reality: Issues and Concepts in Documentary* (Bloomington, IN, 1991); Paula Rabinowitz, "History in Your Own Home: Cinéma Vérité, Docudrama, and America's Families," in *They Must Be Represented: The Politics of Documentary* (London, 1994), 130–154; Fatima Tobing Rony, *The Third Eye: Race, Cinema, and Ethnographic Spectacle* (Durham, NC, 1996); and Brian Winston, "The Documentary Film as Scientific Inscription," in *Theorizing Documentary*, ed. Michael Renov (New York, 1993), 37–57.

9. Kantor and Lehr, *Inside the Family*, ix.

10. Murray Bowen to Norman Q. Brill, May 21, 1959, drawer 3, folder "NIMH Correspondence A through D"; and [Murray Bowen?], "A Description of a Family Research Project for the Study and Treatment of Schizophrenic Patients and Their Families," c. 1959 (since he was still seeking foundation funding for writing project report), folder "Project Prospectus," both in Bowen Archive.

11. Other studies typically focused on office-based therapy sessions, psychological testing, standardized interviews, or methodologies from small group studies. For a thorough bibliography of family therapy research in the 1950s and 1960s, see Ira D. Glick and Jay Haley, *Family Therapy and Research: An Annotated Bibliography of Articles and Books Published 1950–1970* (New York, 1971).

12. Murray Bowen to Wilson Thiede, June 24, 1955, drawer 2, folder "Correspondence— Personal (Dr. Bowen)," 2, Bowen Archive.

13. Murray Bowen to Gilbert J. Dalldorf, August 29, 1957, drawer 3, folder "NIMH Correspondence A through D," 1, Bowen Archive.

14. [Bowen?], "Description of a Family Research Project," 1.

15. The annual reports from NIMH during the 1950s indicate that there were many intramural research projects on schizophrenia in these two divisions. Outside NIMH there was also significant attention devoted to schizophrenia research and treatment: e.g., Alfred Auerback, ed., *Schizophrenia: An Integrated Approach* (New York, 1959); Don D. Jackson, ed., *The Etiology of Schizophrenia* (New York, 1960); David Rosenthal and Seymour Kety, eds., *The Transmission of Schizophrenia* (Oxford, 1968); John Romano, ed., *The Origins of Schizophrenia* (Amsterdam, 1967); and Carl A. Whitaker, ed., *Psychotherapy of Chronic Schizophrenia Patients* (Boston, 1958). On the history of schizophrenia, see Sander L. Gilman, "Constructing Schizophrenia as a Category of Mental Illness," in *Disease and Representation: Images of Illness from Madness to AIDS* (Ithaca, 1988), 202–230; Sheldon Gelman, *Medicating Schizophrenia: A History* (New Brunswick, NJ, 1999); John G. Howells, ed., *The Concept of Schizophrenia: Historical Perspectives* (Washington, DC, 1991); Jonathan Metzl, *The Protest Psychosis: How Schizophrenia Became a Black Disease* (Boston, 2009); and Richard Noll, *American Madness: The Rise and Fall of Dementia Praecox* (Cambridge, MA, 2011).

16. Murray Bowen, "Report on the Research Activity of Laboratory of Adult Psychiatric Investigations, General Staff Meeting, NIMH, March 15, 1955," drawer 3, folder "NIMH— Report to General Staff (Dr. Bowen)," 1, Bowen Archive.

17. Ibid.

18. See Georges Canguilhem, *The Normal and the Pathological*, trans. Carolyn R. Fawcett (New York, 1991).

19. Bowen, "Report on the Research Activity," 1.

20. Murray Bowen et al., "Analysis of NIH Program Activities: Project Description Sheet: Influence of the Early Mother-Child Relationship in the Development of Schizophrenia," NIMH, Laboratory of Adult Psychiatry, Serial No. NIMH 170 (C), December 1955, drawer 2, folder "3-East Project," 1, Bowen Archive.

21. Murray Bowen to Robert Cohen, transfer letter, October 28, 1955, drawer 2, Family 2H/daughter clinical folder, Bowen Archive. My references to patients' clinical files follow a randomized coding system developed to ensure patient anonymity.

22. For a useful survey of the literature on mothering and schizophrenia, see Carol Eadie Hartwell, "The Schizophrenogenic Mother Concept in American Psychiatry," *Psychiatry* 59, no. 3 (Fall 1996): 274–97.

23. "Last summer during the short period of my intensive work with her, we could see very clearly the intense 'symbiotic' relationship with the mother. I approached from the standpoint that I would be with the patient and make an attempt to give her whatever strength she could get from the relationship with me to make her own stand against the mother. In other words, I did not go in the direction of trying to help two people understand the intense attachment for one another and thereby give each other up but went in the direction of helping the patient understand it, hoping that she would get enough strength to make her own stand. I felt at the time that we went into this last summer that it was bound to fail. . . . In the passing months, I discussed the problem with a number of psychiatrists, including both child psychiatrists and adult psychiatrists. Child psychiatrists were unanimous in saying that this is a kind of problem that is often met in their work. They feel the only approach to it is to work psychotherapeutically simultaneously with mother and child. One child psychiatrist told me that when he approached such a problem, he put his best psychiatrist on the mother and the person with the lesser talent on the patient." Progress note, January 13, 1954, black binder with cover title "Papers, Schizophrenic Notes, Etc., Dr. Bowen," drawer 2, Bowen Archive.

24. Consultation record, March 25, 1954, "Papers, Schizophrenic Notes" (emphasis added).

25. Untitled report beginning, "There are a large number of clinical experiences that suggest. . ." c. 1955 (based on approach to data collection described in report, which fit with project's early phase), drawer 2, folder "3-East Project," 1, Bowen Archive.

26. Bowen, "Report on the Research Activity," 6. My analysis of this point echoes aspects of Joan Fujimura's discussion of "doable research problems," concisely summarized in Adele E. Clarke and Joan H. Fujimura, "What Tools? Which Jobs? Why Right?," in *The Right Tools for the Job: At Work in Twentieth-Century Life Sciences*, ed. Adele E. Clarke and Joan Fujimora (Princeton, 1992), 8–9.

27. Bowen et al., "Analysis of NIH Program Activities," 2.

28. "Also hypothesized is that this is something of a universal phenomenon, but subjects were chosen in which mothers and daughters had never been able to achieve any real independence of one another. Three mother-daughter pairs have been admitted. To meet the criteria of this close a relationship automatically means patients who are quite impaired and in whom the treatment process can be expected to be long-term." Bowen, "Report on the Research Activity," 6.

29. Drawer 2, Family R9/daughter clinical folder, "Clinical History," Bowen Archive. Referral information is in the clinical files of each patient. In a paper presented at the American Psychiatric Association meeting in May 1957, Bowen also emphasized the weight given to the intensity of the bond between mother and daughter:

> Three young adult schizophrenic women and their mothers were chosen for the project. The goal was to admit pairs with the most intense attachments that could be found. This was done on the principle that it is easier to see the characteristics of a poorly understood phenomenon in a gross form than in a subtle form. Intensity of symbiotic attachment was considered more important than intensity of, or configuration of, schizophrenic symptoms. It was assumed that this degree of attachment would imply a maximum degree of personality impairment which in turn would imply slower therapeutic response. ("Family Participation in Schizophrenia," paper presented at the annual meeting of the American Psychiatric Association, Chicago, May 15, 1957, drawer 1, folder "NIMH Research Reports," 3–4, Bowen Archive)

30. Family 2H/daughter clinical folder.

31. Bowen, "Family Participation in Schizophrenia," 4.

32. Ibid.

33. Drawer 2, Family R9/daughter clinical folder, "Family History," Bowen Archive.

34. *JCT*, March 13, 1956. Extended discussion of the Palo Alto group's research on schizophrenia and communication can be found in chapter 2.

35. Report beginning, "There are a large number of clinical experiences."

36. On the role of time in the history of the relationship between science and film, see Hannah Landecker, "Microcinematography and the History of Science and Film," *Isis* 97 (2006): 121–132. As Landecker argues, "Whether in the microscopic or the macroscopic realm, film presented the haunting possibility of capturing over time phenomena that had escaped static means of representation such as histology, photography, or drawing. This led to an explosion in experiments with and on film in scientific and medical disciplines from astronomy to psychiatry" (122). On time and cinema, see also Mary Ann Doane, *The Emergence of Cinematic Time: Modernity, Contingency, the Archive* (Cambridge, MA, 2002).

37. Milieu therapy has a much longer history that can be traced back through the moral therapies of the nineteenth century, on which there is a significant literature such as Nancy Tomes, *A Generous Confidence: The Art of Asylum-Keeping: Thomas Story Kirkbride and the Origins of American Psychiatry* (Philadelphia, 1994); and Andrew Scull, *Social Order/Mental Disorder: Anglo-American Psychiatry in Historical Perspective* (Berkeley, 1989).

38. "The Family Project," c. July–August 1945, drawer 2, folder "3-East Project," 2–3, Bowen Archive.

39. Family 2H/daughter clinical folder.

40. Bowen et al., "Analysis of NIH Program Activities," 2.

41. On the complex relationship between clinical research and treatment, see Susan E. Lederer, *Subjected to Science: Human Experimentation in America before the Second World War* (Baltimore, 1995); and Harry Marks, *The Progress of Experiment: Science and Therapeutic Reform in the United States, 1990–1990* (Cambridge, UK, 1997).

42. Family 2H/daughter clinical folder.

43. Murray Bowen to mother of Family 4R, September 21, 1956, drawer 2, folder for Family 4R, Bowen Archive. The family did not enroll in the project.

44. Bowen wrote, "It is a clinical fact that these relationship harmonies are present in the families of schizophrenic people. Often the disharmonies are more undercover than overtly recognized. Who can answer whether the disharmony preceded and helped bring about the schizophrenia or perhaps came later. It is also fairly factual that the schizophrenic one does better when the disharmonies can be at least partially resolved." Ibid.

45. Notes, January 14, 1958, drawer 2, folder for Family K5, Bowen Archive. The family did not enroll in the project. "The one point that [the father] pushed was whether drugs or something would be done to keep [daughter] from hallucinating or regressing. We clarified the project's view on this, how we found that drugs only slowed up working on family problems and [the father] had referred to [daughter]'s needing someone and it was pointed out that here she would have her family and it was quite different from her being in a hospital by herself. Also that drugs have been given patients on the project because of the family's anxiety but that if we did this we wanted it to be clear why it was being done."

46. Bowen et al., "Analysis of NIH Program Activities," 2.

47. Family 2H/daughter clinical folder. Cf. Alfred H. Stanton and Morris S. Schwartz, *The Mental Hospital: A Study of Institutional Participation in Psychiatric Illness and Treatment* (New York, 1954). Stanton and Schwartz conducted their well-known study at Chestnut Lodge. Their results showed that patients' symptoms were exacerbated during periods of disagreement among the staff.

48. "The Family Project," 3.

49. Murray Bowen, "Adult Psychiatry Branch: Section on Ward 3-E," *Annual Report of Program Activities, NIH: National Institute of Mental Health* (Washington, DC: National

Institutes of Health, Public Health Service, U.S. Department of Health, Education, and Welfare, 1957), 11.

50. Ibid.

51. On the connections between observational practices and visual culture, see Marita Sturken and Lisa Cartwright, *Practices of Looking: An Introduction to Visual Culture* (New York, 2001).

52. Bowen, "Adult Psychiatry Branch," 10.

53. "The Family Project," 3.

54. Bowen et al., "Analysis of NIH Program Activities," 1.

55. For the project's technical definition of "move," see "The Family Project," 3, and Report beginning "There are a large number of clinical experiences," 2–7.

56. Report beginning "There are a large number of clinical experiences," 1.

57. Murray Bowen to Marc Rubenstein, August 9, 1965, drawer 5, folder ["Correspondence and Notes, ca. 1963–1966"], Bowen Archive.

58. Murray Bowen, clinical history, drawer 2, Family 9U/daughter clinical folder, Bowen Archive.

59. "The Development of Techniques of Dealing with Five Family Units and Some Patterns Observed in the Transaction of These Families," c. late 1956–57, drawer 2, folder "3-East Project," 14, Bowen Archive, narrates the conceptual, therapeutic, and research shifts in orientation.

60. Bowen et al., "Analysis of NIH Program Activities," 2.

61. Ibid., 2, 3.

62. Ibid., 3.

63. Murray Bowen to [former patient's parent], January 7, 1957, drawer 3, folder "NIMH Correspondence I-K," 1–2, Bowen Archive.

64. Bowen, "Adult Psychiatry Branch," 11.

65. "This capacity to evoke powerful responses in others is historically a characteristic of these families." Ibid., 13.

66. Ibid.

67. [Bowen?], "Description of a Family Research Project," 5.

68. Murray Bowen to Alexander Gralnick, October 21, 1958, drawer 3, folder "NIMH Correspondence F-H," 1, Bowen Archive.

69. Murray Bowen, "Family Psychotherapy," *American Journal of Orthopsychiatry* 31 (January 1961): 40–60, reprinted in Bowen, *Family Therapy in Clinical Practice* (New York, 1978), 72–75.

70. This information comes from individual clinical files of the participant families.

71. For example, in one recruitment letter sent to the father of a potential participant family, Bowen wrote,

We do have some openings for new families in our family research project. This led to my contacts with the doctors at [X] State Hospital to see if they knew of any patients and families they might wish suggest for this treatment program. I reviewed your daughter's record and felt there was some possibility that she and your family might fit in. Our research approach regards schizophrenia in the patient as a problem that involves the entire family. Our thesis is that the entire family is much more capable of making the schizophrenia resolve than the patient alone. It requires considerable effort from the family, especially the father and mother, to participate in the program. So, our program has to be for those families who are willing to make this kind of effort in their own behalf. [Continues about setting up appointment, goal of admitting new families within next three weeks]. Sincerely yours, Murray Bowen, MD. (January 10, 1968, drawer 3, folder for Family 8S, Bowen Archive)

72. Murray Bowen to Peter Fleming, February 7, 1956, drawer 3, folder "NIMH Correspondence E-H," 2, Bowen Archive.

73. "Two months ago I was wondering how I could get fathers to drop their businesses and come in. I was feeling that I probably would have to be content with those who were unattached and unemployed. My experiences in dealing with prospective admissions the past six weeks or so has been to the contrary. The very busy business man will protest, but when he is asked which is more important, to put his family together or hold his business together, he rather readily decides that family comes first and if we will take him, he will get the business worked out." Ibid.

74. Murray Bowen to Z3 family/mother, January 1, 1958, drawer 3, folder "NIMH Correspondence E-H," Bowen Archive.

75. On the history of chlorpromazine and other antipsychotic medications, see Gelman, *Medicating Schizophrenia*.

76. Marjorie Kvarnes, "Orienting Nursing Personnel to a Research Project in Psychiatry," October 18, 1957, drawer 2, "3-East Project,"1–7, Bowen Archive. As Bowen wrote in response to an initial contact from the mother of a soon-to-enroll family,

> Our research effort is devoted to the idea that a schizophrenic illness in the patient involves every member of the family and that there is a better chance for treatment success when the entire family can work together in the treatment effort. Our research project is designed to work in that direction. We have a 14 bed ward set aside for this in our new research hospital. Our living space consists of seven double bed rooms that make up into living room space in the daytime and sleeping rooms at night. We have about four families consisting of father, mother and patient and these families divide up the living space in the most convenient way for themselves. . . . As you know, it requires considerable change in family life to participate in this effort and some families find it easier to make such changes than others. (Bowen to mother of Z3 family)

77. "Development of Techniques," 14.

78. Evidence for the families' perspectives comes from written notes made by family members while they were on the unit, which were saved and filed by project staff.

79. Betty Basamania, preadmission note, June 29, 1956, drawer 2, clinical folder for Family 4R, Bowen Archive.

80. Kvarnes, "Orienting Nursing Personnel," 4, 6.

81. Bowen, "Adult Psychiatry Branch," 11.

82. "Development of Techniques," 15–16.

83. Historians, anthropologists, and sociologists of science have written widely on representation, abstraction, and scientific inscriptions; see, e.g., Michael Lynch and Steve Woolgar, eds., *Representation in Scientific Practice* (Cambridge, MA, 1990).

84. [Bowen?], "Description of a Family Research Project," 8.

85. Ibid.

86. Murray Bowen to Ray L. Birdwhistell, June 11, 1958, drawer 3, folder "NIMH Correspondence A through D," 1, Bowen Archive.

87. Doane, *Emergence of Cinematic Time*, 33.

88. [Bowen?], "Description of a Family Research Project," 8.

89. Murray Bowen to Leslie Osborn, December 30, 1958, drawer 1, folder "Hold Box," 2–3, Bowen Archive.

90. Ibid.

91. Grob, *From Asylum to Community*, 100–114.

92. Murray Bowen to J. Brooks Dugan, May 21, 1956, drawer 2, folder "Correspondence—Personal (Dr. Bowen)," 2, Bowen Archive.

93. Ibid., 3.

94. Kvarnes, "Orienting Nursing Personnel," 4.

95. [Brodey et al.?], "Medical Services 3-E," undated, drawer 1, folder "Medical Service 3 East," 1, Bowen Archive.

96. Ibid.

97. Bowen to Dugan, 2. Bowen also wrote to Dugan, "Administrative anxiety was rising in relation to moves within the project to give responsibility to the family groups. . . . All the while, Dr. Cohen [director of Clinical Investigations] and the administrative people honestly expressed their verbal approval of us giving responsibility to patients and of wanting us to handle the project operation as we saw fit, BUT when we gave responsibility (some new move), there would be a new dozen of questions about research design."

98. "Development of Techniques," 1.

99. Bowen et al., "Analysis of NIH Program Activities," 2–3. However, their project was not as unique as they thought. Christian Midelfort, a psychiatrist, ran an inpatient program for families in LaCrosse, Wisconsin, in the early 1950s in which relatives of psychiatric patients stayed in the hospital. In contrast to the research focus of Bowen's NIMH project, the focus in Midelfort's program was clinical, with family members serving "as nurses' aides and companions in constant attendance to supervise occupational, recreational, and insulin therapies, to minimize suicidal risk, fear, aggression, and insecurity and to take part in therapeutic interviews with patient and psychiatrist." Midelfort, *The Family in Psychotherapy* (New York, 1957), quoted in Carlfred B. Broderick and Sandra S. Schrader, "The History of Professional Marriage and Family Therapy," in *Handbook of Family Therapy*, ed. Alan S. Gurman and David P. Kniskern (New York, 1981), 20–21.

100. They subsequently heard of other projects in which whole families were hospitalized. In an untitled draft of a paper most likely from 1959 (since it begins, "The work of the project in its fourth and final year is seen as part of an evolutionary process that followed the previous three years"), they wrote,

> As soon as patients and mothers were in a living situation together, we began to see phenomena not adequately explained by our concepts developed for the individual. At that time we believed we were the first to have parents and patients in this situation together but we have since heard of many places where this has been done for a long time. Just this week we received a report of a family project conducted by the Department of Psychiatry, National Taiwan University Hospital, Taipei, Formosa. Shortage of nurses during the war required that family members nurse the patients in the hospital. This policy was continued after the war by the Department of Psychiatry. This is one of several such efforts we have heard about. (folder "3E Project," 1)

101. These presentations included Basamania, "The Family as a Unit"; Brodey, "The Study of Five Hospitalized Families Each with a Schizophrenic Member: Narcissistic Relationships and Reality Testing"; and Bowen, "Psychotherapy of the Family as a Unit" (Annual Meeting of the American Orthopsychiatric Association, New York, March 7, 1958); Bowen, Dysinger, and Basamania, "The Role of the Father in Families with a Schizophrenic Patient" (Annual Meeting of the American Psychiatric Association, New York, May 16, 1957); Bowen, "Family Relationships in Schizophrenia" (Hawaiian Division Meeting of the American Psychiatric Association, Honolulu, May 20, 1958); Bowen, "Family Dynamics in Schizophrenia" (Wisconsin Psychiatric Institute, Madison, September 12, 1958); and Bowen, "Role of the Family in Therapy of Schizophrenia" (Conference on Schizophrenia, Temple University, Philadelphia, October 10, 1958). This list comes from *Annual Report of Program Activities, 1958 NIH-NIMH* (Public Health Service, U.S. Department of Health, Education, and Welfare, 1958), 228. Drafts and typescripts of most talks are in Bowen's papers.

102. Murray Bowen to Eugene Goforth, January 28, 1958, drawer 3, folder "NIMH Correspondence F-H," Bowen Archive.

103. July 17, 1959, according to a memo from Bowen to William C. Jenkins, June 25, 1959, drawer 3, folder "NIMH Correspondence I-K," 4, Bowen Archive.

104. Mother in Family Z3 to Robert A. Cohen, October 19, 1958, Family Z3/mother clinical folder, Bowen Archive.

105. Contract, November, 1, 1960, drawer 5, folder "Basic Books Publishing Co., Inc.," Bowen Archive.

106. Murray Bowen, with Robert H. Dysinger, MD, and Betty Basamania, MSW, "The Role of the Father in Families with a Schizophrenic Patient," *American Journal of Psychiatry* 155 (1959): 1017–1020. Bowen initially presented this material at the Annual Meeting of the American Orthopsychiatric Association in May 1958. The number of reprint requests is in "Description of a Research Project," 16.

107. Murray Bowen et al., "The Role of the Father in Families with a Schizophrenic Patient," reprinted in Bowen, *Family Therapy in Clinical Practice*, 17.

108. [Bowen?], "Description of a Family Research Project," 14.

109. Canguilhem, *Normal and the Pathological*, 125, 140–141.

110. Ibid., 243. Canguilhem argues,

The abnormal, as ab-normal, comes after the definition of the normal, it is its logical negation. However, it is the historical anteriority of the future abnormal which gives rise to a normative intention. The normal is the effect obtained by the execution of the normative project, it is the norm exhibited in the fact. In the relationship of the fact there is then a relationship of exclusion between the normal and the abnormal. But this negation is subordinated to the operation of negation, to the correction summoned up by the abnormality. Consequently it is not paradoxical to say that the abnormal, while logically second, is existentially first.

111. See the section "Observing New Things: Objects," in Daston and Lunbeck, *Histories of Scientific Observation*, 277–368, for further reflections on the relationship between observation and its objects in the cases of society, economy, emotion, and radiation.

112. E.g., Oscar Lewis, *Five Families* (New York, 1959).

113. Jules Henry, "My Life with the Families of Psychotic Children," in *The Psychosocial Interior of the Family*, 2d ed., ed. Gerald Handel (Chicago, 1972), 30. Henry first delivered this paper in February 1964 at Forest Hospital, Des Plaines, Illinois, and published it in 1965 in *The American Family in Crisis*.

114. Jules Henry, *Culture against Man* (New York, 1963), 3. See Irving Howe, "This Age of Conformity," *Partisan Review* 20 (1954): 7–33; C. Wright Mills, *White Collar: The American Middle Classes* (New York, 1951); David Reisman, *The Lonely Crowd: A Study of the Changing American Character* (New Haven, 1950); and William Whyte Jr., *The Organization Man* (New York, 1956).

115. Jules Henry, "Common Problems of Research in Anthropology and Psychiatry," *American Journal of Orthopsychiatry* 18 (1948): 698–703, cited in Henry, *Pathways to Madness* (New York, 1965), xi.

116. Henry, *Pathways to Madness*, xv.

117. Ibid.

118. Henry, "My Life with the Families of Psychotic Children," 35.

119. Ibid., 36. On the relationship between observation and interpretation and the related debates within the philosophy of science about theory-laden observation, see Ian Hacking, *Representing and Intervening: Introductory Topics in the Philosophy of Natural Science* (Cambridge, UK, 1983), including chap. 10 on observation; and Lorraine Daston and Elizabeth Lunbeck's introduction to *Histories of Scientific Observation*.

120. Henry, "My Life with the Families of Psychotic Children," 31. The relevant secondary literature on scientific instruments and visual technologies is substantial. Useful sources related to the history of modern science and medicine include Lisa Cartwright, *Screening the Body: Tracing Medicine's Visual Culture* (Minneapolis, 1995); Jonathan Crary, *Techniques of the Observer: On Vision and Modernity in the Nineteenth Century* (Cambridge, MA, 1990); Lorraine Daston and Peter Galison, "The Image of Objectivity," *Representations* 40 (Fall 1992): 81–128; Barron H. Lerner, "The Perils of 'X-Ray Vision': How Radiographic Images Have Historically Influenced Perception," *Perspectives in Biology and Medicine* 35 (1992): 382–397; and Joel Snyder, "Visualization and Visibility," in *Picturing Science, Producing Art*, ed. Caroline A. Jones and Peter Galison (New York: Routledge, 1998), 379–397.

121. "It is a commonplace of scientific history that the first valuable hypotheses are developed out of good observations of natural-occurring phenomena. . . . In this book, I will try to show how understanding human beings is furthered and the opportunities for new theoretical insights are provided by a return from the laboratory and the consulting room to man in his natural surroundings." Henry, *Pathways to Madness*, xvi.

122. Ibid., xx.

123. Ibid.

124. E.g., ibid., 374.

125. Henry, "My Life with the Families of Psychotic Children," 46.

126. Henry, *Pathways to Madness*, 457.

127. Henry, "My Life with the Families of Psychotic Children," 31–34.

128. Henry, *Pathways to Madness*, xix.

129. Ibid., 421, 439.

130. Ibid., 439.

131. "In this book I offer no 'typologies' because human phenomena do not arrange themselves obligingly in types, but, rather, afford us the spectacle of endless overlapping. Hence I have no family 'types' and no statistics, only intensive analyses of the variety of family experience. The less we know about family life the easier it is to set up categories." Ibid., xvi.

132. Ibid., 373–74.

133. E.g., in a letter to Henry, Palo Alto researcher John Weakland expressed interest in Henry's upcoming presentation at the American Orthopsychiatric Association meeting, "The Naturalistic Observation of the Families of Psychotic Children." John Weakland to Jules Henry, January 17, 1961, Weakland file "Correspondence," Jackson Archive. In his reply, Henry explained that he was preparing a book on his research, which was carried out under a Ford Foundation grant to the Sonia Shankman Orthogenic School of the University of Chicago. He was also familiar with Weakland et al.'s work, opening his letter with the exclamation, "Everybody knows about the double bind!" Jules Henry to John Weakland, January 23, 1961, Weakland file "Correspondence," Jackson Archive.

134. Kantor and Lehr, *Inside the Family*, 1.

135. Ibid., 9.

136. Ibid., 38.

137. Ibid., 39.

138. Ibid., 1.

139. Ibid., 224–231.

140. Summarized in Lynn Hoffman, *Foundations of Family Therapy: A Conceptual Framework for Systems Change* (New York, 1981), 67–104.

141. Ibid., 160–162.

142. Ibid., 98. Hoffman summarized Kantor and Lehr's model in this way:

> The closed family is highly structured, hierarchical, and rule-governed; the individual is subordinate to the group. In its flawed version it becomes a rigid, hollow shell. . . . The anarchistic or random family sets a high value on personal individuation. "Do your own thing" is the motto, and there are few rules and little attention to boundaries. In the flawed version this family becomes totally chaotic; turbulence, caprice and contradiction take over. Still, struggles of individual members to reestablish some kind of control may end in a shift to an authoritarian, closed system or alternatively, fragmentation and dispersal will occur, or outside authorities will take over. The democratic or open system, which seems like a golden mean between the other two styles, balances order with flexibility and the rights of the individual with those of the group. In its flawed version this family type tends toward schism and divorce. Its most characteristic stress comes from the bind that results from taking features from both closed and random systems which, if not compatible, can lead to strain and impasse. (Hoffman, *Foundations of Family Therapy*, 99)

143. Kantor and Lehr, *Inside the Family*, 116 (emphasis in original).

144. Ibid., 157.

145. Ibid., 162.

146. Ibid., 162–63.

147. Henry, *Pathways to Madness*, 439.

148. Ibid., 457–459.

5. Visions of Family Life

1. *Rebel Without a Cause*, directed by Nicholas Ray. Warner Brothers, 1955.

2. Nathan W. Ackerman, *Treating the Troubled Family* (New York, 1966), viii, ix.

3. On the status of cinematic claims to represent reality, see, e.g., Bill Nichols, *Representing Reality: Issues and Concepts in Documentary* (Bloomington, IN, 1991); Philip Rosen, *Change Mummified: Cinema, Historicity* (Minneapolis, 2001); and Tom Gunning, "Moving Away from the Index: Cinema and the Impression of Reality," *differences* 18 (2007): 29–52.

4. E.g., Hans Strupp and Carl Rogers. Sample films of therapy sessions with Rogers from the 1950s and 1960s can be streamed at http://www.carlrogers.info/video.html#therapy. On the use of film by psychoanalysts interested in "truth serums" and memory, see Alison Winter, "Screening Selves: Sciences of Memory and Identity on Film, 1930–1960," *History of Psychology* 7, no. 4 (November 2004): 367–401. On psychoanalyst René Spitz's use of film in his studies of infant deprivation, see Lisa Cartwright, "'Emergencies of Survival': Moral Spectatorship and the 'New Vision of the Child' in Postwar Child Psychoanalysis," *Journal of Visual Culture* 3, no. 1 (2004): 35–49.

5. Murray Bowen, *Family Therapy in Clinical Practice* (New York, 1978), 49–50.

6. Jay Haley, "An Editor's Farewell," *Family Process* 8, no. 2 (September 1969) (emphasis added).

7. In addition to the visual techniques and technologies discussed here, family therapists relied on more traditional didactic methods, such as lectures, reading lists, and training manuals.

8. Peggy Papp, "Family Choreography," in *Family Therapy: Theory and Practice*, ed. Philip J. Guerin (New York, 1976), 471.

9. Ibid., 471, 478.

10. Nathan W. Ackerman, "Family Psychotherapy and Psychoanalysis: The Implications of Difference," *Family Process* 1, no. 1 (March 1962): 30–43, reprinted in *Family Process*, ed. Nathan W. Ackerman (New York, 1970), 12.

11. Andrew Lakoff, "Freezing Time: Margaret Mead's Diagnostic Photography," *Visual Anthropology Review* 12, no. 1 (1996): 2–10; and Anthony R. Michaelis, *Research Films in Biology, Anthropology, Psychology, and Medicine* (New York, 1955), 241–243. In a personal communication, March 1999, Salvador Minuchin recounted that the inspiration for his use of a one-way mirror was the one-way viewing screen at Bank Street.

12. Mark Pendergrast, *Mirror, Mirror: A History of the Human Love Affair with Reflection* (New York, 2003), 247–248.

13. Stephen W. Kempster and Elias Savitsky, "Training Family Therapists through 'Live' Supervision," in *Expanding Theory and Practice in Family Therapy*, ed. Nathan W. Ackerman, Frances L. Beatman, and Sanford N. Sherman (New York, 1967), 125–134.

14. Donald Bloch, former director, Ackerman Institute for the Family, New York City, personal communication to author, February 1999.

15. Don D. Jackson, "Comments on Training at the Mental Research Institute," 1966, folder "Proposals and Field Reports," 1, Jackson Archive.

16. Don D. Jackson, "Palo Alto Research Foundation, Mental Research Institute Summary Report for 1961," December 30, 1961, folder "Proposals and Field Reports," 2, Jackson Archive.

17. Don D. Jackson, "Final Progress Report—Public Health Service Grant No. M-5959: Conjoint Family Therapy: Theory and Practice," January 1963, folder "Proposals and Field Reports," 2, Jackson Archive.

18. Ibid., 10.

19. Paul Watzlawick, "A Structured Family Interview," *Family Process*, 5, no. 2 (September 1966).

20. Ibid. Transcripts of several Structured Family Interviews are accessible at the Jackson Archive.

21. "Summary of Training Program: A Proposal to Train Specialists in Educational, Preventative, and Reparative Application of Human Communication and Group Interaction Principles, with Special Emphasis on Well Family Service," c. 1963–67, folder "Variety of Materials from Jules Riskin's Files," 6, Jackson Archive (emphasis in original).

22. This argument appeared in many publications. E.g., Don D. Jackson, "The Question of Family Homeostasis," *Psychiatric Quarterly Supplement* 31 (1957): 79–90.

23. Lorraine Daston and Peter Galison, *Objectivity* (New York, 2007), 311.

24. Tal Golan, "The Emergence of the Silent Witness: The Legal and Medical Reception of X-Rays in the USA," *Social Studies of Science* 34, no. 4 (August 2004): 469–499. See also Cristina Grasseni, *Skilled Visions: Between Apprenticeship and Standards* (New York, 2007), for an anthropological take on debates about the denigration of vision, as well as discussion of the training of the eye and the links between practices and artifacts or technologies of looking.

25. Salvador Minuchin et al., *Families of the Slums: An Exploration of Their Structure and Treatment* (New York, 1967.

26. Janet Malcolm, "The One-Way Mirror," *New Yorker*, May 15, 1978, 39–41.

27. Mara Selvini Palazzoli et al., *Paradox and Counterparadox* (New York, 1978).

28. *In and Out of Psychosis*, produced by Nathan W. Ackerman in cooperation with the Jewish Family Service of New York City and the Family Institute, Inc., 107 min., Family Institute, New York, 1962 (VHS).

29. Nichols, *Representing Reality*, 34–38.

30. On documentary realism and cinematic indexicality, see ibid.,149–198. Recent work on cinema and the trace of the real by film scholars such as Mary Ann Doane, Tom Gunning, Laura Mulvey, and Philip Rosen has turned to the semiotic system of Charles Sanders Peirce, who defined the index as a sign that was distinguished from other types of signs (particularly icons and symbols) by its physical or causal connection to that which it represented, for example through the material trace of a fingerprint, a footprint in the sand, or the photochemical production of a photograph. The indexical quality of photography and film is based on their temporal and physical relation to the things or events being photographed or filmed, and this relation undergirds those media's claims to representing reality.

31. Christian Beels and Andrew Ferber, "Family Therapy: A View," *Family Process* 8, no. 2 (1969): 280–318.

32. On the *Hillcrest Family Series*, see M. L. Friedlander, P. S. Highlen, and W. L. Lassiter, "Content Analytic Comparison of Four Expert Counselors' Approaches to Family Treatment: Ackerman, Bowen, Jackson, and Whitaker," *Journal of Counseling Psychology* 31 (1984): 477–487. Originially produced on 16-mm color film by Ray Birdwhistell at the Eastern Pennsylvania Psychiatric Institute, a copy of the series is available on VHS at the Jackson Archive. On the history of twentieth-century American educational films outside of psychology, see Devin Orgeron, Marsha Orgeron, and Dan Streible, eds., *Learning with the Lights Off: Educational Film in the United States* (New York, 2012).

33. Winter, "Screening Selves."

34. For example, Normal Paul, "Effects of Playback on Family Members of Their Own Previously Recorded Conjoint Therapy Material," *Psychiatric Research Report* 20 (1966): 175–187; and Ian Alger and Peter Hogan, "Enduring Effects of Videotape Playback Experience on Family and Marital Relationships," *American Journal of Orthopsychiatry* 39 (1969): 86–94.

35. The original tapes were produced on two-inch tape, and in later years the researchers used three-quarter-inch videotapes. The full runs of both couples' therapy sessions are stored at the National Library of Medicine. Clips from several years of these sessions are included on "Psychotic Reaction: A Family Systems Phenomenon," videotape, 1976, Bowen Archive.

36. On the complex implications of time, editing, and archiving for the history of film and its relationship with science, see, e.g., Hannah Landecker, "Microcinematography and the History of Science and Film," *Isis* 97 (2006): 121–132; Scott Curtis, "Between Observation and Spectatorship: Medicine, Movies and Mass Culture in Imperial Germany," in *Film 1900: Technology, Perception, Culture*, ed. Klaus Kreimeier and Annemone Ligensa (Bloomington, IN, 2009), 87–98; and Mary Ann Doane, *The Emergence of Cinematic Time: Modernity, Contingency, the Archive* (Cambridge, MA, 2002).

37. Wendy Kozol, *Life's America: Family and Nation in Postwar Photojournalism* (Philadelphia, 1994), vii.

38. Ibid. The "visual portrait of domesticity" represented in *Life* magazine was also on display on television. See, e.g., Lynn Spigel, *Welcome to the Dreamhouse: Popular Media and Postwar Suburbs* (Durham, NC, 2001).

39. On the complex relationship between observation and spectatorship and the attendant relationship between scientific and popular viewing, see Curtis, "Between Observation and Spectatorship"; Gregg Mitman, *Reel Nature: America's Romance with Wildlife on Film* (Cambridge, MA, 1999); and Leslie J. Reagan, Nancy Tomes, and Paula A. Treichler, eds., *Medicine's Moving Pictures: Medicine, Health, and Bodies in American Film and Television* (Rochester, NY, 2008).

40. John Weakland, "Family Interaction and Mental Health," luncheon address to the conference "What's Happening to the Family in Suburbia?," San Fernando Valley State College, CA, 1961, Jackson Archive, 38–39 (emphasis in original).

41. David Reisman, *The Lonely Crowd: A Study of the Changing American Character* (New Haven, 1950); and William Whyte Jr., *The Organization Man* (New York, 1956). On Reisman, see Nathan W. Ackerman, "Behavior Trends and Disturbances of the Contemporary Family," in *The Family in Contemporary Society*, ed. Iago Galdston (New York, 1958), 57.

42. *The Fine Line*, 1959, videotape, Jackson Archive.

43. Minuchin et al., *Families of the Slums*, 43.

44. E.g., Derek Russell Davis, "A Re-Appraisal of Ibsen's 'Ghosts,'" *Family Process* 2 (March 1962): 81–94 ; and Frank S. Pittman, III, and Kalman Flomanhaft, "Treating the Doll's House Marriage," *Family Process* 9 (June 1970): 143–156 .

45. Robert E. Kantor and Lynn Hoffman, "Brechtian Theater as a Model for Conjoint Family Therapy," *Family Process* 5 (September 1966): 218–229; Fred M. Sander, "Family Therapy or Religion: A Re-reading of T. S. Eliot's *The Cocktail Party*," *Family Process* 9 (September 1979): 279–298; Howard F. Stein, "'All in the Family' as a Mirror of Contemporary Culture," *Family Process* 13 (September 1974): 279–316; and Anne Plone, "Marital and Existential Pain: Dialectic in Bergman's 'Scenes from a Marriage,'" *Family Process* 14 (September 1975): 371–378. Stein articulated the goal of his article on *All in the Family* in the following terms: "By exploring the dynamics of the Bunker household, I hope to show that the psychoanalytic, intrapsychic model and the transactional systems/communications model are not contradictory, but complementary."

46. Don D. Jackson to Mike Nichols, March 17, 1965, unlabeled folder of correspondence, Jackson Archive.

47. Salvador Minuchin et al., *Families of the Slums*. They had previously published aspects of their work in journal articles, such as S. Elbert et al., "A Method for the Clinical Study of Family Interaction," *American Journal of Orthopsychiatry* 34 (1964): 885–894.

48. James Gilbert, *A Cycle of Outrage: America's Reaction to the Juvenile Delinquent in the 1950s* (New York, 1986); James T. Patterson, *America's Struggle against Poverty, 1900–1994* (Cambridge, MA, 1994); and Alice O'Connor, *Poverty Knowledge: Social Science, Social Policy, and the Poor in Twentieth-Century US History* (Princeton, 2001).

49. Karen Anderson, *Wartime Women: Sex Roles, Family Relations, and the Status of Women during World War II* (Westport, CT, 1981), 95–105; and Gilbert, *Cycle of Outrage*.

50. Ibid., ix.

51. "No Man's Land: An Interview with Charles R. Fulweiler, Ph.D.," in Jay Haley and Lynn Hoffman, *Techniques of Family Therapy* (New York, 1967).

52. Ibid., 89, 35.

53. Minuchin et al., *Families of the Slums*, 6.

54. Ibid., 298.

55. Ibid., 299–302. Minuchin et al.'s description of the Family Task procedure includes all of the recorded questions and tasks.

56. Ibid., 302–303.

57. David G. Winter, "'Toward a Science of Personality Psychology': David McClelland's Development of Empirically Derived TAT Measures," *History of Psychology* 1 (1998): 130–153.

58. Minuchin et al., *Families of the Slums*, 333.

59. On the notion of the self associated with the Rorschach, Peter Galison argues that "the massive popularity of the Rorschach test over the course of the twentieth century signals (and conditions) a specific concept of self. That historical apperceptive self is picked out by its insistence on relations of depth and surface, inner and outer life, and the inseparability of ideation and affect." Peter Galison, "Image of Self," in *Things That Talk: Object Lessons from Art and Science*, ed. Lorraine Daston (New York: 2008), 277.

60. Minuchin et al., *Families of the Slums*, 330.

61. Ibid.

62. See Evelynn M. Hammonds, "New Technologies of Race," in *Processed Lives: Gender and Technology in Everyday Life*, eds. Jennifer Terry and Melodie Calvert (New York, 1997), 75–76.

63. UNESCO, *The Race Question* (Paris, 1950). The historical literature on scientific studies of race is substantial. A useful starting point is John P. Jackson Jr. and Nadine M. Weidman, *Race, Racism, and Science: Social Impact and Interaction* (New Brunswick, NJ, 2006).

64. Minuchin et al., *Families of the Slums*, 218.

65. Ibid., 219.

66. Ibid., 10–11.

67. Ibid., 23–24. See also Ruth Feldstein, *Motherhood in Black and White: Race and Sex in American Liberalism, 1930–1965* (Ithaca, 2000); Ellen Herman, *The Romance of American Psychology: Political Culture in the Age of Experts* (Berkeley, 1995); and Daryl Michael Scott, *Contempt and Pity: Social Policy and the Image of the Damaged Black Psyche* (Chapel Hill, NC, 1997).

68. Minuchin et al., *Families of the Slums*, 269–270.

69. Ibid., 264.

70. Ibid., 268–269 (emphasis in original).

71. In their interest in the internalization of the unseen observer, the Wiltwyck team mobilized for therapeutic ends a type of surveillance that resonated with Jeremy Bentham's eighteenth-century architectural model of the Panopticon, in which an unseen observer in a central tower could exert control by continuous visual monitoring of the inmates in a prison or other institutions such as a factory or lunatic asylum. Unlike Bentham's architectural model, Minuchin and his colleagues' use of a one-way mirror was designed neither to be maintained long-term nor to monitor inmates. However, their framing of the productive effects of unseen observers on those being observed aligns with Michel Foucault's well-known meditation on the role of surveillance in the functioning of power in the Panopticon:

> Hence the major effect of the Panopticon: to induce in the inmate a state of conscious and permanent visibility that assures the automatic functioning of power. So to arrange things that the surveillance is permanent in its effects, even if it is discontinuous. . .; in short, that the inmates should be caught up in a power situation of which they are themselves the bearers. To achieve this, it is at once too much and too little that the prisoner should be constantly observed by an inspector: too little, for what matters is that he knows himself to be observed; too much, because he has no need in fact of being so. (Michel Foucault, *Discipline and Punish: The Birth of the Prison*, trans. Alan Sheridan [1975; repr., New York, 1977], 201)

72. Minuchin et al., *Families of the Slums*, 36.

73. Ibid., 219.

74. Kathleen W. Jones, *Taming the Troublesome Child: American Families, Child Guidance, and the Limits of Psychiatric Authority* (Cambridge, MA, 1999); and Elizabeth Ann Danto, *Freud's Free Clinics: Psychoanalysis & Social Justice, 1918–1938* (New York, 2005).

75. Minuchin et al., *Families of the Slums*, 259.

76. Salvador Minuchin, *Psychosomatic Families* (Cambridge, MA, 1978).

77. August Napier, introduction to *The Book of Family Therapy*, ed. Andrew Ferber, M. Mendensohn, and August Napier (New York, 1972), quoted in Malcolm, "One-Way Mirror," 45.

78. Ackerman, *Family Process*, xiii.

79. Cf. Fatima Tobing Rony, *The Third Eye: Race, Cinema, and Ethnographic Spectacle* (Durham, NC, 1996), 197, who discusses the implications of ethnographic filmmakers' turning the camera over to their subjects in the context of anthropology's growing self-reflexivity about its representational practices during the 1970s. For a genealogy of autoethnographic films from the 1966 Navajo Film Project to the 2004 film *Born into Brothels* and a critique of their liberating rhetoric, see Pooja Rangan, "Immaterial Child Labor: Media Advocacy, Autoethnography, and the Case of *Born into Brothels*," *Camera Obscura* 25, no. 3 (2011): 142–177.

80. Jay Haley, *Wither Family Therapy?*, produced by Jay Haley and Madeleine Richeport-Haley, 50 min. (Triangle Productions, 1997), videotape.

6. Epilogue

1. Anne Roiphe, "Things Are Keen but Could Be Keener," *New York Times*, February 18, 1973, reprinted in Ron Goulart, *An American Family* (New York, 1973), 9–27; and Lynn Young, "The Broken Family: The Divorce of the Year," *Newsweek*, March 12, 1973, 48–49. *Newsweek* covered the impact of the Loud series in conjunction with a longer article on divorce and the American family.

2. Steven Mintz and Susan Kellogg, *Domestic Revolutions: A Social History of American Family Life* (New York, 1988), 201. Mintz and Kellogg describe in more detail the dramatic changes in the rates of marriage and divorce, average number of children per family, attitudes toward sexuality, influx of married women into paid labor, and frequency of single-parent households (see pp. 203–237).

3. Natasha Zaretsky, *No Direction Home: The American Family and the Fear of National Decline, 1968–1980* (Chapel Hill, 2007).

4. Patricia Loud, "Letter to *The Forum for Contemporary History*," February 23, 1973, reprinted in Goulart, *An American Family*, 235.

5. I have situated *An American Family* as an outgrowth of the earlier history of cinema verité. For analyses of the series as a precursor of reality television, see Susan Murray and Laurie Ouellette, eds., *Reality TV: Remaking Television Culture* (New York, 2004). The literature on reality TV more generally underscores the inextricable relations between the familial and the therapeutic in contemporary American culture.

6. Paula Rabinowitz, "History in Your Own Home: *Cinema Verité*, Docudrama, and America's Families," in *They Must Be Represented: The Politics of Documentary* (London, 1994), 130. See also Jeffrey Ruoff, *An American Family: A Televised Life* (Minneapolis, 2002).

7. Jamie Cohen-Cole, *The Open Mind: Cold War Politics and the Sciences of Human Nature* (Chicago, forthcoming); Peter Galison, "The Americanization of Unity," *Daedalus* 127 (Winter, 1998): 45–71; and David A. Hollinger, "Science as a Weapon in *Kulturkampfe* in the United States during and after World War II," *Isis* 86 (1995): 440–454.

8. Minuchin et al., *Families of the Slums*, 370.

9. Salvador Minuchin and Michael P. Nichols, *Family Healing: Tales of Hope and Renewal from Family Therapy* (New York, 1993). Similarly, Phebe Sessions recounts that in an interview with her, Minuchin "was somewhat critical of the model of practice at that time, feeling that they were 'naïve' about the importance of social institutions in the lives of poor people." Sessions, "Family Therapy and Urban Poverty: Structural Family Therapy in Context" (PhD diss., Brandeis University, 1991), 212.

10. Herman elaborated on this point:

Experts charged with managing populations felt they had no choice but to navigate the murky depths of the interior psyche in order to accomplish their goals. Experts moved to aid suffering individuals resolved that only social alternatives could alleviate pain and facilitate growth. Thus did the concerns of behavioral science and clinical healing merge, complicating the meaning of social engineering and personal liberation alike. . . . Developments such as these offer fresh vantage points from which to view post-war history in the United States and provide insights into some of its characteristic features: the blurring of public and private boundaries, the overlap between political culture and cultural politics, the anxious standoff between self and society. (*The Romance of American Psychology: Political Culture in the Age of Experts* [Berkeley, 1995], 305, 310, 315)

11. Jerome Agel, ed., *Radical Therapist: The Radical Therapist Collective* (New York, 1971).

12. R. D. Laing, *The Politics of the Family, and Other Essays* (New York, 1969); and R. D. Laing and Aaron Esterson, *Sanity, Madness, and the Family: Families of Schizophrenics*, 2nd ed. (1964; repr., London, 1970). On the history of antipsychiatry, see Michael E. Staub, *Madness Is Civilization: When the Diagnosis Was Social, 1948–1980* (Chicago, 2011).

13. Mari Jo Buhle, *Feminism and Its Discontents: A Century of Struggle with Psychoanalysis* (Cambridge, MA, 1998); Alice Echols, *Daring to Be Bad: Radical Feminism in America, 1967–1975* (Minneapolis, 1989); Herman, " The Curious Courtship of Psychology and Women's Liberation, " in *Romance of American Psychology*, chap. 10; and Nancy Whittier, *The Politics of Child Sexual Abuse: Emotion, Social Movements, and the State* (New York, 2009). See also Betty Friedan, *The Feminine Mystique* (New York, 1963), and on its history, Stephanie Coontz, *A Strange Stirring: The* Feminine Mystique *and American Women at the Dawn of the 1960s* (New York, 2011); Daniel Horowitz, *Betty Friedan and the Making of the Feminine Mystique: The American Left, the Cold War, and Modern Feminism* (Amherst, MA, 1998); and Rebecca Jo Plant, *Mom: The Transformation of Motherhood in Modern America* (Chicago, 2010).

14. C.f. Regina G. Kunzel, *Fallen Women, Problem Girls: Unmarried Mothers and the Professionalization of Social Work, 1890–1945* (New Haven, 1993).

15. E.g., Rachel T. Hare-Mustin, "A Feminist Approach to Family Therapy," *Family Process* 17 (1978): 181–194; Marion Lindblad-Goldberg, ed., *Clinical Issues in Single-Parent Households* (Rockville, MD, 1987); Deborah A. Luepnitz, *The Family Interpreted* (New York, 1988); and Marianne Walters et al., *The Invisible Web: Gender Patterns in Family Relationships* (New York, 1988). For a historical account of the feminist family therapy movement based on oral histories with twelve prominent therapists, see Sukie Magraw, "Feminism and Family Therapy: An Oral History" (PhD diss., California School of Professional Psychology at Berkeley/Alameda, 1992).

16. E.g., Monica McGoldrick, John K. Pearce, and Joseph Giordano, eds., *Ethnicity and Family Therapy* (New York, 1982).

17. Monica McGoldrick, ed., *Re-Visioning Family Therapy: Race, Culture, and Gender in Clinical Practice* (New York, 1998), viii.

18. The literature on narrative therapy is extensive. See Michael White and David Epston, *Narrative Means to Therapeutic Ends* (New York, 1990). On the stakes of the discursive turn in family therapy, see Salvador Minuchin, "Where is the Family in Narrative Family Therapy?" *Journal of Marital and Family Therapy* 24, no. 4 (1998): 397–403, and comments on Minuchin's article by Gene Combs and Jill Freedman, Karl Tomm, and Carlos E. Sluzki in the same issue.

19. Richard Simon, "The Larger Story: Reflections on 20 Years of the *Networker*," *The Psychotherapy Networker*, 2002, http://www.psychotherapynetworker.org/larger_story.htm.

20. E.g., Raymond J. Corsini and Danny Wedding, ed., *Current Psychotherapies*, 8th ed. (Belmont, CA 2008); and Jeffery K. Zeig, ed., *The Evolution of Psychotherapy: The Third Conference* (New York, 1995). There is also a family therapy section of the American Psychological Association.

21. Alan S. Gurman and David P. Kniskern, preface to"Preface," in Alan S. Gurman and David P. Kniskern, eds., *The Handbook of Family Therapy*, ed. Alan S. Gurman and David P. Kniskern (New York, 1981), xiii; and http://www.aamft.org/about/Aboutaamft.htm.

22. R. W. Manderscheid and M. A. Sonnenchein, "An Update on Human Resources in Mental Health," Center for Mental Health Services, DHHS Pub. No. (SMA) 96–3098 (Washington, DC: U.S. Government Printing Office Supt. of Docs., U.S. Govt. Print. Off., 1996), quoted at http://www.aamft.org/Press_Room/Press_releases/compare.htm.

23. Mimi White, *Tele-Advising: Therapeutic Discourse in American Television* (Chapel Hill, NC, 1992), 6. Her analysis of the family therapy episode of *The Simpsons* is particularly sharp (173–178). On reality TV, see, e.g., Laurie Ouellette and James Hay, *Better Living through Reality TV: Television and Post-Welfare Citizenship* (Oxford, 2008); and Susan Murray and Laurie Ouellette, eds., *Reality TV: Remaking Television Culture* (New York, 2004).

24. E.g., N. R. Kleinfield, "Baby Makes Four, and Complications," *New York Times*, June 19, 2011, MB1; and Laura M. Holson, "Who's on the Family Tree? Now It's Complicated," *New York Times*, July 5, 2011, A1. See Sarah Franklin and Susan McKinnon, eds., *Relative Values: Reconfiguring Kinship Studies* (Durham, NC, 2001).

25. Lauren Berlant argues that "the intimate public sphere of the U.S. present tense renders citizenship as a condition of social membership produced by personal acts and values, especially acts originating in or directed toward the family sphere," in *The Queen of America Goes to Washington City: Essays on Sex and Citizenship* (Durham, NC, 1997), 5.

BIBLIOGRAPHY

Archival Collections

Ackerman Institute for the Family, New York.

American Psychological Association, Library of Congress, Washington, DC.

Gregory Bateson papers. MS 98. Special Collections and Archives, University Library, University of California, Santa Cruz.

Bowen Archive, Bowen Center for the Study of the Family, Washington, DC. NB: Murray Bowen's papers were donated to the National Library of Medicine after the research for this project ended. Notes to Bowen's papers reference the filing system at the Bowen Center because the collection remains unprocessed at the NLM.

Don D. Jackson Archive (the Mental Research Institute, Palo Alto, CA), stored at the Marriage and Family Therapy Program, University of Louisiana at Monroe.

Oskar Diethelm Library for the History of Psychiatry at New York Hospital-Cornell Medical Center, New York.

Philadelphia Child and Family Therapy Training Center, Philadelphia.

Published Sources

Abraham, Tara. "(Physio)logical Circuits: The Intellectual Origins of the McCulloch-Pitts Neural Networks." *Journal of the History of the Behavioral Sciences* 38 (2002): 3–25.

Ackerman, Nathan W. "Adolescent Problems: A Symptom of Family Disorder." *Family Process* 1, no. 2 (1962): 202–213.

——, ed. *Exploring the Base for Family Therapy.* New York: Family Service Association of America, 1961.

——. "The Family as a Social and Emotional Unit." *Bulletin of the Kansas Mental Hygiene Society* 12 (1937): 2.

——, ed. *Family Process.* New York: Basic Books, 1970.

——. *The Psychodynamics of Family Life: Diagnosis and Treatment of Family Relationships.* New York: Basic Books, 1958.

——. *Treating the Troubled Family.* New York: Basic Books, 1966.

——. "The Unity of the Family." *Archives of Pediatrics* 55 (1938): 51–62.

Ackerman, Nathan W., Frances L. Beatman, and Sanford N. Sherman, eds. *Expanding Theory and Practice in Family Therapy*. New York: Family Service Association of America, 1967.

Ackerman, Nathan W., and Marie Jahoda. *Anti-Semitism and Emotional Disorder*. Studies in Prejudice, edited by Max Horkheimer. New York: Harper & Brothers, 1950.

Adorno, T. W., Else Frenkel-Brunswik, Daniel J. Levinson, and R. Nevitt Sanford. *The Authoritarian Personality*. Studies in Prejudice, edited by Max Horkheimer. New York: Harper & Brothers, 1950.

Agel, Jerome, ed. *Radical Therapist: The Radical Therapist Collective*. New York: Ballantine Books, 1971.

Alger, Ian, and Peter Hogan. "Enduring Effects of Videotape Playback Experience on Family and Marital Relationships." *American Journal of Orthopsychiatry* 39 (1969): 86–94.

Allport, Gordon. *The Nature of Prejudice*. Reading, MA: Addison-Wesley, 1954.

——. *Personality and Social Encounter: Selected Essays*. Boston: Beacon Press, 1960.

Anderson, Karen. *Wartime Women: Sex Roles, Family Relations, and the Status of Women during World War II*. Westport, CT: Greewood Press, 1981.

Apple, Rima D. *Mothers and Medicine: A Social History of Infant Feeding, 1890–1950*. Madison: University of Wisconsin Press, 1987.

——. *Perfect Motherhood: Science and Childrearing in America*. New Brunswick, NJ: Rutgers University Press, 2006.

Apple, Rima D., and Janet Golden, eds. *Mothers & Motherhood: Readings in American History*. Columbus: Ohio State University Press, 1997.

Ash, Mitchell G. *Gestalt Psychology in German Culture, 1890–1967: Holism and the Quest for Objectivity*. Cambridge: Cambridge University Press, 1995.

Attneave, Carolyn L. "Therapy in Tribal Settings and Urban Network Intervention." *Family Process* 8, no. 2 (1969): 192–210.

Auerback, Alfred, ed. *Schizophrenia: An Integrated Approach*. New York: Ronald Press Company, 1959.

Auerswald, Edgar H. "Interdisciplinary Versus Ecological Approach." In *Family Process*, edited by Nathan W. Ackerman, 202–215. New York: Basic Books, 1970.

Back, Les, and John Solomos, eds. *Theories of Race and Racism: A Reader*. London: Routledge, 2000.

Bailey, Beth L. *From Front Porch to Back Seat: Courtship in Twentieth-Century America*. Baltimore: Johns Hopkins University Press, 1988.

——. *Sex in the Heartland*. Cambridge, MA: Harvard University Press, 2002.

Ball, Terence. "The Politics of Social Science in Postwar America." In *Recasting America: Culture and Politics in the Age of Cold War*, edited by Lary May, 76–92. Chicago: University of Chicago Press, 1989.

Banks, Marcus, and Howard Morphy. *Rethinking Visual Anthropology*. New Haven: Yale University Press, 1997.

Barkan, Elazar. *The Retreat of Scientific Racism: Changing Concepts of Race in Britain and the United States between the World Wars*. Cambridge: Cambridge University Press, 1992.

Bassi, Virginia Marie. "The Genesis of Family Therapy: An Oral History of the Years 1945–1960." PhD diss., California School of Professional Psychology at Berkeley/Alameda, 1991.

Bateson, Gregory. "Cultural Problems Posed by a Study of Schizophrenic Process." In *Schizophrenia: An Integrated Approach*, edited by Alfred Auerback, 125–143. New York: Ronald Press, 1959.

——. *Mind and Nature: A Necessary Unity*. New York: Bantam Books, 1979.

——. *Naven: A Survey of Problems Suggested by a Composite Picture of the Culture of a New Guinea Tribe Drawn from Three Points of View*. Stanford: Stanford University Press, 1936.

——. *Perceval's Narrative: A Patient's Account of His Psychosis.* Stanford: Stanford University Press, 1961.

——. *Steps to an Ecology of Mind: Collected Essays in Anthropology, Psychiatry, Evolution and Epistemology.* New York: Ballantine Books, 1972.

Bateson, Gregory, Don D. Jackson, Jay Haley, and John Weakland. "A Note on the Double Bind—1962." *Family Process* 2 (1963): 154–161.

——. "Toward a Theory of Schizophrenia." *Behavioral Science* 1 (1956): 251–264.

Bateson, Gregory, and Margaret Mead. *Balinese Character: A Photographic Analysis.* New York: New York Academy of Sciences, Special Publications 2, 1942.

Bederman, Gail. *Manliness & Civilization: A Cultural History of Gender and Race in the United States, 1880–1917.* Chicago: University of Chicago Press, 1995.

Beels, C. Christian. "Notes for a Cultural History of Family Therapy." *Family Process* 41 (2002): 67–82.

Beels, Christian, and Andrew Ferber. "Family Therapy: A View." *Family Process* 8, no. 2 (1969): 280–318.

Bell, Norman W., and E. F. Vogel, eds. *A Modern Introduction to the Family.* Glencoe, IL: Free Press, 1960.

Benedict, Ruth. *The Chrysanthemum and the Sword.* Boston: Houghton Mifflin, 1946.

——. *Patterns of Culture.* Boston: Houghton Mifflin, 1934.

Berger, Milton, ed. *Beyond the Double Bind: Communication and Family Systems, Theories and Techniques with Schizophrenics.* New York: Brunner/Mazel, 1978.

Berlant, Lauren. *The Queen of America Goes to Washington City: Essays on Sex and Citizenship.* Durham, NC: Duke University Press, 1997.

Bertalanffy, Ludwig von. *General System Theory: Foundations, Developments, Applications.* New York: George Braziller, 1968.

——. *Modern Theories of Development: An Introduction to Theoretical Biology.* London: Oxford University Press, 1933.

——. *Problems of Life: An Evaluation of Modern Biological and Scientific Thought.* New York: Harper & Brothers, 1952.

——. *Robots, Men and Minds.* New York: George Braziller, 1967.

Bertrando, Paolo. "The Evolution of Family Interventions for Schizophrenia: A Tribute to Gianfranco Cecchin." *Journal of Family Therapy* 28 (2006): 4–22.

Bettelheim, Bruno. *The Empty Fortress.* New York: Free Press, 1967.

Bettelheim, Bruno, and Morris Janowitz. *Dynamics of Prejudice: A Psychological and Sociological Study of Veterans.* Studies in Prejudice, edited by Max Horkheimer and Samuel H. Fowerman. New York: Harper & Brothers, 1950.

Bhabha, Homi K. *The Location of Culture.* London: Routledge, 1994.

Bleuler, Eugen. "The Fundamental Symptoms of Dementia Praecox or the Group of Schizophrenia." In *The Origins of Modern Psychiatry*, edited by C. Thompson, 165–209. Chichester, UK: John Wiley, 1987.

Blitsten, Dorothy R. *The Social Theories of Harry Stack Sullivan.* New York: William-Frederick Press, 1953.

Bloch, Donald, ed. *Techniques of Family Psychotherapy.* New York: Grune and Stratton, 1973.

Bloch, Donald, and Robert Simon, eds. *The Strength of Family Therapy: Selected Papers of Nathan W. Ackerman.* New York: Brunner/Mazel, 1982.

Blum, John Morton. *V Was for Victory: Politics and Culture during World War II.* San Diego: Harcourt Brace Jovanovich, 1976.

Bono, James L. "Science, Discourse, and Literature: The Role/Rule of Metaphor in Science." In *Literature and Science: Theory & Practice*, edited by Stuart Peterfreund, 59–89. Boston: Northeastern University Press, 1990.

Boszormenyi-Nagy, Ivan, and James L. Framo, eds. *Intensive Family Therapy.* New York: Harper and Row, 1965.

Bowen, Murray. "Adult Psychiatry Branch: Section on Ward 3-E." In *Annual Report of Program Activities, NIH: National Institute of Mental Health*. Washington, DC: National Institutes of Health, Public Health Service, U.S. Department of Health, Education, and Welfare, 1957.

——. *Family Therapy in Clinical Practice*. New York: Jason Aronson, 1978.

Boyer, Paul. *By the Bomb's Early Light: American Thought and Culture at the Dawn of the Atomic Age*. Chapel Hill: University of North Carolina Press, 1985.

Brandt, Allan M. *No Magic Bullet: A Social History of Venereal Disease in the United States Since 1880*. New York: Oxford University Press, 1987.

Braslow, Joel. *Mental Ills and Bodily Cures: Psychiatric Treatment in the First Half of the Twentieth Century*. Berkeley: University of California Press, 1997.

Braverman, Lois. *A Guide to Feminist Family Therapy*. London: Harrington Park Press, 1988.

Breines, Wini. *Young, White, and Miserable: Growing Up Female in the Fifties*. Boston: Beacon Press, 1992.

Brick, Howard. *The Age of Contradiction: American Thought and Culture in the 1960s*. New York: Twayne, 1998.

Brockman, John, ed. *About Bateson: Essays on Gregory Bateson*. New York: E. P. Dutton, 1977.

Broderick, Carlfred B., and Sandra S. Schrader. "The History of Professional Marriage and Family Therapy." In *Handbook of Family Therapy*, edited by Alan S. Gurman and David P. Kniskern, 5–35. New York: Brunner/Mazel, 1981.

Brodkin, Adele M. "Family Therapy: The Making of a Mental Health Movement." *American Journal of Orthopsychiatry* 50, no. 1 (1980): 4–17.

Brodsky, Carroll M. "The Social Recovery of Mentally Ill Housewives." *Family Process* 7, no. 2 (1968): 170–183.

Brookeman, Christopher. *American Culture and Society since the 1930s*. London: Macmillan, 1984.

Brown, Bruce. *Images of Family Life in Magazine Advertising: 1920–1978*. New York: Praeger, 1981.

Brumberg, Joan Jacobs. *Fasting Girls: The Emergence of Anorexia Nervosa as a Modern Disease*. Cambridge, MA: Harvard University Press, 1988.

Bryson, Dennis. "Lawrence K. Frank, Knowledge, and the Production of the 'Social.'" *Poetics Today* 19, no. 3 (Autumn 1998): 401–21.

Buhle, Mari Jo. *Feminism and Its Discontents: A Century of Struggle with Psychoanalysis*. Cambridge, MA: Harvard University Press, 1998.

Burnham, John C. "The Influence of Psychoanalysis upon American Culture." In *American Psychoanalysis: Origins and Development*, edited by Jacques M. Quen and Eric T. Carlson, 52–72. New York: Brunner/Mazel, 1978.

——. "The New Psychology: From Narcissism to Social Control." In Burnham, ed., *Paths into American Culture*, 69–93. Philadephia: Temple University Press, 1988.

——, ed. *Paths into American Culture: Psychology, Medicine, and Morals*. Philadelphia: Temple University Press, 1988.

Butler, Judith. "Is Kinship Always Already Heterosexual?" *differences* 13 (2002): 14–44.

Byars, Jackie. *All That Hollywood Allows: Re-reading Gender in 1950s Melodrama*. Chapel Hill: University of North Carolina Press, 1991.

Byng-Hall, John. "An Appreciation of John Bowlby: His Significance for Family Therapy." *Journal of Family Therapy* 13 (1991): 5–16.

Canguilhem, Georges. *The Normal and the Pathological*. 1966. Reprint, New York: Zone Books, 1991.

Cannon, Walter B. *The Wisdom of the Body*. New York: Norton, 1932.

Caplan, Eric. *Mind Games: American Culture and the Birth of Psychotherapy*. Berkeley: University of California Press, 1998.

Capshew, James H. *Psychologists on the March: Science, Practice, and Professional Identity in America, 1929–1969*. Cambridge: Cambridge University Press, 1999.

Cartwright, Lisa. "'Emergencies of Survival': Moral Spectatorship and the 'New Vision of the Child' in Postwar Child Psychoanalysis." *Journal of Visual Culture* 3 (2004): 35–49.
——. *Screening the Body: Tracing Medicine's Visual Culture.* Minneapolis: University of Minnesota Press, 1995.
Celello, Kristen. *Making Marriage Work: A History of Marriage and Divorce in the Twentieth-Century United States.* Chapel Hill: University of North Carolina Press, 2009.
Cherlin, Andrew J. *Marriage, Divorce, Remarriage.* 2nd ed. Cambridge, MA: Harvard University Press, 1992.
Christensen, H. T., ed. *Handbook of Marriage and the Family.* Chicago: Rand McNally, 1964.
Ciompi, Luc. *The Psyche and Schizophrenia: The Bond between Affect and Logic.* Translated by Deborah Lucas Schneider. Cambridge. MA: Harvard University Press, 1988.
Clark, Clifford E., Jr. "Ranch-House Suburbia: Ideals and Realities." In *Recasting America: Culture and Politics in the Age of Cold War*, edited by Lary May, 171–191. Chicago: University of Chicago Press, 1989.
Clark, Kenneth. *Dark Ghetto: Dilemmas of Social Power.* New York: Harper & Row, 1965.
Clarke, Adele E., and Joan Fujimura, eds. *The Right Tools for the Job: At Work in Twentieth-Century Life Sciences.* Princeton: Princeton University Press, 1992.
Clifford, James. *The Predicament of Culture: Twentieth-Century Ethnography, Literature and Art.* Cambridge, MA: Harvard University Press, 1988.
Clifford, James, and George E. Marcus, eds. *Writing Culture: The Poetics and Politics of Ethnography.* Berkeley: University of California Press, 1986.
Cloud, Dana L. *Control and Consolation in American Culture and Politics.* Thousand Oaks, CA: Sage Publications, 1998.
Cloward, Richard A., and Lloyd E. Ohlin. *Delinquency and Opportunity: A Theory of Delinquent Gangs.* Glencoe, IL: Free Press, 1960.
Cohen, Albert K. *Delinquent Boys: The Culture of the Gang.* Glencoe, IL: Free Press, 1955.
Cohen, Lizabeth. *A Consumers' Republic: The Politics of Mass Consumption in Postwar America.* New York: Knopf, 2003.
Cohen-Cole, Jamie. *The Open Mind: Cold War Politics and the Sciences of Human Nature* Chicago: University of Chicago Press, forthcoming.
Collier, John, Jr., and Malcolm Collier. *Visual Anthropology: Photography as a Research Method.* Rev. and exp. ed. 1967. Reprint, Albuquerque: University of New Mexico Press, 1986.
Coontz, Stephanie. *The Social Origins of Private Life: A History of American Families, 1600–1900.* London: Verso, 1988.
——. *A Strange Stirring: The* Feminine Mystique *and American Women at the Dawn of the 1960s.* New York: Basic Books, 2011.
——. *The Way We Never Were: American Families and the Nostalgia Trap.* New York: Basic Books, 1992.
Coontz, Stephanie, Maya Parson, and Gabrielle Raley, eds. *American Families: A Multicultural Reader.* New York: Routledge, 1999.
Cooter, Roger, ed. *In the Name of the Child: Health and Welfare, 1880–1940.* London: Routledge, 1992.
Corsini, Raymond J., and Danny Wedding, eds. *Current Psychotherapies.* 8th ed. Belmont, CA: Thomson Brooks/Cole, 2008.
Cott, Nancy F. *Public Vows: A History of Marriage and the Nation.* Cambridge, MA: Harvard University Press, 2000.
Crary, Jonathan. *Techniques of the Observer: On Vision and Modernity in the Nineteenth Century.* Cambridge: MIT Press, 1990.
Cravens, Hamilton. "Behaviorism Revisited: Developmental Science, the Maturation Theory, and the Biological Basis of the Human Mind, 1920s-1950s." In *The Expansion of American Biology*, edited by Keith R. Benson, Jane Maienschein, and Ronald Rainger, 133–163. New Brunswick, NJ: Rutgers University Press, 1991.

——. "Child-Saving in the Age of Professionalism, 1915–1930." In *American Childhood: A Research Guide and Historical Handbook*, edited by Joseph M. Hawes and N. Ray Hiner, 415–488. Westport, CT: Greenwood, 1985.

——. "Scientific Racism in America, 1970s–1990s." *Prospects* 21 (1996): 471–490.

Crnic, Meghan. "Better Babies: Social Engineering for 'a Better Nation, a Better World.'" *Endeavour* 33 (2009): 13–18.

Cross, Stephen J., and William R. Albury. "Walter B. Cannon, L. J. Henderson, and the Organic Analogy." *Osiris* 3 (1987): 165–192.

Curtis, Scott. "Between Observation and Spectatorship: Medicine, Movies and Mass Culture in Imperial Germany." In *Film 1900: Technology, Perception, Culture*, edited by Klaus Kreimeier and Annemone Ligensa, 87–98. Bloomington: Indiana University Press, 2009.

Cushman, Philip. *Constructing the Self, Constructing America: A Cultural History of Psychotherapy*. Reading, MA: Addison-Wesley, 1995.

Cyrus, Della D. "What's Wrong with the Family?" *Atlantic Monthly*, November 1946, 67–73.

Dann, Kevin, and Gregg Mitman. "Essay Review: Exploring the Borders of Environmental History and the History of Ecology." *Journal of the History of Biology* 30 (1997): 291–302.

Danto, Elizabeth Ann. *Freud's Free Clinics: Psychoanalysis & Social Justice, 1918–1938*. New York: Columbia University Press, 2005.

Danziger, Kurt. *Constructing the Subject: Historical Origins of Psychological Research*. Cambridge: Cambridge University Press, 1990.

Darnell, Regna. *And Along Came Boas: Continuity and Revolution in Americanist Anthropology*. Amsterdam: John Benjamins, 1998.

Daston, Lorraine. "The Coming into Being of Scientific Objects." In *Biographies of Scientific Objects*, edited by Lorraine Daston, 1–14. Chicago: University of Chicago Press, 2000.

Daston, Lorraine, and Peter Galison. "The Image of Objectivity." *Representations* 40 (1992): 81–128.

——. *Objectivity*. New York: Zone Books, 2007.

Daston, Lorraine, and Elizabeth Lunbeck, eds. *Histories of Scientific Observation*. Chicago: University of Chicago Press, 2011.

Davidoff, Leonore, and Catherine Hall. *Family Fortunes: Men and Women of the English Middle Class, 1780–1850*. Chicago: University of Chicago Press, 1987.

Davis, Derek Russell. "A Re-Appraisal of Ibsen's 'Ghosts.'" *Family Process* 2 (March 1962): 81–94.

Davis, Rebecca L. *More Perfect Unions: The American Search for Marital Bliss*. Cambridge, MA: Harvard University Press, 2010.

Degler, Carl N. *At Odds: Women and the Family in America from the Revolution to the Present*. New York: Oxford University Press, 1980.

——. *In Search of Human Nature: The Decline and Revival of Darwinism in American Social Thought*. New York: Oxford University Press, 1991.

de Marneffe, Daphne. "Looking and Listening: The Construction of Clinical Knowledge in Charcot and Freud." In *Gender and Scientific Authority*, edited by Barbara Laslett, Sally Gregory Kohlstedt, Helen Longino, and Evelynn Hammonds, 241–281. Chicago: University of Chicago Press, 1996.

D'Emilio, John, and Estelle B. Freedman. *Intimate Matters: A History of Sexuality in America*. New York: Harper & Row, 1988.

Demos, John. *A Little Commonwealth: Family Life in Plymouth Colony*. New York: Oxford University Press, 1970.

——. "Oedipus and America: Historical Perspectives on the Reception of Psychoanalysis in the United States." In *Inventing the Psychological: Toward a Cultural History of Emotional Life in America*, edited by Joel Pfister and Nancy Schnog, 63–83. 1978. Reprint, New Haven: Yale University Press, 1997.

——. *Past, Present, and Personal: The Family and Life Course in American History*. New York: Oxford University Press, 1986.

Demos, John, and Sarane Spence Boocock, eds. *Turning Points: Historical and Sociological Essays on the Family*. Chicago: University of Chicago Press, 1978.

Digby, Ann. *Madness, Morality, and Medicine: A Study of the York Retreat, 1796–1914*. Cambridge, UK: Cambridge University Press, 1985

Doane, Mary Ann. *The Emergence of Cinematic Time: Modernity, Contingency, the Archive*. Cambridge, MA: Harvard University Press, 2002.

Dolnick, Edward. *Madness on the Couch: Blaming the Victim in the Heyday of Psychoanalysis*. New York: Simon & Schuster, 1998.

Donzelot, Jacques. *The Policing of Families*. Translated by Robert Hurley. 1977. Reprint, New York: Random House, 1979.

Douglas, Ann. *The Feminization of American Culture*. New York: Knopf, 1977.

——. *Terrible Honesty: Mongrel Manhattan in the 1920s*. New York: Farrar, Straus, and Giroux, 1995.

Dumit, Joseph. "A Digital Image of the Category of the Person: PET Scanning and Objective Self-Fashioning." In *Cyborgs & Citadels: Anthropological Interventions in Emerging Sciences and Technologies*, edited by Gary Lee Downey and Joseph Dumit, 83–102. Sante Fe, NM: School of American Research Press, 1997.

Echols, Alice. *Daring to Be Bad: Radical Feminism in America, 1967–1975*. Minneapolis: University of Minnesota Press, 1989.

Edwards, Paul N. *The Closed World: Computers and the Politics of Discourse in Cold War America*. Cambridge, MA: MIT Press, 1996.

Eisenberg, Leon. "The Social Imperatives of Medical Research." *Science* 198 (1977): 1105–1110.

Elizur, Joel, and Salvador Minuchin. *Institutionalizing Madness: Families, Therapy, and Society*. New York: Basic Books, 1989.

Erenberg, Lewis A., and Susan E. Hirsch, eds. *The War in American Culture: Society and Consciousness during World War II*. Chicago: University of Chicago Press, 1996.

Family Process, 1962–72.

Fass, Paula S. "The Child-Centered Family? New Rules in Postwar America." In *Reinventing Childhood after World War II*, edited by Paula S. Fass and Michael Grossberg, 1–18. Philadelphia: University of Pennsylvania Press, 2012.

——. *The Damned and the Beautiful*. New York: Oxford University Press, 1977.

Faulkner, Howard J., and Virginia D. Pruitt, eds. *Dear Dr. Menninger: Women's Voices from the Thirties*. Columbia: University of Missouri Press, 1997.

Feldstein, Ruth. "Antiracism and Maternal Failure in the 1940s and 1950s." In *"Bad" Mothers: The Politics of Blame in Twentieth Century America*, edited by Molly Ladd-Taylor and Lauri Umansky, 145–168. New York: New York University Press, 1998.

——. *Motherhood in Black and White: Race and Sex in American Liberalism, 1930–1965*. Ithaca: Cornell University Press, 2000.

Ferber, Andrew, M. Mendensohn, and August Napier, eds. *The Book of Family Therapy*. New York: Science House, 1972.

Fields, Barbara J. "Ideology and Race in American History." In *Region, Race and Reconstruction*, edited by J. Morgan Kousser and James MacPherson, 143–177. New York: Oxford University Press, 1982.

Fleming, Donald. "Walter B. Cannon and Homeostasis." *Social Research* 51 (1984): 609–640.

Flugel, J. C. *The Psycho-analytic Study of the Family*. London: Hogarth Press, 1921.

Foster, Hal, ed. *Vision and Visuality*. Discussions in Contemporary Culture, edited by Dia Art Foundation. Seattle: Bay Press, 1988.

Foucault, Michel. *Discipline and Punish: The Birth of the Prison*. Translated by Alan Sheridan. 1975. Reprint, New York: Vintage Books, 1977.

——. *The History of Sexuality: An Introduction*. Translated by Robert Hurley. Vol. 1. New York: Vintage Books, 1978.

——. "Nietzsche, Genealogy, History." In *Language, Counter-Memory, Practice: Selected Essays and Interviews*, edited by Donald F. Bouchard, 139–164. Ithaca: Cornell University Press, 1977.

Framo, James, ed. *Family Interaction: A Dialogue between Family Researchers and Family Therapists*. New York: Springer, 1972.

Frankenberg, Ruth. *White Women, Race Matters: The Social Construction of Whiteness*. Minneapolis: University of Minnesota Press, 1993.

Franklin, Sarah, and Susan McKinnon, eds. *Relative Values: Reconfiguring Kinship Studies*. Durham, NC: Duke University Press, 2001.

Frazier, E. Franklin. *The Negro Family in the United States*. Chicago: The University of Chicago Press, 1939.

Freedheim, Donald K., ed. *History of Psychotherapy: A Century of Change*. Washington, DC: American Psychological Association, 1992.

Freedman, Jonathan. "From *Spellbound* to *Vertigo*: Alfred Hitchcock and Therapeutic Culture in America." In *Hitchcock's America*, edited by Jonathan Freedman and Richard Millington, 77–98. New York: Oxford University Press, 1999.

Freud, Sigmund. *Totem and Taboo: Some Points of Agreement between the Mental Lives of Savages and Neurotics*. Translated by James Strachey. 1913. Reprint, London: Routledge & Kegan Paul, 1950.

Friedan, Betty. *The Feminine Mystique*. New York: Norton, 1963.

Friedlander, M. L., P. S. Highlen, and W. L. Lassiter. "Content Analytic Comparison of Four Expert Counselors' Approaches to Family Treatment: Ackerman, Bowen, Jackson, and Whitaker." *Journal of Counseling Psychology* 31 (1984): 477–487.

Fromm-Reichmann, Frieda. "Notes on the Development of Treatment of Schizophrenics by Psychoanalytic Psychotherapy," *Psychiatry* 11, no. 3 (August 1948): 263–273.

——. *Psychoanalysis and Psychotherapy: Selected Papers*. Chicago: University of Chicago Press, 1959.

Galdston, Iago, ed. *The Family in Contemporary Society*. New York: International Universities Press, 1958.

——, ed. *The Interface between Psychiatry and Anthropology*. New York: Brunner/Mazel, 1971.

Galison, Peter. "The Americanization of Unity." *Daedalus* 127, no. 1 (1998): 45–71.

——. "Image of Self." In *Things That Talk: Object Lessons from Art and Science*, edited by Lorraine Daston, 257–294. New York: Zone Books, 2008.

——. "The Ontology of the Enemy: Norbert Wiener and the Cybernetic Vision." *Critical Inquiry* 21 (1994): 228–266.

Gardner, Richard A. "A Four-Day Diagnostic-Therapeutic Home Visit in Turkey." *Family Process* 9 (1970): 301–330.

Gelman, Sheldon. *Medicating Schizophrenia: A History*. New Brunswick, NJ: Rutgers University Press, 1999.

Gerhard, Jane. *Desiring Revolution: Second-Wave Feminism and the Rewriting of American Sexual Thought, 1920–1982*. New York: Columbia University Press, 2001.

Gerovitch, Slava. *From Newspeak to Cyberspeak: A History of Soviet Cybernetics*. Cambridge, MA: MIT Press, 2002.

Gilbert, James. *Another Chance: Postwar America, 1945–1968*. Philadelphia: Temple University Press, 1981.

——. *A Cycle of Outrage: America's Reaction to the Juvenile Delinquent in the 1950s*. New York: Oxford University Press, 1986.

——. *Men in the Middle: Searching for Masculinity in the 1950s*. University of Chicago Press: Chicago, 2005.

Gilkeson, John S., Jr. "The Domestication of 'Culture' in Interwar America, 1919–1941." In *The Estate of Social Knowledge*, edited by Joanne Brown and David K. Van Keuren, 153–174. Baltimore: Johns Hopkins University Press, 1991.

Gilman, Sander L. "Black Bodies, White Bodies: Toward an Iconography of Female Sexuality in Late Nineteenth-Century Art, Medicine, and Literature." *Critical Inquiry* 12 (Autumn 1985): 204–242.

——. "Constructing Schizophrenia as a Category of Mental Illness." In *Disease and Representation: Images of Illness from Madness to AIDS*, 202–230. Ithaca: Cornell University Press, 1988.

Gitre, Edward J. K. "The Great Escape: World War II, Neo-Freudianism, and the Origins of U.S. Psychocultural Analysis." *Journal of the History of the Behavioral Sciences* 47, no. 1 (2011): 18–43.

Glazer, Nathan, and Daniel P. Moynihan. *Beyond the Melting Pot: The Negroes, Puerto Ricans, Jews, Italians, and Irish of New York City*. Cambridge, MA: MIT Press, 1963.

Glick, Ira D., and Jay Haley. *Family Therapy and Research: An Annotated Bibliography of Articles and Books Published 1950–1970*. New York: Grune & Stratton, 1971.

Glick, Paul. "Types of Families: An Analysis of Census Data." *American Sociological Review* 6, no. 6 (1941): 830–838.

Glueck, Sheldon, and Eleanor T. Glueck. *Delinquents in the Making: Paths to Prevention*. New York: Harper & Brothers, 1952.

Goffman, Erving. *Asylums: Essays on the Social Situation of Mental Patients and Other Inmates*. Garden City, NY: Anchor Books, 1961.

Golan, Tal. "The Emergence of the Silent Witness: The Legal and Medical Reception of X-Rays in the USA." *Social Studies of Science* 34, no. 4 (August 2004): 469–499.

Goldenberg, Herbert, and Irene Goldenberg. *Family Therapy: An Overview*. 7th ed. Belmont, CA: Thomson Brooks/Cole, 2008.

Goode, William J. *The Family*. Englewood Cliffs, NJ: Prentice-Hall, 1964.

Goodrich, Thelma Jean, Cheryl Rampage, Barbara Ellman, and Kris Halstead. *Feminist Family Therapy: A Casebook*. New York: Norton, 1988.

Gordon, Linda. *Pitied but Not Entitled: Single Mothers and the History of Welfare, 1890–1935*. New York: Free Press, 1994.

Gordon, Michael, ed. *The American Family in Social-Historical Perspective*. 2nd ed. New York: St. Martin's, 1978.

Gorer, Geoffrey, and John Richman. *The People of Great Russia*. London: Cresset Press, 1949.

Goulart, Ron. *An American Family*. New York: Warner Paperback Library, 1973.

Graebner, William. *The Age of Doubt: American Thought and Culture in the 1940s*. Boston: Twayne, 1991.

——. "The Unstable World of Benjamin Spock: Social Engineering in Democratic Culture, 1917–1950." *Journal of American History* 67, no. 3 (1980): 612–629.

Grant, Julia. *Raising Baby by the Book: The Education of American Mothers*. New Haven: Yale University Press, 1998.

Grasseni, Cristina. *Skilled Visions: Between Apprenticeship and Standards*. New York: Berghahn Books, 2007.

Grinker, Roy R., and John P. Spiegel. *Men under Stress*. Philadelphia: Blakiston, 1945.

Griswold, Robert L. *Fatherhood in America: A History*. New York: Basic Books, 1993.

Grob, Gerald N. *From Asylum to Community: Mental Health Policy in Modern America*. Princeton: Princeton University Press, 1991.

——. *Mental Illness and American Society, 1875–1940*. Princeton: Princeton University Press, 1983.

——. "Origins of DSM-I: A Study in Appearance and Reality." *American Journal of Psychiatry* 148 (1991): 421–431.

——. "Psychiatry and Social Activism: The Politics of a Specialty in Postwar America." *Bulletin of the History of Medicine* 60 (1986): 477–501.

Grönseth, Erik. "Research on Socialization in Norway." *Family Process* 3, no. 2 (1964): 302–322.

Gross, Martin L. *The Psychological Society: A Critical Analysis of Psychiatry, Psychotherapy, Psychoanalysis and the Psychological Revolution*. New York: Touchstone/Simon and Schuster, 1978.

Grosser, George H., and Norman L. Paul. "Ethical Issues in Family Group Therapy." *American Journal of Orthopsychiatry* 34 (1964): 875–885.

Grossmann, Atina. *Reforming Sex: The German Movement for Birth Control and Abortion Reform, 1920–1950*. New York: Oxford University Press, 1995.

Guerin, Philip J., ed. *Family Therapy: Theory and Practice*. New York: Gardner Press, 1976.

Gunning, Tom. "Moving Away from the Index: Cinema and the Impression of Reality." *differences* 18 (2007): 29–52.

Gurin, Gerald. *Americans View Their Mental Health: A Nationwide Interview Survey; A Report to the Staff Director, Jack R. Ewalt*, Joint Commission on Mental Health Monograph Series 4. New York: Basic Books, 1960.

Gurman, Alan S., and David P. Kniskern, eds. *The Handbook of Family Therapy*. New York: Brunner/Mazel, 1981.

Gutman, Herbert G. *The Black Family in Slavery and Freedom, 1750–1925*. New York: Pantheon Books, 1976.

Hacking, Ian. *Representing and Intervening: Introducing Topics in the Philosophy of Natural Science*. Cambridge: Cambridge University Press, 1983.

Hale, Nathan G., Jr. *Freud and the Americans: The Beginnings of Psychoanalysis in the United States, 1876–1917*. New York: Oxford University Press, 1971.

——. "From Berggasse XIX to Central Park West: The Americanization of Psychoanalysis, 1919–1940." *Journal of the History of the Behavioral Sciences* 14 (1978): 290–315.

——. *The Rise and Crisis of Psychoanalysis in the United States: Freud and the Americans, 1917–1985*. New York: Oxford University Press, 1995.

Haley, Jay. "Approaches to Family Therapy." *International Journal of Psychiatry* 9 (1970): 233–242.

——. "The Art of Being Schizophrenic." *Voices* 1 (1965): 133–147.

——, ed. *Changing Families: A Family Therapy Reader*. New York: Grune & Stratton, 1971.

——. "The Family of the Schizophrenic: A Model System." *Journal of Nervous and Mental Disease* 129 (1959): 357–374.

——. *The Power Tactics of Jesus Christ, and Other Essays*. New York: Grossman Publishers, 1969.

——. *Problem-Solving Therapy: New Strategies for Effective Family Therapy*. San Francisco: Jossey-Bass, 1976.

——. *Strategies of Psychotherapy*. New York: Grune & Stratton, 1963

——. *Uncommon Therapy: The Psychiatric Techniques of Milton Erickson, M.D.* New York: Norton, 1973.

Haley, Jay, and Lynn Hoffman. *Techniques of Family Therapy*. New York: Basic Books, 1967.

Halpern, Orit. "Dreams for Our Perceptual Present: Temporality, Storage, and Interactivity in Cybernetics." *Configurations* 13, no. 2 (2005): 283–319.

Hamilton, Peter, ed. *Talcott Parsons: Critical Assessments*. London: Routledge, 1992.

Hammonds, Evelynn M. "New Technologies of Race." In *Processed Lives: Gender and Technology in Everyday Life*, edited by Jennifer Terry and Melodie Calvert, 74–85. New York: Routledge, 1997.

Handel, Gerald, ed. *The Psychosocial Interior of the Family: A Sourcebook for the Study of Whole Families*. 2nd ed. 1967. Reprint, Chicago: Aldine, 1972.

Handler, Richard. "Boasian Anthropology and the Critique of American Culture." *American Quarterly* 42, no. 2 (1990): 252–273.

Haralovich, Mary Beth. "Sitcoms and Suburbs: Positioning the 1950s Homemaker." *Quarterly Review of Film and Video* 11, no. 1 (1989): 61–83.

Haraway, Donna. "The Biopolitics of Postmodern Bodies: Determinations of Self in Immune System Discourse." *differences* 1 (1989): 3–43.

——. "The High Cost of Information in Post-World War II Evolutionary Biology: Ergonomics, Semiotics, and the Sociobiology of Communication Systems." *Philosophical Forum* 13 (1981–82): 244–78.

——. "Universal Donors in a Vampire Culture: It's All in the Family: Biological Kinship Categories in the Twentieth-Century United States." In *Uncommon Ground: Rethinking the Human Place in Nature*, edited by William Cronon, 321–366. New York: Norton, 1996.

Harden, Victoria. *Inventing the NIH: Federal Biomedical Research Policy, 1887–1937.* Baltimore: Johns Hopkins University Press, 1986.

Hare-Mustin, Rachel T. "A Feminist Approach to Family Therapy." *Family Process* 17 (1978): 181–194.

Haring, Douglas G., ed. *Personal Character and Cultural Milieu.* Syracuse: Syracuse University Press, 1948.

Harries-Jones, Peter. *A Recursive Vision: Ecological Understanding and Gregory Bateson.* Toronto: University of Toronto Press, 1995.

Harrington, Anne. *Reenchanted Science: Holism in German Culture from Wilhelm II to Hitler.* Princeton: Princeton University Press, 1996.

Harrington, Michael. *The Other America: Poverty in the United States.* New York: Macmillan, 1962.

Harris, Miriam Lynnell. "From Kennedy to Combahee: Black Feminist Activism from 1960 to 1980." PhD diss., University of Minnesota, 1997.

Harrison, Tom. *Bion, Rickman, Foulkes and the Northfield Experiments: Advancing on a Different Front.* London: Jessica Kingsley, 2000.

Hartmann, Susan M. *The Home Front and Beyond: American Women in the 1940s.* Boston: Twayne, 1982.

——. "Prescriptions for Penelope: Literature on Women's Obligations to Returning World War II Veterans." *Women's Studies* 5 (1978): 223–239.

Hartwell, Carol Eadie. "The Schizophrenogenic Mother Concept in American Psychiatry," *Psychiatry: Interpersonal and Biological Processes* 59 (Fall 1996): 274–297.

Hayles, N. Katherine. "Boundary Disputes: Homeostasis, Reflexivity, and the Foundations of Cybernetics." *Configurations* 2, no. 3 (1994): 441–467.

——. "Designs on the Body: Norbert Wiener, Cybernetics, and the Play of Metaphor." *History of the Human Sciences* 3, no. 2 (1990): 211–228.

——. *How We Became Posthuman: Virtual Bodies in Cybernetics, Literature, and Informatics.* Chicago: University of Chicago Press, 1999.

Hedgecoe, Adam. "Schizophrenia and the Narrative of Enlightened Geneticization." *Social Studies of Science* 31 (2001): 875–911.

Hegeman, Susan. *Patterns for America: Modernism and the Concept of Culture.* Princeton: Princeton University Press, 1999.

Heims, Steve Joshua. *Constructing a Social Science for Postwar America: The Cybernetics Group, 1946–1953.* Cambridge, MA: MIT Press, 1993.

——. "Gregory Bateson and the Mathematicians: From Interdisciplinary Interaction to Societal Functions." *Journal of the History of the Behavioral Sciences* 13 (1977): 141–159.

Helly, Dorothy O., and Susan Reverby, eds. *Gendered Domains: Rethinking Public and Private in Women's History: Essays from the Seventh Berkshire Conference on the History of Women.* Ithaca: Cornell University Press, 1992.

Henry, Jules. *Culture against Man.* New York: Random House, 1963.

——. *Pathways to Madness.* New York: Vintage Books, 1965.

Herman, Ellen. *Kinship by Design: A History of Adoption in the Modern United States.* Chicago: University of Chicago Press, 2008.

——. *The Romance of American Psychology: Political Culture in the Age of Experts.* Berkeley: University of California Press, 1995.

Herzberg, David. *Happy Pills in America: From Miltown to Prozac.* Baltimore: Johns Hopkins University Press, 2009.

Herzig, Rebecca. *Suffering for Science: Reason and Sacrifice in Modern America.* New Brunswick, NJ: Rutgers University Press, 2005.

Hesse, Mary. *Revolutions and Reconstructions in the Philosophy of Science.* Brighton, UK: Harvester Press, 1980.

Hill, Reuben. "The American Family: Problem or Solution?" *American Journal of Sociology* 53 (September 1947): 125–130.

Hodes, Martha. *White Women, Black Men.* New Haven: Yale University Press, 1998.

Hoffman, Lynn. *Foundations of Family Therapy: A Conceptual Framework for Systems Change.* New York: Basic Books, 1981.

Hollinger, David A. *In the American Province: Studies in the History and Historiography of Ideas.* Baltimore: Johns Hopkins University Press, 1985.

——. "Science as a Weapon in *Kulturkampfe* in the United States during and after World War II." *Isis* 86 (1995): 440–454.

Hollingshead, August B., and Fredrick C. Redlich. *Social Class and Mental Illness.* New York: Wiley, 1958.

Holson, Laura M. "Who's on the Family Tree? Now It's Complicated." *New York Times,* July 5, 2011, A1.

Honey, Maureen. *Creating Rosie the Riveter: Class, Gender, and Propaganda during World War II.* Amherst: University of Massachusetts Press, 1984.

——. "Maternal Welders: Women's Sexuality and Propaganda on the Home Front during World War II." *Prospects* 22 (1997): 479–520.

——. "The Working-Class Woman and Recruitment Propaganda during World War II: Class Differences in the Portrayal of War Work." *Signs* 8 (1983): 672–687.

Hopkins, Patrick D., ed. *Sex/Machine: Readings in Culture, Gender, and Technology.* Bloomington: Indiana University Press, 1998.

Horn, Margo. *Before It's Too Late: The Child Guidance Movement in the United States, 1922–1945.* Philadelphia: Temple University Press, 1989.

Hornstein, Gail A. *To Redeem One Person Is to Redeem the World: The Life of Frieda Fromm-Reichmann.* New York: Free Press, 2000.

Horowitz, Daniel. *Betty Friedan and the Making of the Feminine Mystique: The American Left, the Cold War, and Modern Feminism.* Amherst: University of Massachusetts Press, 1998.

Horowitz, Frances D., and Lloyd L. Lovell. "Attitudes of Mothers of Female Schizophrenics." *Child Development* 31 (June 1960): 299–305.

Howard, Ronald L. *A Social History of American Family Sociology, 1865–1940.* Westport, CT: Greenwood Press, 1981.

Howe, Irving. "This Age of Conformity." *Partisan Review* 20 (1954): 7–33.

Howells, John G., ed. *The Concept of Schizophrenia: Historical Perspectives.* Washington, DC: American Psychiatric Press, Inc., 1991.

——, ed. *Theory and Practice of Family Therapy.* New York: Brunner/Mazel, 1971.

Hughes, Thomas P. "Spread of the Systems Approach." In *Rescuing Prometheus,* edited by Thomas P. Hughes, 141–195. New York: Pantheon Books, 1998.

Hulbert, Ann. *Raising America: Experts, Parents, and a Century of Advice about Children.* New York: Knopf, 2003.

Irvine, Judith T., ed. *Edward Sapir: The Psychology of Culture.* Berlin: Mouton de Gruyter, 1994.

Jackson, Don D. *Communication, Family and Marriage.* Palo Alto: Science and Behavior Books, 1967.

——, ed. *The Etiology of Schizophrenia.* New York: Basic Books, 1960.

——. "Family Rules: Marital Quid Pro Quo." *Archives of General Psychiatry* 12 (1965): 589–594.

——. "The Question of Family Homeostasis." *Psychiatric Quarterly Supplement* 31 (1957): 79–90.

———. "The Study of the Family." *Family Process* 4 (March 1965): 1–20.

———. *Therapy, Communication and Change.* Palo Alto: Science and Behavior Books, 1967.

Jackson, John P. Jr., and Nadine M. Weidman. *Race, Racism, and Science: Social Impact and Interaction.* New Brunswick, NJ: Rutgers University Press, 2006.

Jackson, Kenneth T. *Crabgrass Frontier: The Suburbanization of the United States.* New York: Oxford University Press, 1985.

Jacob, Theodore. "Family Interaction and Psychopathology: Historical Overview." In *Family Interaction and Psychopathology: Theories, Methods, and Findings,* edited by Theodore Jacob, 3–22. New York: Plenum Press, 1987.

Jacobson, Matthew Frye. *Whiteness of a Different Color: European Immigrants and the Alchemy of Race.* Cambridge, MA: Harvard University Press, 1998.

Jardine, Nicholas. "The Laboratory Revolution in Medicine as Rhetorical and Aesthetic Accomplishment." In *The Laboratory Revolution in Medicine,* edited by A. Cunningham and P. Williams, 304–323. Cambridge: Cambridge University Press, 1992.

Jay, Martin. *Permanent Exiles: Essays on Intellectual Migration from Germany to America.* New York: Columbia University Press, 1985.

Jenkins, Henry, ed. *The Children's Culture Reader.* New York: New York University Press, 1998.

Joint Commission on Mental Illness and Health. *Action for Mental Health: Final Report of the Joint Commission on Mental Illness and Health.* New York: Basic Books, 1961.

Jones, Caroline A., Peter Galison, and Amy Slaton, eds. *Picturing Science, Producing Art.* New York: Routledge, 1998.

Jones, David S. "Visions of a Cure: Visualization, Clinical Trials, and Controversies in Cardiac Therapeutics, 1968–1998." *Isis* 91, no. 3 (2000): 504–541.

Jones, Gerard. *Honey, I'm Home! Sitcoms: Selling the American Dream.* New York: Grove Weidenfeld, 1992.

Jones, Jacqueline. *Labor of Love, Labor of Sorrow: Black Women, Work, and the Family from Slavery to the Present.* New York: Basic Books, 1985.

Jones, Kathleen W. ""Mother Made Me Do It": Mother-Blaming and the Women of Child Guidance." In *"Bad" Mothers: The Politics of Blame in Twentieth Century America,* edited by Molly Ladd-Taylor and Lauri Umanksy, 99–124. New York: New York University Press, 1998.

———. *Taming the Troublesome Child: American Families, Child Guidance, and the Limits of Psychiatric Authority.* Cambridge, MA: Harvard University Press, 1999.

Jordanova, Ludmilla. "Naturalizing the Family: Literature and the Bio-Medical Sciences in the late Eighteenth Century." In *Languages of Nature: Critical Essays on Science and Literature,* edited by Ludmilla Jordanova, 86–116. London: Free Association Books, 1986.

———. *Sexual Visions: Images of Gender in Science and Medicine between the Eighteenth and Twentieth Centuries.* Madison: University of Wisconsin Press, 1989.

———. "The Social Construction of Medical Knowledge." *Social History of Medicine* 8 (1995): 361–381.

Kahana, Jonathan. *Intelligence Work: The Politics of American Documentary.* New York: Columbia University Press, 2008.

Kaiser, David. *Drawing Theories Apart: The Dispersion of Feynman Diagrams in Postwar Physics.* Chicago: University of Chicago Press, 2005.

Kaffman, Mordechai. "Family Conflict in the Psychopathology of the Kibbutz Child." *Family Process* 11, no. 2 (1972): 171–189.

Kaledin, Eugenia. *Mothers and More: American Women in the 1950s.* Boston: Twayne, 1984.

Kantor, David, and William Lehr. *Inside the Family: Toward a Theory of Family Process.* San Francisco: Jossey-Bass, 1975.

Kantor, Robert E., and Lynn Hoffman. "Brechtian Theater as a Model for Conjoint Family Therapy." *Family Process* 5 (September 1966): 218–229.

Kaplan, Bert, ed. *Studying Personality Cross-Culturally.* New York: Harper & Row, 1961.

Kaplan, E. Ann. "Motherhood and Representation: From Postwar Freudian Figurations to Postmodernism." In *Psychoanalysis and Cinema*, edited by E. Ann Kaplan. New York: Routledge, 1990.

Kardiner, Abram, R. *The Psychological Frontiers of Society*. With the collaboration of Cora DuBois Linton and J. West. New York: Columbia University Press, 1945.

Kardiner, Abram, and Lionel Ovesey. *The Mark of Oppression: A Psychosocial Study of the American Negro*. New York: Norton, 1951.

Kasanin, J. S., ed. *Language and Thought in Schizophrenia*. New York: Norton, 1964.

Kaslow, Florence W. "The Art and Science of Family Psychology: Retrospective and Perspective." *American Psychologist* 46 (1991): 621–626.

——. "Marital and Family Therapy." In *Handbook of Marriage and the Family*, edited by Marvin B Sussman and Suzanne K. Steinmetz, 835–859. New York: Plemum Press, 1987.

Kay, Lily E. "Cybernetics, Information, Life: The Emergence of Scriptural Representations of Heredity." *Configurations* 5, no. 1 (1997): 23–91.

——. *Who Wrote the Book of Life? A History of the Genetic Code*. Stanford: Stanford University Press, 2000.

Keller, Evelyn Fox. *Making Sense of Life: Explaining Biological Development with Models, Metaphors, and Machines*. Cambridge, MA: Harvard University Press, 2002.

——. *Refiguring Life: Metaphors of Twentieth-Century Biology*. New York: Columbia University Press, 1995.

Kempster, Stephen W., and Elias Savitsky. "Training Family Therapists through 'Live' Supervision." In *Expanding Theory and Practice in Family Therapy*, edited by Nathan W. Ackerman, Frances L. Beatman, and Sanford N. Sherman, 125–134. New York: Family Service Association of America, 1967.

Kerber, Linda K. "Separate Spheres, Female Worlds, Woman's Place: The Rhetoric of Women's History." *Journal of American History* 75 (1988): 9–39.

——. *Women of the Republic: Intellect and Ideology in Revolutionary America*. Chapel Hill: University of North Carolina Press, 1980.

Kessler-Harris, Alice. *Out to Work: A History of Wage-Earning Women in the United States*. New York: Oxford University Press, 1982.

Kevles, Daniel J. *In the Name of Eugenics: Genetics and the Uses of Human Heredity*. New York: Knopf, 1985.

Kimmel, Michael S. "Consuming Manhood: The Feminization of American Culture and the Recreation of the Male Body, 1832–1920." *Michigan Quarterly Review* 33 (1994): 7–36.

——. *Manhood in America: A Cultural History*. New York: Free Press, 1996.

Kingsland, Sharon E. *Modeling Nature: Episodes in the History of Population Ecology*. Chicago: University of Chicago Press, 1985.

Kinzie, David, P. C. Suchama, and Mary Lee. "Cross-Cultural Family Therapy—A Malaysian Experience." *Family Process* 11, no. 1 (1972): 59–67.

Kirkebøen, Geir. "From a Naked Emperor to Just Clothes: The Rise and Fall of Cybernetic Family Therapy." *Social Science Information* 34 (1995): 31–65.

Klaus, Alisa C. *Every Child a Lion: The Origins of Maternal and Infant Health Policy in the United States and France, 1890–1920*. Ithaca: Cornell University Press, 1993.

Kleinfield, N. R. "Baby Makes Four, and Complications." *New York Times*, June 19, 2011, MB1.

Kleinman, Arthur. *The Illness Narratives: Suffering, Healing and the Human Condition*. New York: Basic Books, 1988.

Kline, Wendy. *Building a Better Race: Gender, Sexuality, and Eugenics from the Turn of the Century to the Baby Boom*. Berkeley: University of California Press, 2001.

Kluckhohn, Clyde, and Henry A. Murray, eds. *Personality in Nature, Society, and Culture*. New York: Knopf, 1948.

Koch, Ellen B. "In the Image of Science? Negotiating the Development of Diagnostic Ultrasound in the Cultures of Surgery and Radiology." *Technology and Culture* (1993): 858–893.

Kohler, Robert E. *Landscapes and Labscapes: Exploring the Lab-Field Border in Biology.* Chicago: University of Chicago Press, 2002.

——. *Lords of the Fly: Drosophila Genetics and the Experimental Life.* Chicago: University of Chicago Press, 1994.

Koven, Seth, and Sonya Michel, eds. *Mothers of a New World: Maternalist Politics and the Origins of Welfare States.* New York: Routledge, 1993.

Kozol, Wendy. *Life's America: Family and Nation in Postwar Photojournalism.* Philadelphia: Temple University Press, 1994.

Kroeber, A. L. *The Nature of Culture.* Chicago: University of Chicago Press, 1952.

Kroeber, A. L., and Clyde Kluckhohn. *Culture: A Critical Review of Concepts and Definitions.* Papers of the Peabody Museum of American Archaeology and Ethnography, vol. 47, no. 1. Cambridge, MA: Peabody Museum of American Archaeology and Ethnography, 1952.

Kuklick, Henrika, and Robert E. Kohler, eds. *Science in the Field.* Osiris, 2nd series, vol. 11. Chicago: University of Chicago Press, 1996.

Kunzel, Regina G. *Fallen Women, Problem Girls: Unmarried Mothers and the Professionalization of Social Work, 1890–1945.* New Haven: Yale University Press, 1993.

Kuper, Adam. *Culture: The Anthropologists' Account.* Cambridge, MA: Harvard University Press, 1999.

Ladd-Taylor, Molly. *Mother-Work: Women, Child Welfare, and the State, 1890–1930.* Urbana: University of Illinois Press, 1994.

Ladd-Taylor, Molly, and Lauri Umansky, eds. *"Bad" Mothers: The Politics of Blame in Twentieth-Century America.* New York: New York University Press, 1998.

Laing, R. D. *The Self and Others: Further Studies in Sanity and Madness.* London: Tavistock Publications, 1961.

——. *The Politics of the Family, and Other Essays.* New York: Vintage Books, 1969.

——. *Knots.* London: Tavistock Publications, 1970.

Laing, R. D., and Aaron Esterson. *Sanity, Madness, and the Family: Families of Schizophrenics.* 2nd ed. 1964. Reprint, London: Tavistock Publications, 1970.

Lakoff, Andrew. "Freezing Time: Margaret Mead's Diagnostic Photography." *Visual Anthropology Review* 12, no. 1 (1996): 1–18.

Lakoff, George, and Mark Johnson. *Metaphors We Live By.* Chicago: University of Chicago Press, 1980.

Landecker, Hannah. "Microcinematography and the History of Science and Film," *Isis* 97 (2006): 121–132.

LaRossa, Ralph. *Of War and Men: World War II in the Lives of Fathers and Their Families.* Chicago: University of Chicago Press, 2011.

Larson, Edward. *Sex, Race, and Science: Eugenics in the Deep South.* Baltimore: Johns Hopkins University Press, 1995.

Lasch, Christopher. *The Culture of Narcissism.* New York: Norton, 1978.

——. *Haven in a Heartless World: The Family Besieged.* New York: Basic Books, 1977.

Lassonde, Stephen. "Family and Demography in Postwar America: A Hazard of New Fortunes?" In *A Companion to Post-1945 America,* edited by Jean-Christophe Agnew and Roy Rosenzweig, 3–19. Malden, MA: Blackwell, 2002.

Lasswell, Harold D. *Psychopathology and Politics.* Chicago: University of Chicago Press, 1930.

Latour, Bruno. "Drawing Things Together." In *Representation in Scientific Practice,* edited by Michael Lynch and Steve Woolgar. Cambridge, MA: MIT Press, 1990.

Lears, T. J. Jackson. "From Salvation to Self-Realization: Advertising and the Therapeutic Roots of the Consumer Culture, 1880–1930." In *The Culture of Consumption:*

Critical Essays in American History, 1880–1980, edited by Richard Wightman Fox and T. J. Jackson Lears, 1–38. New York: Pantheon Books, 1983.

——. *No Place of Grace: Antimodernism and the Transformation of American Culture, 1880–1920.* Chicago: University of Chicago Press, 1981.

Lederer, Susan E. *Subjected to Science: Human Experimentation in America before the Second World War.* Baltimore: Johns Hopkins University Press, 1995.

Lemons, J. Stanley. "The Shepherd-Towner Act: Progressivism in the 1920s." *Journal of American History* 55 (March 1969): 776–786.

Lenoir, Timothy. *Instituting Science: The Cultural Production of Scientific Disciplines.* Stanford: Stanford University Press, 1997.

Lerner, Barron H. "The Perils of 'X-Ray Vision': How Radiographic Images Have Historically Influenced Perception." *Perspectives in Biology and Medicine* 35 (1992): 382–397.

Levey, Jane F. "Imagining the Family in Postwar Popular Culture: The Case of *The Egg and I* and *Cheaper by the Dozen.*" *Journal of Women's History* 13, no. 3 (2001): 125–150.

Lewis, Oscar. *Five Families.* New York: Basic Books, 1959.

Lidz, Theodore. "The Intrafamilial Environment of Schizophrenic Patients: II. Marital Schism and Marital Skew." *American Journal of Psychiatry* 114 (1957): 241–248.

Lidz, Theodore, Stephen Fleck, and A. R. Cornelison. *Schizophrenia and the Family.* New York: International Universities Press, 1965.

Light, Jennifer S. *From Warfare to Welfare: Defense Intellectuals and Urban Problems in Cold War America.* Baltimore: Johns Hopkins University Press, 2003.

Lindblad-Goldberg, Marion, ed. *Clinical Issues in Single-Parent Households.* Rockville, MD: Aspen, 1987.

Linton, Ralph. *The Cultural Background of Personality.* New York: Appleton-Center-Crofts, 1945.

Lipset, David. *Gregory Bateson: The Legacy of a Scientist.* Englewood Cliffs, NJ: Prentice-Hall, Inc., 1980.

Lipset, Seymour Martin, and Leo Lowenthal, eds. *Culture and Social Character: The Work of David Reisman Reviewed.* New York: Free Press of Glencoe, 1961.

Lipset, Seymour Martin, and Neil J. Smelser, eds. *Sociology: The Progress of a Decade.* Englewood Cliffs, NJ: Prentice-Hall, 1961.

Lipsitz, George. *Time Passages: Collective Memory and American Popular Culture.* Minneapolis: University of Minnesota Press, 1990.

Lovett, Laura L. *Conceiving the Future: Pronatalism, Reproduction, and the Family in the United States, 1890–1938.* Chapel Hill: University of North Carolina Press, 2007.

Luepnitz, Deborah A. *The Family Interpreted.* New York: Basic Books, 1988.

Lunbeck, Elizabeth. *The Psychiatric Persuasion: Knowledge, Gender, and Power in Modern America.* Princeton: Princeton University Press, 1994.

Lynch, Michael, and Steve Woolgar, eds. *Representation in Scientific Practice.* Cambridge, MA: MIT Press, 1990.

Lynd, Robert S., and Helen Merrell Lynd. *Middletown: A Study in Contemporary American Culture.* New York: Harcourt, Brace, 1929.

Mabee, Carleton. "Margaret Mead and Behavioral Scientists in World War II: Problems in Responsibility, Truth, and Effectiveness." *Journal of the History of the Behavioral Sciences* 23 (1987): 3–13.

Mace, David. "The Marriage Guidance Council." *Probation,* January–February 1947, 86.

MacGregor, Robert. "Communicating Values in Family Therapy." In *Family Therapy and Disturbed Families,* edited by Gerald Zuk and Ivan Boszormenyi-Nagy, 178–185. Palo Alto: Science and Behavior Books, 1967.

——. "Multiple Impact Psychotherapy with Families." *Family Process* 1 (March 1962): 15–29

Magraw, Sukie. "Feminism and Family Therapy: An Oral History." PhD, California School of Professional Psychology at Berkeley/Alameda, 1992.

Malcolm, Janet. "The One-Way Mirror." *New Yorker*, May 15, 1978, 39–114.

Manganaro, Marc. *Culture, 1922: The Emergence of a Concept.* Princeton: Princeton University Press, 2002.

Manson, William C. *The Psychodynamics of Culture: Abram Kardiner and Neo-Freudian Anthropology.* New York: Greenwood Press, 1988.

Marcus, George E., and Michael M. J. Fischer. *Anthropology as Cultural Critique: An Experimental Moment in the Human Sciences.* Chicago: University of Chicago Press, 1986.

Markowitz, Gerald, and David Rosner. *Children, Race, and Power: Kenneth and Mamie Clark's Northside Center.* Charlottesville: University Press of Virginia, 1996.

Marks, Harry. *The Progress of Experiment: Science and Therapeutic Reform in the United States, 1990–1990.* Cambridge: Cambridge University Press, 1997.

Marling, Karal Ann. *As Seen on TV: The Visual Culture of Everyday Life in the 1950s.* Cambridge, MA: Harvard University Press, 1994.

Marsh, Margaret. "From Separation to Togetherness: The Social Construction of Domestic Space in American Suburbs, 1840–1915." *Journal of American History* 76, no. 2 (1989): 506–527.

——. *Suburban Lives.* New Brunswick, NJ: Rutgers University Press, 1990.

——. "Suburban Men and Masculine Domesticity, 1870–1915." *American Quarterly* 40 (1988): 165–186.

Masserman, Jules H., ed. *Individual and Familial Dynamics.* New York: Grune and Stratton, 1959.

Matthews, Fred. "In Defense of Common Sense: Mental Hygiene as Ideology and Mentality in Twentieth-Century America." *Prospects* 4 (1979): 459–516.

——. "Social Scientists and the Culture Concept, 1930–1950: The Conflict between Processual and Structural Approaches." *Sociological Theory* 7 (1989): 87–101.

——. "The Utopia of Human Relations: The Conflict-Free Family in American Social Thought, 1930–1960." *Journal of the History of the Behavioral Sciences* 24 (1988): 343–362.

Matthews, J. Rosser. *Quantification and the Quest for Medical Certainty.* Princeton: Princeton University Press, 1995.

May, Elaine Tyler. "Explosive Issues: Sex, Women, and the Bomb." In *Recasting America: Culture and Politics in the Age of Cold War*, edited by Lary May, 154–70. Chicago: University of Chicago Press, 1989.

——. *Homeward Bound: American Families in the Cold War Era.* New York: Basic Books, 1988.

May, Lary, ed. *Recasting America: Culture and Politics in the Age of Cold War.* Chicago: University of Chicago Press, 1989.

McCall, Laura, and Donald Yacavone, eds. *A Shared Experience: Men, Women, and the History of Gender.* New York: New York University Press, 1998.

McCarthy, Anna. *The Citizen Machine: Governing by Television in 1950s America.* New York: New Press, 2010.

McGoldrick, Monica, ed., *Re-Visioning Family Therapy: Race, Culture, and Gender in Clinical Practice.* New York: Guilford Press, 1998.

McGoldrick, Monica, John K. Pearce, and Joseph Giordano, eds. *Ethnicity and Family Therapy.* New York: Guildford Press, 1982.

McKinlay, John B. "From 'Promising Report' to 'Standard Procedure': Seven Stages in the Career of a Medical Innovation." *Milbank Memorial Fund Quarterly* 59 (1981): 233–270.

McLean, Athena Helen. "Family Therapy Workshops in the United States: Potential Abuses in the Production of Therapy in an Advanced Capitalist Society." *Social Science and Medicine* 23, no. 2 (1986): 179–190.

———. "The Social Production of Clinical Knowledge: A Case Study of Family Therapy in the United States, 1937–1978." PhD diss., Temple University, 1990.

Mead, Margaret. *And Keep Your Powder Dry: An Anthropologist Looks at America.* New York: Morrow, 1942.

———. "What's the Matter with the Family?" *Harper's,* April 1945, 393–399.

Mead, Margaret, and Rhoda Metraux. *The Study of Culture at a Distance.* Chicago: University of Chicago Press, 1953.

Mechling, Jay. "Mind, Messages, and Madness: Gregory Bateson Makes a Paradigm for American Cultural Studies." *Prospects* 8 (1983): 11–30.

Meckel, Richard A. *Save the Babies: American Public Health Reform and the Prevention of Infant Mortality, 1850–1929.* Baltimore: Johns Hopkins University Press, 1990.

Merton, Robert K. *The Sociology of Science: Theoretical and Empirical Investigations.* Chicago: University of Chicago Press, 1973.

Metzl, Jonathan. *The Protest Psychosis: How Schizophrenia Became a Black Disease.* Boston: Beacon Press, 2009.

———. *Prozac on the Couch: Prescribing Gender in the Era of Wonder Drugs.* Durham, NC: Duke University Press, 2003.

Meyerowitz, Joanne. "'How Common Culture Shapes the Separate Lives': Sexuality, Race, and Mid-Twentieth-Century Social Constructionist Thought." *Journal of American History* 96 (2010): 1057–1084.

———, ed. *Not June Cleaver: Women and Gender in Postwar America, 1945–1960.* Philadephia: Temple University Press, 1994.

Michaelis, Anthony R. *Research Films in Biology, Anthropology, Psychology, and Medicine.* New York: Academic Press, 1955.

Michel, Sonya. "American Women and the Discourse of the Democratic Family in World War II." In *Behind the Lines: Gender and the Two World Wars,* edited by Margaret Randolph Higonnet, Jane Jenson, Sonya Michel and Margaret Collins Weitz, 154–167. New Haven: Yale University Press, 1987.

———. *Children's Interests/Mothers' Rights: The Shaping of America's Child Care Policy.* New Haven: Yale University Press, 1999.

———. "Danger on the Home Front: Motherhood, Sexuality, and Disabled Veterans in American Postwar Films." *Journal of the History of Sexuality* 3, no. 1 (1992): 109–128.

Milkman, Ruth. "Redefining 'Women's Work': The Sexual Division of Labor in the Auto Industry during World War II." *Feminist Studies* 8 (1982): 337–372.

Miller, Brent C. *Family Research Methods.* Beverly Hills, CA: Sage Publications, 1986.

Miller, Peter, and Nikolas Rose. "On Therapeutic Authority: Psychoanalytical Expertise under Advanced Liberalism." *History of the Human Sciences* 7, no. 3 (1994): 29–64.

Mills, C. Wright. *White Collar: The American Middle Classes.* New York: Oxford University Press, 1951.

Mintz, Steven. *Huck's Raft: A History of American Childhood.* Cambridge, MA: Harvard University Press, 2006.

Mintz, Steven, and Susan Kellogg. *Domestic Revolutions: A Social History of American Family Life.* New York: Free Press, 1988.

Minuchin, Salvador. *Families & Family Therapy.* Cambridge, MA: Harvard University Press, 1974.

———. *Family Kaleidoscope.* Cambridge, MA: Harvard University Press, 1984.

———. "The Leap to Complexity: Supervision in Family Therapy." In *The Evolution of Psychotherapy: The Third Conference,* edited by Jeffery K. Zeig, 271–281. New York: Brunner/Mazel, 1995.

———. *Psychosomatic Families.* Cambridge, MA: Harvard University Press, 1978.

———. "Where is the Family in Narrative Family Therapy?" *Journal of Marital and Family Therapy* 24, no. 4 (1998): 397–403.

Minuchin, Salvador, and Avner Barcai. "Therapeutically Induced Family Crisis." In *Science and Psychoanalysis: Childhood and Adolescence*, vol. 14, edited by Jules H. Masserman, 199–205. New York: Grune and Stratton, 1969.

Minuchin, Salvador, and H. Charles Fishman. *Family Therapy Techniques.* Cambridge, MA: Harvard University Press, 1981.

Minuchin, Salvador, Braulio Montalvo, Bernard G. Guerney, Bernice L. Rosman, and Florence Schumer. *Families of the Slums: An Exploration of Their Structure and Treatment.* New York: Basic Books, 1967.

Minuchin, Salvador, and Michael P. Nichols. *Family Healing: Tales of Hope and Renewal from Family Therapy.* New York: Free Press, 1993.

Minuchin, Salvador, Wai-Yung Lee, and George M. Simon. *Mastering Family Therapy.* New York: Wiley, 1996.

Mishler, Elliot G., and Nancy E. Waxler. *Family Processes and Schizophrenia.* New York: Jason Aronson, Inc., 1968.

Mitman, Gregg. *Reel Nature: America's Romance with Wildlife on Film.* Cambridge, MA: Harvard University Press, 1999.

——. *The State of Nature: Ecology, Community, and American Social Thought, 1900–1950.* Chicago: University of Chicago Press, 1992.

Montagu, M. F. Ashley, ed. *The Concept of Race.* London: Free Press of Glencoe, 1964.

——, ed. *Culture and the Evolution of Man.* New York: Oxford University Press, 1962.

——. *Man's Most Dangerous Myth: The Fallacy of Race.* 2nd ed. New York: Columbia University Press, 1945.

Morawski, Jill G., "Organizing Knowledge and Behavior at Yale's Institute of Human Relations." *Isis* 77, no. 2 (1986): 219–242.

Morton, Patricia. *Disfigured Images: The Historical Assault on Afro-American Women.* New York: Greenwood Press, 1991.

Moskowitz, Eva S. *In Therapy We Trust: America's Obsession with Self-Fulfillment.* Baltimore: Johns Hopkins University Press, 2001.

——. "'It's Good to Blow Your Top': Women's Magazines and a Discourse of Discontent, 1945–1965." *Journal of Women's History* 8 (1996): 66–98.

Murdock, George Peter. *Social Structure.* New York: Macmillan, 1949.

Murphy, Michelle. *Sick Building Syndrome and the Problem of Uncertainty: Environmental Politics, Technoscience, and Women Workers.* Durham, NC: Duke University Press, 2006.

Murray, Susan, and Laurie Ouellette, eds. *Reality TV: Remaking Television Culture.* New York: New York University Press, 2004.

Myrdal, Gunnar. *An American Dilemma: The Negro Problem and Modern Democracy.* New York: Harper and Row, 1944.

Narain, D. "Growing Up in India." *Family Process* 3, no. 1 (1964): 127–154.

Nathiel, Susan Lenore. "Toward a Critical Social History of the Profession of Family Therapy." PhD diss., University of Connecticut, 1997.

Neill, John R., and David P. Kniskern, eds. *From Psyche to System: The Evolving Therapy of Carl Whitaker.* New York: Guilford Press, 1982.

Nichols, Bill. *Representing Reality: Issues and Concepts in Documentary.* Bloomington: Indiana University Press, 1991.

Nichols, Michael P., and Richard C. Schwartz. *Family Therapy: Concepts and Methods.* 4th ed. Boston: Allyn and Bacon, 1998.

Noll, Richard. *American Madness: The Rise and Fall of Dementia Praecox.* Cambridge, MA: Harvard University Press, 2011.

Nuckolls, Charles W. *Culture: A Problem That Cannot Be Solved.* Madison: University of Wisconsin Press, 1998.

O'Connor, Alice. *Poverty Knowledge: Social Science, Social Policy, and the Poor in Twentieth-Century US History.* Princeton: Princeton University Press, 2001.

Orgeron, Devin, Marsha Orgeron, and Dan Streible, eds. *Learning with the Lights Off: Educational Film in the United States.* New York: Oxford University Press, 2012.

Omi, Michael, and Howard Winant. *Racial Formation in the United States: From the 1960s to the 1990s.* 2nd ed. New York: Routledge, 1994.

Ophir, Adi, and Steven Shapin. "The Place of Knowledge: A Methodological Survey." *Science in Context* 4, no. 1 (1991): 3–21.

Opler, Marvin K. "Social and Cultural Influences on the Psychopathology of Family Groups." In *Family Therapy and Disturbed Families*, edited by Gerald Zuk and Ivan Boszormenyi-Nagy, 133–158. Palo Alto: Science and Behavior Books, 1967.

Orr, Jackie. "The Ecstasy of Miscommunication: Cyberpsychiatry and Mental Dis-Ease." In *Doing Science + Culture*, edited by Roddey Reid and Sharon Traweek, 151–176. New York: Routledge, 2000.

Ostow, Mortimer. "The New Drugs." *Atlantic Monthly* July 1961, 92–96.

Ouellette, Laurie, and James Hay. *Better Living through Reality TV: Television and Post-Welfare Citizenship.* Oxford: Blackwell, 2008.

Pang, Alex Soojung-Kim. "Victorian Observing Practices, Printing Technology, and Representations of the Solar Corona, (1): The 1860s and 1870s." *Journal of the History of Astronomy* 25 (1994): 249–274.

——. "Victorian Observing Practices, Printing Technology, and Representations of the Solar Corona, (2): The Age of Photomechanical Reproduction." *Journal of the History of Astronomy* 26 (1995): 63–75.

Papajohn, John, and John P. Spiegel. *Transactions in Families: A Modern Approach for Resolving Cultural and Generational Conflicts.* San Francisco: Jossey-Bass, 1975.

Papp, Peggy, ed. *Family Therapy: Full Length Case Studies.* New York: Gardner Press, 1977.

——. *The Process of Change.* Guilford Family Therapy Series, edited by Alan S. Gurman. New York: Guilford Press, 1983.

Parsons, Talcott. *Social Structure and Personality.* London: Free Press of Glencoe, 1964.

Parsons, Talcott, and Robert F. Bales. *Family, Socialization, and Interaction Process.* Glencoe, IL: Free Press, 1955.

Patterson, James T. *America's Struggle against Poverty, 1900–1994.* Enl. ed. Cambridge, MA: Harvard University Press, 1994.

——. *Freedom Is Not Enough: The Moynihan Report and America's Struggle over Black Family Life.* New York: Basic Books, 2010.

Paul, Diane B. *Controlling Human Heredity, 1865 to the Present.* Atlantic Highlands, NJ: Humanities Press, 1995.

Paul, Norman. "Effects of Playback on Family Members of Their Own Previously Recorded Conjoint Therapy Material." *Psychiatric Research Report* 20 (1966): 175–187.

Pendergrast, Mark. *Mirror, Mirror: A History of the Human Love Affair with Reflection.* New York: Basic Books, 2003

Perry, Helen Swick. *Psychiatrist of America: The Life of Harry Stack Sullivan.* Cambridge, MA: Harvard University Press, 1982.

Pettigrew, Thomas F. *A Profile of the Negro American.* Princeton: D. Van Nostrand, 1964.

Pfister, Joel, and Nancy Schnog, eds. *Inventing the Psychological: Toward a Cultural History of Emotional Life in America.* New Haven: Yale University Press, 1997.

Pickering, Andrew. *The Cybernetic Brain: Sketches of Another Future.* Chicago: University of Chicago Press, 2010.

——, ed. *Science as Practice and Culture.* Chicago: University of Chicago Press, 1992.

Pittman, III, Frank S., and Kalman Flomanhaft. "Treating the Doll's House Marriage." *Family Process* 9 (June 1970): 143–156.

Plant, Rebecca Jo. *Mom: The Transformation of Motherhood in Modern America.* Chicago: University of Chicago Press, 2010.

Plone, Anne. "Marital and Existential Pain: Dialectic in Bergman's 'Scenes from a Marriage.'" *Family Process* 14 (September 1975): 371–378.

Pols, Johannes C. "Managing the Mind: The Culture of American Mental Hygiene, 1910–1950." PhD diss., University of Pennsylvania, 1997.

Porter, Roy. "The Patient's View: Doing Medical History from Below." *Theory and Society* 14 (1985): 175–198.

Poster, Mark. *Critical Theory of the Family*. New York: Seabury Press, 1978.

Prescott, Heather Munro. *A Doctor of Their Own: The History of Adolescent Medicine*. Cambridge, MA: Harvard University Press, 1998.

Pressman, Jack David. *Last Resort: Psychosurgery and the Limits of Medicine*. Cambridge: Cambridge University Press, 1998.

Quen, Jacques M., and Eric T. Carlson, eds. *American Psychoanalysis: Origins and Developments*. New York: Brunner/Mazel, 1978.

Rabinowitz, Paula. "History in Your Own Home: *Cinéma Vérité*, Docudrama, and America's Families." In *They Must Be Represented: The Politics of Documentary*, 130–154. London: Verso, 1994.

Rainwater, Lee, and William L Yancey. *The Moynihan Report and the Politics of Controversy, Including the Full Text of* The Negro Family: The Case for National Action, *by Daniel Patrick Moynihan*. Cambridge, MA: MIT Press, 1967.

Rangan, Pooja. "Immaterial Child Labor: Media Advocacy, Autoethnography, and the Case of *Born into Brothels*." *Camera Obscura* 25, no. 3 (2011): 142–177.

Reagan, Leslie J., Nancy Tomes, and Paula A. Treichler, eds. *Medicine's Moving Pictures: Medicine, Health, and Bodies in American Film and Television*. Rochester: University of Rochester Press, 2008.

Reich, Wilhelm. *The Mass Psychology of Fascism*. Translated by Vincent Carfagno. 1933. Reprint, New York: Farrar, Straus and Giroux, 1970.

Reisman, David. *The Lonely Crowd: A Study of the Changing American Character*. New Haven: Yale University Press, 1950.

Renov, Michael, ed. *Theorizing Documentary*. New York: Routledge, 1993.

Reverby, Susan. *Ordered to Care: The Dilemma of American Nursing, 1850–1945*. Cambridge: Cambridge University Press, 1987.

Reverby, Susan, and David Rosner. "Beyond the Great Doctors." In *Health Care in America*, edited by Susan Reverby and David Rosner, 3–16. Philadelphia: Temple University Press, 1979.

Rice, Laura N., and Leslie S. Greenberg. "Humanistic Approaches to Psychotherapy." In *History of Psychotherapy: A Century of Change*, edited by Donald K. Freedheim, 197–224. Washington, DC: American Psychological Association, 1992.

Richards, Graham. *"Race," Racism and Psychology: Towards a Reflexive History*. London: Routledge, 1997.

Richardson, Theresa R. *The Century of the Child: The Mental Hygiene Movement and Social Policy in the United States and Canada*. Albany: State University of New York Press, 1989.

Rieff, Philip. *The Triumph of the Therapeutic*. Chicago: University of Chicago Press, 1966.

Riley, Denise. *War in the Nursery: Theories of the Child and Mother*. London: Virago Press, 1983.

Risse, Guenter, and John Harley Warner. "Reconstructing Clinical Activities: Patient Records in Medical History." *Social History of Medicine* 5 (1992): 183–205.

Ritterman, Michele Klevens. "Paradigmatic Classification of Family Therapy Theories." *Family Process* 16 (1977): 29–48.

Roediger, David. *The Wages of Whiteness: Race and the Making of the American Working Class*. London: Verso, 1991.

Rogers, Daniel T. "In Search of Progressivism." *Reviews in American History* 10 (1982): 113–132.

Rogin, Michael. "Kiss Me Deadly: Communism, Motherhood, and Cold War Movies." *Representations* 6 (1984): 1–36.

Rogler, Lloyd H., and August B. Hollingshead. *Trapped: Families and Schizophrenia.* New York: Wiley, 1965.

Romano, John, ed. *The Origins of Schizophrenia.* Amsterdam: Excerpta Medica Foundation, 1967.

Rony, Fatima Tobing. *The Third Eye: Race, Cinema, and Ethnographic Spectacle.* Durham, NC: Duke University Press, 1996.

Rose, Elizabeth. *A Mother's Job: The History of Day Care, 1890–1960.* New York: Oxford University Press, 1999.

Rose, Nikolas. *Governing the Soul: The Shaping of the Private Self.* 2nd ed. 1989. Reprint, London: Free Association Books, 1999.

Rose, Nikolas, and Peter Miller. *Governing the Present: Administering Economic, Social and Personal Life.* Cambridge: Polity Press, 2008.

Rose, Jacqueline. *Sexuality in the Field of Vision.* London: Verso, 1986.

Rosen, John. *Direct Analysis: Selected Papers.* New York: Grune & Stratton, 1953.

Rosen, Philip. *Change Mummified: Cinema, Historicity.* Minneapolis: University of Minnesota Press, 2001.

Rosenberg, Bernard, and David Manning White, eds. *Mass Culture: The Popular Arts in America.* London: Free Press, 1957.

Rosenberg, Charles E. *The Cholera Years: The United States in 1832, 1849, and 1866.* Chicago: University of Chicago Press, 1962.

——, ed. *The Family in History.* Philadephia: University of Pennsylvania Press, 1975.

——. "Framing Disease: Illness, Society, and History." In *Framing Disease: Studies in Cultural History*, edited by Charles E. Rosenberg and Janet Golden, xiii–xxvi. New Brunswick, NJ: Rutgers University Press, 1992.

Rosenblueth, Arturo, Norbert Wiener, and Julian Bigelow. "Behavior, Purpose, and Teleology." *Philosophy of Science* 10 (1943): 18–24.

Rosenthal, David. *The Genian Quadruplets: A Case Study and Theoretical Analysis of Heredity and Environment in Schizophrenia.* New York: Basic Books, 1963.

Rosenthal, David, and Seymour Kety, eds. *The Transmission of Schizophrenia.* Oxford: Pergamon, 1968.

Rotskoff, Lori. *Love on the Rocks: Men, Women, and Alcohol in Post-World War II America.* Chapel Hill: University of North Carolina Press, 2002.

Rotundo, E. Anthony. *American Manhood: Transformations in Masculinity from the Revolution to the Modern Era.* New York: Basic Books, 1993.

Ruesch, Jurgen, and Gregory Bateson. *Communication: The Social Matrix of Psychiatry.* New York: Norton, 1951.

Ruoff, Jeffrey. *An American Family: A Televised Life.* Minneapolis: University of Minnesota Press, 2002.

Rupp, Leila J. *Mobilizing Women for War: German and American Propaganda, 1939–1945.* Princeton: Princeton University Press, 1978.

Ryan, Mary P. *Cradle of the Middle Class: The Family in Oneida County, New York, 1790–1865.* Cambridge: Cambridge University Press, 1981.

Sacks, Sheldon, ed. *On Metaphor.* Chicago: University of Chicago Press, 1978.

Safilios-Rothschild, Constantina. "Deviance and Mental Illness in the Greek Family." *Family Process* 7, no. 1 (1968): 100–117.

Sahlins, Marshall. "'Sentimental Pessimism' and Ethnographic Experience, or, Why Culture Is Not a Disappearing 'Object.'" In *Biographies of Scientific Objects*, edited by Lorraine Daston, 158–202. Chicago: University of Chicago Press, 2000.

Said, Edward. *Orientalism.* New York: Pantheon Books, 1978.

Sander, Fred M. "Family Therapy or Religion: A Re-reading of T. S. Eliot's *The Cocktail Party*." *Family Process* 9 (September 1979): 279–298.

Satir, Virginia. *Conjoint Family Therapy: A Guide to Theory and Technique.* 2nd ed. 1964. Reprint, Palo Alto: Science and Behavior Books, 1967.

Scheff, Thomas J. *Being Mentally Ill: A Sociological Theory.* Chicago: Aldine, 1966.
———. *Labeling Madness.* Englewood Cliffs, NJ: Prentice-Hall, 1975.
Scheflen, Albert E. *Communicational Structure: Analysis of a Psychotherapy Transaction.* Bloomington: Indiana University Press, 1973.
———. "Living Space in an Urban Ghetto." *Family Process* 10, no. 4 (1971): 429–450.
Scott, Daryl Michael. *Contempt and Pity: Social Policy and the Image of the Damaged Black Psyche.* Chapel Hill: University of North Carolina Press, 1997.
Scott, Joan Wallach. "The Evidence of Experience." *Critical Inquiry* 17, no. 4 (1991): 773–797.
———. *Gender and the Politics of History.* New York: Columbia University Press, 1988.
Scull, Andrew. *Social Order/Mental Disorder: Anglo-American Psychiatry in Historical Perspective.* Berkeley: University of California Press, 1989.
Seed, David. "Brainwashing and Cold War Demonology." *Prospects* 22 (1997): 535–574.
Seldman, Steven. *Romantic Longings: Love in America, 1830–1989.* New York: Routledge, 1992.
Seltzer, Mark. *Bodies and Machines.* New York: Routledge, 1992.
Selvini Palazzoli, Mara. *Self-Starvation.* New York: Jason Aronson, 1974.
Selvini Palazzoli, Mara, Luigi Boscolo, Gianfranco Cecchin, and Guiliana Prata. *Paradox and Counterparadox.* New York: Jason Aronson, 1978.
Sessions, Phebe. "Family Therapy and Urban Poverty: Structural Family Therapy in Context." PhD diss., Brandeis University, 1991.
Sheehy, Peter Phillips. "The Triumph of Group Therapeutics: Therapy, the Social Self, and Liberalism in America, 1910–1960." PhD diss., University of Virginia, 2002.
Sherman, Murray H., Nathan W. Ackerman, Sanford N. Sherman, and Celia Mitchell. "Non-Verbal Cues and Reenactment of Conflict in Family Therapy." *Family Process* 4, no. 1 (1965).
Sherry, Michael S. *In the Shadow of War: The United States since the 1930s.* New Haven: Yale University Press, 1995.
Shortland, Michael. "Screen Memories: Towards a History of Psychiatry and Psychoanalysis in the Movies." *British Journal in the History of Science* 20 (1987): 421–452.
Silver, Ann-Louise S. *Psychoanalysis and Psychosis.* Madison, CT: International Universities Press, 1989.
Silverman, Milton, and Margaret Silverman. "Psychiatry inside the Family Circle." *Saturday Evening Post,* July 28–August 4, 1962, 46–51.
Simmons, Christina. *Making Marriage Modern: Women's Sexuality from the Progressive Era to World War I.* New York: Oxford University Press, 2009.
Singer, Milton. "A Survey of Culture and Personality Theory and Research." In *Studying Personality Cross-Culturally,* edited by Bert Kaplan, 9–90. New York: Harper & Row, 1961.
Skolnick, Arlene. *Embattled Paradise: The American Family in an Age of Uncertainty.* New York: Basic Books, 1991.
Sluzki, Carlos E., and Donald C. Ransom, eds. *Double Bind: The Foundation of the Communicational Approach to the Family.* New York: Grune and Stratton, 1976.
Smith, Judith E. *Visions of Belonging: Family Stories, Popular Culture, and Postwar Democracy, 1940–1960.* New York: Columbia University Press, 2006.
Smith, Steven. "Personalities in the Crowd: The Idea of the 'Masses' in American Popular Culture." *Prospects* 19 (1994): 225–288.
Snyder, Joel. "Visualization and Visibility." In *Picturing Science, Producing Art,* edited by Caroline A. Jones and Peter Galison, 379–397. New York: Routledge, 1998.
Spickard, Paul R. *Mixed Blood: Intermarriage and Ethnic Identity in Twentieth-Century America.* Madison: University of Wisconsin Press, 1989.
Spigel, Lynn. *Make Room for TV: Television and the Family Ideal in Postwar America.* Chicago: University of Chicago Press, 1992.
———. *Welcome to the Dreamhouse: Popular Media and Postwar Suburbs.* Durham, NC: Duke University Press, 2001.

Srole, Leo, Thomas S. Langner, Stanley T. Michael, Price Kirkpatrick, Marvin K. Opler, and Thomas A. C. Rennie. *Mental Health in the Metropolis: The Midtown Manhattan Study*. Rev. and enl. ed. 1962. Reprint, New York: Harper Torchbooks, 1975.

Stanton, Alfred H., and Morris S. Schwartz. *The Mental Hospital: A Study of Institutional Participation in Psychiatric Illness and Treatment*. New York: Basic Books, 1954.

Star, Susan Leigh, and James R. Griesemer. "Institutional Ecology, 'Translations' and Boundary Objects: Amateurs and Professionals in Berkeley's Museum of Vertebrate Zoology, 1907–39." *Social Studies of Science* 19, no. 3 (August 1989): 387–420.

Staub, Michael E. *Madness Is Civilization: When the Diagnosis Was Social, 1948–1980*. Chicago: University of Chicago Press, 2011.

Stearns, Peter N. *Anxious Parents: A History of Modern Childrearing in America*. New York: New York University Press, 2003.

Stein, Howard F. "'All in the Family' as a Mirror of Contemporary Culture." *Family Process* 13 (September 1974): 279–316.

Stepan, Nancy Leys. "Race and Gender: The Role of Analogy in Science." In *The "Racial" Economy of Science: Toward a Democratic Future*, edited by Sandra Harding, 359–376. Bloomington: Indiana University Press, 1993.

——. "Race, Gender, Science, and Citizenship." *Gender & History* 10, no. 1 (1998): 26–52.

Stern, Alexandra Minna. "Better Baby Contests at the Indiana State Fair: Child Health, Scientific Motherhood and Eugenics in the Midwest." In *Formative Years: Children's Health in the United States, 1880–2000*, edited by Alexandra Minna Stern and Howard Markel, 121–152. Ann Arbor: University of Michigan Press, 2002.

——. *Eugenic Nation: Faults and Frontiers of Better Breeding in Modern America*. Berkeley: University of California Press, 2005.

Sterns, Peter N. *Anxious Parents: A History of Modern Childrearing in America*. New York: New York University Press, 2004.

Stewart, John. "The Scientific Claims of British Child Guidance, 1918–1945." *British Journal for the History of Science* 42, no. 3 (September 2009): 407–432.

Stocking, George W., Jr., ed. *Malinowski, Rivers, Benedict and Others: Essays on Culture and Personality*. Madison: University of Wisconsin Press, 1986.

——. *Race, Culture and Evolution: Essays in the History of Anthropology*. New York: Free Press, 1968.

——. "The Turn of the Century Concept of Race." *Modernism/Modernity* 1 (1993): 4–16.

——. *Victorian Anthropology*. New York: Free Press, 1987.

Stone, Lawrence. "The Rise of the Nuclear Family in Early Modern England: The Patriarchal Stage." In *The Family in History*, edited by Charles Rosenberg, 13–57. Philadephia: University of Pennsylvania Press, 1975.

Strecker, Edward. *Their Mothers' Sons*. New York: Lippincott, 1946.

Sturken, Marita, and Lisa Cartwright. *Practices of Looking: An Introduction to Visual Culture*. New York: Oxford University Press, 2001.

Sugrue, Thomas J. "Reassessing the History of Postwar America." *Prospects* 20 (1995): 493–509.

Sullivan, Harry Stack. *Schizophrenia as a Human Process*. New York: Norton, 1962.

——. *The Collected Works of Harry Stack Sullivan*. New York: Norton, 1953.

Sulman, A. Michael. "The Humanization of the American Child: Benjamin Spock as a Popularizer of Psychoanalytic Thought." *Journal of the History of the Behavioral Sciences* 9 (1973): 258–265.

Susman, Warren. "Did Success Spoil the United States? Dual Representations in Postwar America." In *Recasting America: Culture and Politics in the Age of the Cold War*, edited by Lary May, 19–37. Chicago: University of Chicago Press, 1989.

——. "'Personality' and the Making of Twentieth-Century Culture." In *Culture as History: The Transformation of American Society in the Twentieth Century*, 271–285. New York: Pantheon Books, 1973.

Taylor, Ella. *Prime-Time Families: Television Culture in Postwar America*. Berkeley: University of California Press, 1989.

Taylor, Lucien, ed. *Visualizing Theory: Selected Essays from V.A.R., 1990–1994*. New York: Routledge, 1994.

Taylor, Peter J. "Technocratic Optimism, H.T. Odum, and the Partial Transformation of Ecological Metaphor after World War II." *Journal of the History of Biology* 21, no. 2 (1988): 213–244.

Terry, Jennifer. "'Momism' and the Making of Treasonous Homosexuals." In *"Bad" Mothers: The Politics of Blame in Twentieth Century America*, edited by Molly Ladd-Taylor and Lauri Umanksy, 169–190. New York: New York University Press, 1998.

Thomson, Mathew. "Mental Hygiene as an International Movement." In *International Health Organisations and Movements, 1918–1939*, edited by Paul Weindling, 283–304. Cambridge: Cambridge University Press, 1995.

Thorne, Barrie, and Marilyn Yalom, eds. *Rethinking the Family: Some Feminist Questions*. Rev. ed. Boston: Northeastern University Press, 1992.

Tomes, Nancy. *A Generous Confidence: The Art of Asylum-Keeping: Thomas Story Kirkbride and the Origins of American Psychiatry*. Philadelphia: University of Pennsylvania Press, 1994.

Tompkins, Michael A. "Family Therapy: Evolution of a Knowledge System." PhD diss., California School of Professional Psychology at Alameda, 1992.

Umanksy, Lauri. *Motherhood Reconceived: Feminism and the Legacy of the Sixties*. New York: New York University Press, 1996.

UNESCO. *The Race Question*. Paris: UNESCO, 1950.

Vicedo, Marga. "The Social Nature of the Mother's Tie to Her Child: John Bowlby's Theory of Attachment in Post-War America." *British Journal of the History of Science* 44, no. 3 (2011): 1–26.

Viner, Russell. "Putting Stress in Life: Hans Selye and the Making of Stress Theory." *Social Studies of Science* 29, no. 3 (1999): 391–410.

von Foerster, Heinz, ed. *Cybernetics: Circular Causal and Feedback Mechanisms in Biological and Social Systems (Transactions of the Sixth–Tenth Conferences)*. New York: Josiah Macy Jr., Foundation, 1949–1953.

Walters, Marianne, Betty Carter, Peggy Papp, and Olga Silverstein. *The Invisible Web: Gender Patterns in Family Relationships*. New York: Guilford Press, 1988.

Watkins, Elizabeth Siegel. *On the Pill: A Social History of Oral Contraceptives, 1950–1970*. Baltimore: Johns Hopkins University Press, 1998.

Watzlawick, Paul. "A Review of the Double Bind Theory." *Family Process* 2 (1963): 132–153.

Watzlawick, Paul, Janet Beavin, and Don D. Jackson. *Pragmatics of Human Communication: A Study of Interactional Patterns, Pathologies, and Paradoxes*. New York: Norton, 1967.

Watzlawick, Paul, and John Weakland, eds. *The Interactional View*. New York: Norton, 1977.

Weakland, John, and William Fry. "Letters of Mothers of Schizophrenics." *American Journal of Psychiatry* 32 (1962): 604–623.

Weidman, Nadine. "Psychobiology, Progressivism, and the Anti-Progressive Movement." *Journal of the History of Biology* 29 (1996): 267–308.

Weinberger, Eliot. "The Camera People." In *Visualizing Theory: Selected Essays from V.A.R., 1990–1994*, edited by Lucien Taylor, 3–26. New York, Routledge: 1994

Weinstein, Deborah F. "Culture at Work: Family Therapy and the Culture Concept in Post-World War II America." *Journal of the History of the Behavioral Sciences* 40, no. 1 (2004): 23–46.

Weiss, Jessica. *To Have and To Hold: Marriage, the Baby Boom and Social Change*. Chicago: University of Chicago Press, 2000.

Weiss, Julie H. "Womanhood and Psychoanalysis: A Study of Mutual Construction in Popular Culture, 1920–1963." PhD diss., Brown University, 1990.

Welter, Barbara. "The Cult of True Womanhood: 1820–1860." *American Quarterly* 18, no. 2 (1966): 151–174.

Westbrook, Robert. "Fighting for the American Family: Private Interests and Political Obligations in World War II." In *The Power of Culture*, edited by Richard Wightman Fox and T. J. Jackson Lears, 195–221. Chicago: University of Chicago Press, 1993.

Whitaker, Carl A., ed. *Psychotherapy of Chronic Schizophrenia Patients*. Boston: Little, Brown, 1958.

Whitaker, Carl A., and Thomas P. Malone. *The Roots of Psychotherapy*. 1953. Reprint, New York: Brunner/Mazel, 1981.

White, Michael, and David Epston. *Narrative Means to Therapeutic Ends*. New York: Norton, 1990.

White, Mimi. *Tele-Advising: Therapeutic Discourse in American Television*. Chapel Hill: University of North Carolina Press, 1992.

Whitfield, Stephen J. *The Culture of the Cold War*. The American Moment, edited by Stanley I. Kutler. Baltimore: Johns Hopkins University Press, 1991.

Whittier, Nancy. *The Politics of Child Sexual Abuse: Emotion, Social Movements, and the State*. New York: Oxford University Press, 2009.

Whyte, William, Jr. *The Organization Man*. New York: Doubleday, 1956.

Wiener, Norbert. *Cybernetics, or Control and Communication in the Animal and the Machine*. 2nd ed. 1948. Reprint, Cambridge, MA: MIT Press, 1961.

——. *The Human Use of Human Beings: Cybernetics and Society*. Boston: Houghton Mifflin, 1950.

Williams, Raymond. *Keywords: A Vocabulary of Culture and Society, Revised Edition*. 1976. Reprint, New York: Oxford University Press, 1985.

Winston, Brian. "The Documentary Film as Scientific Inscription." In *Theorizing Documentary*, edited by Michael Renov, 37–57. New York: Routledge, 1993.

Winter, Alison. "Film and the Construction of Memory in Psychoanalysis, 1940–1960." *Science in Context* 19, no. 1 (2006): 111–136.

——. "Screening Selves: Sciences of Memory and Identity on Film, 1930–1960." *History of Psychology* 7, no. 4 (November 2004): 367–401.

Winter, David G. "'Toward a Science of Personality Psychology': David McClelland's Development of Empirically Derived TAT Measures." *History of Psychology* 1 (1998): 130–153.

Witmer, Helen Leland, and Ruth Kotinsky, eds., *Personality in the Making: The Fact-Finding Report of the Midcentury White House Conference on Children and Youth*. New York: Harper & Brothers, 1952.

Wylie, Philip. *Generation of Vipers*. 1942. Reprint, New York: Holt, Rinehart and Winston, 1955.

Wynne, Lyman C. "Reflections on Blame and Responsibility for Schizophrenia." In *Origins of Psychopathology: Problems in Research and Public Policy*, edited by David F. Ricks and Barbara S. Dohrenweld, 205–213. Cambridge: Cambridge University Press, 1983.

——. "Responses of the Theorists." In *Family Processes and Schizophrenia*, edited by Elliot G. Mishler and Nancy E. Waxler. New York: Jason Aronson, Inc., 1968.

Wynne, Lyman C., Rue L. Cromwell, and Steven Matthysse, eds. *The Nature of Schizophrenia: New Approaches to Research and Treatment*. New York: Wiley, 1978.

Wynne, Lyman C., Irving M. Rychoff, Juliana Day, and Stanley I. Hirsch. "Pseudo-Mutuality in the Family Relations of Schizophrenics." *Psychiatry* 21 (1958): 205–220.

Yans-McLaughlin, Virginia. "Science, Democracy and Ethics: Mobilizing Culture and Personality for World War II." In *Malinowski, Rivers, Benedict and Others: Essays on Culture and Personality*, edited by George W. Stocking Jr., 184–217. Madison: University of Wisconsin Press, 1986.

Yates, JoAnne. *Control through Communication: The Rise of System in American Management*. Baltimore: Johns Hopkins University Press, 1989.

Young, Allan. *The Harmony of Illusions: Inventing Post-Traumatic Stress Disorder.* Princeton: Princeton University Press, 1995.

Young, Lynn. "The Broken Family: The Divorce of the Year." *Newsweek*, March 12, 1973, 48–49.

Young-Bruehl, Elisabeth. *The Anatomy of Prejudices.* Cambridge, MA: Harvard University Press, 1996.

Zaretsky, Eli. *Secrets of the Soul: A Social and Cultural History of Psychoanalysis.* New York: Vintage Books, 2004.

Zaretsky, Natasha. *No Direction Home: The American Family and the Fear of National Decline, 1968–1980.* Chapel Hill: University of North Caroline Press, 2007.

Zeig, Jeffery K., ed. *The Evolution of Psychotherapy: The Third Conference.* New York: Brunner/Mazel, 1995.

Zuckerman, Michael. "Dr. Spock: The Confidence Man." In *The Family in History*, edited by Charles Rosenberg, 179–207. Philadelphia: University of Pennsylvania Press, 1975.

Zuk, Gerald. "Family Therapy." *Archives of General Psychiatry* 16 (1967): 71–79.

Zuk, Gerald, and Ivan Boszormenyi-Nagy, eds. *Family Therapy and Disturbed Families.* Palo Alto: Science and Behavior Books, Inc., 1967.

INDEX